ITALIAN FESTIVAL FOOD

RECIPES AND TRADITIONS FROM ITALY'S
REGIONAL COUNTRY FOOD FAIRS

ANNE BIANCHI

MACMILLAN—USA

MACMILLAN
A Pearson Education Macmillan Company
1633 Broadway
New York, NY 10019-6785

A catalogue record is available from the Library of Congress.

Designed by Amy Trombat

Printed in the United States of America
10 9 8 7 6 5 4 3 2 1

For RDH, who is always there, always involved, always wise,
and always ready with the ultimate reminder
that now it's time for a vacation.

CONTENTS

ACKNOWLEDGMENTS IX
INTRODUCTION XI
HOW TO USE THIS BOOK XV
INGREDIENTS XVII

I
Appetizers and Salads 1
Piedmont: Blessed are the Humble

II
Polenta and Risotto 53
Trentino–Alto Adige: Boundaries of the Mind

III
Pasta and Gnocchi 95
Emilia–Romagna: The Succulent Flavor of the Earth

IV
Vegetables 153
Tuscany: Ancient Ruins and Modern Permutations

V
Soups, Breads, Focaccias, and Pizzas 193
Sardinia: Sacred Rites and Profane Pleasures

VI
Eggs, Cheeses, and Savory Tarts 249
Campania: The Drawbacks of Being Boring

VII
Meats, Game, and Poultry 295
Puglia: Going Once, Going Twice

VIII
Fish and Seafood 353
Calabria: A Belief in Believing

IX
Desserts 407
Sicily: Of Boundaries and Separation

APPENDICES
A *Basic Recipes* 458
B *Italian Wines* 464
C *Calendar of Festivals* 466
D *Mail-Order Sources* 476

INDEX 477

ACKNOWLEDGMENTS

WHERE TO BEGIN AFTER A MULTIYEAR JOURNEY THROUGH TINY VILLAGES IN EVERY corner of the Italian peninsula—a journey that brought me into contact with—and dependent on—literally thousands of people? Thank you, first of all, to Douglas Hatschek, photographer extraordinaire, for bumping along beside me in that antiquated Panda, always searching for the one image that would say it all. I know it was a trial, *amore*—never more so than in Sicily, when that farcical mechanic looked under the hood—smoke streaming out from all directions—and, in his best deadpan manner, declared, "Signora, this is just not your lucky day."

Thanks also to Marco Francesconi, Franca Costa, Enzo Russo, Giuseppe Santoro, Bette Maraillat, Carmen Wallace Giuggia, and all the people at Slow Food Arcigola for providing me with contacts, lodging, material, and technical support.

In Liguria, thank you to Gianfranco, Rosa, Mario, Giulio, Sandra, and Marco. In Piedmont, to Aldo, Mauro, Paolo, Martilda, Bishop Taurisio, Beatrice, Donatella, and that nameless man who, amidst the tumult of a *robbiolo* festival in Rocco Grimaldo, simply said, "I have an abandoned villa at the top of that hill—stay there as long as you like." In Val d'Aosta, to Gigi, Beppe, Ulianio, Eliza, Cicci, and Roberto at the Merlano campground for coaxing me out of my tent before lightning would have precipitously ended my journey. In Trentino, to Reno, Vera, Mauro, and the Contessa Vagliani. In Friuli, to Marta and Sauro (you were right—there is *never* any place to stay in Venice). In Emilia, to Sandro, Marisa, Anna, and Gianluca. In Le Marche, to all the people at the Ascoli Picena tourist office for an amazing job with securing contacts and places to stay. In Campania, to Nicolo, Michele, Alfredo, Don Francesco, Giuliana, and Mini. In Puglia, to Don Pierino, Tonio, Allesandro, Silvestro, Mariana, Elena, and the Commandante of the Altamura police force. In Calabria, to Don Reggio, Franca, Robertino, Paolo, Tina, Loreta, Duilio, and Moreno. In Sardinia, to Calistro, Gianpaolo, Marzia, and all the people at the Cagliari Tourist Board for extending themselves far beyond anything I could have imagined. In Sicily, to Ciro and Maria in the Sicilian tourist office, as well as to Beppe, Mariano, Mariella, Teresita, Michele, and Claudio.

A huge thank you to all the people mentioned in my stories—most of you were already great friends; some of you have now become so. The experiences we shared will always be larger and more vivid than what I could possible ever hope to chronicle with mere words.

As always, thanks to Sandra Lotti—cousin, friend, reseacher, colleague, recipe tester, and co-owner of our cooking school. Whatever made you think I had fallen off the edge of existance in the Veneto and needed to be rescued by the federal police?

Also in the "as always" department, thank you to Tom Gelinne for his expert recipe checking and general culinary knowledge. The fear that you will yell at me over whether or not I have used enough eggs keeps me forever on my toes, darling.

Grazie to my mother, who—again—provided lodging, food, the occasional cash infusion, and a consistent pessimistic sense that my car would never make yet another long trip. *Avevi ragione mamma.*

Thank you to my agent, Susan Lescher, for believing in this project and helping me shape it into a manageable form.

Thank you to Jennifer Griffin and Jim Willhite, for kicking this book into shape.

And finally, thank you to all the extraordinary friends who people my American life and consistently make me feel that I have roots in New York City, despite long periods on the road. It is wonderful to travel around Italy making new friends and living new experiences, but it is absolutely crucial to come home and be embraced in a way that says "We haven't forgotten that you exist."

INTRODUCTION

There are more festivals in Italy in one month than in any other country in one year.

STENDAHL

TO ITALIANS, THE WORD *festa* CAN MEAN ANYTHING FROM A PARTY, TO A HOLIDAY, to a celebration in honor of a specific food or religious patron. *È festa* if someone gets married or has a birthday. *È festa* if people have off from work for the June 2 Proclamation of the Republic. And of course, *è festa* when the Tuscan town of Barghecchia reaps its chestnut harvest or when Palermo pays tribute to Santa Rosalia for saving it from the ravages of a seventeenth-century plague.

In Italy, each *festa,* or *sagra,* as they are often called, comes with its own food. From the massive plates of spaghetti consumed during Trastevere's *Festa de' Noantri,* to the extraordinary *bomboloni* associated with Lucca's *Luminaria,* Italians are unquestionably of one mind when it comes to which factor most defines a festival.

While researching this book, I spent the better part of the last few years eating my way from one festival to another—not an easy task, regardless of how wonderful it sounds to the uninitiated. Italians well understood my plight—fiercely regional when it comes to both the folkloric charm of their particular festival and the excellence of its associated food, they never understood in the first place why I would want to travel to any other festival when I could simply stay put at theirs. But my American friends maintained throughout that I had been touched by the right hand of God—that I should cease my whining about such things as Italian inefficiency and summer crowds at *vaporetto* terminals and, by the way, did I need an assistant?

That I did my share of whining, I will be the first to admit. What other response makes sense when stuck in a leaky tent on a cold, rainy night in the Dolomites? Or how about having your car engine burn out fifteen minutes after getting off the ferry in Sicily?

In the end, however, those moments have seamlessly blended with the glorious sunset over the Ionian Sea the night I picnicked on the beach with members of Soverato's civic band. With the night spent in an abandoned fourteenth-century villa on a hilltop in the Piedmont only to find that, during the night, the estate's caretaker had deposited outside my door a mountain of cherry tree boughs laden with ripe red fruit. With the adorable teenagers in Brescia who offered to take me to "the best restaurant in Lombardy," which turned out to be an IKEA.

The festivals were breathtaking—all of them. Having only ever read about the passionate devotion of southern Italians to their particular patron saints, I went armed with cynicism regarding the authenticity of the lavish festivals mounted in their honor. Happily, I was wrong. The floats reaching forty-foot heights, the windows along the procession route proudly draped with colorful rugs and hand-made tapestries, the praying and chanting and weeping with joy as the saint's statue passes by—it is all as genuine as the gracious offers I received from individual participants to join their postfestival dinners.

One of the things that most impressed me was the incredible difference between festivals in the north and their southern counterparts. When it comes to festivals, the two are truly separate enclaves. In the north, the majority of the celebrations are secular in nature; *sagras*—originally centered on the dedication of a church—are now largely country fairs featuring one or more local ingredients. Thus, Piediluco celebrates fish; Gubbio, truffles; Umbertide, the chestnut; Panicale, the grape; Massarosa, the crab; Pieve a Elici, soup; and Bozzello, the artichoke. In fact, there is hardly a food that is not, at some point, celebrated somewhere. From polenta to *ciccioli* (porkskin scraps), *gelato* to rosemary, sea urchins to thrushes—there's even a *sagra* devoted to a particular type of summer melon grown without irrigation!

The north also mounts a large number of *palios*—games of rivalry between various factions of the same city. In Livorno, a seaside resort, the *palio marinaro* features a regatta of ornate boats competing against each other along the city's atmospheric canals. Arezzo's palio is famous for its vigorous jousts staged before stands packed with noble dignitaries. But the most famous of all the palios is Siena's with its thrilling horse races and seventeen *contrade* (factions) outfitted in stunning medieval costumes.

There is something charmingly accessible about the more local palios, however, many with the same types of horse races as Siena's, some with donkeys standing in for the horses, some featuring pigs, and all with elaborate costumes, impressive flags, and bands whose musicians have more than likely inherited the role from their great-grandfathers.

Although not nearly as numerous as in the south, the north has its share of religious festivals and celebrations. One of my favorites is Viareggio's pre-Lenten Carnival, famous throughout Europe for the political and satirical theme of many of its huge papier-mâché floats. Another favorite is Venice's *Festa del Redentore*, with its bridge of boats built across the Giudecca Canal to the Church of the Redentore. Thousands row out to picnic on the water and then stay for the midnight fireworks.

In the south, however, most festivals are *patronale*—held in honor of a patron saint. While all share certain commonalities—a procession, a band, a mass, a statue (with or without attending relics)—each has its own distinct identity having to do with both the local character of the town and the individual personality of the saint. Unlike God or the Virgin Mary (who are thought to be too busy to attend to such things as finding someone a job or guaranteeing a bountiful harvest) the saints once lived as ordinary mortals and are thus considered to be a living testimony to the trials of being human.

So St. Lucy is beseeched by people with eye problems; St. Blaise, by those with sore throats; St. Agatha, by women with breast cancer; St. Anna, by those about to bear children; and St. Paul, by anyone bothered with snake infestations. Festivals held in their respective honors incorporate each of those specialties; many of the villages which have adopted Paul as their patron, for example (presumably after his intercession cleared their village of snakes), feature live snakes hung around the necks of specialized *cerauli,* or snake handlers.

I was amazed at the number of religious festivals with pagan overtones. While I was no stranger to the Catholic predilection for replacing pagan rites with Christian celebrations (as in Christmas, which turned the birth of the sun into the Birth of the Son), I was not expecting the ease with which southern Italians have homogenized the two belief systems. In Sicily, the custom of tossing of grain onto the waters to commemorate the rebirth of Adonis, Aphrodite's *inamorata* (Aphrodite being the goddess who sprang from the sea) has simply merged with Easter, which commemorates the rebirth of Christ. Instead of throwing the grains on the waters, Sicilian women now place them on a plate, carry them into the church, and lay them on the altar.

In the end, all Italian festivals—regardless of type or location—have one uniting factor: food. Some feature grand platters of meats and fish and pastas and desserts offered free or for sale as part of the festival itself. Included in this category are both the *Ravioli Sagras* with seven different types of ravioli listed on the menu board, and Camogli's *Fish Sagra,* where the fish is handed out for free in small paper cones.

Other festivals are associated with certain foods, but those foods are consumed only in private homes or restaurants following the scheduled festivities. Many are the families that invited me to join them for *pranzo* after we had spent the morning processing side by side behind a statue of St. Anthony.

It is through these latter experiences that I eventually realized the true significance of festivals to Italians, whether north or south. No matter what they celebrate or how they do it, festivals are—all—a direct extension of family, an unbroken link to the parents and grandparents who celebrated in the same way and with the same foods. Whether 25 years ago or 355 years ago, the members of the DiPaola family in Bari walked the same streets carrying the statue of St. Anthony and afterward sat down (more often than not, in the same house) to eat the same meals as Vito, Mariella, Pippo, Andrea, and all the rest of the DiPaolas do today.

I learned much during my research, but nothing was more important than this realization. To everyone who travels to Italy and experiences a festival through the eyes of a tour book writer who limits his description to time, price, historical origins, and a listing of events, I say, delve deeper. You are missing the heart and soul of why Italy is the festival capital of the world.

Yes, Italians are festive people and yes, they are blessed with all the elements that make for a good *festa:* extraordinary weather, incomparable landscapes, a history that has always favored the creation of art over the devastation of war, and, of course, an incomparable mastery when it comes to turning out good, simple food.

But more than any of that is the deep emotional attachment to people—to family, including those living and those who have gone before. It does not matter how many times they flock to the streets at 3:00 A.M. to arrange the floral carpets for Corpus Domini. Nor that, afterward, they sit at long wooden tables and eat the same *zuppa di cozze* and *agnello ai ferri.* There is a freshness about their faces—a blazing torch behind their eyes—that makes them luminous with the energy of those for whom this encounter with tradition is the most important element of their lives.

And so it is. More than the car they drive, more than how much money they have, more than what they wear and the status significance of the label on their sunglasses, festivals define Italians. As the most obvious manifestation of Italy's traditional rites and rituals, festivals define the very aspect of being Italian that makes the Italian people able to thrive in small villages, take the same evening *passegiatta,* and choose the same bread for breakfast every morning of their lives.

This is what I learned—me who grew up as a Tuscan but with the American overtones of one who spent half the year here, half there. What I realized is that, despite having always called Tuscany "home," I had missed this link to all the Bianchis who had gone before. Somehow, they were not as real to me as they have always been to my cousins and aunts and uncles and all my relatives who would rather be fired from their jobs than miss the procession through the cemetery of Saint Iacopo on All Soul's Day.

My mother has always been of the impression that Italians were the greatest people in the world. This book has given me the opportunity to realize just exactly what she meant.

ANNE BIANCHI
Tuscany, 1999

HOW TO USE THIS BOOK

IN ASSEMBLING THE RECIPES FOR THIS BOOK, I TRIED TO GIVE EACH OF ITALY'S eighteen regions their due. The recipes themselves are either traditional ones that have been associated with certain festivals from time immemorial, or individually divined creations that start and end with one household or set of households intent on establishing more modern traditions. Some have been refined by me according to both my understanding of American palates and a personal passion for esthetic presentation. Others are exactly as I experienced them while eating or cooking alongside festival participants. All entail the use of ingredients that are either readily available in American markets or can be ordered by mail from the list of sources on page 476.

Each recipe is followed by the amount of preparation time required, calculated from the minute you approach the recipe to the minute you place it on the table. Next comes the level of difficulty: *Easy* means the recipe involves minimal directions and simple preparations; *Moderate,* that there are a number of directions, but no difficult techniques or preparations; *Advanced* recipes involve one or more techniques or preparations that require prior knowledge or experience.

I have also included information on which parts of the recipe can be prepared ahead of time or stored for future use, as well as recommendations for the various ways in which the recipe can be served. In no way should you limit yourself to my serving advice, however. The extraordinary thing about Italian cuisine—and what most differentiates it from French cooking—is its egalitarian nature, its receptivity to infinite experimentation. Take many liberties and remember to guide yourself, not only by taste, but by smell, feel, look, and attitude. If you want to use more rosemary, or think the dish would be better with a tablespoon or two of heavy cream, do it. Remember: What separates a master chef from a competent technician is a certain proclivity toward experimentation.

The postrecipe section concludes with a wine-pairing suggestion. The suggested wines are defined broadly according to type: Dry White, Medium-Sweet White, Medium-Bodied Red, and Full-Bodied Red. While the categories speak for themselves, I have added in Appendix B, a list of specific types of wine arranged according to region for those desiring a little more guidance. Again, you should not consider my wine suggestions to be absolute truth. As one who always prefers red wine over white, I tend to lean more toward pairing borderline dishes (those like certain chicken or fish preparations that can conceivably take either a red or a white) with light reds, instead of the classic white.

The book opens with a list of ingredients, because I firmly believe it is hard either to get started or produce a wonderful recipe if your ingredients are not of the very finest quality. Italians have a saying: *prima ti fornisci, dopo fai.* First you equip yourself with the right tools, then you do.

The stories preceding each recipe section represent nine of Italy's eighteen regions, arranged north to south. So the first takes place in Piedmont, the last, in Sicily. All narrate a certain experience or transformation I underwent because of my interactions with the wonderful people of that area. From the questioning of belief systems that pervaded my thoughts while watching the Bishop of Naples elevate the vial of San Gennaro's blood over his head, to the still-churning consternation over the dubious exorcism I witnessed in Calabria, my problem was never assembling enough material, but rather how was I going to limit myself to only nine stories. In addition to this experiential narrative, each of the stories also describes a local festival and highlights, regional foods, and food traditions.

The book concludes with a series of appendices, one of which presents basic recipes used throughout the book: meat broth, egg pasta, pizza dough, and more. In addition to serving as the underlying element for specific recipes, these basic preparations can also be used on their own to create an endless series of culinary variations.

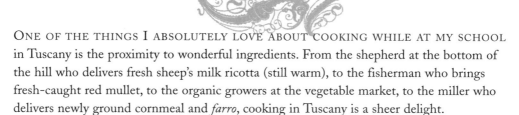

INGREDIENTS

ONE OF THE THINGS I ABSOLUTELY LOVE ABOUT COOKING WHILE AT MY SCHOOL in Tuscany is the proximity to wonderful ingredients. From the shepherd at the bottom of the hill who delivers fresh sheep's milk ricotta (still warm), to the fisherman who brings fresh-caught red mullet, to the organic growers at the vegetable market, to the miller who delivers newly ground cornmeal and *farro*, cooking in Tuscany is a sheer delight.

In the States, especially for those of you who live far away from big cities, finding the right ingredients can sometimes entail a bit of a search. Fortunately, the food revolution seems to have affected even the smallest town out in the middle of what was formerly hot-dogs-and-beans country. In fact, I remember two students from Edmonton, Oklahoma, who came to my cooking school in the fall of 1997—Bob and Joy Heiman. "Why, I can get fresh porcini mushrooms right at my local market," Joy declared in her wonderful Oklahoma accent. "And if there's something I want that they don't have, my grocer says he'll order it." A few weeks after their class had ended, Joy e-mailed me to say that her grocer had ordered a case of San Marzano tomatoes. "Just for me," she beamed.

Edmonton grocers notwithstanding, finding items such as fresh salsify or *marzolino* cheese is still a bit of a stretch for most people. And fresh-ground chestnut flour—well, you might as well ask for the moon. But there's always mail order (see page 476 for a list of purveyors) as well as an ever-increasing number of specialty and gourmet food stores that stock high-quality ingredients. The key is knowing the difference between what's okay and what's simply divine. Just keep in mind this old Tuscan proverb: *la buona cucina origina in dispensa*—the success of a recipe begins with your ingredients.

Balsamic vinegar   Let's put the important information up front: good balsamic vinegar costs as much as a very fine bottle of aged barolo. Is it worth it? Yes, but you may want to keep on hand a variety of grades so that you're not pouring $100-a-bottle balsamic indiscriminately over salad greens. Good balsamic vinegar is made from boiled-down grape juice. After spending a year each in different types of wood barrels (woods can include oak, chestnut, mulberry, ash, and/or juniper), the juices concentrate into a thick, aromatic syrup. The older the syrup, the less of it there is (due to evaporation) and the more expensive it becomes—so much so that Italians once willed balsamic vinegar to their descendants. Balsamic vinegar is a trademark ingredient that can only be produced in a strictly controlled area of Emilia-Romagna, around Modena. Do not be swayed by bottles that gratuitously read "*Aceto Balsamico di Modena.*" The fact is, that unless it comes from Modena (or one of a few towns surrounding Modena), it cannot be called balsamic vinegar in the first place. So how to differentiate good from less good? Price. Bottles that cost $3.99 are commercially produced blends of boiled down grape juice mixed with regular vinegar, darkened with caramel and aged as little as one year. Blend these into salad dressings or use in cooked sauces and keep the real balsamic for drizzling (sparingly) over grilled meats or vanilla ice cream or hunks of Parmigiano-Reggiano or ripe red strawberries.

Olive oil By now, everyone knows that olive oil not only tastes good, but also is good for you. Less well known however, is that unless you choose wisely, you're getting neither health nor flavor. In fact, extra virgin olive oil is the only grade that can unequivocally deliver both advantages. Produced without chemicals from stone-crushed olives, extra virgin oil has an acidity level of less than 1 percent. The better the grade, the lower the acidity; hence, the best hover around .5 or .6 percent. All other grades of olive oil (from virgin, to pure olive to pomace) are blends, some—or all—of the components of which may be chemically pressed and colored. Good olive oils vary widely in flavor, depending on type of olive, growing conditions, geography, and soil composition. Some are good with grilled fish, others as a base for a good *aioli*. Ideally, your pantry will have three or four types of olive oil and you will be able to pick and choose which one to pair with a specific dish.

Cheeses Italians use either Parmigiano-Reggiano or pecorino for grating. Which depends on tradition, recipe, and palate. Parmigiano-Reggiano is known as the "king of cheeses," both for its subtle flavor and the fact of its strictly controlled production. As with balsamic vinegar, Parmigiano is a trademark ingredient that can come only from Emilia-Romagna. By law, only cow's milk and rennet can be used and the finished product must be aged for at least eighteen months. The best wheels have "Parmigiano-Reggiano" etched in small red or green dots on the rind and cost anywhere from $13 to $25 per pound. Wheels found to have a few too many air holes have a line through the dots and the resulting cheese can be purchased for somewhat less, around $8 to $12 per pound. As with most things in life, you get what you pay for, although the less expensive Parmigiano is perfectly fine for all-purpose use. Grate the cheese as needed and keep refrigerated in a tightly sealed plastic container. Domestic "Parmesan" is a completely different product and should be routinely avoided.

Pecorino is a catchall name for a wide variety of sheep's milk cheeses (*pecora* means sheep), the texture, color, and flavor of which differ according to the type of grass used for grazing, the length of aging, and the technique utilized by the cheese maker. Hard pecorinos (aged varieties) are generally used for grating, while softer, younger types work best when paired either with fruits or briny foods such as olives or pickled onions.

Ricotta is a soft, delicate cheese made from milk whey that comes from either cows, sheep, or goats. Used in everything from ravioli to cakes to stuffing for chestnut crepes, ricotta is best when eaten within a few days of production. Always purchase the fresh variety from a specialty foods or cheese shop; prepackaged ricotta sold in supermarket containers bears no relation to the real thing.

Canned tomatoes   In this country, the best canned plum tomatoes are the San Marzano variety. Since San Marzano is a geographic location as well as a type of tomato as well as a widely distributed brand name, read the label carefully. Some say "San Marzano–style," which simply means the contents are plum tomatoes, generally hard and as far from vine-ripened as the those offered by supermarkets in February. When you open a good can of tomatoes, you should find tomatoes ripe enough to be hand-shredded floating in a thick, syrupy juice. As with so many of the ingredients listed here, price is a perfect determinant for separating good canned tomatoes from those best left on the shelf.

Herbs   While many people presume that all herbs are better in their fresh, natural state, the reality is that dried herbs serve just as valuable a function, albeit a different one. Dried herbs are more concentrated in flavor and release their oils over a long period of time, which makes them perfect for soups, stews, or any other dish that requires long cooking. Unlike their fresh counterparts, dried herbs tend to have sharp, intense flavors and are better used in small quantities—a pinch is generally enough. Of the green herbs, chervil, parsley, and chives have little culinary value in their dried state. Better those that grow on woody stems—thyme, rosemary, sage, marjoram, winter savory, and oregano—all wonderful in such dishes as hearty tomato sauce or thick, rustic minestrones. Dried basil is a personal preference—some cooks (myself included) like its zesty, spicy flavor added to winter soups; others claim that drying dissipates basil's essential oils and renders it worthless.

Fresh herbs have milder flavors than their dried counterparts and can be used in greater quantity. Since their flavor releases immediately, fresh herbs such as basil, fennel, lovage, parsley, rosemary, sage, tarragon, chives, thyme, and mint should be sprinkled onto cooked or raw vegetables, or used in sautés, grills, stir fries and other quick-cooked dishes. Woodier varieties, such as thyme and tarragon, can also be layered into a slow-cooked dish, with one amount added early enough to thoroughly blend into the basic flavor, and a second portion sprinkled onto the dish just before serving for freshness and appearance. And, of course, any combination of minced fresh herbs works wonderfully stirred into a salad vinaigrette. Try also blending fresh herb minces with olive oil, lemon zest, crushed garlic, and chopped nuts for a wonderful paste that can be stirred into hot soups or used as a topping for pizza, pasta, or grilled meats and vegetables.

Salt   I always try to include salt tastings in my cooking school classes so that students can see for themselves how much different salts vary in flavor. All salt comes from the sea, but is processed in different ways. What we call common table salt is really finely ground crystals mixed with starch and phosphate of lime to keep the crystals free flowing. The consequence is a generally flat and metallic taste. Iodized salt goes through a heavy refinement process that strips it of its natural iodine and then replaces it in the form of sodium iodide; the result is a muddy, acrid flavor. Kosher salt, which has no additives, got its name because its large grains were once used to draw blood from meat in accordance with Jewish dietary laws. Of all the commerically available salts, it is the cleanest tasting and its coarse grains make it very easy to use.

Sea salt is generally obtained by evaporating seawater in protected areas. This purification process leaves it with a high percentage of sodium chloride and many trace elements, which can include magnesium, zinc, calcium, iron, and potassium. Available in both fine and coarse grains, sea salt has a much fuller flavor, which of course means that a little goes farther. I tend to use only sea salt in my cooking, both for health reasons and because it has much more flavor than any other variety. I either bring it back from Italy (where all salt is sea salt) or use La Baleine, a commercial brand that comes from the Mediterranean and is generally available in most supermarkets, and has a fresh, bright flavor that works well with almost any dish.

Many specialty markets now also stock salt from Brittany, where the cold, active North Sea currents impart a unique and flavorful mix of minerals. The salt is harvested from ocean water channeled into pristine ponds edged with natural waterways, wild grasses, and other green plants. Wind and sun evaporate the ocean water, leaving a mineral-rich brine from which the salt crystals form. Somewhat more expensive than La Baleine (sold for about $3 for a $1^1/_2$-pound container), Brittany sea salt ranges from $10 to $56 per pound and can be ordered through the Grain and Salt Society (800/867-7258). Another salt from Brittany, Fleur de Sel, costs about $25 per pound and can be purchased at specialty stores (see page 476).

Pepper One of the most underutilized of all spices, pepper offers a palette of colors and flavors that can transform an ordinary slab of fish into a succulent, peppercorn-encrusted grilled salmon masterpiece. Green, black, and white peppercorns all start out the same way— as the fruit of a perennial shrub called *Piper nigrum.* The green, unripe variety always comes either pickled or freeze-dried; its flavor is so mild that pickled peppercorns must be rinsed before using or the brine will overwhelm the taste of the spice. Because its fruity flavor fades almost immediately, green pepper is always added to a dish as close to serving time as possible.

Black peppercorns also start out as underripe green berries, but are then sundried and fermented until withered. The smoky, pungent flavor that results is somewhat longer lasting than that of the green variety, but black pepper should still be ground just before using.

White pepper berries are the only ones allowed to ripen and redden on the vine. Their outer skins are then buffed free of color and, when ground, used mainly in light-colored foods that would otherwise look dirty if speckled with flecks of black. Of the three, white pepper is my least favorite; its flavor always seems clawing and bitter.

Pink peppercorns are not, botanically speaking, part of the peppercorn family. Used mainly for their appearance, their faint hint of fruit and pine fades too quickly for any use other than esthetic.

Porcini mushrooms   Porcini mushrooms (*Boletus edulis*) are large, bulbous tubers that grow under chestnut trees mainly in fall. The most flavorful of all mushroom varieties, porcini have rust-brown caps and are plump, with stems that flare at the base. They may also be pale or almost white, depending on the sun exposure of the part of the forest where they grew. Increasingly available in farmers' markets in their fresh state, porcini mushrooms can also be purchased dry at specialty food stores. The difference between fresh and dry is one of both flavor and intensity, and the two should not be automatically interchanged. When purchasing fresh, look for smooth, creamy-colored caps with a firm, springy texture and a mild odor. Dried specimens should be large (avoid bags filled with tiny pieces), as light colored as possible (the lighter the more expensive), and not too hard in texture. Dried porcini should be soaked in warm water for 30 to 45 minutes, drained (liquid strained to remove grit and reserved), and rinsed before using.

Cornmeal   Used for making polenta, cornmeal can be purchased at specialty food stores in either fine or coarse grain. The best brands specify how the corn was ground (stone ground is preferable) and when (since all flours and grains lose moisture as they age, look for the most recent date). To store cornmeal, wrap tightly and keep in a dark, dry pantry or in the freezer.

Semolina   Another term for semolina is hard durum wheat. Milled from the heart of wheatberries, semolina is a high-gluten grain used in Italy mainly for making pasta. In English-speaking countries, it is also milled into a very fine grain and sold as "cream of wheat."

Appetizers and Salads

FONDUA
Fontina Cheese and White Truffle Fondue

ROBBIOLA IN SALSA
Rounds of Robiola Cheese Marinated in Tomato Sauce and Balsamic Vinegar

SPIEDINI DI FRITTATA CON CREMA DI CECI
Frittata Kebabs Stuffed with Creamed Chick Peas

MEDAGLIE DI RISO
Sicilian Rice and Pecorino Cheese Croquettes

PEVERADA DI FUNGHI
Porcini Mushroom Sauté

CARPACCIO DI ZUCCHINE AL PEPE VERDE
Zucchini Carpaccio with Green Peppercorn Dressing

PILLAS
Sardinian Semolina Terrine

PANADAS DI PECORINO
Pecorino Empanadas

BRUSCHETTA DI TARTUFO ALLO SPELLO
Bruschetta with Truffles

FUNGHI E FILETTO DI CINGHIALE
Porcini Canapés Served with Wild Boar Prosciutto

PANINI DI NOCE E MOZZARELLA
Walnut, Mozzarella, and Prosciutto Sandwiches

RONDELLI DI POLENTA CON SALSA DI NOCE
Polenta Rounds with Walnut Sauce

INSALATA DI TAROCCI
Blood Orange and Red Onion Salad

CARPACCIO DI TONNO
Tuna Carpaccio with Lemon–Parsley Sauce

CAPONÉT
Stuffed Zucchini Blossoms

OLIVE RIPIENE
Green Olives Stuffed with Meat, Battered, and Fried

PALLINE DI RICOTTA AI PISTACCHI
Mixed Green Salad Topped with Ricotta Rolled in Pistachios

CALAMARETTI CON AGLIATA
Baby Shrimp with Garlic Sauce

BURLENGHI
Rosemary Crepes

CALZONI PUGLIESI
Cheese, Anchovy, and Caper-stuffed Calzones

INSALATA DI FARRO
Farro Salad

SPIEDINI DI COZZE
Pancetta-wrapped Mussels Grilled on Skewers

OLIVE CONDITE
Olive and Blood Orange Salad

*Quando dal Po in autunno, come fantasmi sorgono le nebbie, io
vi perdo, o mei cari.*

*When in autumn the fog rises from the Po like a ghostly spectre,
I lose you, oh my loved ones.*

CORRADO GOVONI

PIEDMONT
Blessed Are the Humble

THE PO RIVER CUTS A HORIZONTAL SWATH through Piedmont and Lombardy and
serves as a de facto border defining northern Italy. With the coming of October, this mighty
waterway produces a thick gray fog that, for the next six months, completely blankets the
lowlands of its two host provinces, collectively known as Padana or the Valley of the Po.
So all-encompassing is this *fantasmo* that to anyone looking down from a mountaintop, the
entire valley seems nothing more than a still, gray lake. To outsiders, the effect is one of
disorientation, of feeling that the real world—the one with a clear line of sight—has somehow
disappeared.

But for those who have always lived here, like my friend Elisa Bottero and her family, the
fog creates an alternative faculty. "We never use our eyes to see during Po winters," says Elisa.
"We use instead a sixth sense that enables us to deduce, from the noises of the countryside—
even the most minimal of noises—the exact location of people and things. It is as if we
become implanted with a spiritual compass."

Elisa works for Slow Food Arcigola, an idiosyncratic organization devoted to undoing
the effect fast food has had on our collective lives. The "official" Slow Food manifesto reads

somewhat like a page taken directly from Lenin: "Born and nurtured under Industrialization, Speed has become our shackles. We have fallen prey to the same virus, the 'fast life' that fractures our customs and assails us even in our own homes, forcing us to ingest fast food. Let us defend ourselves against the universal madness of fast living with tranquil material pleasure. To escape the tediousness of fast food, let us rediscover the rich varieties and aromas of local cuisines, historical food culture, and old-fashioned food traditions."

Phenomenally successful since its inception in 1989, Slow Food Arcigola is the brainchild of businessman Carlo Petrini, who organized the original conference in reaction to the opening of a McDonald's on his beautiful historic block in central Rome. Headquartered in the Piemontese city of Bra and featuring a snail as its logo, Slow Food is now active in 40 countries and embraces over 80,000 members, 25,000 of which are—not surprisingly—in Italy, the world-renowned home of the three-hour lunch.

"You laugh," Elisa says every time I teasingly insinuate that it would just not be possible for Italians to be any more hedonistic about food than they already are, "but things are changing quickly, even here. Already, we are seeing the erosion of the ritualistic *pranzo* (the long family lunch), albeit only in big cities."

I have come to Bra both to spend time with Elisa and to take part in what we hope will be a moving tribute to her father, Pietro, who, for the past thirty-five years, has served as the chief cook for the Polenta Festival held in his village of Cherasco. On Saturday, the last day of this year's event, festival organizers plan to award him a beautiful silver plaque in gratitude for his long years of devotion. After which Don Fausto from the village church is slated to make a short speech and the hope is that Pietro will also say a few words.

THE PROBLEM IS that Pietro is Piemontese. And what that means, exactly, is that he refuses to be lauded on this or any other day of the year. The Piemontese are noted for existing in the shadows, for preferring behind-the-scenes situations to spotlights and applause, for hiding, so to speak, behind their native fog. "We all made the polenta," Pietro argues for the sixth time in the last few hours. "How does that qualify me for an award?"

In contrast to other groups of Italians who have little compunction about sharing their multiple virtues (I am thinking primarily here of Tuscans and Neapolitans), the Piemontese have an almost neurotic aversion to absolutely any hint of either emotional exhibition or self-aggrandizement. Understated in all things, they are known throughout Italy as *I Verbalmente Parsimoniosi*—The Verbally Parsimonious.

Elisa tells a story that perfectly illustrates the extent of this reticence. "In 1862, shortly after Torino became the capital of the newly created Kingdom of Italy, King Vittorio Emanuele II of the House of Savoy was frequently seen riding around the city in an ornate carriage drawn by four white horses. There was also, however, a local chocolatier who rode around in a carriage drawn by *six* horses. And so, one day, a member of the royal court suggested to the king that he might want to commission a new carriage, maybe one pulled by six, or even eight, horses. To which the king replied, 'Why would I consider such a thing. I am not, after all, a chocolatier.'"

"Remember," she tells me when I ask what she thinks will happen on Saturday, "Piemonte is known throughout Europe for its truffles, which—understand—also grow perfectly well in Tuscany and Umbria. But the character of a *trifolau*—truffle hunter—is so quintessentially Piemontese that I wonder why we have not yet adopted this dark character as our regional symbol." She hunches her shoulders and hides her head in a dramatic portrayal of the truffle hunter's stance. "The strong, silent man leaving his house after dark to wander through fog-encumbered forests, alone except for his loyal dog. Who else would take so perfectly to this kind of existence?"

She throws back her head in an abject gesture of futility. "Where did they ever get the idea for this award in the first place. It is so very unlike the Piemontese."

Despite our best efforts to convince Pietro otherwise, the closer we get to Saturday, the more made up his mind becomes. "I am not going to accept this award and don't you also try to talk me into it," he warns, as we negotiate our way through the dense fog.

"It has nothing to do with my appreciaton for the thought behind the award," he says, returning to the main subject. "I am not the ingrate Mariella [his wife] would have you believe. It is just that I shy away from public gestures. Nothing more, nothing less."

We pass a group of welders working on one of the many bridges swept away by the horrendous floods of 1994. Despite an aggressive schedule of reconstruction, Piemonte has still to climb out from under the massive damage sustained.

"It is already too ostentatious having everyone know I have worked at the festival for thirty-five years. Now I am to be stuffed into a suit, hauled onto a stage, and awarded a plaque. No, no, no. I will stay in the kitchen and cook the polenta the way I have always done."

He hunches slightly over the wheel to see through an especially thick fog patch. "*Chi monta piu alto che non deve, cade piu basso che non crede,*" he declares after we emerge into somewhat of a clearing. He who climbs higher than he should, falls much further than he would ever have thought.

At this point, I am beginning to wonder why he is still on the subject of the award, given his stated aversion to even thinking about it. Nothing I have said has in any way advanced the theme. In fact, I have rarely even spoken, given his unusual verbosity on this dreary afternoon.

"Don't you think your grandsons would be proud to see their beloved *nonno* accepting an award?" I finally venture. "They would remember it for the rest of their lives."

Silence.

"You could even have them accompany you onto the stage. Erico, you could carry and Claudio could be holding your hand."

Silence.

"Perhaps Claudio could even say a few words on your behalf and then you would not have to say anything at all."

This last idea ventured a bit too far upstream. I realized it as soon as the words had exited my lips.

"*Sì,*" he says sarcastically. "And then I could have my two daughters displaying photos showing what a good father I have always been."

"*Non è mica una brutta idea,*" I joke. Not a bad idea.

Three hours later, Pietro and I climb back into the car and wind our way once again through the fog en route to lunch. "Mariella said she was making *panissa,*" he informs me, knowing I will be pleased. *Panissa* is a traditional dish of the Piemonte region—a heavenly combination of Arborio rice cooked in homemade beef broth with freshly shelled cranberry beans, herbs, and salami.

"Mariella is a gastronomic treasure," I tell him.

"Yes, but she does not know how to make polenta."

I wonder if this comment is intended to return us to the question of the Saturday festival, but then he segues into an analysis of whether the government should allow the royal Savoy family to return to Italy after over thirty long years of exile and the next thing I know, we are sitting at the table and Elisa is asking if I will pass the basket of bread.

"*Le petits batôns de Turin,*" she says, taking a breadstick and holding it up for me to see. "Napolean loved breadsticks." She stuffs her hand into her shirtfront in parody of the teensy dictator. "When Torino (Piemonte's capital) was under French rule, every bakery in the city competed for his patronage."

Her comment reminds me that Torino has long been a powerful gastronomic force. Vermouth was invented here as was *gianduja* (hazelnut chocolate). In fact, Piemonte as a whole is no stranger to culinary superlatives—a fact that is wholly appropriate for the largest of Italy's eighteen mainland regions. A sophisticated blend of Northern Italian peasant staples and elegant French garnishes, the Piemontese kitchen is based largely on the use of butter, cheese, mushrooms, and truffles. Its great cheeses are too numerous to mention; suffice to say that eight have long held the prestigious D.O.C. denomination—more than any other region. Its wines—specifically barolo, barbaresco, and barbera—are among the world's finest.

"SO," MARIELLA SAYS when everyone's plate is filled with *panissa,* "did you and Anna talk at all about tomorrow night?" Her question is directed toward Pietro, but he is conveniently involved with his grandson Erico, into whose mouth he is trying to fit a spoonful of mashed peas.

"*Babbo,*" Elisa says, addressing him directly. "Have you made a decision?"

He pours himself a glass of wine and holds it up to the light.

"*Babbo!*"

"I will be in the kitchen cooking the same way I have been for thirty-five years," he answers, and then adds in a *sotto voce* mutter designed—obviously—to test the waters: "*If* this sore throat of mine does not materialize into something too serious."

CHERASCO'S *SAGRA DELLA POLENTA* is held in the village's main piazza, which is dominated by the Church of Saint Agatha. The kitchen is in the festival room—*Sala don Bosco*—adjacent to the church, and has long been used for a continuous series of community events like the recent dinner held for residents over seventy years of age (the waiters and waitresses ranged from nine to fifteen years). It is a very well-equipped kitchen, especially tonight, with its array of huge cauldrons brought in specifically for this festival.

The menu is varied, as it is at any of today's Italian food festivals. At one time, polenta festivals offered polenta exclusively, perhaps prepared variously with meat sauce, melted cheese, mushrooms, truffles, or fried and spread with stracchino cheese (so versatile is polenta, in fact, that in some places in Piemonte, it is referred to as "Traviata" because, like its operatic counterpart, this culinary headliner can "prostitute" itself to accommodate any number of preparations).

Earlier festivals were highly focused: If roasted pork was what you wanted the night of a polenta *sagra*, you had to go elsewhere. No longer. Today's food festivals offer menus ripe with choices, although it is always true that the featured food reigns as main attraction.

THERE ARE AT LEAST TWENTY COOKS working tonight in St. Agata's kitchens, all wearing white caps and aprons and all busy at their individual stations, chopping herbs, making sauces, basting chickens, stuffing eggplants. Pietro's role is that of supervisor, making sure that everything runs smoothly. In addition, he is in charge of the huge copper cauldron, dating back to the fifteenth century, in which the polenta will eventually be cooked over an open wood fire.

"Polenta is the great unifier of northern Italy," he says when I ask why Cherasco chose polenta as its patron. "From the Alpine villages of Val d'Aosta to the palaces of Torino and Milan to the fishing villages of the Veneto to the German enclaves scattered throughout Alto Adige—everyone loves polenta, regardless of ancestry or class."

In fact, he adds, "Polenta is one of the few grains in our history consumed as much by peasants as by kings. Peasants, of course, ate it plain or perhaps with a small drizzle of oil, while kings served it accompanied by great platters of grilled meats." He stops to answer a question about whether the red peppers should be chopped or slivered. "But regardless of class," he continues, "it was always eaten at long wooden tables analogous to those well-oiled slabs of wood residing today in Milan's executive dining rooms. A pity that bankers rarely choose polenta for their elevated gastronomic experiences. What better food than one so clearly evocative of pure gold?"

He strolls over to the cauldron of boiling water in which he will make tonight's polenta. I am told it holds twenty-five gallons of water, which means that, at the rate of one pound flour per two quarts water, Pietro will be cooking more than fifty pounds of polenta! I cannot imagine how anyone could do a good job working with such quantities, but I am told that Pietro's polenta is renowned throughout the province.

He works with a long-handled wooden spoon—*la mestola*—which is the traditional instrument for stirring polenta (so you're not scalded by the blips of boiling corn flour that occasionally jump out of the pot) and stirs in a counterclockwise fashion. "Some say polenta should always be stirred clockwise," I comment.

He laughs. "You hear all kinds of dicta when it comes to stirring polenta. Some swear by one method, others another, still others say you should stir first in one direction and then switch when the polenta is halfway cooked. *Ascolta bene*—listen well—the only thing that is absolutely important is that the polenta be stirred. How is of absolutely no importance."

I ask about the type of polenta flour he uses, and it is clearly a question he would rather not address. "True polenta, meaning that eaten for centuries, was dense, crisp, and dark," he says sadly. "Today it is difficult to make something comparable, even when you adhere to the strictest of culinary techniques. The fact is that the corn I remember from my youth was different from today's hybrid varieties. Then the cobs were small, oddly shaped, and reddish in color."

"What happened?"

"Let's just say that ancient varieties yielded thirty *quintali per ettaro* (about 15,000 pounds per 100 acres) and today's yield more than three times as much. *Comprende?*—Understand?"

He begins the process of stirring as a tall, red-haired teenager pours the polenta into the steaming cauldron in a practiced steady stream (I later learn that the position of "pourer" has long been a coveted one and that this particular teenager—Orlando—has been so honored as to be chosen by Pietro three years in a row).

"There is one place I know of, however, that still grows that old-style corn," says Pietro holding up his hand to indicate that Orlando should pour even slower. "In Mapello, near Bergamo [in Lombardia]. Scotti, it is called. They not only grow authentic corn, but also grind it the way we used to when I was young—simply using a giant stone wheel that crushes the kernels without the heat of electrical machines. The resulting polenta flour is more consistently granular and maintains more of its nutritional value."

He looks up from his stirring. "There is also a place you can go to to eat this genuine polenta," he says, struggling to remember the name. "*Aspetta, aspetta* (wait, wait). *Si! La Polenteria* in Torino. It is the only place in Italy with a menu devoted exclusively to polenta. Everything is prepared traditionally, with a wood fire and a giant copper cauldron like this." He gives his "personal" cauldron a resounding slap.

Five minutes later, when the polenta has completely melded with the water, Pietro rises to his feet and a clearly reverent Orlando removes the small stool on which "Il Capo" sat during his initial stirring phase. From now until the polenta is cooked in about ninety minutes, "The Boss" will stand with his feet spread in a stance wide enough to give him the leverage necessary for stirring this mountainous mass of dense golden gruel. Actually, as Elisa told me yesterday, nowadays Pietro only stirs the first and last few minutes. "Orlando is more and more taking over the job," she said, clearly saddened by her beloved *babbo's* advancing age.

ELISA, MARIELLA, AND I EAT OUTSIDE, at a table filled with aunts and uncles and cousins and friends. The air is laced with the fragrance of cooking aromas weaving in between the wisps of fog. There are over 400 people tonight in this piazza, most wearing silk scarves and wool blazers and sitting elbow to elbow at long tables, eating polenta and drinking wine. In a few minutes, the band will begin playing and the chairs surrounding the dance floor will be appropriated by elderly residents rising majestically for the occasional *liscio*—slow dance.

"When is the presentation supposed to take place?" I ask Elisa.

"In about an hour. What do you think will happen?" she asks nervously.

"I don't know. I can't imagine your father creating a scene, which is what will happen if they announce his name and he refuses to come out of the kitchen."

Mariella chimes in. "I asked Don Fausto if he had spoken to Pietro and he said he'd rather just do things according to the schedule."

"What does that mean?" Elisa storms.

"I have no idea," Mariella admits. "But I think it is clear that by now the award ceremony is going to take place and Pietro will have no choice but to accept."

Just at that moment, we see Pietro exiting the kitchen door with his friend Loreno. The two stroll over to a table where four men sit playing cards. Lighting their cigars, Pietro and Loreno choose positions behind one of the card players and begin the routine practice of offering advice.

"Is it my imagination," Elisa asks. "Or is my father's hair gelled?"

"I think you're right," Mariella answers. "And he has on a silk cravat, which he only wears on Christmas Day."

"Well, I guess that answers the question of whether or not he plans to accept the plaque," I say, grinning.

I'M NOT SURE WHAT I WAS EXPECTING, but the so-called awards ceremony exceeded even my wildest expectations of Piemontese-style moderation. The band ceased playing, Don Fausto said a few words about the upcoming procession in honor of the Feast of All Saints, and ended with these exact words: "And now we have a little plaque we want to give Pietro Bottero in honor of the thirty-five years he has worked at this *Sagra*."

There was a round of applause, Pietro climbed onto the stage accompanied—yes—by his grandson Claudio—and took the plaque from Don Fausto's hands. "*Grazie,*" he said into the standing microphone. "*Grazie.*" Everyone applauded a bit more and then he walked off the stage and returned to the kitchen, where I'm sure everyone continued about their business with, perhaps, the occasional *auguri*—congratulations.

"All this anxiety for *that*?" I asked Elisa.

"This is, after all, Piemonte," she said, laughing. "What were you expecting—the Oscars?"

FONDUA

Fontina Cheese and White Truffle Fondue

❦ Piemonte ❧

ON APRIL 23, THE PEOPLE OF SUSA IN WESTERN PIEMONTE HONOR THEIR VILLAGE'S *patron saint San Giorgio with a festival called the Dance of the Sabers. Dressed in traditional red-and-white striped costumes dating back to the fourteenth century, dozens of young, handsome swordsmen reenact a series of ancient rituals designed to guarantee the soil's fertility and, thus, a plentiful harvest. The grand finale—a fascinating bacchanalia of colors and sounds—involves two swordsmen holding firm a large, flower-festooned hoop through which twelve female dancers (signifying the months of the year) pass twice, the twenty-four passages signifying the hours of the day.*

The food for the festival revolves mainly around Piemonte's traditional cheeses, fontina being one of the most famous. This souplike appetizer can be eaten as a soup or, as presented in this recipe, served as a dip for the bread cubes that sit alongside the bowl.

serves 4

Time: 40 minutes (excluding the 2-hour resting period for the cheese)

Level of Difficulty: Easy

12 ounces high-quality fontina cheese, cut into 1-inch cubes
1 cup whole milk
4 large egg yolks, lightly beaten
4 tablespoons unsalted butter at room temperature
Freshly ground white pepper to taste

1 Put the cheese in a small bowl with the milk, cover with a clean cotton cloth, and let sit for at least 2 hours.

2 Transfer the milk and cheese mixture to a medium-size heavy-gauge casserole (terra-cotta works best) and stir in the eggs and butter until well blended.

3 Place the casserole over a pot of boiling water, reduce the heat to low, and cook for 10 to 15 minutes, whisking constantly, until the mixture is dense and creamy. Immediately remove from the heat and season with a hefty dose of pepper.

*For maximum freshness, truffles should be sliced directly onto each plate at the table. The best implement for achieving perfect, wafer-thin slices is, appropriately, called an affetatartufi, *or truffle-slicer. A mandoline can also be used, although without the same visual flourish.*

4 Pour the fondua into four heated bowls, top with thinly sliced truffles, arrange the bread cubes around the rim of the bowls, and serve immediately.

Serve With Can be a hefty appetizer followed by a light fish and vegetable entrée, or can serve as an entree on its own accompanied by a green salad and fresh, crusty bread.

Wine Suggestion Dry White or Medium-Sweet White

2 ounces white truffles (or fresh porcini or other wild mushrooms)*
Eight 3/4-inch-thick slices peasant-style bread, toasted and cut into 1-inch cubes

9

ROBBIOLA IN SALSA

Rounds of Robbiola Cheese Marinated in Tomato Sauce and Balsamic Vinegar

❦ Piemonte ❦

TWO OTHER PIEMONTESE MOUNTAIN VILLAGES CELEBRATE THE APRIL 23 FEAST *of San Giorgio with swordplay demonstrations: Bagnasco a Fenestrelle and Rocca Grimalda. All three evoke the same underlying theme: the positive force of the soil's fertility pitted against the negative force of the winter death cycle. My favorite part of the Rocco Grimalda festival was watching the twenty-four graceful (and spectacularly costumed) swordsmen perform their ritualistic dances, slicing the earth with their sabers as if to liberate the Goddess of Fertility herself. Even better, however, was the cheese tasting that followed. Wedges of local cheese, their fresh, tart flavor perfectly counter-balanced by the sweetness of the tomato-garlic-balsamic marinade, were arranged on a display table and spectators helped themselves.*

For those who want to sample the joys of robbiola cheese in absolute purity, head to Vesime, in the Alba region of Piemonte, on the first Sunday of June for the Sagra della Robbiola which, in addition to the free giveaway of quarti fritti *(fried squares of dough) spread with robbiola, features a stunning parade of vintage cars, including a 1947 Alfa Romeo sports coupe that, according to the announcer, once belonged to Marcello Mastroianni.*

serves 4

Time: 20 minutes, excluding the 2 to 3 hour marinating time

Level of Difficulty: Easy

🜊

2 cloves garlic, peeled
4 tablespoons fresh, roughly
    chopped Italian parsley
2 tablespoons tomato paste*
1 cup extra virgin olive oil

1 Chop the garlic with the parsley until the consistency is homogenous and pastelike. Place in a bowl and add the tomato paste, oil, vinegar, salt and pepper. Mix well until all ingredients are blended into a thick emulsion.

2 Slice the rounds of cheese into thick wedges. Arrange in a nonreactive pan and cover with the tomato emulsion. Marinate for 2 to 3 hours, spooning the marinade over the wedges every 20 to 30 minutes. To serve, arrange the wedges on a platter

*The best quality tomato pastes are made from San Marzano tomatoes. In most cases, tubes of paste are better than cans, which tend to have a slightly metallic taste.

surrounded by parsley sprigs and topped with the marinade.

How to Serve Works well served as an appetizer accompanied by a basket of various breads and olives, and perhaps a raw vegetable platter.

Wine Suggestion Dry White, Medium-Sweet White, or Medium-bodied Red

3 tablespoons good balsamic
 vinegar
Salt to taste
Freshly ground black pepper
 to taste
Six 8-ounce rounds of very fresh
 robbiola cheese**
Parsley sprigs for garnish

11

**Robbiola is a D.O.C. cheese made of goat's and cow's milk; its inimitable flavor comes from grazing pastures that abound in wild thyme and blackthorn. Goat's milk cheese can be substituted.*

SPIEDINI DI FRITTATA CON CREMA DI CECI

Frittata Kebabs Stuffed with Creamed Chick Peas

❧ Umbria ❧

UMBRIA'S MOST SPECTACULAR PROCESSION TAKES PLACE ON MAY 15 IN HONOR OF *Gubbio's patron, Saint Ubaldo, a bishop who lived in the twelfth century. Ubaldo's body is interred in the church that bears his name, located on Mount Ingino. Originally, residents walked up to the mountain sanctuary holding small candles and singing simple songs. Over the years, the candles have evolved into huge wooden flatbeds bearing octagonal prisms filled with colored lights and topped with dioramas depicting scenes from the saint's life. Thousands of spectators line the route but the atmosphere remains solemn and respectful nonetheless.*

I bought these kebabs at a food stall at the base of the mountain. Frittatas are one of the foods traditionally associated with Saint Ubaldo, the proprietor told me, and then added that she had tired of making the same types of frittatas year in and year out and so had created this charmingly creative version.

serves 4

Time: 45 to 60 minutes

Level of Difficulty: Easy

⚶

4 large eggs, lightly beaten

Salt to taste

1/2 dried chili, crumbled

2 tablespoons unsalted butter

1 1/2 cups canned chick peas,
    drained, rinsed, and drained

Juice of 1 lemon

1 tablespoon lemon zest

2 tablespoons extra virgin olive oil

1 small onion, minced

1 Beat the eggs with the salt and chili in a medium bowl. Heat 1 tablespoon butter in a 6-inch nonstick skillet over medium heat and pour in a ladleful of the egg mixture. Cook until the underside is set. Slide onto a dish, cover with another dish, turn upside down and return to the skillet. Cook until both sides are set. Continue making frittatas until the egg mixture is used up. Keep the frittatas warm.

2 Meanwhile, place all but about 15 chick peas in a food processor with the lemon, lemon zest, oil, onion, parsley, spinach, and salt. Blend until pureed.

3 Spread a dollop of chick-pea puree onto each frittata and roll into a tight cylinder. Cut into

1-inch-thick slices and thread the slices onto skewers, alternating with cherry tomatoes and the reserved chick peas. Arrange the skewers on a bed of lettuce and serve at room temperature.

Make Ahead The frittatas can be made in advance, refrigerated, and then heated in a lightly oiled skillet or in a warm oven just before serving.

How to Serve The skewers can serve as an entire appetizer or as part of an appetizer plate that also includes a braised leek or a small quantity of panfried artichokes.

Wine Suggestion Dry White, Medium-Sweet White or Medium-bodied Red

1 tablespoon freshly chopped parsley

1/4 cup chopped fresh or frozen spinach

20 to 24 cherry tomatoes

Lettuce to line the platter

20 to 24 skewers

13

MEDAGLIE DI RISO

Sicilian Rice and Pecorino Cheese Croquettes

❦ Sicilia ❦

IN THE LATE AFTERNOON EVERY SEPTEMBER 7, THOUSANDS OF PILGRIMS JOURNEY *to a mountain sanctuary in Tindari, Sicily, to celebrate the feast of the Black Madonna. A huge ceramic statue, the Madonna was supposedly placed on this spot at the end of the eighth century by Byzantine sailors forced by a hurricane to land in Tindari's port. Since then, as any citizen of Tindari will hasten to inform you, she has performed literally hundreds of miracles, the most famous being the 1927 resurrection of a young girl who had drowned while playing on the shoals.*

Later the same day, the town hosts a grand festival on the central piazza, complete with dancing and a sumptous display of traditional foods, including the following croquettes whose delicate flavor emanates primarily from the use of fresh pecorino cheese.

serves 4

Time: 60 to 75 minutes

Level of Difficulty: Moderate

4 cups short-grained white rice
4 ounces freshly grated pecorino
4 ounces pecorino (as young as possible), cut into 1-inch cubes
1 cup fresh tomato sauce
2 large eggs, lightly beaten
1/2 cup unflavored breadcrumbs
Olive oil for frying

1 Put the rice in a large pot of boiling salted water and cook for about 18 minutes or until tender to the point of stickiness. Drain and place the rice on a large cotton cloth, spreading the rice with the back of a chef's knife until you have a large circle that is uniformly 1/4 inch thick.

2 Press a 2-inch-round cookie cutter or the rim of an overturned juice glass into the rice to delineate a small, round medallion. Leave the medallion in place and continue delineating circles until the rice is divided into as many medallions as possible. Make sure to wet the rim of the glass in cold water each time before using. Let the rice cool to room temperature.

3 Spread half the cooled medallions with the following ingredients, one at a time: a dusting of

14

grated cheese, 2 or 3 cheese cubes, and 1 teaspoon sauce.

4 Using a spatula, lift off a plain rice medallion and carefully place over one spread with cheese. Press slightly with the back of the spatula to seal. Continue until all the medallions have been paired into croquettes.

5 Place the eggs in a small bowl and the breadcrumbs on a large plate. Pour 2 inches of oil into a medium skillet and place over medium heat. Carefully lift the croquettes from the cloth, one at a time. Dip each croquette first into the beaten eggs, making sure to dampen each side, and then roll in breadcrumbs until all surfaces are coated. When the oil reaches 375°F, fry the croquettes, 4 or 5 at a time, until golden on both sides.*

6 Remove with a slotted spatula and drain on paper towels. Place on a bed of greens and serve immediately.

Make Ahead The rice medallions may be made up to a week in advance and refrigerated. Return to room temperature before spreading with the filling mixture and finishing.

How to Serve Makes a perfect appetizer on its own or works equally well as a light entrée served on a bed of roasted vegetables.

Wine Suggestion If used on its own as an appetizer, serve with a Dry White or Medium-bodied Red. If served as an entree bedded on roasted vegetables, try pairing with something bigger—a Medium- or Full-bodied Red.

To test the temperature of the oil, use a thermometer or dip a small bread cube into the hot oil; if the edges sizzle and the bread turns golden almost immediately, the oil is hot enough for frying. Avoid overcrowding, as it will lower the temperature of the oil and prevent proper frying.

15

PEVERADA DI FUNGHI

Porcini Mushroom Sauté

❧ Veneto ❧

THE COMING OF THE NEW YEAR HAS ITS ASSOCIATED RITUALS, MANY BASED ON *long-held superstitions. Throughout the Veneto and even in Friuli, if the first falls on a Sunday or Wednesday, all will be well; if on Tuesday, wars will be fought; if on Friday, the winter will be long and dark. Years containing a seven or its multiple, furthermore, will bring bad harvests and years containing a three will produce a plethora of male babies. Another New Year's ritual involves throwing zoccoli (wooden clogs) down the stairs. If they land together, it will be a good year; if not, terrible. To ascertain the future of a love affair, Venetians pour an egg yolk into a bottle and leave it overnight. If the yolk gels in a round position, marriage is on the horizon; if ovular, nothing.*

The first meal of the New Year leans heavily on superstitions whose basic assumptions can be reduced to one simple dictum: the more the better. Bad omens hover over festival tables bearing few courses consisting of simple, quick-and-easy food. Better to stick with exquisite flavors such as the following dish of sautéed mushrooms folded into a smooth, creamy sauce and served with toast wedges.

serves 4

Time: 60 minutes

Level of Difficulty: Easy

1 pound fresh porcini mushroom
    caps
2 ounces dried porcini
    mushrooms*
2 tablespoons unsalted butter
Salt to taste
Freshly ground white pepper
    to taste

1 Clean the mushroom caps using a damp cloth (do not place under running water) and cut into wafer-thin slices. Grate the dried mushrooms using a hand grater or food processor.

2 Melt the butter in a skillet, add both the fresh and the grated mushrooms, season with salt and pepper, cover, and cook over very low heat for 35 to 40 minutes, stirring frequently with a wooden spoon.

3 Meanwhile, place the breadcrumbs, cream, marrow, and broth in a saucepan, cover, and cook over very low heat for 30 minutes, stirring frequently until the sauce is dense and smooth.

4 Add the marrow sauce and lemon zest to the mushrooms and stir until all ingredients are well blended. Continue to cook over low heat, uncovered, for 2 to 3 minutes. Remove from the heat and transfer to a heated platter. Surround with wedges of toasted bread and serve immediately.

Make Ahead The mushroooms can be prepared through Step 2 earlier in the day. Heat through before proceeding.

How to Serve Works perfectly as either an appetizer on its own or as an entrée when accompanied by a mixed green salad. The finished mushrooms can also be used as a topping for pasta, rice, or polenta.

Wine Suggestion I find this dish works well with every type of wine from Dry White to Full-bodied Red. Listen to your taste buds for absolute guidance.

4 tablespoons unflavored
   breadcrumbs
1/4 cup heavy cream
2 ounces beef marrow**
2 cups good-quality beef broth
3 tablespoons lemon zest

Dried mushrooms can also be grated in a pepper, spice, or coffee grinder. Placed in a tightly sealed glass jar, the resulting pow-der can be conserved without refrigeration for 8 to 9 months and used for flavoring sauces, soups, stews, and salad dressings.

Beef marrow can be found at butcher shops where the butcher will extract it from the insides of bones.

CARPACCIO DI ZUCCHINE AL PEPE VERDE

Zucchini Carpaccio with Green Peppercorn Dressing

18

❧ Lazio ❧

WHEN I HAPPENED UPON *LE PASSATE* (SEE PAGE 50), I WANDERED AROUND THE *festival for about an hour before an old, wrinkled woman accosted me and asked what I was doing there. "I'm writing a book about festival food," I told her, hoping she might take me under her wing and share some scrumptious recipes. "Then let me show you this fresh zucchini dish," she said, pulling me toward her kitchen. "I had made it for my family for years and always called it* Insalata di Zucchini. *But recently my daughter came down from Rome and added green pepper as an extra ingredient. As well as mixing grated cheese into the dressing, she also shaved the cheese and placed it on top. Finally, she called it carpaccio, a word I had never before heard but it sounded so wonderful that I now bring it to the festival and tell everyone it is a carpaccio of zucchini. Most people are not willing to taste something new, but the younger participants order more of it than I can make."*

serves 4

Time: 25 to 35 minutes, including resting time

Level of Difficulty: Easy

⚸

4 small zucchini, trimmed and shaved with a potato slicer into very thin lengthwise strips
4 tablespoons extra virgin olive oil
Juice of 1 lemon
2 tablespoons finely diced fresh Italian parsley

1 Put the zucchini in a bowl. In a separate bowl, whisk together the oil, lemon, parsley, and salt until emulsified. Toss the zucchini with the lemon vinaigrette until well coated.

2 Stir in the green pepper and cheese shavings. Let rest for 10 to 15 minutes, then arrange on a platter and serve with fresh country-style bread.

Make Ahead The entire recipe can be made up to a day in advance, except for the cheese shavings, which should be added just before serving.

---

*Cheese can be shaved with a common vegetable peeler or with a wide-blade potato peeler. Wide-blade shavers created specifically for cheese can be purchased at specialty stores.

How to Serve Can stand on its own as an appetizer; can also be used as a salad course, served either independently or as a salad accompaniment to an entrée.

Wine Suggestion Dry White

Salt to taste

1 teaspoon green peppercorns in brine, drained and crushed

1/4 cup freshly shaved Parmigiano-Reggiano*

19

PILLAS

Sardinian Semolina Terrine

❦ Sardegna ❧

SASSARI IS ONE OF SARDINIA'S MAIN CITIES AND ON THE AUGUST FOURTEENTH *Feast of the Assumption, of the Virgin, what seems like most of the city's inhabitants turn out to celebrate* I Candelieri di Sassari, *an event combining ancient tradition, incredible foods, and breathtaking fireworks. The festival dates back to 1580, when a ferocious pestilence decimated most of the population only to end precisely on August 14 with the miraculous discovery of an herbal cure. Celebrants process from the Church of the Rosary in the city's northern end, to the piazza in front of the city's Municipal Palace where there is a colorful and masterly display of flagmanship (the flags and swords dating back to the sixteenth century), to the final destination: the Church of Saint Maria of Betlem after which the merriment begins in earnest with much dancing and spectacular recipes like the following semolina tart, sliced into appetizer portions and served lukewarm on paper napkins.*

serves 6

Time: 2 hours

Level of Difficulty: Moderate

1 quart whole milk

1 1/2 cups finely ground semolina
   or cream of wheat

Salt to taste

2 large egg yolks

8 tablespoons (1 stick) unsalted
   butter

1 cup freshly grated pecorino

12 ounces ground sirloin

1 cup dry white wine

Freshly ground black pepper
   to taste

1 Place the milk in a saucepan and, over low heat, bring to a gentle boil. Add the semolina or cream of wheat, pouring in a steady stream and whisking constantly. Season with salt, reduce the heat to low, and cook, uncovered, for 20 minutes, or until the whisk stands up by itself in the center. Remove from heat and whisk in the eggs, 3 tablespoons of the butter, and all but 4 tablespoons of the grated cheese. Whisk until all the ingredients are thoroughly blended. Rinse an 8 x 10-inch metal pan with cold water and do not dry it. Pour in the semolina mixture, level the surface with a spatula, and cool to room temperature. Dip the spatula into cold water from time to time to help spread the mixture more easily.

2 Meanwhile, melt 3 tablespoons butter in a skillet over medium heat and add the chopped sirloin. Sauté, separating the meat with a fork and stirring constantly until it has lightly browned. Pour in the wine and cook until completely evaporated, about 3 to 5 minutes. Season with salt and pepper, add 2 tablespoons cold water, cover, reduce the heat to low, and cook for 30 minutes.

3 Preheat the oven to 350°F. Butter a 16 x 20-inch ovenproof baking pan. Cut the cooled semolina into small pieces and arrange a single layer on the bottom of the pan. Cover with a layer of meat, 2 or 3 slices Parma ham, tomato sauce, and grated cheese. Top with another layer of semolina pieces and continue layering until all the ingredients, except for the 4 tablespoons of reserved cheese, are used up. The final layer should be semolina.

4 Dot the semolina with the remaining butter, sprinkle with the cheese, and bake for 30 minutes. Cool for 30 minutes, cut into squares, and serve.

Make Ahead The entire casserole can be made up to a day or two in advance and kept refrigerated.

How to Serve In addition to serving as a wonderfully hearty appetizer, this terrine also works well as an entrée accompanied by a mixed green salad.

Wine Suggestion Medium- or Full-bodied Red

8 ounces Parma ham or other type of prosciutto, thinly sliced
2 cups good-quality tomato sauce

21

PANADAS DI PECORINO

Pecorino Empanadas

❧ Sardegna ❧

ANOTHER EXAMPLE OF THE LUSCIOUS KINDS OF FINGER FOOD SERVED AT SARDINIA'S Candelieri *festival is the following panadas, whose origin and Spanish-sounding name date back to the seventeenth century when Catalans emigrated in great numbers to this rugged island's western coast. The panadas are filled with a simple mixture of finely chopped mint and that delicious mainstay of the Sardinian kitchen, pecorino cheese. If possible, try to find pecorino sardo, a harder, more peppery type of pecorino than most.*

makes about 10 to 12 panadas

Time: 65–75 minutes

Level of Difficulty: Advanced

1 cup unbleached all-purpose
    flour, sifted

4 ounces rendered salt pork or
    bacon fat

Salt to taste

1 tablespoon cold water

1 1/2 cups freshly grated pecorino
    sardo (other varieties of aged
    pecorino can be substituted)

10 tablespoons finely minced
    fresh mint

Freshly ground black pepper
    to taste

Olive oil for frying

Fresh mint leaves for garnish

1 Heap the flour on a flat surface and create a well in the center. Pour the rendered salt pork or bacon fat with a pinch of salt and 1 tablespoon cold water into the well. Using a fork, stir the liquid ingredients in a clockwise fashion, each time incorporating a little of the flour wall (see Basic Egg Pasta, page 461 for more detailed instructions). Continue incorporating flour until you have a soft, elastic ball of dough. Divide the dough into 2 equal parts and, using a rolling pin or pasta machine, roll each part into a 6 x 15-inch rectangle about 1/8 inch thick. Let it rest for 20 to 30 minutes.

2 Meanwhile, place the minced mint in a bowl with the grated cheese, season with pepper, and stir until all ingredients are well blended.

3 Using a teaspoon, place walnut-size dollops of the mint and cheese mixture 2 1/2 to 3 inches apart on the bottom half of each dough rectangle.

Carefully fold the top half over the bottom and, with your fingers, press down on the area around the dollops, making sure the edges are thoroughly sealed. Using a ravioli cutter or butter knife, cut the dough into 3-inch-square panadas.

4 Heat 2 inches of olive oil in a skillet until the temperature reaches 375°F.* Fry the panadas, 4 or 5 at a time, turning once until both sides are golden brown.** Drain on paper towels and serve hot garnished with the fresh mint.

Make Ahead The dough can be made up to a day in advance, refrigerated, and returned to room temperature before using, or frozen and thawed completely. The panadas can also be made up to a day ahead of time and reheated in the oven before serving (although I must stress that they are much better made fresh).

How to Serve As part of an appetizer plate also containing a few wedges of tomato salad, or as finger food for a party or buffet.

Wine Suggestion Medium-Sweet White

*In lieu of using a thermometer to determine when the oil is ready for frying, immerse a small bread cube in the center of the pan. The edges of the bread should sizzle and the bread itself should turn golden almost immediately.

**For a lower-fat alternative, the panadas can also be brushed with oil and baked at 350°F for 20 minutes per side, 40 minutes total.

BRUSCHETTA DI TARTUFO ALLO SPELLO

Bruschetta with Truffles

❧ Umbria ❧

THE END OF THE OLIVE HARVEST ROUGHLY COINCIDES WITH TRUFFLE SEASON AND *in Spello, fifteen miles outside of Perugia in Umbria, the two are honored together in an event called* La Festa dell'olivo e La Sagra della bruschetta *held about the last Sunday in November. Spello's main claim to fame lies in its stunning collection of Pinturicchio frescoes located inside the Church of Santa Maria Maggiore—in the Baglioni chapel. Food for the festival consists solely of various types of bruschetta (slices of rustic-style bread rubbed with garlic), all brushed with oil before serving. And wine of course. There's the traditional bruschetta, with its simple topping of oil, a drizzle of vinegar, salt, and pepper. And then there's everyone's favorite: Bruschetta with Truffles. After all the eating and drinking, there's also dancing under the stars to a lively band, enamored of traditional music like* Il Saltarello.

makes 8 bruschettas or 4 appetizer servings

Time: 25 minutes, excluding the 1-hour rest time

Level of Difficulty: Easy

4 ounces fresh black truffles, cleaned carefully with a vegetable brush, or 2 ounces truffle paste

6 tablespoons extra virgin olive oil

1 clove garlic

2 tablespoons unsalted butter

Salt to taste

2 tablespoons fresh lemon juice

2 to 3 anchovy fillets, finely minced*

1 Cut the truffle roughly into small pieces and, using a mezzaluna or a chef's knife, mince until you have a pastelike consistency.

2 Heat 3 tablespoons of the oil in a skillet over medium heat and sauté the garlic for 2 minutes. Remove the garlic with a slotted spoon and discard.

3 Pour the hot oil into a small bowl. Add the truffles, butter, a pinch of salt, the lemon juice, and the anchovies. Mix until all ingredients are well blended.

4 Pour the remaining oil into a skillet and fry the bread over moderate heat on both sides until golden. Drain on paper towels and spread with the truffle mixture. Arrange the bruschette on a large

platter garnished with the fennel fronds. Let sit for
1 hour before serving.

Make Ahead The truffle spread can be made earlier
in the day.

How to Serve On its own as an appetizer or as part
of an appetizer buffet. Also works well when used as
the bread accompaniment to thin soups such as
onion or various types of broths.

Wine Suggestion Medium- or Full-bodied Red

Eight 3/4-inch-thick slices rustic
bread
Fennel fronds for garnish

25

*If at all possible, buy salt-packed anchovies, which are bigger, meatier, and less briny tasting than oil-packed anchovies
in cans or jars. Rinse before using and remove the backbone. Salt-packed anchovies generally come in one-pound cans;
the remainder can be filleted, packed in oil, and stored in a cool, dry place for future use.*

FUNGHI E FILETTO DI CINGHIALE

Porcini Canapés Served with Wild Boar Prosciutto

❦ Toscana ❦

RUFINA, A TOWN IN THE CHIANTI REGION OF TUSCANY JUST OUTSIDE FLORENCE, *is best known for the exceptional quality of its wines. On the last Saturday of October, the town's inhabitants gather to celebrate the Feast of San Michele with a festival centered completely around the benediction of its wines and their imbibing. Included are processions of antiquated wagons piled high with wine-filled demijohns and pulled by huge white steers as well as open admission to the Poggio Reale, one of Italy's seven wine museums where visitors can view a host of ancient tools used for preparing, bottling, and drinking wine. Also on display at the town's many* bancarelli— *festival tables—are endless quantities of traditional foods designed to enhance the wine's oh-so-eloquent bouquet.*

These particular canapés are served as the bread accompaniment to wild boar prosciutto, which is darker in color, leaner, and slightly gamier in flavor than the traditional pork variety.

serves 4

Time: 50 minutes

Level of Difficulty: Easy

8 ounces fresh porcini mushroom
    caps, cleaned with a soft
    brush, or shiitakes or
    chantarelles
5 tablespoons extra virgin olive oil
1 clove garlic
5 tablespoons freshly minced
    Italian parsley
Salt to taste

1 Cut the cleaned mushroom caps into thin slices.

2 Heat the oil in a skillet over low heat and sauté the garlic and 4 tablespoons of the parsley for 4 minutes. Add the mushrooms, season with salt and pepper, and cook for 25 to 30 minutes, stirring occasionally. In the last 5 minutes, stir in the flour.

3 Toast the bread squares on both sides, top with mushrooms, and sprinkle with the remaining parsley. Arrange the canapés on one side of a serving platter and the prosciutto cylinders on the other.

How to Serve In addition to making a wonderful appetizer (especially when served with bowls of various *sott-olios* and *sott-acetos*—oil and vinegar-marinated vegetables), the mushroom mixture makes an ideal topping for pasta and rice.

Wine Suggestion Full-bodied Red

Freshly ground black pepper to taste

1 tablespoon unbleached all-purpose flour

Eight 3/4-inch-thick slices day-old bread, cut into about 3-inch squares

4 ounces wild boar prosciutto, sliced very thin and rolled lengthwise into cylinders, or other types of prosciutto

PANINI DI NOCE E MOZZARELLA

Walnut, Mozzarella, and Prosciutto Sandwiches

❦ Lazio ❧

IN THE LAZIO REGION OF ITALY, AUGUST MARKS THE WALNUT HARVEST.
And in Caprarola, a tiny village located in the Cimini mountains of northern Lazio, the harvest is celebrated with a no-holds-barred sagra that takes place the last two Saturdays and Sundays of August and includes a huge variety of foods, all centered around walnuts. To the Caprarolese, walnuts have always had an importance far beyond their highly prized flavor; well protected in a hard outer shell, la noce *was said to signify an interior wisdom.*

And so it is that sage residents of Caprarola have traditionally dredged the following sandwich—a succulent mouthful of mozzarella and prosciutto—in ground walnuts before frying.

serves 6

Time: 45 to 60 minutes, excluding the 1-hour resting period

Level of Difficulty: Easy

1 cup shelled walnuts

1/2 cup unbleached all-purpose flour

1 round loaf of day-old rustic bread (about 1 1/2 pounds)

1 pound fresh bufala mozzarella or cow's milk mozzarella, cut into 1-inch cubes

12 thin slices prosciutto

1 cup milk

3 large eggs, lightly beaten with a pinch of salt

1 Place the walnuts and flour in a food processor and reduce to a fine powder. Transfer to a large plate.

2 Cut the bread into six 2-inch-thick slices. Remove the crusts and, using a sharp knife, cut a deep slit lengthwise into each slice in order to create a pocket. Fill each pocket with 4 to 5 cubes of mozzarella and 2 slices prosciutto.

3 Place the milk in a wide bowl. Dredge the sandwiches in the walnut flour, dip in the milk, and place side by side in a glass dish. Pour the eggs over the sandwiches and set aside for at least 1 hour.

4 Heat 2 inches oil in a skillet and fry the sandwiches 6 to 8 minutes, or until golden brown on each side. Drain on paper towels and serve immediately on a bed of lettuce.

Make Ahead The sandwiches can be prepared earlier in the day up to Step 3. Keep refrigerated.

How to Serve For use as part of an appetizer buffet, the finished sandwiches can be sliced into small, almost bite-size portions. The sandwiches also make a wonderful lunch entrée, ccompanied by a mixed green or green bean salad.

Wine Suggestion Dry White or Medium-bodied Red

Olive oil for frying
Lettuce leaves for garnish

29

RONDELLI DI POLENTA CON SALSA DI NOCE

Polenta Rounds with Walnut Sauce

❦ Lazio ❧

ANOTHER OF THE WONDERFUL FOODS SERVED AT CAPRAROLA'S WALNUT SAGRA *is the following appetizer consisting of fried circles of polenta served with a gremolatalike sauce that pairs the meatiness of walnuts with the creaminess of fresh sheep's milk ricotta.*

makes approximately 12 to 15 rounds

Time: 90 minutes

Level of Difficulty: Moderate

POLENTA

2 1/2 quarts salted water for cooking

12 ounces coarsely ground cornmeal

Salt to taste

Olive oil for frying

SAUCE

1 cup shelled walnuts

1 clove garlic, peeled

1 tablespoon freshly chopped marjoram (parsley can be substituted)

Salt to taste

6 ounces fresh sheep's milk ricotta or high-quality cow's milk ricotta

1/2 cup extra virgin olive oil

1 Heat the 2 1/2 quarts water to a boil over medium heat. Pour the cornmeal in a steady stream into the boiling water, whisking constantly until the liquid has significantly thickened. Reduce the heat to low and cook for 30 to 40 minutes, whisking frequently, until the cornmeal begins to detach from the sides of the pot and the whisk can stand by itself in the center. Pour into a moistened 8 x 10-inch baking pan and, using a spatula, level the surface. Cool completely.

2 Meanwhile, put the nuts, garlic, marjoram, and salt in a mortar. Using a pestle, pound the mixture into a dense, homogenous paste. A food processor can also be used although the texture will be grainier, drier, and less pastelike. Transfer to a bowl and add the ricotta and oil. Mix well until all ingredients are thoroughly blended.

3 Using a large ravioli cutter, the rim of a juice glass, or a knife, cut the cooled polenta into rounds about 2 1/2 inches in diameter. Heat 1 inch of the oil in a skillet and fry the polenta 3 minutes per side, or until lightly browned.* Drain on paper towels.

4 Just before serving, stir the grated Parmigiano-Reggiano into the walnut mixture. Spread the fried polenta rounds with the mixture and arrange on a large platter garnished with sprigs of fresh marjoram or parsley.

6 tablespoons freshly grated
    Parmigiano-Reggiano
5 to 6 sprigs fresh marjoram or
    parsley for garnish

Make Ahead The polenta rounds can be fried or baked earlier in the day and kept warm or reheated in a warm oven. The topping can be made up to a day in advance, refrigerated, and brought to room temperature before serving.

How to Serve Stands on its own as an appetizer. To create a grander appetizer or enlarge to a light entrée, form a circle of six finished rounds on each plate and arrange three thick, overlapping slices of bufala mozzarella in the center. Dust the mozzarella with freshly ground black pepper and drizzle with extra virgin olive oil or truffle oil.

Wine Suggestion Dry White or Medium-Sweet White

The polenta rounds can also be arranged on a baking sheet and baked at 350°F for 10 minutes, or until the edges are slightly browned. To add flavor and moisture, the tops of the rounds can be basted with olive oil before baking.

INSALATA DI TAROCCI

Blood Orange and Red Onion Salad

32

❧ Sicilia ❧

COMBINE A DOZEN OR SO MEN WITH LARGE SNAKES DRAPED OVER THEIR SHOULDERS; *ox-drawn carts bearing the image of San Paolo (himself holding a snake and a book in one hand, a sword pointing to the heavens in the other); squads of flagbearers and swordsmen; a cotillion of old men with black berets playing an indescribable array of instruments (many homemade); a piazza packed with local residents dressed in Sunday finery; and long tables filled with all manner of food and beverage, and you have a beginner's idea of what to expect if you find yourself in Aragona in southern Sicily on June 29, the feast of St. Paul. (If you decide to visit the church however, you no longer have to fear the ritual called* La benedizione deglie serpe, *whereby residents presented snakes to the priest for benediction. The ritual was done away with a few years ago.)*

If you do venture to Aragona for this festival, the blood orange and red onion salad presented here is one of the many foods you're likely to sample. Although any type of orange can be substituted, the following is made with tarocci, *or blood oranges, which are one of Sicily's most famous products. Exceptionally high in vitamin C, strongly fragrant, and with brilliant red peel and pulp, the tarocco is widely used in salads, frozen ice cream desserts, and sorbets.*

serves 4

Time: 30 minutes

Level of Difficulty: Easy

⚶

4 blood oranges or other small, sweet oranges

1 small red onion, cut into very thin slices*

4 tablespoons extra virgin olive oil

1 Peel the oranges and remove the pith. Cut horizontally into thin slices. Put in a bowl and set aside.

2 Separate the onion slices into individual layers and put in the bowl with the oranges. Add the oil and half the parsley to the bowl, season with salt and pepper, and toss until all ingredients are well coated.

3 Arrange the orange and onion slices in a circular pattern on a round platter. Drizzle with the

Italians have become very fond of cipolle di tropea, *a type of sweet red onion that comes from Calabria and is not yet available in the U.S. To achieve the same sweetness, soak the sliced red onion in water for thirty minutes before using.*

oil left in the bowl, sprinkle with the remaining parsley, and serve.

Make Ahead   The oranges can be tossed with the marinade earlier in the day.

How to Serve   On its own as a midsummer appetizer, followed by a light pasta, or as a salad course accompanying an especially piquant entrée.

Wine Suggestion   Medium-Sweet White

3 tablespoons freshly chopped
   Italian parsley, stems
   discarded
Salt to taste
Freshly ground black pepper
   to taste

33

CARPACCIO DI TONNO

Tuna Carpaccio with Lemon-Parsley Sauce

❧ Sicilia ❧

LA FESTA DI SAN PAOLO CELEBRATES THE FEAST DAY OF A SAINT WHO IS GENERALLY *depicted in a brown tunic and completely surrounded by a bevy of serpents. Legend credits him with being the first of the* serpari—*men who chase away snakes. His powers apparently stem from an incident that took place on the island of Malta, where he was bitten by a poisonous snake and survived, and from then on, according to legend, Maltese snakes never again bit anyone. Modern-day festivalgoers seeking the same immunity can often be heard chanting this prayer: San Paulu, ciaráulu ammazza a chissu, ca é nimicu di Diu e sarva a mia ca sugnu figgiu di Maria. St. Paul, great snake chaser that you are, kill this serpent who is God's enemy and save me, son of Mary.*

Following is another of the simple and delicious dishes I ate while at Aragona's St. Paul festival. Like other types of seviche, the tuna "cooks" in the acidic lemon juice.

serves 4

Time: 20 minutes, excluding the 1-to-2 hour refrigeration period

Level of Difficulty: Easy

12 ounces fresh tuna*, cut into
    very thin slices
3 tablespoons extra virgin olive oil

1 Place the tuna on a platter. Whisk together the oil, lemon juice, salt, pepper, oregano, and parsley until emulsified. Pour the sauce over the tuna, cover with plastic, and refrigerate for 1 to 2 hours, turning the tuna once or twice during that period.

2 Arrange the greens on a serving platter, top with tuna, and serve, garnished with lemon slices.

Swordfish and seabass can be served the same way; if using sea bass, eliminate the oregano.

How to Serve Works equally well as an appetizer or as a light summer entrée served with couscous or another type of room-temperature grain salad.

Wine Suggestion Dry White

Juice of 3 lemons

Salt to taste

Freshly ground black pepper
    to taste

1 tablespoon freshly
    chopped oregano

2 tablespoons freshly chopped
    Italian parsley

8 ounces mixed greens,
    washed and dried

1 lemon, cut into thin slices,
    for garnish

35

CAPONÉT

Stuffed Zucchini Blossoms

❦ Piemonte ❦

BEING A HUGE FAN OF ZUCCHINI BLOSSOMS, I TRY NEVER TO MISS SANTENA'S Sagra Primaverile *held on or about the third Sunday of May. Primaverile means springtime, and the foods prepared by the small corps of volunteers revolve largely around spring cheeses and vegetables, such as spring onions, artichokes, asparagus, and zucchini blossoms. Located just eight miles southwest of Torino, Santena has somehow managed to miss the "touristification" that has taken place in other nearby villages. Local housewives still work through the night cleaning vegetables, setting up chairs, and folding napkins.*

serves 4

Time: 60 minutes

Level of Difficulty: Moderate

⚶

16 large zucchini blossoms with
    at least 1 1/2-inch-long
    stems intact
12 ounces veal cutlet
Salt to taste
4 ounces cooked salami
1 tablespoon freshly chopped
    Italian parsley, stemmed
1 clove garlic
2 large eggs, lightly beaten
3 tablespoons freshly grated
    grana padana (Parmigiano-
    Reggiano can be substituted)
Olive oil for frying

1 Wash and dry the zucchini blossoms. Using a paring knife, peel the stems all the way up to the crown of the blossom.

2 Put the veal in a saucepan with a few tablespoons salted water and boil for 10 minutes. Drain and place on a cutting board with the salami. Using a mezzaluna or a chef's knife, chop the two until you have a very fine dice. Place in a bowl and set aside.

3 Using the same mezzaluna or chef's knife, mince the parsley with the garlic and place in the bowl with the meats. Add the eggs and cheese and mix until all ingredients are well blended.

4 Divide the meat fillling into 16 ping-pong-size balls and stuff one inside each of the zucchini blossoms.

5 Heat 1 inch oil in a skillet over medium heat and fry the blossoms, 4 or 5 at a time, until all sides are golden. Drain on paper towls. To serve, arrange the blossoms in a circle on a round platter, blossom end out, and fan the edges of the blossoms to form a sort of golden-orange frill around the outer edge of the platter.

Make Ahead The meat filling can be made up to 2 to 3 days in advance, refrigerated, and brought to room temperature before using.

How to Serve On its own as an appetizer or as a side dish accompanying a plate of cold roasted chicken.

Wine Suggestion Dry White or Medium-bodied Red

OLIVE RIPIENE

Green Olives Stuffed with Meat, Battered, and Fried

❧ Le Marche ❧

NEVER ONES TO OVERLOOK AN OCCASION FOR THROWING A FESTIVAL, MANY ITALIANS *even celebrate the fact of having reached the halfway point during Lent. In San Lorenzo in Campo, residents burn a huge puppet representing death while around their necks hang garlands of sausages and sweets—both forbidden until the end of the forty-day period. Spectators throw oranges and lemons at the burning puppet and sometimes also at each other (the practice was outlawed under Fascism because it was deemed too dangerous to allow opposing party members a day when it was all right to pelt each other with hard objects). In olden days (when people really adhered to the fasting traditions), these olives were stuffed with a simple mixture of breadcrumbs, parsley, cheese, and eggs. At the home of Paolo and Giulia Segali, where I experienced the* Mezzaquaresima, *as it is called, both that simple and this more luxurious version were served.*

makes 40 olives

Time: 2 hours

Level of Difficulty: Moderate

⚖

2 tablespoons extra virgin olive oil

4 ounces pancetta, minced

2 ounces veal cutlet, roughly chopped

2 ounces pork loin, roughly chopped

2 ounces chicken breast, roughly chopped

2 ounces prosciutto, chopped

2 tablespoons tomato sauce

1 Heat the 2 tablespoons oil in a skillet over low heat and sauté the pancetta for 3 minutes. Add the veal, pork, chicken, prosciutto, and tomato sauce and cook for 1 hour, stirring frequently with a wooden spoon and adding a few tablespoons of water as needed. Remove the meats with a slotted spoon and, using a mezzaluna or chef's knife, chop finely. Return to the skillet and deglaze the pan by mixing the juices into the finely chopped meat to create a thick paste.

2 Transfer the meat to a bowl. Add 1 egg, 1 tablespoon breadcrumbs, the cheese, milk, nutmeg, and salt. Mix well until all ingredients are well blended.

3 In a separate bowl, lightly beat the remaining egg. Stuff the olives with the meat mixture, dredge in flour, dip into the egg, and then roll in the remaining breadcrumbs.

4 Heat 1 inch oil in a skillet over medium heat. Fry the olives, 9 or 10 at a time, until all surfaces are golden brown. Drain on paper towls. Transfer to a serving platter and garnish with sliced lemons.

Make Ahead The stuffing mixture can be made up to a day in advance and refrigerated until needed.

How to Serve Serve on its own or as part of an appetizer plate that also includes a small bruschetta topped with sautéed mushrooms.

Wine Suggestion Medium- or Full-bodied Red

2 large eggs

4 tablespoons unflavored breadcrumbs

2 tablespoons freshly grated grana padana (Parmigiano-Reggiano can be substituted)

1/2 cup whole milk

2 tablespoons extra virgin olive oil

1/8 teaspoon freshly grated nutmeg

Salt to taste

40 large green olives, pitted

Flour for dredging

Olive oil for frying

Sliced lemons for garnish

PALLINE DI RICOTTA AI PISTACCHI

Mixed Green Salad Topped with Ricotta Rolled in a Pistacchio Crust

40

※ Le Marche ※

THIS IS ANOTHER OF GIULIA SEGALI'S PERSONAL RECIPES (SEE PAGE 38) FOR THE Mezzaquaresima, *or Halfway Through Lent Festival. Very quick and easy to make, this salad is much enhanced by using both very fresh ricotta and a fruit-flavored vinegar, such as the one Signora Segali makes from the raspberries that habitually overrun the back half of her property.*

serves 4

Time: 45 minutes excluding the 1-hour refrigeration period

Level of Difficulty: Easy

8 ounces shelled pistachios

8 ounces fresh ricotta, preferably sheep or goat's milk

2 tablespoons unsalted butter at room temperature

5 tablespoons freshly grated grana padana or Parmigiano-Reggiano

1/8 teaspoon paprika

Salt to taste

Freshly ground black pepper to taste

1 To peel the pistachios, immerse in boiling water for 3 minutes. Drain and rub against a hard mesh sieve until the peels come loose. Remove and discard the peels. Finely chop the peeled nuts and place in a bowl.

2 Pass the ricotta through a food mill to give it a smooth, creamy consistency. Place in a bowl and add the butter, cheese, paprika, salt, and pepper, stirring until blended. Form this mixture into walnut-size balls and roll in the pistachios until well coated. Place on a platter, cover, and refrigerate for 1 hour.

3 Toss the greens with a vinaigrette made from whisking together the oil, vinegar, salt, and pepper. Arrange on a serving platter and sprinkle with raspberries. Distribute the ricotta balls over the surface and serve immediately.

Make Ahead The pistachio balls can be made up to 1 day in advance, wrapped tightly in plastic, and refrigerated until needed.

How to Serve As an appetizer on its own, as a salad course, or as a light lunch entrée accompanied by thin slices of fresh focaccia.

Wine Suggestion **Dry White**

8 ounces *misticanza*—mixed greens (arugula, sorrel, lemon balm, curly endive, mache), washed and roughly torn

2 tablespoons extra virgin olive oil

1 tablespoon raspberry vinegar or other fruit vinegar

1 cup raspberries or other berries

CALAMARETTI CON AGLIATA

Baby Shrimp with Garlic Sauce

❧ Liguria ❧

IF YOU ARE EVER IN LIGURIA IN MID-MAY, RACE TO CAMOGLI FOR THAT VILLAGE'S *spectacular Fish Sagra. Residents fry almost two tons of fish in a twelve-foot-diameter pan set on the beach. Each of the thousands of participants gets—for free—a paper cone filled with fried fish and a chunk of lemon. Numerous stands set up around the fish fry area sell desserts and a host of other fish specialties, including the following.*

serves 6

Time: 25 to 30 minutes

Level of Difficulty: Easy

3 cloves garlic

5 to 6 slices day-old bread, crusts removed

1 tablespoon red wine vinegar

4 tablespoons finely chopped Italian parsley

Salt to taste

Freshly ground black pepper to taste

1 1/3 cups extra virgin olive oil

2 pounds small to medium shrimp, peeled, deveined, rinsed, and dried

2 cloves garlic, crushed

1/2 cup dry white wine

Thin slices lemon for garnish

1 To make the *agliata,* place the 3 whole garlic cloves in the bowl of a food processor and puree. Add the bread, vinegar, parsley, salt, and pepper and turn on the motor, pouring 1 cup of the oil through the feed tube in a steady stream until the sauce is the consistency of wet paste. Transfer to a bowl and place the bowl in the center of a serving platter.

2 To make the shrimp, heat the remaining oil in a skillet and sauté the crushed garlic for 2 minutes over low heat. Using a slotted spoon, remove the garlic and discard. Increase the heat to high, add the shrimp, and cook for 8 minutes, stirring constantly. Pour in the wine and cook until evaporated, about 3 minutes. Season with salt and arrange on the serving platter around the bowl of agliata. Garnish with the lemon slices.

Make Ahead The agliata sauce can be made earlier in the day, covered, and set aside until needed.

How to Serve A wonderful appetizer in its own right, this dish also works very well as an entrée served with a green salad.

Wine Suggestion Dry- or Medium-Sweet White

BURLENGHI

Rosemary Crepes

❦ Emilia-Romagna ❦

IN CERVIA, A COASTAL TOWN IN EMILIA-ROMAGNA, VERY RELIGIOUS RESIDENTS *celebrate the feast day of San Lorenzo (August 10) by immersing themselves seven times in the waters of the Adriatic. Those that are less religious go in only once since, as the local proverb says: "One bath on San Lorenzo's day is worth seven any other time." The custom dates back to 1927, when an outbreak of malaria was cured through the intercession of San Lorenzo, who stipulated that the sick should be carried to the beach and immersed in the cold Adriatic waters seven times in one day.*

The festivities begin in early morning with a procession through the town's pine forests and continues into late afternoon with a huge communal swim accompanied by music from a marching band assembled right on the beach. After the sun goes down, there is much eating and drinking and finally, the incomparable fireworks display over the gray-green waters of the Adriatic.

makes about 8 crepes

Time: 45 to 60 minutes

Level of Difficulty: Moderate

1 clove garlic, peeled

2 tablespoons chopped fresh
   rosemary

2 ounces *lardo* (salt pork) or
   pancetta, minced

1 1/2 cups unbleached all-purpose
   flour, sifted

Salt to taste

1/2 cup water

2 tablespoons extra virgin olive oil

1 Using a mezzaluna or a chef's knife, chop together the garlic, rosemary, and lardo or pancetta to make a paste.

2 Place the flour, salt, and 1/2 cup water in a food processor and blend until smooth and liquid, adding additional water as needed, 1 tablespoon at a time.

3 Heat 1 tablespoon oil in a nonstick 8-inch skillet with sloped sides over low heat. Pour 1/4 cup of the batter into the pan, swirling it around to create a thin crêpe. Cook for 2 to 3 minutes, or until set. Turn with a spatula and cook for 2 minutes on the other side. Transfer to a heated plate and spread with

1 teaspoon of the rosemary mixture and a dusting of grated cheese. Fold in half so that the mixture is enclosed and then in half again. Place on a heated platter and keep warm. Repeat until all ingredients have been used. To serve, arrange the crepes on a platter and garnish with the sprigs of fresh rosemary.

4 ounces freshly grated grana padana or Parmigiano-Reggiano

4 to 5 sprigs fresh rosemary for garnish

45

Make Ahead The rosemary spread can be made up to 3 days in advance, refrigerated, and returned to room temperature before using. The crepe batter can be made earlier in the day, covered, and set aside until needed. If too thick, add more water, 1 tablespoon at a time and blend until smooth.

How to Serve As an appetizer, an entrée accompanied by a vegetable salad, and, certainly, as a brunch treat.

Wine Suggestion **Dry White**

CALZONI PUGLIESE

Cheese, Anchovy, and Caper-stuffed Calzones

46

❧ Puglia ❧

PUGLIA'S CHILDREN RECEIVE THEIR CHRISTMAS GIFTS ON DECEMBER 6, THE FEAST *of San Nicola. According to legend, Nicola—accompanied by an old man carrying on his shoulders two large sacks, one filled with toys, one with coal—arrives on a ship sailing up the Adriatic and disembarks onto Puglian soil on the night of the fifth surrounded by a shimmery golden halo. Behind him come a band of angels whose harps and cornets imbue the air with music so sweet as to lull children into slumber sound enough for Nicola to creep into their houses unnoticed and—hopefully— deliver the toys of their dreams. To guarantee that he reaches into the proper bag however, the children of Puglia (more likely, their mothers) prepare for him platters filled with these wonderful cheese and anchovy-stuffed calzones.*

makes 6 calzones

Time: 75 minutes

Level of Difficulty: Moderate

DOUGH
1/2 teaspoon yeast
1 cup warm water
1 1/2 cups unbleached all-purpose
   flour, sifted
Salt to taste
2 tablespoons extra virgin olive oil

FILLING
5 tablespoons extra virgin olive oil
1 large onion, minced

1 Stir the yeast into 1/2 cup of the warm water. Place the cup in a saucepan filled with enough hot tap water to come two-thirds of the way up the sides of the cup. Let rest until the surface of the yeast is foamy, about 10 to 20 minutes.

2 To make the dough, put the flour in a food processor with a pinch of salt. Turn on the motor and pour the yeast water through the feed tube. Continue to process, adding another 1/2 cup warm water and the oil. When the dough has formed a ball, transfer to a floured counter and knead for 10 minutes, adding more flour as needed to create a smooth, elastic ball. Place the ball in a bowl, cover with a cloth, and let sit for 1 hour, or until doubled in bulk.

3 Meanwhile, heat 3 tablespoons oil in a skillet over medium-low heat and sauté the onions for 7 minutes, stirring constantly.

4 Preheat the oven to 500°F.

5 Using a floured rolling pin and working on a lightly floured surface, roll the dough into roughly a 10 x 15-inch rectangle, about $1/8$ inch thick. Cut the rectangle into 6 circles, each 4 inches in diameter. Divide the onions among the circles, positioning them on the lower half. Add the anchovies, capers, olives, and cheese. Fold the circles in half and seal the edges with a fork.

6 Scatter the cornmeal over the surface of a large baking sheet or pizza stone.* Using a spatula, transfer the calzones to the sheet, brush the tops lightly with the remaining oil, and bake for 15 minutes, or until the surface of the dough is a light golden color. Remove from the oven and serve immediately or when lukewarm.

Make Ahead The dough for the calzones can be made earlier in the day and refrigerated in a tightly sealed plastic bag until needed. Return to room temperature before using. The dough can also be frozen for up to 3 weeks, again in a tightly sealed plastic bag. Thaw and warm to room temperature before using.

How to Serve As appetizers on their own or as an entrée served with a tomato salad.

Wine Suggestion Medium-bodied Red

2 ounces salt-packed anchovies, minced (see page 25 about anchovies)

2 tablespoons capers, rinsed

6 tablespoons pitted and minced Gaeta olives or other type olive

$1/2$ cup freshly grated pecorino

4 tablespoons coarsely ground cornmeal

Pizza stones must be preheated for 20 minutes before using. Terra-cotta baking tiles can also be used but make sure they are American-made and, therefore, lead-free.

INSALATA DI FARRO

Farro Salad

48

❧ Toscana ❧

THROUGHOUT FLORENCE, ST. JOHN THE BAPTIST'S FEAST DAY (JUNE 24) USED TO BE *an occasion for citywide fairs, tournaments, processions, jousts, masked balls, and even wild animal hunts. All that has remained of this bacchanalia is a soccer tournament held in the Piazza Santa Croce. The game is preceded by a procession that weaves its way through the city. The four participating teams, consisting of twenty-seven members each, dress in different colors.*

Following the game, everyone repairs to nearby restaurants and trattorias, which all offer special St. John's Day menus. Among the most popular menu items of recent years is the following salad, made with farro from the Garfagnana region of Tuscany.

serves 6

Time: 60 minutes

Level of Difficulty: Moderate

2 cups farro*
1 small red onion, thinly sliced
4 very ripe tomatoes, chopped
10 leaves fresh basil, chopped
1/2 cup extra virgin olive oil
3 tablespoons red wine vinegar
Salt to taste
Freshly ground black pepper
  to taste
Arugula for the platter

Cook the farro in boiling salted water for 45 to 60 minutes, or until tender. Drain in a colander and cool to room temperature. Place in a bowl and add the onions, tomatoes, basil, oil, and vinegar. Season with salt and pepper and toss to blend all ingredients. Serve on a bed of arugula or other greens.

Make Ahead This can be made up to 2 days in advance, refrigerated, and served cold or at room temperature. Add the tomatoes at the last minute.

How to Serve As an appetizer, salad, or light summer entrée.

Wine Suggestion Medium-bodied Red

Farro can be purchased in specialty food stores. Do not confuse it with spelt, which is a softer look-alike that will have much too mushy a texture for this salad.

SPIEDINI DI COZZE

Pancetta-wrapped Mussels Grilled on Skewers

❧ Molise ❧

THE FOLLOWING IS A WONDERFUL FOOD ASSOCIATED WITH CAMPOBASSO'S *CORPUS DOMINI festival. The Molisani use pancetta, or unsmoked bacon, for flavoring. Bacon or prosciutto can be substituted.*

serves 4

Time: 30 minutes

Level of Difficulty: Easy

1¹/₂ pounds large blue mussels, scrubbed, bearded, and washed under running water

¹/₂ cup dry white wine

4 ounces pancetta, thinly sliced and cut into pieces about 3 inches long

12 skewers

Lettuce leaves and thin lemon slices for garnish

1 Put the mussels in a large skillet with the wine and cook over high heat, covered, for 3 to 5 minutes, or until the mussels open. Discard any unopened mussels. Strain the pan juices through a fine sieve and keep warm.

2 Remove the mussels from their shells and wrap each in a piece of pancetta. Thread the mussels onto the skewers.

3 Prepare a charcoal grill or preheat the broiler.

4 Grill the mussels or broil for 2 to 3 minutes per side, or until the pancetta is golden brown and crispy. Place on a bed of lettuce and surround with the lemon slices. Drizzle with a tablespoon or two of the mussel broth and serve immediately.

Make Ahead The mussels can be wrapped in pancetta earlier in the day and refrigerated until ready to grill.

How to Serve In addition to serving as an appetizer, this dish can also be used as an entrée presented on a bed of rice cooked in fish broth.

Wine Suggestion Dry White or Medium-bodied Red

OLIVE CONDITE

Olive and Blood Orange Salad

❦ Lazio ❦

MAY 14, *LE PASSATE*, IS ONE OF THE FOUR MOST IMPORTANT DAYS OF THE YEAR IN *Marta, a small village on Lake Bolsena in the Lazio—the day on which almost every one of the 983 inhabitants turns out to honor its* contadini—*the hardworking men and women who sow the crops and bring in the catch. I am told that in the past the festival was more genuine, each of the participants in the plays and processions an actual laborer. Today, apparently, the event has evolved into more of a touristic one, with actors and actresses playing the roles of yesterday's fieldworkers and fishermen. Nevertheless,* Le Passate *is a wonderful opportunity to witness the simple elegance of ancient tools (the 500-year-old threshing machine made entirely of bamboo canes is my particular favorite) and to sample the foods from what may have been a poorer past, but certainly not one lacking in gastronomic eloquence.*

serves 4

Time: 30 to 45 minutes, excluding the 1- to 2-hour resting time

Level of Difficulty: Easy

⚶

1 pound oil-cured olives
1 blood orange or other type orange
2 cloves garlic, peeled and very thinly sliced
2 tablespoons chopped wild fennel or 1 tablespoon fresh chopped rosemary
5 tablespoons extra virgin olive oil
Salt to taste
Freshly ground black pepper to taste

1 Place the olives in a large bowl, cover with lukewarm water, and soak for 10 minutes. Drain, shake dry, and set aside.

2 Zest the orange rind, making uniform and equidistant cuts. Place the zest in the bowl with the olives. Peel the orange, making sure to remove all of the pith and cut into very thin horizontal slices. Arrange the slices around the perimeter of a serving plate, overlapping the slices slightly.

3 Toss the olives with the garlic, fennel, and oil. Season with salt and pepper. Mound the dressed olives over the oranges, leaving 1 inch of orange border showing. Let rest for 1 to 2 hours and then serve.

Make Ahead The olives can be dressed up to 3 or 4 days in advance and placed on the orange slices an hour or two before serving.

How to Serve Works very well as part of an appetizer buffet or in any situation where a bowl of olives might be served. For an extra dose of both flavor and visual delight, add 2 tablespoons fresh-squeezed lemon juice and a sprinkle of lemon zest.

Wine Suggestion Medium-bodied Red

Polenta and Risotto

Polenta

POLENTA SULLA SPIANATORA
Polenta Served on a Wooden Board

POLENTA PASTICCIATA
Baked Polenta with Meat Sauce

SPIEDINI DI POLENTA FRITTA
Fried Polenta and Fontina Cheese Kebabs

CASOEÛLA
Polenta with Braised Duck and Winter Cabbage

POLENTA CON OSEI
Polenta with Skewered Meats

BATUFFOLI
Polenta Layered with Meat Sauce

POLENTA FRITTA COL STRACCHINO
Fried Polenta with Stracchino Cheese

GULASCH E POLENTA
Goulash with Polenta

POLENTA DI GRANO SARACENO AL FORNO
Baked Buckwheat Polenta

PASTUCCIA
Baked Polenta with Sausage and Raisins

POLENTA DI NIEL
Creamy Polenta with Beef Stew

Risotto

RISOTTO AL' TARTUFO
Risotto with Truffles

TIELLA DI RISO E ZUCCHINI
Baked Rice Casserole with Zucchini and Potatoes

PANISSA
Rice and Beans, Piedmont-style

RISOTTO CON ASPARAGI SELVAGGI
Risotto with Wild Asparagus

RISOTTO AI FUNGHI AL SALTO
Twice-cooked Porcini Mushroom Risotto

PALLINE DI RISOTTO FRITTE
Fried Risotto Croquettes

RISOTTO CON CILIEGIE
Risotto with Black Cherries

BRODERA
Risotto with Spareribs

TRENTINO-ALTO ADIGE
Boundaries of the Mind

I HAVE COME TO APPIANO IN ALTO ADIGE for the October apple harvest and the annual *Sagra del risotto*—Rice Festival—for which my friend Virgilio Maronelli provides the musical entertainment. Virgilio's wife, Maria, called me a few weeks ago to report that they had just finished this year's grape pressing and that the resultant batch of red wine was the best in a decade. "Hurry," she said. "We are waiting for you to toast the end of the season."

Generally, I come to this area in May, when the cherries are literally falling off the trees and no one minds if you pause in their front garden to pick a basketful or two. This, in fact, was how I met my other friends, Dora and Alfred Birkenheim, all those years ago, when they strolled out of their house to find me munching on the fruits of their orchard.

"*Aspetta,*" Dora called out in her heavily Germanized Italian. "*Ni do un sacco!*" Wait. I will give you a bag! As it turns out, she also gave me a slice of cherry streudel and a jar of cherry preserves and, the following day, I transferred from my hotel in Caldaro to her charming guesthouse in this picturesque mountain village three miles west of Bolzano.

The area from Bolzano north is a semi-autonomous region known as the *Sudtirol* (South Tirol). A stunning assemblage of quaint villages, towering castles (of which there are more than 120), and the stunning limestone spires of the Dolomites, the Sudtirol is 160 square miles in area and home to a large population of ethnic Germans. It is also part of a larger region—Trentino-Alto Adige—that is ripe with an ethnic tension simmering just beneath the surface of any interaction between the minority Germans and the predominantly Italian-speaking population.

The Germans consider the area to be theirs by virtue of history. But what they want on a more practical level is to be able to live as Germans without having to speak Italian (which they all do) and having their desires consistently overruled by the Italian majority. On the other side of the coin lie the Italians, whose point of view is based on the fact that the Sudtirol is now under Italian rule and, therefore, its people should live as Italians, not as Germans. Very few Italians speak German.

The situation dates back to the 1800s, when Napoleon conquered this integral part of the Holy Roman Empire, only to relinquish it to the Austro-Hungarians a few years later. At the end of World War I, the entire region fell under Italian rule and with the ascendance of Mussolini came a series of brutal attempts at completely eradicating any hint of German presence.

"Mussolini insisted that all names be changed to Italian," says Dora, "and so our city became known as 'Appiano' instead of 'Eppan,' which is what people had called it for over a thousand years. And that was only the beginning. As children, we all had to go to Italian schools, where it was a crime to speak German. Teachers taught in Italian, which we barely understood, and badgered us every day to buy the obligatory *tessere*—Fascist membership cards—which cost five lire. They would demand the money and beat us with wooden sticks if we didn't have it. Then, of course, we would go home and tell our parents we needed five lire for the dreaded *tessere* and get another beating for even suggesting such a thing." She cups her hands together as if in prayer. "How can we be expected, today, to forget the past?"

According to the Birkenheims, the area north of Bolzano is two-thirds Italian and one-third German, with Germans assigned all the lower-end jobs. "If the fields are planted each spring, it is because Germans have done the planting," Alfred says. "All the industries are owned by Italians and Italians control all the banks."

"Now, Alfred!" Dora chides. "We *are* part of Italy, after all.

"That's true," Alfred concedes. "But it would be nice not to constantly feel like part of an undesirable minority. Not that things would have been any better under Hitler, but at least from him, we had the promise of a better life."

Over the years I have known Alfred and Dora, I have listened to many stories of life in the Sudtirol before and after World War II. Their personal account, naturally, gives greater credence to the German point of view—to the fact that Hitler offered them jobs and autonomy and so they gave him their loyalty. "We never knew," Alfred says when I ask about Hitler's failings. "Everyone had twelve to sixteen children, and we were too poor to have a radio or buy a newspaper. How could we have known what was happening in Germany?"

The argument has its aura of credibility, but more so than whether or not Sudtiroleans were aware of Hitler's ultimate design, is the reality of self-interest, especially as applied to people who were chronically short of even the most basic necessities.

"We were told we would be able to speak German and wear our German dirndls," says Dora. "Whenever Hitler came here, he always ended his speeches with the words, 'This is your home.'"

"After the war, the Americans came," Alfred volunteers. "And at first we thought our days of poverty and starvation had come to an end. But soon we realized that, to them, we were the losers and that, in return, they planned to turn the Sudtirol into an industrial zone."

"When the peacemakers talked about us at all, they referred to our land as 'that little place near Austria,'" Dora interrupts. "They didn't even know where we were and already the plans had been drawn up to evacuate us from the area so they could begin building their industrial villages."

"By then," Alfred continues, "the Sudtirol was flooded with Italians brought from the South by Mussolini as a way to Italianize the area. And because of that—because the Americans felt they owed a debt of gratitude to the Italians who had ultimately fought at their side—we were all spared the fate of losing our homes to a valley of factories."

"Our life has been a good one," Alfred declares. "We have no right to complain. But the truth is, we have always had to make do with what little was tossed our way."

The Birkenheims' stories run counter to the usual image of Germans and Italians. Generally, Germans are the bankers and financiers and Italians the tillers of the soil. But here the industries and businesses and banks are mostly owned by Italians, and it is the Germans who toil as public servants and rent out rooms to tourists.

"If all you say is true, why have the two of you never considered moving to Germany?" I once asked Dora.

When she finally answered, her words were heavy with the pain my question had obviously caused. "It is a very good question, but the answer is simple: We are Tiroleans, not Germans, and this is our home."

We spend the next few days picking apples and I finally learn how to make Dora's famous apple bread, in which she combines six grains bought in bulk from the local market. She grinds the grains herself in an amazing German-made milling machine the size of a small food processor. "The grain is crushed with a granite stone," she explains. "Not with a motor-driven blade. A motor would give off too much heat and all the vitamins would be lost."

As we work, she tells me of her concerns regarding the imminent finalization of the European Economic Union, a federation that will unify the previously fragmented national economies of Europe. Its goals are to completely eliminate trade barriers and replace national currencies with one European currency, the Euro.

"We're told we have a lot to gain," Dora says. "But no one talks about everything that will be lost, like our most distinctive fruit and vegetable varieties."

According to Dora, the EEU has already issued directives specifying the size, shape, and color of produce that will be acceptable to all countries of the Union. With respect to apples, for example, only thirteen of Trentino-Alto Adige's forty-seven cultivars will do.

"The way I see it, we are moving toward a Europe dominated by large distributors whose interests lie in eradicating both local sources of production and regional varieties. Ten years from now, for example, you will not be able to buy, anywhere in this region, *susine di Dro"* (a local variety of small, slightly tart, greenish-purple plums).

By way of another example, she tells the story of her friend Nilda, who "makes the best *lardo* in the region." (*Lardo* is the slab of fat taken from the back of the pig. Throughout Italy, it is marinated for three to six months with spices and herbs and used as a flavoring agent in soups and sautés).

According to Dora, Nilda's family has been marinating *lardo* in marble casks for over 300 years. But with the onslaught of new hygienic directives designed to safeguard and standardize food production—directives issued as a condition of Italy's full participation in the EEU— Nilda may be forced to cease production.

"Imagine, if you will, that Nilda's only source of income is her small *alimentari* (grocery store)—the back room of which contains three marble casks—and that, in those casks, she marinates perhaps as little as twenty-five pounds of *lardo*, most of which is consumed by family and friends.

"Now she is being told she must install two bathrooms and set aside a separate room for the casks. Not only that, but the room must have a stainless steel double sink and maintain a constant temperature as measured by a government-issued thermometer. Having completed all the installations, she must then, of course, apply for and purchase a license to sell artisan-produced foods. All to make twenty-five pounds of *lardo*!"

"So what will happen to all the people who cure their own speck and distill their own grappa?" I ask.

"Homemade grappa has already been outlawed," she replies. "But we are very close to seeing the virtual end of all the products that define our regional diversity. Pietro, down the road, is a skilled pork butcher who, for thirty-four years, has been turning our pigs into delicious sausages and salamis, using the recipes taught him by his grandfather. But last year, he was visited by the *guardia di finanza*—the finance police—and told he must apply for a special permit.

"Even if you concede, as some do, that Pietro *should* have a permit if he is going to work with pork meat, everyone knows a permit is just the beginning. In the end, the only sausages available are going to be those produced by giant factories who can afford the necessary equipment. And this is what we will call progress."

That Saturday night, Dora and Alfred and I set out for Appiano's Risotto Festival. Even before we have made it all the way to the top of the hill, I can hear Virgilio's accordian booming its addictive blend of simple harmonies and complex chord structures. I first heard Virgilio play at an asparagus festival in Bolzano in 1995. At the time, I had journeyed to Alto Adige, *Kompass Wanderkarte* in hand, to hike the Dolomites with Dr. Hannsjörg Hager, a noted Alpinist; the festival was my Last Supper before heading out.

That night, Virgilio had played his heart out—waltzes, mazurkas, polkas, two-steps, tarantellas, and even, after midnight, a medley of disco favorites. At the end of it all, I had edged up to the bandstand to tell him how much I'd enjoyed his repertoire and we somehow wound up talking about gnocchi. When I returned from the hike, I spent four days with Virgilio and his wife, Maria, cooking and eating.

Tomorrow, I am scheduled to join them for *Törggelen,* an ancient harvest ritual that traditionally started on St. Martin's Day, November 11, and ended on November 25, the feast of St. Catherine. In its original form, *Törggelen* consisted of walking from one *maso* (upland farm) to another, sampling the fruits of the harvest, especially newly fermenting wine. Today's event spans eight weeks from September to November, during which a blend of locals and tourists hike (or, more often, drive) through the countryside, stopping occasionally for small feasts consisting of fresh-sliced speck (the regional version of prosciutto), chestnuts, whole-grain breads, cheeses, and newly pressed wine.

"Anna!" Maria calls out as soon as the Birkenheims and I have crested the hill. "Over here!" She has saved places at her table. "Virgilio thought you were coming much earlier."

In truth, I had planned to arrive much earlier, but Dora and I got involved in making apple-stuffed tortellini and the time passed much more quickly than we had imagined.

"What's on the menu this year?" Alfred teases. The menu has been the same for at least ten years: eight types of risotto, grilled chicken with fried potatoes, roast pork with apple fritters, and ice cream. Every now and then, someone suggests an addition or modification, but when the committee meets to decide on food and decorations, the vote is always to retain what has been a highly successful formula.

One year, someone suggested changing the basic nature of the *sagra* itself. "The only connection Appiano has to rice is that its residents eat it in great quantity," the man supposedly pleaded. "Why not have an apple festival or a cherry festival or even a wine festival?"

But he was quickly overruled on the basis of there being dozens of apple, cherry, wine, and even speck festivals scattered throughout Alto Adige. "Appiano's festival is successful because everybody loves risotto. So what if we don't actually produce rice in the immediate vicinity?

This region is part of Italy's northeast, is it not? And is the northeast not Italy's principal rice-growing region?"

It depends how you look at it. The greatest *quantity* of rice is grown in the northwest, in the Vercelli and Lomellina areas of northern Piemonte. In fact, if you drive from Torino to Milano, you can't help but notice the extensive stretches of paddies: green in spring when the new shoots have just sprouted, and dark brown in fall when the grain is ripe and ready for harvest. But the best *quality* rice is grown in the northeast, in the lowlands below Verona.

Italian rice is classified into four categories (*commune, semifino, fino,* and *superfino*) depending on the length and shape of the kernels. The classification is based on the fact that Italian rice is cultivated almost exclusively to be eaten as *risotto*—a uniquely northern Italian method of gradually cooking rice in rich broth until the kernels' intrinsic starches have been transformed into a rich, creamy consistency. Hence, the size and shape of various rices refer to how much broth they can absorb and still retain that *al dente*—firm—consistency essential to a good risotto.

In essence, the better the quality, the longer the rice will take to cook, which, of course, means it absorbs more liquid. Those classified as *commune* (*Originario* and *Balilla*) are small and round and their thirteen- to fourteen-minute cooking time makes them better suited for soups and desserts. *Semifini* (*Maratalli* and *Ardizzone*) are plump, long-grained varieties that can be used for risotto although their fifteen-minute cooking time is not as optimal as the next two types. *Fini* (*R.B., Razza 77, Rizzotto,* and *Vialone Nano*—this last considered by many to be the Ferrari of rice varieties) are narrow, long-grained rices that take sixteen minutes to cook and absorb great quantities of liquid. *Superfini* varieties (*Arborio, Carnaroli,* and *Sesia*) are the narrowest and longest-grained of all and their eighteen-minute cooking time gives them the greatest advantage with respect to making risotto.

According to Virgilio, Italy's best rice is, today, produced by artisans adhering to ancient methods of cultivation and processing. "The northeast contains a number of small *risaie,*" he explains, "and they grow and harvest the rice the way it has been done for centuries. They carefully regulate the flooding and draining of the fields to create the best growing conditions, use carp to eliminate pests from the flooded paddies, slow polish the grains to minimize the loss of vitamins, and hand sieve the kernels to ensure that the grains are equal in size and, hence, cook in the same amount of time."

"When I buy rice, I always check to make sure the grains are whole," his wife, Mariella, once told me. "Broken grains dissolve during cooking and turn the risotto into mush."

Dora also inspects the rice for color and brilliance. "If the grains are opaque, they have not achieved full maturity and will liquefy when cooked. If they are yellowish, it means they have been exposed to humidity and are in the process of fermenting."

To make sure the kernels are fresh and new, she advises me to bury my fist in a mound of rice. "If it comes out dusted with white powder, the rice is old. Don't buy it."

Our table orders a variety of risottos: with mushrooms, with yellow squash, with truffles, *alla Trentino,* which means with a variety of cheeses, and *milanese*—with saffron. They are all superb and I am not surprised. The chefs at this *sagra* are some of Appiano's best home cooks. "There's a new volunteer this year," Alfred had told me before we arrived. "His name is Walter and, at the last meeting, he was one of the ones who wanted to change the menu to include a few new varieties—a desire that initially made him somewhat unpopular with the rest of the group. But then they tasted his four-cheese risotto and decided he would be a wonderful addition."

Alfred takes the first bite of Walter's risotto. "All the same," he says, giving voice to his unswervingly traditional nature, "it's not exactly the way Dora would have made it."

The conversation turns to the topic of Giovanni Freti, second-in-command to Bolzano's long-term mayor. The day before I arrived, it seems, Freti was convicted of having embezzled the money for the new sports stadium planned for the city's north end.

"Everyone knew something was wrong," says Virgilio, who has joined us on his break. "Freti owns two houses, a string of gas stations, and a brand-new Mercedes. How could he have bought those things on the salary of an assistant mayor?"

"The part that really makes Virgilio and me mad is that Freti is one of the few Italians ever to hold that office," Maria tells me. "Being Italian ourselves, we felt personally responsible for his actions."

"This is not a question of Italian or German," Alfred says gently, although I strongly suspect he believes otherwise. "It is about a man who subjected us to the highest level of personal deceit and then was spared having to pay even the most minimal of penalties."

"He was tried by the regional government," Dora explains and I understand her words to insinuate the fact that the regional government is under Italian control. "They gave him two years' probation with the requirement that he perform twenty hours of social work per week."

Alfred shakes his head. "They should have gone to his house and confiscated everything and anything of value. What good does it do us if Freti works in the local hospital for two years and then goes back to living his life of luxury?"

"Bolzano has had the same mayor for over thirty years," Dora adds. "Whenever there was any kind of event, you could be sure he would take part. Not Freti. No one ever saw him or knew what his job actually entailed."

I ask about the Northern League, the separatist movement led by Umberto Bossi that threatens to turn the affluent north into its own country, called Padania. "Is Alto Adige in support of Bossi?"

Virgilio gives a sarcastic laugh. "Only if it wants to go from the frying pan into the fire."

"If Bossi succeeds, the Sudtirol will also push for secession," says Alfred vehemently. "As long as we are part of Italy, we are part of Italy, but if Italy ceases to exist, then our future lies in establishing our own country."

"And what about the Italians who live here?" I ask. "What will happen to them if the Sudtirol secedes?" My question is greeted with a unanimous silence.

"I don't know," Virgilio finally says. "But I don't think we have to worry about ever finding out."

The hesitation in his voice reminds me that the great joy I always feel in coming here and sending time with my friends—Alfred and Dora, who are German, and Virgilio and Maria, who are Italians—has also always paralleled a constantly shifting point of view with respect to the ever-present ethnic tension. The region is one of Italy's most beautiful, with picturesque, ordered villages and charming, hospitable guesthouses. But the streets of Bolzano are also lined with police and there is no choice but to notice the increased paramilitary presence from the moment one ventures into the geographical area marked "Alto Adige." On the surface, everyone always seems to get along well, and yet there is an undercurrent of rancor that accompanies the constant series of compromises.

"Yes," I press on. "But what about the fact that Germans and Italians consider themselves separate factions of the same geographical area?"

The four of them look a bit confused.

"I think you are forgetting that this is Italy, " Maria eventually proffers. "We were not even a country until 1871 when Count Cavour masterminded the diplomatic agreement that created a united kingdom. Until then, this peninsula consisted of hundreds of rival fiefdoms."

"National unity is a concept that has yet to take root here," says Virgilio. "In fact, the country's strength, as you well know, lies in its regional diversity."

Dora laughs. "Is that not, in fact, why you came here this week? To sample our diversity? To get recipes from regional festivals?"

Once again, I feel my point of view shifting. "Yes, but what if regionality begins to take precedence over unity?" I plead.

Alfred pats my shoulder. "In Europe, that threat is ever present," he says with great seriousness in his voice. "You Americans never even think about your country splitting apart. Maybe the fact that you are all of different heritages gives you a kind of willfully imposed unity. Or maybe your differences are too recent to be ingrained. But ours are thousands of years in the making and they are constantly in front of us, like wisps of lashes splayed across the surface of our eyeballs. One or another of us is always insisting on the sovereignty of our rights."

"And yet we go forward," Maria adds.

I leave the Sudtirol four days later with—as usual—many wonderful memories and great food for thought. As I ease onto the autostrada, I see a sign that says "*Garibaldi, 1, Bossi, 0*" a reference to Umberto Bossi's recent bout of supidity. Weeks earlier, his secessionist movement had commandeered a tank and—somehow—driven it into Piazza San Marco in the center of Venice to garner publicity for its cause. The media coverage was explosively damning and Bossi's subsequent loss of stature is temporarily considered a win for Garibaldi, the military leader whose victories helped unite Italy in the mid-1800s.

"This is Italy." I relive Maria's words.

Yes, I remind myself, this *is* Italy. And I hope it will always remain so.

POLENTA SULLA SPIANATORA*

Polenta Served on a Wooden Board

❧ Abruzzo ❧

TWELFTH NIGHT CONCLUDES THE PERIOD WHEN THE OLD YEAR MOVES INTO THE *new one, initiated on Christmas. In Abruzzo, the event is called* pasquella—*the little coming (in the same way the Abruzzese refer to any religious feast by tacking on the term* pasqua *or* pasquetta, *which they use to mean "the coming of." So* pasqua *all by itself means "the coming of Christ";* pasqua di Resurrezione *means "the coming of the Resurrection";* pasqua di natale *means "the coming of Christmas." Traditionally, on* Pasquella *(referred to elsewhere in Italy as the Epiphany to commemorate the coming of the Wise Men to Bethlehem) young men and women parade through the streets, stopping in front of various homes to sing one or two verses of an ancient song which begins—*

> *Da lontan abbiam saputo*
> *Che ammazzato il porco avete*
> *Qualche cosa ci darete*
> *O polenta or mortadella*
> *Viva viva la Pasquella.*
>
> From far way we have heard
> That you have killed the pig
> Something you will surely give us
> Or polenta or mortadella [a type of bologna]
> Viva viva the Pasquella.

At the end of the song, one of two things happen: Either the singers are invited in to eat or residents come outside bearing gifts of food. If invited in, they will most likely be offered the following, served with a platter of prosciutto, mortadella, and cotto (ham).

serves 4 to 6

Time: 50 minutes

Level of Difficulty: Moderate

♊

1 Heat the oil in a large skillet over low heat. Sauté the onion, garlic, celery, and basil for 8 minutes, stirring frequently, until the celery is soft and the onion translucent. Add the tomato sauce

---

In olden days, the term spianatora referred to a large wooden table. The polenta would be poured onto the table and diners would eat directly from there, using their forks to scrape, or spianare, the polenta towards them.

and 1 cup warm water. Cook for 10 minutes, then add the sausage. Season with salt and pepper and cook for 30 minutes, stirring occasionally.

2 Meanwhile, make the polenta. Bring 8 cups salted water to a rolling boil over medium heat in a heavy-gauge saucepan. Reduce the heat to low, pour in the polenta in a steady stream, and cook, whisking constantly. Cook for 30 to 40 minutes, whisking frequently until the polenta comes away from the sides of the pan and the whisk stands up by itself in the center of the polenta.‡

3 Pour the polenta onto a 16-inch-round wooden board, a similar-size clean cloth, or a 16 x 20-inch rectangular board. Cool for 5 minutes and then pour half the sauce on top. Cut the polenta into wedges using a large serving spoon or cake server, place the wedge on a plate, and drizzle with the remaining sauce.

Make Ahead The sauce can be made up to 2 days in advance, refrigerated in a sealed container, and reheated just before serving. It can also be frozen for up to 3 weeks.

How to Serve This dish will often be presented alongside a platter of turnip greens that have been sautéed in garlic and oil.

Wine Suggestion Medium- or Full-bodied Red

4 tablespoons extra virgin olive oil

1 medium onion, minced

2 cloves garlic, minced

1 celery stalk, minced

8 to 10 basil leaves, ripped into shreds by hand"

1 cup tomato sauce

1 cup warm water

4 links sweet fennel sausage, removed from casing and crumbled

Salt to taste

Freshly ground black pepper to taste

8 cups salted water

2 cups coarsely ground cornmeal†

"Basil should be ripped by hand to avoid the darkening of leaves that occurs when it's cut with a knife. Alternatively, referred to as chiffonading, stack the basil leaves on top of each other and roll into a tight lengthwise cylinder. Using a very sharp knife, slice (don't chop) into thin slivers.

†Cornmeal, or polenta, is sold at specialty stores. If sold in bulk, it can be ground coarsely or finely or any variant in between. Italians vary their grades, sometimes choosing fine (generally in early autumn, when new polenta becomes available), other times choosing coarse. Nevertheless, cooking times are similar.

‡A less enery-intensive method for preparing polenta is to add the cornmeal to the boiling salted water as described above. When all the polenta has been added and absorbed, transfer the mixture to a large stainless steel bowl and set the bowl over a large pasta pot containing about 4 inches of simmering water that does not touch the bottom of the bowl. Seal the bowl tightly with foil and cook for about 1 hour and 15 minutes, stirring well every 20 minutes. Remember to reseal the bowl after stirring so that no moisture escapes. The polenta is done when it is smooth, creamy, and comes away from the sides of the bowl.

POLENTA PASTICCIATA

Baked Polenta with Meat Sauce

❧ Piemonte ❧

L'ESTATE DI SAN MARTINO DURA TRE GIORNI E UN POCHININO, A PIEMONTESE PROVERB maintains. The summer of St. Martin lasts three days and a little bit, a reference to the fact that the saint's feast day falls on November 11—after the rains of October and just before the dreaded cold of winter. November 11 also coincides with the end of the grape harvest and, in fact, San Martino festivals generally encompass as much drinking of new wine as they do eating autumnal foods; hence, the saying: Chi non gioca a Natale, chi non balla a Carnevale, chi non beve a San Martino, è un amico malandrino. *If you don't play at Christmas or dance at Carnival or drink on St. Martin's Day, you are a roguish friend indeed.*

Following is a traditional polenta served on the Feast of St. Martin—of course, with plenty of rich red wine.

serves 4

Time: 90 minutes

Level of Difficulty: Moderate

3 tablespoons unsalted butter
1 medium onion, minced
5 ounces ground pork
5 links pork sausage, removed
    from casing and crumbled
1 cup tomato sauce
Salt to taste
1/2 cup whole milk
4 cups coarsely ground cornmeal
6 tablespoons freshly grated
    grana padana or
    Parmigiano-Reggiano

1 Heat 2 tablespoons of the butter in a braising pan or Dutch oven over low heat. Sauté the onion for 4 minutes, then add the ground pork and crumbled sausage. Cook for 5 minutes, stirring constantly. Add the tomato sauce, season with salt, cover, and cook for 1 hour, adding 1 tablespoon milk at a time as needed to keep the sauce liquid. Make sure to use all the milk.

2 Meanwhile, make the polenta according to Step 2 in the directions for Polenta sulla spianatora (page 63) or see the note on the same page. When the polenta is cooked, pour into a 16 x 20-inch baking pan rinsed in cold water and still wet. Cool to room temperature.

3 Preheat the oven to 350°F. Using the remaining butter, grease a decorative baking pan, approximately 10 x 12 x 3 inches.

4 Cut the polenta into slices, about 2 x 5 inches. Transfer the slices to the baking pan, layering them with sauce and a dusting of grated cheese. The final layer should be polenta. Dust with cheese and bake for 30 minutes, or until the surface is crispy and golden.

Make Ahead The sauce can be made up to 2 days in advance, refrigerated in a sealed container, and reheated just before serving. It can also be frozen for up to 3 weeks.

How to Serve Like the Polenta sulla spianatora (see page 62), this dish is traditionally served with some type of sautéed green.

Wine Suggestion Medium- or Full-bodied Red

SPIEDINI DI POLENTA FRITTA

Fried Polenta and Fontina Cheese Kebabs

❧ Piemonte ❧

UNTIL THE END OF WORLD WAR II, TORINO WAS THE CENTER OF THE ITALIAN *fashion world. As such it was inhabited by thousands of young girls who worked as tailors and were called* caterinette *after St. Catherine of Alessandria, who was their patron saint by virtue of having been martyred at the young age of eighteen. At one time, very young girls received gifts on Catherine's feast day (November 25), while older ones were entitled to invite a young man of their choice for dinner. The name caterinette originated in Paris to which Torino had always been culturally tied. The Parisians still widely celebrate the feast of St. Catherine while, in Torino, the event is largely forgotten. I was given this recipe by Marialuisa Gros, who once worked for a designer of wedding dresses and remembered with great nostalgia both the caterinette festivals and how popular was this typical dish of crispy skewered polenta.*

serves 6, 2 skewers each

Time: 30 minutes

Level of Difficulty: Easy

1 recipe cooked polenta (see page 63), cooled to room temperature

12 ounces fontina cheese, cut into 1-inch cubes

1 large egg, lightly beaten

1 cup unflavored breadcrumbs

12 skewers

Olive oil for frying

1 Cut the polenta into 1-inch cubes and thread onto the skewers, alternating with cubes of fontina.

2 Dip the skewered ingredients first into the beaten egg, then in the breadcrumbs. Heat 1 inch of oil in a skillet over medium heat, and fry the polenta and cheese until golden brown and crispy. Serve immediately.

How to Serve As an appetizer followed by roast loin of pork with sautéed broccoli.

Wine Suggestion Medium-Sweet White

CASOEÛLA

Polenta with Braised Duck and Winter Cabbage

❧ Lombardy ❧

THROUGHOUT LOMBARDY, ST. MARTIN'S DAY, NOVEMBER 11, IS CELEBRATED WITH A *host of scrumptious foods, many including duck. This dates back to 371, when a monk named Martin was elected Bishop of Tours. Preferring his solitude, Martin hid in the woods until a flock of ducks revealed his whereabouts.*

As Italian food traditions go, polenta (or granoturco, the name of the uncooked flour) is fairly recent. Corn flour arrived in Italy only in the early 1500s, shortly after Columbus made his fortuitous journey. When it first arrived at the port of Venice, no one knew what to call it, but since most foods at that time arrived from Turkey, it was given the name granoturco, or "grain from Turkey."

serves 4

Time: 1 hour

Level of Difficulty: Moderate

3 tablespoons unsalted butter
1 medium onion, minced
2 small carrots, diced
1 celery stalk, diced
1 small head savoy cabbage
    (about 2 pounds), cored
    and shredded
1 small duck breast (about 1
    pound), cut into thin strips
Salt to taste
Freshly ground black pepper
    to taste
1/4 cup tomato sauce
2 cups coarsely ground cornmeal
Fresh parsley sprigs for garnish

1 Heat the butter in a heavy-gauge skillet over low heat and sauté the onion for 5 minutes, or until soft. Add the carrots, celery, and cabbage and cook, stirring frequently, for 10 minutes. Cover and cook for another 10 minutes, or until softened.

2 Add the duck, and cook until browned, 3 to 5 minutes. Season with salt and pepper and pour in the tomato sauce. Cook for 30 minutes, stirring frequently.

3 Meanwhile, make the polenta according to Step 2, page 63, or see note, page 63. Serve with polenta and casoeûla. Garnish with the parsley.

Make Ahead The duck can be prepared an hour or two in advance and kept warm until ready to use.

How to Serve Pair with crisply fried artichoke slivers.

Wine Suggestion Full-bodied Red

POLENTA CON OSEI

Polenta with Skewered Meats

❦ Friuli-Venezia-Giulia ❦

OSEI MEANS SMALL BIRDS—THRUSHES, SPARROWS, FINCHES. TINY DELICACIES WITH *a long gastronomic tradition and many passionate aficionados, small birds are generally prepared grilled, stewed (in umido), or skewered and sautéed. But in the last ten years, their numbers have decreased because of overhunting, and most of those that are left are now thankfully protected by strict antihunting laws—all of which might have put a crimp in Livenza's annual* Sagra degli Osei, *a festival held every third Sunday in August for 721 years. But the people of this region, just fifty miles south of Switzerland and thirty-five miles west of Slovenia, are extremely resourceful in the way that cities on the old merchant trails between Europe and Asia have always been, and a variety of other meats—prepared the same way—now accompany the few birds actually served. The festival itself is widely attended and, in addition to the food, encompasses open-air concerts in Piazza Centrale, art shows, an outdoor cabaret, and a variety of stands selling crafts. In the following recipe, one of the more popular of the sagra, pork, beef, and veal have been substituted for the birds.*

serves 4

Time: 1 hour

Level of Difficulty: Moderate

⚖

8 ounces pancetta, sliced

8 ounces round of beef fillets

12 leaves fresh sage

1 pound pork loin, cut into fillets

4 ounces veal cutlet

12 skewers

4 links fennel sausage, removed from casing and cut into chunks

1 Place 1 slice of pancetta on each beef fillet. Cover with a piece of sage and roll into a tight cylinder. Do the same for the pork and veal. Thread the rolled meats onto the skewers, alternating with chunks of sausage and cubes of pancetta.

2 Meanwhile, make the polenta according to Step 2, page 63, or see note, page 63.

3 While the polenta is cooking, heat the butter in a skillet over low to moderate heat and cook the skewers a few minutes per side until golden. Season with salt and pepper and continue to cook for 15 minutes, adding broth as necessary to keep the meats from sticking.

4 Spoon the cooked polenta onto a serving platter. Stick the skewers into the surface of the polenta so that they are standing up straight, and serve.

How to Serve With a platter of sautéed greens.

Wine Suggestion Medium- or Full-bodied Red

4 ounces pancetta, cubed
2 cups coarsely ground cornmeal
3 tablespoons unsalted butter
About 1/2 cup Basic Meat Broth
    (page 460)
Salt to taste
Freshly ground black pepper
    to taste

69

BATUFFOLI

Polenta Layered with Meat Sauce

❦ Tuscany ❧

LITERALLY TRANSLATED, *BATUFFOLI* MEANS "WAD." AS UNAPPETIZING AS THAT *sounds, the word is more than appropriate for describing this traditional dish assembled by layering heaping spoonfuls, or wads, of polenta in a serving bowl and covering each spoonful with a dollop of rich, hearty meat sauce. At the* Sagra della Polenta *in the western Tuscan village of Villa Basilica (held every Saturday and Sunday from mid-June to mid-August), batuffoli is one of the main attractions, both for its delicious flavor and for the memories it sparks of a traditional* cucina casalinga.

serves 4

Time: 1 hour

Level of Difficulty: Moderate

꽃

1 clove garlic

1 medium onion

1 small carrot

1 celery stalk

1/4 cup packed fresh Italian
    parsley leaves

4 tablespoons extra virgin olive oil

8 ounces freshly chopped sirloin

2 tablespoons tomato paste

2 tablespoons hot water

2 ounces dried porcini
    mushrooms, soaked in
    warm water for 20 minutes,
    squeezed dry, and finely
    chopped

1 Put the garlic, onion, carrot, celery, and parsley on a cutting board. Using a mezzaluna or a chef's knife, chop all the ingredients together into a uniform paste. Heat the oil in a skillet over low heat and sauté the paste for 4 minutes, stirring constantly. Add the meat, stirring with a wooden spoon to separate the clumps. Cook for 5 minutes.

2 Dilute the tomato paste in 2 tablespoons hot water and add to the skillet, stirring until all ingredients are well blended. Cook for 1 hour, then add the mushrooms. Season with salt and pepper and cook for 1 more hour.

3 Meanwhile, make the polenta according to Step 2, page 63, or see note, page 63. Transfer it, 1 heaping spoonful at a time, into a serving bowl. Top each spoonful of polenta with 1 spoonful of sauce and a dusting of cheese. Continue until all ingredients are used up, making sure to end up with a layer of sauce and cheese. Let rest for 10 minutes before serving.

Salt to taste
Freshly ground black pepper
  to taste
2 cups coarsely ground cornmeal
8 tablespoons freshly grated
  Parmigiano-Reggiano

71

Make Ahead The sauce can be made up to 2 days in advance and refrigerated in a sealed container until ready to use. It can also be frozen for up to 3 weeks.

How to Serve As with other polenta dishes, this one pairs best with a platter of bitter greens (turnip tops, broccoli rabe, chard) sautéed in garlic and oil.

Wine Suggestion Medium- or Full-bodied Red

POLENTA FRITTA COL STRACCHINO

Fried Polenta with Stracchino Cheese

❦ Tuscany ❦

ANOTHER FAVORITE OF THE HUGE CROWDS ATTENDING VILLA BASILICA'S *Sagra della Polenta is the following dish, which works especially well when one has some leftover polenta. Stracchino is a rich, buttery cheese produced in many of Italy's northern regions. Best eaten when fresh and young, it is especially appropriate for recipes requiring a cheese that spreads easily. Gorgonzola and taleggio are both members of the stracchino family.*

serves 4

Time: 90 minutes

Level of Difficulty: Moderate

2 cups coarsely ground cornmeal

6 tablespoons extra virgin olive oil

8 ounces stracchino cheese or any soft cheese, such as brie, taleggio, triple cream, or even fresh ricotta

5 to 6 sprigs fresh rosemary or other herb for garnish

Note The polenta rectangles can also be fried in olive oil instead of baked.

1 Make the polenta according to Step 2, page 63, or see note, page 63. Spoon onto a large, wet baking sheet and smooth with a wet spatula until 1 inch thick. Cool completely.

2 Preheat the oven to 400°F.

3 Cut the cooled polenta into 2 x 3-inch rectangles and brush both sides with oil. Place the slices on a baking sheet and bake for 15 minutes, turn the slices over, and bake for another 15 minutes. Top the baked polenta with a scoop of stracchino, spreading the cheese over the entire surface. Arrange the slices on a serving platter and garnish with the fresh herbs.

Make Ahead The polenta can be made up to 3 days in advance, cut into rectangles, sealed in plastic wrap, and refrigerated until needed.

How to Serve Works very well as part of a party buffet or as an appetizer followed by grilled sausages and sautéed greens.

Wine Suggestion Medium Sweet White

GULASCH E POLENTA

Goulash with Polenta

❧ Trentino-Alto Adige ❧

TRENTINO-ALTO ADIGE IS ONE OF ITALY'S MAJOR PRODUCERS OF WINE. ON THE THIRD *Sunday of September, the picturesque village of Settequerce holds its harvest festival,* La Sagra dell'Uva, *to celebrate another year's vintage. Complete with traditional floats, games dating back to the fifteenth century, carafes of new wine, and a host of hearty dishes, the sagra is a most authentic Alpine experience. The following recipe, a blend of German-style goulash and Italian polenta, is a perfect evocation of the region's bilingual–bicultural flavor.*

serves 4

Time: 2 hours

Level of Difficulty: Moderate

1 pound top round beef, fat
    removed and cut into
    1-inch cubes
Flour for dredging
1 large onion, halved
1 tablespoon unsalted butter
1 tablespoon extra virgin olive oil
1 clove garlic, crushed
Salt to taste
1 teaspoon paprika
1 cup dry, full-bodied red wine
2 cups coarsely ground cornmeal
12 sprigs fresh parsley for garnish

1 Dredge the meat in the flour and set aside. Cut half the onion into thin slices; dice the other half. Heat the butter and oil in a large ovenproof skillet over medium heat and sauté the diced onion for 4 minutes, stirring constantly. Add the meat and cook, stirring, until all sides are golden brown.

2 Preheat the oven to 350°F. Add the sliced onion and crushed garlic to the skillet, season with salt and paprika, and pour in the wine. Add as much water as need to completely cover the meat, cover, and bake for 1$^{1}/_{2}$ hours.

4 Meanwhile, make the polenta according to Step 2, page 63, or see note, page 63. Spoon the cooked polenta onto a serving platter and create a well in the center. Spoon the goulash into the well, garnish with parsley, and serve.

Make Ahead The meat can be cooked up to 1 day in advance, refrigerated, and reheated when ready to use.

How to Serve As an entrée accompanied either with sautéed bitter greens or a green salad.

Wine Suggestion Medium-bodied Red

POLENTA DI GRANO SARACENO AL FORNO

Baked Buckwheat Polenta

74

❧ Trentino-Alto Adige ❧

BUCKWHEAT POLENTA IS AS MUCH A STAPLE IN THIS COLORFUL ALPINE REGION *as is hard durum wheat in more southern parts of Italy. In the following recipe, a favorite of the participants in Settequerce's* Sagra dell'Uva, *the darker, finer speckled flour is used to make a wonderfully hearty polenta that is generally consumed with sautéed greens and hunks of two- to three-year-old grana padana.*

serves 4

Time: 60 minutes

Level of Difficulty: Moderate

8 cups salted water for cooking

1¹/₂ cups buckwheat polenta* or coarsely ground cornmeal

4 tablespoons unsalted butter

4 anchovy fillets, spines removed (see page 25 about anchovies)

¹/₂ cup dry white wine

4 tablespoons freshly grated grana padana or Parmigiano-Reggiano

1 Make the polenta according to Step 2 in the directions for Polenta sulla Spinatora (page 63) or see note, page 63.

2 Meanwhile, heat 2 tablespoons of the butter in a skillet over low heat and sauté the anchovies until dissolved.

3 Preheat the oven to 400°F. Butter a 10 x 12-inch baking pan.

4 Stir the wine into the cooked polenta and pour into the pan. Top with the anchovies, dust the surface with the cheese, and dot with the remaining butter. Bake for 10 minutes. Serve hot.

How to Serve As an entrée with sautéed greens and hunks of hard cheese, such as grana padana or Parmigiano-Reggiano.

Wine Suggestion Dry White

Buckwheat polenta, often called granturco alla saracena, *can be found in specialty food stores.*

PASTUCCIA

Baked Polenta with Sausage and Raisins

❧ Abruzzo ❧

SAINT ANTHONY IS THE PATRON SAINT OF DOMESTICATED ANIMALS AND ON HIS FEAST *day, January 17, many small southern Italian villages assemble all their pigs, cats, dogs, donkeys, and horses outside the church for an annual benediction—a custom immortalized by Goethe in the account of his journeys to the mezzogiorno. In Cansano in Abruzzo, the day is celebrated by killing a specially selected pig— purchased during the first week of September and allowed to wander freely around the village with a bell around its neck. The day is an orgy of eating and drinking—each course, naturally, revolving around pork. I coaxed this unusual recipe from Signora Ada Maltazzano, a seventy-five-year-old resident of Cansano.*

serves 4

Time: 60 minutes

Level of Difficulty: Moderate

2 cups very finely ground cornmeal

1/2 teaspoon salt

8 ounces pork sausage, removed from casing and crumbled

1/4 cup golden raisin, soaked in warm water for 10 minutes, drained, and squeezed dry

4 ounces pork loin, thinly sliced, then diced

2 tablespoons extra virgin olive oil

2 large egg yolks

1 Place the cornmeal and salt in a large bowl and add boiling water, 1 tablespoon at a time, whisking until the resulting dough is moist and comes away easily from the sides of the bowl. Stir in half the sausage, half the raisins, and half the pork loin. Mix well to blend.

2 Preheat the oven to 350°F. Oil a glass baking dish.

3 Stir the egg yolks into the polenta mixture and pour into the dish, smoothing the surface with a spatula. Sprinkle the remaining sausage, raisins, and pork loin over the surface, drizzle with the oil, and bake for 45 minutes. Slice into wedges, and serve hot.

How to Serve This dish works well in a variety of settings, from appetizer to party food to entrée—serve on a bed of greens accompanied by broccoli gratin.

Wine Suggestion Full-bodied Red

POLENTA DI NIEL

Creamy Polenta with Beef Stew

❧ Val d'Aosta ❧

THE ARNEODO FAMILY LIVES IN SANCTO LUCIO DI COUMBOSCURO, JUST ON THE *other side of the Alps from France. Thirty years ago, Sergio Arneodo and his wife founded the Centre Prouvençal Coumboscuro, an ethnographic museum documenting the lives of the farmers and field-workers who lived centuries past in this bilingual (French/Italian), mountainous region. Today, along with their six children, the Arneodos publish books, record traditional music, and organize two cultural festivals a year attended by residents of the area as well as by hordes of French provenzale, many of whom pilgrimage across the Alps on foot. In fact, the Arneodo home has become a mecca for the safekeeping of provenzale traditions.*

The following recipe comes from Matilda Arneodo, who generally makes it for the festival, which is held at the end of August. Its name dates back to another ancient festival—La Polentata di Niel—held nearby, in the village of Niel.

serves 6

Time: 45 minutes

Level of Difficulty: Moderate

⚕

1 quart whole milk
1 quart water
2 cups coarsely ground cornmeal
2 tablespoons unsalted butter
2 tablespoons extra virgin olive oil
2 ounces pancetta, finely diced
2 cloves garlic, minced
1 bay leaf
1 1/2 pounds chopped sirloin

1 Bring the milk and salted water to a boil over medium heat in a heavy-gauge saucepan. Reduce the heat to low, pour in the polenta steadily, and cook, whisking constantly, until the polenta becomes smooth and creamy.

2 Meanwhile, heat the butter and oil in a skillet over low heat and sauté the pancetta for 4 minutes, or until translucent. Add the garlic and bay leaf and continue to cook, stirring constantly, until the garlic starts to brown. Increase the heat to medium, crumble the meat into the skillet, season with salt, pepper, and the clove, and cook for 10 to 15 minutes, or until the meat is dry and completely browned.

3 Pour the wine over the meat, and cook for 10 minutes, stirring occasionally. Add the broth, and cook for 20 minutes, or until the mixture has thickened to stewlike consistency.

4 Divide the polenta among four bowls. Top with the meat and serve hot.

Make Ahead The meat can be prepared earlier in the day and reheated when ready to use. Add extra broth if the consistency is too thick.

How to Serve As an entrée, pair with gratinéed broccoli, asparagus, or brussels sprouts.

Wine Suggestion Medium-bodied Red

Salt to taste
Freshly ground black pepper
   to taste
1 whole clove
2 cups dry red wine
1 cup Basic Meat Broth
   (page 460)

77

RISOTTO AL'TARTUFO

Risotto with Truffles

78

❦ Umbria ❦

IN THE DAYS WHEN KING VITTORIO EMANUELE ENTERTAINED VISITING NOBLES BY *leading them on an early morning search for truffles, truffle foraging was considered to be a serious and authoritative sport, much like fox hunting. Its adherents were defined by their knowledge, experience, and absolute obedience to a rigid code of conduct. Today, unfortunately, professional truffle hunters (*trifolai*) are increasingly outnumbered by greedy and ignorant amateurs. "These cretini dig anywhere and everywhere and even forget to close the holes behind them," says Franco Maltieri, a professional* trifolau *who lives in Perugia. "They know nothing about the truffle's reproductive cycle and take what they find without any concern for whether they leave enough root for the truffle to regenerate. Maltieri supplies a great number of the pungent tubers for Alba's Truffle Sagra, a madcap marathon of eating and merrymaking that takes place every November. Maltieri also helps with the cooking and from him comes the following recipe.*

serves 4

Time: 35 to 40 minutes

Level of Difficulty: Moderate

〽

5 tablespoons unsalted butter
1 small onion, minced
3 ounces pancetta, finely diced
1 ounce prosciutto, finely diced
2 cups Carnaroli or Arborio or
    Vialone Nano rice*
1 1/2 quarts Basic Meat Broth,
    (page 460), simmering
1/2 cup freshly grated
    Parmigiano-Reggiano

1 Heat 3 tablespoons butter in a heavy-gauge saucepan or Dutch oven over low heat and add the onion. Cook, stirring frequently, for 5 minutes. Add the pancetta and prosciutto and cook, stirring constantly, for 5 minutes longer, or until the onion turns translucent.

2 Add the rice and cook for 3 minutes, stirring constantly, until the grains are completely coated with oil. Pour 1 ladleful of broth over the rice and cook, stirring constantly, until the liquid has been completely absorbed. Add another ladleful and stir until it has been completely absorbed. Continue cooking for about 20 minutes, or until the rice is tender and the consistency resembles a thick soup.

3 Stir the remaining butter and the cheese into the rice and distribute among four plates. Thinly slice the truffle or mushroom over each serving and serve immediately. If you use truffle paste, stir into the risotto just before serving.

Make Ahead **Many restaurants prepare risotto to the point where it is half cooked, and then complete the process when the customer orders. But risotto should always be served *al onda*, which means "wavy"—a reference to its soupy texture—and it is very difficult to attain that texture unless the rice is cooked all the way through without interruption.**

How to Serve **With steamed asparagus.**

Wine Suggestion **Dry White or Full-bodied Red**

1 ounce white truffle, 1 teaspoon truffle paste, or 1 fresh porcini mushroom

79

Carnaroli and Vialone Nano are two types of superfino Arborio rice produced in small quantities mainly in the flatland area south of Verona. Known for their nutty flavor and as well as their capacity for absorbing great quantities of liquid, the two rice varieties are generally grown in risaie using techniques dating back over 300 years.

TIELLA DI RISO E ZUCCHINI

Baked Rice Casserole with Zucchini and Potatoes

❧ Calabria ❧

SPINATI IS THE NAME FOR THE MAIN PROTAGONISTS OF REGGIO CALABRIA'S
San Rocco di Montpellier *Festival, held every August 16 in Palmi. Literally translated, the word means "pricked by spines"—a reference to the hundreds of people who, that entire day, encase their near-naked bodies in a head-to-foot cage made of spiny twigs, then march through the town trailing blood on the streets. The practice is not unique to Palmi; southern Italy contains many villages where residents practice some form of self-mutilation in expiation for their sins. What makes this festival stand out is that the number of spinati—both men and women—seems to grow exponentially with every passing year.*

My tolerance for this genre of spectacle is not very high, however, and so I ducked into my friend Mariarosa's house immediately after the first wave of bleeding men and women had passed by. Fortunately, she was just finishing up the preparation for that day's pranzo, *and I was able to settle my stomach with a "preview" bowl of this casserole, a traditional dish for the feast of Palmi's patron saint.*

serves 4

Time: About 90 minutes

Level of Difficulty: Moderate

❧

2 large onions, thinly sliced
2 cloves garlic, minced
3 tablespoons freshly chopped
    Italian parsley
3 cups packed cherry tomatoes,
    halved

1 Preheat the oven to 350°F.

2 Arrange half the onion slices in the bottom of an ovenproof 10-inch-round casserole with sides at least 2 inches high. Top with half the garlic, half the parsley, and half the tomatoes, arranged cut side up. Dust with half the cheese and season with salt and pepper. Top with a layer of potatoes, arranged in slightly overlapping fashion. Rinse and drain the rice and layer evenly over the potatoes. Top this with a layer of sliced zucchini.

3 Add the remaining parsley and garlic, a layer of the remaining onions, a layer of the remaining tomatoes, and the remaining potatoes. Drizzle with oil, season again with salt and pepper, and pour in the broth. Sprinkle with the breadcrumbs and cover tightly with foil.

4 Bake for 20 minutes. Remove the foil and bake for another 35 minutes, or until the rice is cooked. Add more broth if the ingredients seem too dry. Serve immediately.

Make Ahead The entire casserole can be prepared earlier in the day, set aside in a warm place, and reheated when needed.

How to Serve Round out with an arugula and radicchio salad.

Wine Suggestion **Medium-Sweet White**

3 tablespoons freshly grated
   Parmigiano-Reggiano
Salt to taste
Freshly ground black pepper
   to taste
1 pound boiling potatoes,
   peeled and thinly sliced
1 1/2 cups Vialone Nano or
   Arborio rice
2 pounds small zucchini,
   cut into thin rounds
5 tablespoons extra virgin
   olive oil
About 4 cups Basic Meat Broth
   (page 460) or canned broth
3 tablespoons plain breadcrumbs

PANISSA

Rice and Beans, Piedmont-style

❦ Piemonte ❦

UNTIL 1962, MOTTALCIATA'S ANNUAL SAGRA WAS STRICTLY DEVOTED TO THE AREA'S *favorite foods: rice and beans. Since then, however, northern Piemonte has evolved more and more into a wine-lover's paradise, with much of the region's hillsides now terraced for nebbiolo, barbera, and barolo. And so, the event's official name is now* La Sagra dell'Uva, Fagioli e Riso—*The Rice, Bean, and Wine Festival.*

The following is one of the sagra's most popular dishes, a heavenly blend of rice, fresh-shelled borlotti *(cranberry beans), hard salami, and homemade beef broth. Not technically a risotto, it nevertheless uses the same technique for plumping the rice by adding liquid a little at a time. So popular is panissa throughout Piemonte that Morano sul Po, a tiny village on the banks of the Po River, devotes its entire annual festival to it. Held on or about the third weekend in June,* La Sagra della Panissa *is a very small and local event, the entire menu consisting of panissa and wine. In other parts of Piemonte, the same dish may be called* paniscia *or* panizza.

serves 6

Time: 2 hours, 45 minutes

Level of Difficulty: Moderate

⚜

BROTH
1 large onion, peeled and halved
3 whole cloves
1 carrot, peeled
1 celery stalk
1 beef bone
8 ounces beef ribs
Salt to taste

1 To make the broth, stud the onion with the cloves and place all ingredients in a large soup pot. Cover and bring to a boil over medium-high heat, reduce the heat to low, and cook for 2 hours, skimming the surface occasionally.

2 Strain the broth and discard the solids. Return the broth to the soup pot, add the beans and the prosciutto rind, cover, and cook over medium-low heat for 30 minutes.

3 Meanwhile, heat the oil and butter in a large skillet over low heat and sauté the onion and salami 8 to 10 minutes, stirring frequently, or until the onion is translucent. Add the rice and cook for 5 minutes, stirring constantly, until slightly toasted.

4 Using a slotted spoon, remove the beans from the broth and add to the skillet. Pour in a ladleful of broth and cook until absorbed, stirring constantly. Add another ladleful of broth and cook, stirring constantly, until it has been absorbed. Continue adding broth, 1 ladleful at a time, and cook for about 15 minutes, or until the rice is tender. Season with salt and pepper, remove from the heat, cover, and let sit for 5 minutes. Serve with a dusting of grated cheese.

Make Ahead The broth can be prepared through Step 2 up to 3 days in advance and refrigerated in a sealed container until needed. It can also be frozen for up to 3 weeks.

How to Serve Mainly a one-dish meal, this recipe also works well when paired with a platter of marinated vegetables such as onions, eggplant, zucchini, mushrooms, artichokes, and peppers.

Wine Suggestion Medium-bodied Red

Freshly ground black pepper
   to taste
2 quarts water

83

RICE AND BEANS

2 cups fresh-shelled cranberry
   beans or other type
   fresh-shelled beans
2 ounces prosciutto rind
   or prosciutto
2 tablespoons extra virgin
   olive oil
2 tablespoons unsalted butter
1 medium onion, minced
2 ounces hard salami, finely diced
2 cups Arborio rice
Salt to taste
Freshly ground black pepper
   to taste
4 tablespoons freshly grated
   grana padana or
   Parmigiano-Reggiano

RISOTTO CON ASPARAGI SELVAGGI

Risotto with Wild Asparagus

84

* Tuscany *

IN TUSCANY, EVERY SEASON HAS ITS CELEBRATED VEGETABLES AND, IN EARLY *spring, that vegetable is wild asparagus. Thinner (most stalks are no thicker than a pencil) than cultivated asparagus and dark purple-green in color, wild asparagus have an earthy, pungent flavor that sends Tuscans racing to the fields and olive orchards as soon as the first tiny sprouts break through the earth. In the Tuscan province of Massa (where beachgoers sun themselves against a scenic backdrop of marble-capped mountains), May 4 is reserved for the* Sagra della Cipolla e Asparago Selvaggio *(The Festival of the Onion and Wild Asparagus) held in the village of Bagnone, just up the road from the area's stunningly restored Sarzana Castle. In the United States, wild asparagus are increasingly available in farmer's markets and specialty produce stores.*

serves 4

Time: 40 minutes

Level of Difficulty: Moderate

1 pound wild asparagus or
   pencil-thin white or green
   cultivated asparagus

1 1/2 quarts chicken broth

2 tablespoons extra virgin
   olive oil

2 tablespoons unsalted butter

1 large sweet onion, finely diced

2 cups Vialone Nano or Arborio
   or Carnaroli rice*

1 Snap off the tough end sections of the asparagus and clean and chop all but 8 to 12 spears. Place the broth in a saucepan and over high heat bring to a boil. Reduce the heat to low and maintain a simmer.

2 In a separate saucepan, boil the 8 to 12 reserved asparagus spears for about 7 minutes, or until limp. Drain and set aside.

3 Heat the oil and butter in a large saucepan or Dutch oven over low heat. Sauté the onion, stirring occasionally, for 8 minutes, or until translucent. Stir in the chopped asparagus and cook for 5 minutes, or until soft. Add the rice and cook, stirring constantly, for about 3 minutes, or until the grains are completely coated.

*See page 79 for an explanation of various rices.

4 Pour in a ladleful of broth and cook until absorbed, stirring constantly. Add another ladleful of broth and cook, stirring, until it has been absorbed. Continue adding broth, 1 ladleful at a time, and cook for about 20 minutes, or until the rice is tender and the consistency resembles a thick soup. Season with salt and pepper, stir in the parsley and grated cheese, garnish each plate with 2 to 3 asparagus spears, and serve immediately.

How to Serve **With a platter of steamed baby vegetables drizzled with oil and lemon.**

Wine Suggestion **Dry White**

Salt to taste

Freshly ground white pepper to taste

2 tablespoons freshly chopped Italian parsley

$1/4$ cup freshly grated Parmigiano-Reggiano

85

RISOTTO AI FUNGHI AL SALTO

Twice-cooked Porcini Mushroom Risotto

❧ Lombardia ❧

ON MAY 7, MILAN CELEBRATES THE FEAST OF ITS PATRON, SANT'AMBROGIO. *In late morning, young boys and girls bring assorted donations to the Basilica of Saint Ambrose and lay them on an altar decorated with dozens of flower displays; at night La Scala Opera House opens its spring season. But with the first light of daybreak, the piazza in front of the basilica teams with a festival called* O bei! O bei!, *which dates back to 1288 when it was held in Piazza Santa Maria Maggiore, the present sight of Milan's imposing Duomo. When construction began on the duomo in 1386, the festival was moved to its present location. The name—o bei! o bei!, which translates roughly to "oh my, oh my"—originated when Pope Pius V invited Gianetto Castiglione, the founder of the Order of Saints Maurizio and Lazzaro, to come to Milan to revive the Order's waning power. As the aristocratic Castiglione paraded into the city, accompanied by his royal court of elegantly dressed nobles, and distributing cakes and biscuits to the assembled throngs, the children in the crowd cried out in joy:* O bei! O bei!

Today, the event draws tens of thousands—sometimes millions—of visitors, who come for the spirit of the festival as well as the wide variety of food offerings. The following is a recipe given me by one of the event's food purveyors, Giovanna d'Amperi, who initially created the dish to deal with postfestival remnants. "Everyone loved it so much," she says, "that I now serve it fresh."

serves 6

Time: 1 hour

Level of Difficulty: Moderate

⚶

About 1¹/2 quarts Basic Meat
    Broth (page 460)

8 tablespoons unsalted butter

1 small onion, minced

12 ounces fresh porcini
    mushroom caps, cleaned
    and diced

1 Place the broth in a saucepan and over high heat bring to a boil. Reduce the heat to low and maintain a simmer.

2 Heat 5 tablespoons of the butter in a saucepan or Dutch oven over low heat. Sauté the onion for 8 minutes, or until translucent. Add the mushrooms, stir for 1 minute, and add the wine. Cook for 4 minutes, or until the wine has almost evaporated, then add the rice, stirring until the grains are completely coated with the mushroom mixture.

3 Pour in a ladleful of broth and cook until absorbed, stirring constantly. Add another ladleful of broth and cook, stirring, until it has been absorbed. Continue adding broth, 1 ladleful at a time, and cook for about 20 minutes, or until the rice is tender and the consistency resembles a thick soup. Season with salt and pepper, stir in the grated cheese, and pour into a bowl. Cool to room temperature.

4 Heat the remaining butter in a skillet. Add the finished risotto, smoothing the surface with a spatula. Cook over medium heat for 10 minutes, or until the rice develops a bottom crust. Slide onto a plate, cover with another plate, and turn upside down. Slide back into the skillet and cook for 8 to 10 minutes on the reverse side. Cut into slices and garnish with the parsley.

Make Ahead The rice can be prepared through Step 3 up to 2 days in advance and refrigerated in a sealed container until needed. Just before using, stir 2 tablespoons hot broth into the rice to soften the consistency.

How to Serve With a platter of oven-roasted tomatoes.

Wine Suggestion Dry White or Medium-bodied Red

1 cup dry white wine

2 cups Vialone Nano or other Arborio rice*

Salt to taste

Freshly ground black pepper to taste

1/2 cup freshly grated Parmigiano-Reggiano

Parsley leaves for garnish

*See page 79 for an explanation of various rices.

PALLINE DI RISOTTO FRITTE

Fried Risotto Croquettes

❦ Lombardia ❦

GIOVANNA D'AMPERI HAS MORE THAN ONE USE FOR WHATEVER RISOTTO IS LEFT *over after Milan's O bei! O bei! festival (see page 86). Following is a recipe for crisply fried croquettes made from the risotto that so characterizes Milan that it carries its name: Risotto alla milanese. Any type of risotto can be used for making these croquettes, however.*

serves 4

Time: 1 hour

Level of Difficulty: Moderate

6 to 7 saffron threads
About 1¹/2 quarts Basic Meat
    Broth (page 460), simmering
4 tablespoons extra virgin
    olive oil
1 small onion, minced
1¹/2 cups Carnaroli or
    Arborio rice
4 ounces freshly grated
    Parmigiano-Reggiano
1 large egg, lightly beaten
Flour for dredging
Olive oil for frying
Arugula and radicchio salad
    dressed with vinaigrette
    for bedding

1 Place the saffron threads in a plastic sandwich bag and press the strands with a rolling pin to pulverize them. Sprinkle the powder over ¹/2 cup hot broth, stir, and set aside.

2 Heat the 4 tablespoons oil in a saucepan or Dutch oven over low heat. Sauté the onion for 8 minutes, stirring constantly. Add the rice and continue to stir for 5 to 7 minutes, or until the grains are lightly toasted.

3 Pour in a ladleful of broth and cook until absorbed, stirring constantly. Add another ladleful of broth and cook, stirring, until it has been absorbed. Continue adding broth, 1 ladleful at a time, and cook for about 20 minutes, or until the rice is tender and the consistency resembles a thick soup. After the last addition of broth, add the broth with the dissolved saffron and stir until the liquid has been absorbed. Stir in the cheese, remove from the heat, transfer to a bowl, and cool to room temperature.

4 Using your hands, form walnut-size balls of risotto, dip the balls in the egg and then dredge with flour. Heat 2 inches of olive oil in a skillet to 375°F.* Fry the balls, 10 or 12 at a time, in the oil until golden brown. Remove with a slotted spoon, drain on paper towels, and serve on a bed of arugula and radicchio leaves.

Make Ahead The uncooked croquettes can be made up to 1 day in advance and refrigerated in a sealed container until ready to use.

How to Serve The finished croquettes can also be placed in boiling broth and served as a soup.

Wine Suggestion **Dry White**

*To test the temperature of the oil, you can put a cube of bread into the skillet. When it sizzles around the edges and turns golden almost immediately, the oil is the right temperature.

RISOTTO CON CILIEGIE

Risotto with Black Cherries

❦ Piemonte ❦

IF YOU HAVE ALWAYS HARBORED AN INSATIABLE LOVE FOR CRISP, FRESH CHERRIES *(especially the creamy white variety), hasten forthwith to Piemonte (or Trentino-Alto Adige, for that matter) during the months of May and June. No matter where you wind up, you're bound to be inundated with cherries and cherry products—so blanketed are the two regions with cherry trees that you can generally wander along any country road picking them off the prodigious number of trees, ignored by residents who simply have had their fill come mid-May.*

You can also choose among dozens of festivals devoted exclusively to this minuscule delight—in Piemonte, there's a Sagra delle Cilegie *in Garbagna (around June 15), in Pecetto T. Se (around June 1), and in Sagliano Micca (around May 20), and that's just a small sampling. One of the more unusual savory recipes containing cherries is the following, pulled from the slightly hesitant lips of Malva Montagiosi, one of the expert cooks behind the success of Garessio's Cherry Festival.*

serves 4

Time: 45 minutes

Level of Difficulty: Moderate

⚖

About 1¹/₂ quarts Basic Meat
    Broth (page 460)
5 tablespoons unsalted butter
1 small onion, minced
4 packed cups ripe black cherries,
    pitted and diced, plus
    4 small bunches fresh
    cherries for garnish

1 Place the broth in a saucepan and over high heat bring to a boil. Reduce the heat to low and maintain a simmer.

2 Heat 3 tablespoons of the butter in a saucepan or Dutch oven over low heat. Sauté the onion for 8 minutes, or until translucent. Add the cherries and cook for 4 minutes, stirring frequently. Add the rice and cook for 4 to 5 minutes, stirring constantly, until the grains are completely coated. Pour in the champagne and cook for 3 minutes, or until evaporated.

3 Pour in a ladleful of broth and cook until absorbed, stirring constantly. Add another ladleful of broth and cook, stirring, until it has been absorbed. Continue adding broth, 1 ladleful at a time, and cook for about 20 minutes, or until the rice is tender and the consistency resembles a thick soup. Season with salt and pepper, stir in the cream and the remaining butter, garnish each plate with a bunch of fresh cherries, and serve.

How to Serve This is a very rich dish and can be used, in very small portions, as first course or as the main course following a platter of steamed vegetables with parsley sauce.

Wine Suggestion **Dry White**

$1^1/2$ cups Carnaroli or
    Arborio rice*
1 cup dry champagne
Salt to taste
Freshly ground black pepper
    to taste
$1/2$ cup heavy cream

91

*See page 79 for an explanation of various rices.

BRODERA

Risotto with Spareribs

❦ Val d'Aosta ❦

ALTHOUGH VAL D'AOSTA IS ITALY'S SMALLEST REGION, IT CONTAINS ONE OF THE *most dramatically scenic stretches of Alpine valleys and snow-capped peaks. Located just on the other side of the Alps from France, the region is autonomous and bilingual, its residents as comfortable speaking French as Italian. In recognition of its Alpine heritage, every year on the third Sunday of October, the people of Croix Noire hold a unique tournament, La Bataille des reines, "reine" meaning "queen," a reference to a highly prized breed of black-horned cow that can be seen roaming the region's mountains and valleys. The cows are pitted against each other in a mild battle for territorial supremacy and the winner crowned with a garland of flowers. The subsequent festival involves much music and dancing and such delights as the following.*

serves 4

Time: About 3 hours

Level of Difficulty: Moderate

⚖

BROTH
2 pounds spareribs, fatty parts removed
1 large onion, halved
1 carrot
1 celery stalk
1 green pepper, cleaned and diced
Salt to taste
2 quarts water

1 To make the broth, place all ingredients in a large soup pot. Cover and bring to a boil over medium-high heat, reduce the heat to low, and cook for 2 hours, skimming the surface occasionally.

2 Using tongs or a slotted spoon, remove the spareribs, cut into individual sections, and keep warm. Strain the broth and discard the solids. Return the broth to the pot, bring to a boil, reduce the heat to low, and simmer.

3 To make the risotto, heat 2 tablespoons of the butter in a heavy-gauge saucepan or Dutch oven over low heat. Sauté the onion for 7 minutes, stirring constantly, until translucent. Add the rice, stirring to coat the grains with the butter.

4 Pour in a ladleful of broth and cook until absorbed, stirring constantly. Add another ladleful of broth and cook, stirring, until it has been absorbed. Continue adding broth, 1 ladleful at a time, and cook for about 15 minutes, or until the rice is tender and the consistency resembles a thick soup. Add the remaining butter and the cheese, season with salt and pepper, and distribute among four plates. Arrange a few ribs to the side, garnish with sage, and serve.

Make Ahead The broth can be made earlier in the day and the spareribs kept warm until needed.

How to Serve With sautéed greens such as spinach or broccoli rabe.

Wine Suggestion Medium or Full-bodied Red

RICE

4 tablespoons unsalted butter
1 medium onion, thinly sliced
2 cups Arborio rice
4 tablespoons freshly grated
    grana padana or
    Parmigiano-Reggiano
Salt to taste
Freshly ground black pepper
    to taste
Fresh sage for garnish

Pasta and Gnocchi

Pasta

ORECCHIETTE STRASCINATE
Homemade Orecchiette with Sundried Tomato Sauce

CULLURZONES AL FORMAGGIO
Chard and Mint Ravioli with Sardinian Pecorino

CASCASA CARLOFORTINA
Couscous with Chick Peas

CIALSÓNS CIARGNEI
Egg Dumplings with Smoked Ricotta and Dark Chocolate

MACCHERONI ALLA PASTORA
Shepherd's Pasta with Fresh Ricotta

SPAGHETTI A CACIO E PEPE
Spaghetti with Black Pepper and Pecorino Cheese

MALFATTI AL MASCARPONE
Pasta Dumplings with Mascarpone

PISARÉI CON CECI E CIME DI RAPA
Gnocchetti with Chick Peas and Broccoli Rabe

SPAGHETTI ALLA CARRETTIERA
Spaghetti with Tuna and Porcini Mushrooms

BIGOLI IN SALSA DI ANATRA
Spaghetti Tubes with Duck Sauce

SPAGHETTI AL NERO DI SEPPIA
Spaghetti with Squid and Squid Ink

PASTICCHIO DI MACCHERONI
Oven-baked Pasta Pie Filled with Porcini Mushroom and Truffles

PIZZOCHERI
Buckwheat Pasta with Potatoes and Cabbage

TAGLIATELLE AL PROSCIUTTO
Wide Ribbon Noodles with Prosciutto

RAVIOLI DOLCE
Oven-baked Sweet Ravioli Filled with Quince

TIMBALLO DI MACCHERONI
Eggplant Timballo

MILLECOSEDDE
Winter Pasta with Chick Peas, Lentils, and White Beans

BUCATINI AL CAVOLFIORE
Hollow Spaghetti with Cauliflower

TRENETTE COL PESTO
Trenette with Pesto

VINCISGRASSI
Stuffed Lasagne

Gnocchi

STRANGOLAPRETI ALLA TRENTINA
Green Gnocchi with Butter and Sage Sauce

GNOCCHI DI ZUCCA
Butternut Squash Gnocchi

GNOCCHI DI SEMOLINO
Baked Semolina Gnocchi

GNOCCHI DI ASPARAGI
Baked Gnocchi Made with Asparagus, Taleggio, and Asiago

GNOCCHI ALLA GORGONZOLA
Potato Gnocchi with Gorgonzola Sauce

EMILIA-ROMAGNA
The Succulent Flavor of the Earth

WHENEVER I JOURNEY BEYOND THE BOUNDS OF CITIES AND TOWNS and venture light-hearted into open sky—green vistas and smells having to do with leaves and hay and pine needles crunching beneath my feet—I have a habit of tasting the earth, of choosing a few select grains and scrutinizing them, using the same critical analysis as sommeliers do with fine wine.

I first search its color for clues as to age, origin, composition, and functionality. Its odor I use to establish locale—to define its heritage, its pedigree, the wars it has witnessed, the floods it has sustained. In good time, I curl my palm around the grains and grind them against each other to see whether they form a clump; are they oily, crumbly, wet, dusty? And finally, I place a few grains on my tongue and let my taste buds complete the profile.

Of course, I then spit the whole thing out, although sometimes the flavor is so exquisite as to make me think earth tartare might work wonderfully as a buffet item at my next party. Take the earth of Emilia-Romagna, for example. In many places, I have found it to be so fat and oily and reeking with the essence of mint and juniper berries that I have wondered how it might taste spread on a thick piece of garlic-rubbed bread. Not at all like the earth in Liguria, which tends to be thin and fishy smelling, with overtones of cheese rinds and overly cooked shell beans.

Also not like Sicilian earth, with its undercurrent of lemon pith and unripe apricots. In some places in Sicily, notably in the interior—in the hot, dry mountains, crusted with a top layer of red Saharan clay—the flavor is somewhat akin to that of licking a cut finger, the ferrous blood gristling reluctantly against one's teeth. In Puglia's case, the earth is so hot it burns the lips and fizzles against the tongue, like dry, burned breadcrumbs.

I remember once, in Tuscany, walking up the hill behind my house and sampling some earth from beneath the large row of cypresses facing the sea. By then, I had not only become quite the connoisseur, but also had developed what I considered an admirable rigor with respect to scientific methodology.

But something propelled me simply to pick up a clump of earth and, without pausing for a second's worth of analysis, put it directly into my mouth. And immediately I was propelled back to the womb. Because it tasted like me, like my skin, my sweat, my saliva, that unique combination of mushrooms, sage, dried figs, and parboiled cardoons that is me and me alone. "We are born of the earth," Catholicism teaches. Finally, I could say I understood.

Never having shared my habit of earth-tasting with anyone ever, I was surprised to find my friend Adriana Chesi similarly disposed. "*Come si può piantare l'orto se non s'asaggia la terra?*" she asked, when the topic first came up by way of talking about our respective gardens. How is it possible to plant vegetables without first tasting the dirt?

Adriana claims to know which spots in the garden are best for planting each type of vegetable purely by tasting. I suspect what she means is that she can taste whether the soil needs more lime or potash or nitrogen or loam. But, despite years of earth tasting and a certain expertise in sensory discrimination, it simply never occurred to me that there was a pragmatic side to what I would have described as a purely esthetic proclivity.

The proof, as they say, is in the sauce although, in Adriana's case, in the flavor and bounty of her vegetables. Which are superb, as I can't help but remark each year when I venture to her house north of Parma in Emilia-Romagna to bring her back for a two-week beach vacation in Tuscany.

Adriana is an old family friend who thrives on living—for fifty weeks a year—a happy but duty-bound existence in the same small village as her dozens of grandchildren. Come September, therefore, this perpetual mermaid of eighty-two years desires nothing more than to bob and weave among the gentle waves of the Tyrrhenian without any little mullets dragging on her tail. So every year, I go to gather her up and, in the process, take in one of my favorite regional festivals, *La sagra del Culatello.*

Culatello is a cured pork product similar to prosciutto in both its origins and long curing process, but different in almost every other way, especially in the scarcity of its production. Taken from the *culo,* or rump, of a pig, *culatello* is largely an artisan-made delicacy, the delicate texture and sweet intensity of which develop only in the fog and humidity of the Po Valley lowlands (contrary to prosciutto, which is aged in the dry mountains around Parma).

Its precise recipe remains a guarded secret known only to a handful of old men. Still warm from the freshly slaughtered pig, the rumps are marinated in an unknown mixture of salt and spices, tied into large, pear-shaped bundles, and hung to cure in open, airy rooms for more than eighteen months. Many spoil as a result of the area's notorious dampness, but the successful few that *do* make it to maturity exhibit a creamy texture and succulent sweetness unmatched by any other cured pork product. Because of culatello's extremely limited production, however, only a few people ever get so far as actually tasting the damn thing.

Which is the main reason I so much enjoy this particular *sagra*—because of the opportunity it presents for shameless indulgence in a delicacy that is otherwise largely unavailable. While it is true that Adriana always brings my mother a gift basket with gastronomic treasures that include an entire culatello, the fact remains that I must share it with my mother, my cousins, and whomever else happens to wander by for a visit. Here at the sagra, I can gorge to my heart's content.

In addition to attending the sagra, Adriana and I also use the opportunity of my being here to cook together in the way we used to do when I was young and my family vacationed in a house not far from hers. I would spend hours in her kitchen, creating one or another type of stuffed pasta, Adriana yelling at me when I was making the ravioli too big or the tortellini too ruffled.

"I never yelled," she maintains about those long-ago sessions, although the reality is she *still* yells at me today when she thinks my *agnolotti* border on the asymmetrical.

In learning at the side of Adriana Chesi, I consider myself to have studied with one of Emilia-Romagna's best pasta makers. The honor is a difficult one to assign since the entire region has long been known not only for the superb quality of its egg pasta, but also for the incredible variety of the shapes generated from that pasta. Ravioli, agnolotti, tortelloni, tortellini, cannelloni, farfalle, tagliatelle, maltagliati, tagliolini, garganelli, maccheroni al pettine . . . each an artistic creation in its own right.

While southern Italy is also known for its extraordinary pasta (I am thinking here of Calabria's fusilli, of Puglia's orecchieti, of the Lazio's bucatini), the difference lies in the fact that southern pasta is made solely with flour and water, which renders it whitish in color and chewy in texture (cooking times for this dense pasta range from ten to sixteen minutes). Emilia's is *pasta all'uovo*—fresh egg pasta with a brilliant yellow color and smooth elasticity that cooks almost as soon as it hits the water. While pasta shapes vary according to who makes it and where they live, the technique is always the same: Flour is heaped onto a table, a well created in the center, eggs added, and, much stirring, kneading, and rolling later, shaped into radiators or hats or butterflies or combs . . . .

But pasta is not the only gastronomic superlative for which Emilia-Romagna is known. There is also Parmigiano-Reggiano, a rich, hard cheese that, to many, symbolizes Italian food at its most distinctive and delicious. The world's entire supply of authentic Parmigiano-Reggiano is made in a geographic area the size of Rhode Island. Its production is strictly regulated and adheres to a methodology dating back to the Etruscans. Boccaccio's *Decameron* in fact, bears this passage: ". . . and there was an entire mountain of Parmigiano cheese, all finely grated, on top of which stood people doing nothing other than making macaroni and ravioli." Molière's biographers tell us that during the great playwright's declining years, he lived primarily on Parmigiano cheese.

The bulk of my information about Parmigiano comes from Adriana's husband, who works for the Parmigiano-Reggiano Consortium in Reggio-Emilia. To be more specific, Amerigo is a cheese tapper and, as such, a member of a small and highly professional group of men who judge the internal structure of cheese simply by tapping the hardened rind. "By tapping both the flat and the convex part of the rind with a small steel hammer," he once explained, "I am able to define the product as premium, second, or third quality."

The image he created with those words has always stayed in my mind, and so as soon as I arrived the day before yesterday, I asked to accompany him one morning during my stay to see exactly how he goes about these determinations.

On the morning in question, we turn into an enormous parking lot and Amerigo drives directly into a spot marked prominently with his name. Only later do I fully comprehend that cheese tappers are like wine tasters—without their expertise, there can be no production. Cherished and revered beyond the realm of even this consortium's senior officers, cheese tappers are coddled to a point just short of an electronic red carpet, rolling out each morning upon their arrival.

"Make sure to bring your sweater," Amerigo reminds me. "The maturing rooms are cold."

I am not at all prepared for my first view of the cheese halls. The rooms are enormous, with hundreds of rows of cheese forms, each row consisting of forty-five forms laid side by side in stacks piled up sixteen forms high. Amerigo reels off a plethora of numbers: each form weighs about seventy-five pounds, the cheese is sold for roughly $8 per pound, and there are approximately 120,000 forms resting in this one consortium. I do a quick massaging of those figures and come up with the unbelievable reality that I am standing in the presence of about $72 million worth of cheese!

Amerigo explains that the consortiums are actually banks in the full sense of the word: They generate profit by lending money and charging interest. No cheese is actually made here; the consortium simply stores the cheese during its eighteen- to twenty-four-month maturation period.

"The hundreds of individual farmers who initially made the cheese have already been paid," Amerigo explains. "But the wholesalers who lay claim to those cheeses can't turn their product around for eighteen to twenty-four months (the maturation period required for cheese to be known as authentic Parmigiano-Reggiano), even though they're expected to pay upon delivery by the farmers. Furthermore, producers have no place to store the cheeses given the constant temperature and humidity required. So the consortium acts as a middleman or banker. It puts up the money to pay the farmers, stores the cheese for the required period, and then collects from the wholesalers—with interest—when the cheese is ready to sell."

If I had heard this explanation without seeing the consortium's storage halls, I might have imagined a small operation involving, perhaps, hundreds of dollars. Now I know we're talking about an enterprise that makes millions of dollars in profit every year simply by collecting interest on cheese.

For the remainder of the morning, I watch as Amerigo goes about his job. His instruments consist of a percussion hammer, a screw needle, and a sampling dowel. With the hammer, he taps the hard rind of an occasional seventy- to eighty-pound wheel at various points while listening carefully to the way the crust takes the blows. "I am like a doctor listening with his stethoscope," he says.

He then pierces the cheese with a screw needle to extract a minute sample of the contents. The resistance of the cheese when it is pierced indicates its internal consistency says Amerigo. The sample itself lets him judge the aroma and the degree of maturation. "I only go on to use the sampling dowel if the hammer and screw needle fail to give me the necessary information."

At one point he tells me that Italy produces more than three million rounds of Parmigiano-Reggiano each year. "All are assessed for commercial value on the basis of information gained by tapping and sampling."

When I express amazement at the number of tappers that must be needed for such an evaluation, he looks at me as if I had just announced that the earth rested on the back of a sea turtle. "Obviously we do not tap *every* wheel," he explains with the same impatience evinced by his wife when I make a mistake with the tortellini. "Tapping is only carried out on a representative sample of cheeses from each production batch."

As the morning advances, I am given a more and more detailed explanation of what I'm witnessing. Tappers, Amerigo tells me, get their information as a result of cracks (called "eyes") that vary in size and number. Apparently, taps create sound waves that travel through the wheels and are analyzed once they reach the other end. Since cracks create variances in what would otherwise be a normal pattern of sound, the variances—though imperceptible to most ears—can be picked up by the extraordinary sensitivity of a good tapper.

"Good tappers must be a very rare breed," I comment at one point.

"You have no idea *how* rare," he answers with evident pride. "It takes at least three years to recognize and train an apprentice who has the necessary sensitivity in his genetic makeup. Several more years are needed to reach a required level of absolute certainty."

He stops what he's doing to drive home the point. "To give you an idea of the kind of certainty I am talking about, a professional tapper takes about four seconds to tap the cheese in various points and render a decision. More importantly, he is very rarely mistaken, even when the defects are minuscule."

By the time we leave the consortium, I am a veritable expert on Parmigiano-Reggiano. I know that it is made from raw cow's milk collected immediately after milking, that the cows are fed a simple diet of grass or hay, and that only cows from Parma, Reggio-Emilia, Modena, Mantua, and Bologna are allowed to take part in the program—if the cows come from anywhere else, the end result must carry a different name.

The actual cheese production takes place on *caselli* (cheese farms) where natural whey culture is added to the milk as a starter along with calf rennet. The only additive permitted is salt; aging lasts on average two years; and the finished cheese is stamped with the words "Parmigiano-Reggiano," repeated at close intervals to differentiate it from lesser cheeses, many lumped together under the generic term "parmesan."

"But there is only one Parmigiano-Reggiano," he says handing me a huge sample. When I attack the hunk as if it were the first food I'd seen in three weeks, he realizes his mistake. "Don't spoil your appetite," he cautions. "It's almost time for lunch."

On the way home, we hear a new report about the ongoing investigation into political money laundering. Paolo Berlusconi has just been indicted and it seems likely that his brother, Silvio, the former right-wing president, will soon face a similar fate.

"Thieves, all of them," Amerigo snaps. "Someday Italians are going to realize they would be far better off under the Communists, who at least make an attempt to share the wealth."

Amerigo and I have never before talked politics. But I would have bet my last lira on his being a Communist. Adriana too. And, for that matter, most of the people of Emilia-Romagna, a region known throughout Italy for having a "slightly pinkish tinge."

"Our most prominent citizens were all Communists," Amerigo claims. "Take Verdi (the composer who was born in the nearby town of Roncole Verdi and spent most of his life in Busseto, also nearby). If ever there was a man at odds with the concept of social elitism, Verdi was he. Just look at the main protagonists of his three most popular operas, *Rigoletto, Il Trovatore,* and *La Traviata.* A hunchback, a gypsy, and a courtesan. Verdi obviously appreciated the bottom rung of the social ladder."

He turns off the highway to a small local road. "Jesus, too," he continues. "You might not have ever thought of it this way, but Jesus was unquestionably a Communist."

Leaving aside Jesus's political affiliations, Emilia-Romagna's Communist tendencies make perfect sense. Created during the mid-1800s unification of Italy by fusing the coastal Romagna to the Emilian plains, the present-day region of Emilia-Romagna has almost no architectural or cultural superlatives, few great urban centers, and still fewer residing aristocrats—all of which might tend to create an elitist bent. The region is basically a flat swatch of very fertile land inhabited by prosperous, hardworking farmers who, today, produce most of northern Italy's pasta flour, fruits, vegetables, and a good deal of its meat.

Its people are unflinchingly tied to the soil and all that that affinity has always entailed: from the social and economic inequities that existed during feudalism, to the coming of the Industrial Revolution, and the resultant rise in both workers' rights movements and, concurrently, the Communist party. "The soil has given us our riches," an early workers' rights slogan maintained, "and in return we give our souls to the cause."

Adriana is waiting with pots steaming and table laid. We begin lunch with a fragrant bowl of *tortellini in brodo* (tortellini in chicken broth), move to *ossobuchi alla reggiana* (veal braised in marsala), and finish up with *torta degli addobati,* which is a delicious rice cake that has traditionally been served during religious festivals, when town residents would drape beautiful tapestries from their windows (*addobati*) to pay tribute to the processions passing by.

When the lunch dishes have been cleared away, Adriana leads me out to the garden, knowing I will gush over every baby beet and sprouting fava. "Emilia-Romagna has the best gardens in all of Italy," she tells me with the regional hubris I have come to expect. "In fact, we have an old proverb—'When an Emilian peasant goes to hell, he always takes his hoe because he knows that, even in hell, there will be earth to till.'

"It's not only our soil, which is dark and sweet and generous," she expounds. "It's also the winds. Without the chill winds, autumn crops would never have the same crisp flavor." She raises her outstretched arms toward the sky. "God bless the *tramontana!*" she cries exuberantly.

The tramontana is generally considered to be Emilia-Romagna's wind in the same way that the *libeccio* belongs to Tuscany, the *grecale* to the Lazio, the *scirocco* to Sicily, and, for that matter, the *mistral* to Provence. Its arrival signals the coming of fall, the retreat indoors, the lighting of the hearth, the gathering together of the generations. "The tramontana waits for me," Adriana once said by way of good-naturedly refusing to extend her late summer visit to Tuscany. "If I do not return, its gusts will abandon us for the Veneto. And then what will happen to our fall cabbages and fennel without the cold to release their essential flavors?"

Much has been written about the tramontana, but no verse is more beautiful than that penned by Curzio Malaparte, that great chronicler of all things Italian: "They call [the tramontana] the cutter because it trims the cypresses and makes them sharp as knives. It brings with it, like a river running full, an odor of wood and chestnuts, warm barns, oak forests, smoke from fireplaces of calm stone. The cleansed air vibrates and hums like a pane of glass; the clear sky curves down and grows distant; the mountains jut out against the pale smooth azure; trees grow fragile and lean; streets seem whiter; water in the river shimmers and breaks against the bank; and a serenity enters into the houses, filling bottles and plates and bowls with azure. A beautiful wind, the tramontana."

Two days before leaving Adriana's, it occurs to me that I have never driven the Via Emilia, the ancient Roman road that winds through each of Emilia-Romagna's great culinary capitals. While I have visited many of the individual cities themselves, I have never had the pleasure of driving from one to the other with no plans other than the simple and unfettered quest for fantastic food.

Built in 187 B.C., the Via Emilia crosses Emilia-Romagna diagonally and joins together its major gastronomic capitals: Piacenza with its excellent (and underrated) wines; Parma, source of both the aforementioned Parmigiano-Reggiano as well as delicious Parma ham (*prosciutto di Parma*); Reggio-Emilia, surrounded by small, local *caselli* (cheese producers); Modena, the home of authentic balsamic vinegar; and, of course, Bologna—*La Grassa* (The Fat)—Emilia-

Romagna's capital and a university town filled from end to end with legendary restaurants. "It is impossible to eat poorly in Bologna," an old proverb maintains.

"Let's journey to Tuscany via a circuitous route," I suggest to Adriana. "We could zigzag our way between the various food purveyors and overnight once or twice in a hotel."

There is no surprise on my part when she immediately agrees, it having been made more than clear that Adriana is ready to begin her vacation. And what better beginning for this ultimate Earth Goddess than a trip designed around the earth's bounty?

She demures just long enough to get her husband's approval. "All right?" she sweet-talks into Amerigo's ear after dinner.

He grabs her face and kisses her square on the lips. "No, it's not all right," he says firmly. "I have eaten enough frozen tortellini to last two lifetimes. This time I'm going to join you."

Surprise is far too mild a word for our reaction. The fact is, we're amazed; in the twenty-three years that Adriana has vacationed in Tuscany, Amerigo has never once wanted to come along.

"The two of you driving directly to Tuscany is one thing," he offers by way of explanation. "But loose on the open roads . . . No, no, no, you will need me to keep you out of trouble."

Our trip eventually takes three days, two of which are filled from dawn to dusk with slow, languorous gluttony. At one point, Adriana wants to extend the food festival by another twenty-four hours so we can stop in the hills just above Bologna to sample a particular type of boiling salami called *cappello da prete*—priest's hats (named so because of their triangular shape). But Amerigo wants to press on to Bologna, where, he says, it will be difficult enough to find a room "without arriving like *malviventi*—delinquents—in the middle of the night."

"*Tesoro,*" coos Adriana, stretching her impressive bosom lushly across the stick shift. "Why should we race across the region when we could take our time and meander? How long has it been since we simply enjoyed journeying from place to place without an agenda? Since before the boys were born, no?" She nibbles his ear and pinches with soft, caressing gestures the fleshy part of his cheek.

It occurs to me that the only other circumstance that generates this type of behavior on her part is when she is working in the garden. The sweet nothings simpered to a luxurious head of cabbage; the endearments lavished on a perfect cardoon; the breathless visage; softened demeanor; the sparkling glow that attends her every brush against the dewy green rows of sweet peas. Earth and Amerigo—the two passions of Adriana Chesi.

The extended trip is not to be, however. "I have to get back to Tuscany," I announce about an instant before Amerigo is slated to cave in to his wife's coercion. "Our first cooking school class starts in four days and I have to start working on menus."

"*Dai,*" says Adriana. Don't be a spoilsport.

But I hold my ground and Amerigo dutifully points the nose of the car toward our last stop, Bologna, where we shuffle past restaurant after restaurant searching for a menu featuring *vincisgrassi*, the extraordinary Emilian lasagna dish containing several dozen ingredients—all of them rich.

"*Incredibile,*" Adriana says, when three heaping plates are finally placed in front of us. "The flavor is so clearly evocative of Emilian earth."

"There she goes again," says Amerigo. "Claiming the earth has a distinctive taste."

"You don't think so?" I ask in my most incredulous tone.

"No I don't think so," he says, mimicking my voice. "And don't tell me you're another one of those lunatics who goes around tasting dirt. I thought my wife had that category all to herself."

He signals the waiter for the check. "Actually," he continues, "if I wanted to be completely accurate, I would claim no opinion one way or the other, since I have never once in my life even considered placing dirt on my tongue."

"Well, then you have no idea what you've missed," says Adriana in her most dismissive tone.

"Try it just once," I beseech him.

"I would sooner give up drinking wine."

"Just once."

"Not even under pain of death."

"One little taste."

"No."

But everything has its own peculiar resolution and, in this case, it seems that the bottle of Amarone we drank with dinner combined with those oh-so-tiny sips of postprandial grappa to soften the fervor of his resolve.

As we leave the restaurant, I race over to the garden plot at the end of the lane and scoop up a handful of dark, rich earth. "Just put a few grains on your tongue and tell us what you taste," I say handing him a tiny pinch.

The rest I divide into two small clumps and hand one over to my partner in crime. Pro that she is, Adriana immediately begins her pretaste analysis—the feel, the smell, the appearence, the texture.

"Ummmm," she says after her analysis has been completed. "Very spicy. Must have added a great deal of nitrogen."

"You two are mad," says Amerigo, as his wife and I argue over whether the taste is more like unripe figs or raw beet greens. But in the very moment of his dismissal, his face grows noticeably more acquiescent and his hand moves ever closer to his lips.

"Make sure you don't swallow it," I add as a final prod.

And then he does it. He presses the tip of his index finger against the dirt and transfers the sticky grains into his mouth.

"Well?" says Adriana with great anticipation. "Figs, right?"

"No, the flavor is much greener," I counter as he quickly spits out his sample. "Much more metallic."

"*Allora?*" we query when a few seconds have gone by with no response. Well?

He looks at both of us with a mixture of resignation and disbelief. "I know I'm going to regret this," he says finally. "But I think I detected a tiny trace of concentrated parsley."

ORECCHIETTE STRASCINATE

Homemade Orecchiette with Sundried Tomato Sauce

❧ Puglia ❧

A SPLENDIDLY DECORATED WHITE STALLION FORMS THE CENTRAL FOCUS OF *Brindisi's* Corpus Domini *celebration. The tradition dates back to the thirteenth century, when the French king, Louis IX, was caught in a storm while journeying on a ship carrying the sacred Eucharist (*Corpus Domini*). Finally able to land on a stretch of beach just outside Brindisi, Louis immediately sent word to his host, the city's bishop, who arrived on a luxurious white stallion.*

Today's Corpus Domini *procession takes place sometime in mid-June and begins begins in Piazza Vittoria, where the stallion's rider, himself elegantly garbed in medieval dress, receives the Eucharist, which he carries through the old city, riding on carpets of flowers arranged in hundreds of different designs. Handwoven tapestries hang at the windows and small children dressed as monks and nuns walk alongside the route, throwing flowers from straw baskets.*

When it is all over, everyone gathers in individual houses for a many-course feast, more often than not starting with these traditional orecchiette (ear-shaped pasta) tossed with a sauce made from sundried tomatoes and grated ricotta salata.

serves 4

Time: About 2 hours

Level of Difficulty: Advanced

⚖

3/4 cup packed sundried tomatoes, soaked in 2 cups warm water for 30 minutes

3 tablespoons extra virgin olive oil

1 dried chili, seeded and crumbled

2 tablespoons freshly chopped oregano

1 Drain the tomatoes, reserving the liquid, and dice finely. Heat the oil in a heavy-gauge skillet over low heat and add the tomatoes and chili. Cook for 10 minutes, stirring constantly. Add the reserved liquid and oregano, season with salt, cover, and cook for 30 minutes, adding additional water to prevent drying out, if needed.

2 Meanwhile, make the pasta. Sift together 3 cups of the flour, a pinch of salt, and the semolina. Place in a large bowl, add 1/4 cup warm water, and work the dough with your hands. Continue adding water,

1 tablespoon at a time, and kneading by hand for about 10 minutes, or until the dough is solid and smooth.

3 Divide the dough into golf ball-size portions, flour a work surface, and roll each ball into a long rope about 3/4 inch wide. Cut one of the ropes into 1-inch-long segments and cover the remaining ropes with a damp towel. Using the curved point of a butter knife, make a slit on the surface of each segment, avoiding cutting through to the other side. Enlarge the slit with your thumb, cupping the sides around the hole with your index and middle fingers. The finished product should resemble a small bowl or ear. Continue until all the dough has been used. Transfer the finished orecchiette to a floured surface and dry for 20 minutes.

4 Bring to a boil 3 quarts salted water over medium-high heat. Add the orecchiette and cook for 12 to 15 minutes, or until tender.

5 Meanwhile, add the grated ricotta to the sauce and cook until heated through. Divide the cooked and drained orecchiette among four bowls. Top with a dollop of sauce and serve.

Make Ahead Both sauce and pasta can be made up to a day or two in advance or frozen, separately, for up to 3 weeks. If freezing, immerse the frozen pasta directly in the boiling water and stir immediately to avoid sticking.

How to Serve Makes a fine one-course meal when served with a green salad and hot, crusty bread.

Wine Suggestion Medium- or Full-bodied Red

Salt to taste

4 cups unbleached all-purpose flour, sifted

1/2 cup semolina

About 1/2 cup warm water plus 3 quarts salted water

4 ounces ricotta salata*, grated

105

Ricotta salata is usually made from ewe's milk, conserved in salt, then left to age until hard. Saltier and creamier than most grating cheeses, it is used throughout southern Italy for grating over pasta. Look for it in most specialty cheese stores.

CULLURZONES AL FORMAGGIO

Chard and Mint Ravioli with Sardinian Pecorino

❧ Sardegna ❧

IN MAMOIADA, A SARDINIAN VILLAGE NOT FAR FROM NUORO, CARNIVAL CELEBRATIONS *retain an almost medieval flavor. The pre-Lenten festivities begin early on Martedi Grasso (Fat Tuesday), with Mamoiada's central piazza buzzing with accordian players, dancers dressed in traditional garb, and a crowd of onlookers, most dressed in black from head to toe. At noon, the merrymaking ceases instantly, the arrival of* maimones, *the Devil, and his accomplices, called* mamuthones, *each one covered in animal pelts and wearing horrific masks. A peculiar ritual then begins, whereby those called* issicadores *and dressed as jailers, begin racing after the demons and capturing them, latching them to the rails of the piazza's gates. After this the festivities resume.*

Cullurzones *(also called* culingiones*) is a typical Sardinian ravioli which can also be filled with potatoes.*

serves 6

Time: 75 minutes, excluding the 45-minute drying period for the pasta

Level of Difficulty: Advanced

⚕

CULLURZONES
4 cups semolina
5 large eggs
Salt to taste

FILLING
1 pound chard, stemmed
4 tablespoons unsalted butter

1 To make the cullurzones, heap the semolina on a work surface and make a well in the center. Add the eggs and a pinch of salt to the well. Using a fork, begin beating the eggs clockwise, incorporating a little of the flour wall each time until the flour is all used. Continue beating for 10 minutes, or until a smooth, elastic dough is formed, adding 1 or 2 tablespoons cold water, if necessary. Knead the dough for 5 minutes, then place in a bowl, cover, and let rest for half an hour.

2 Meanwhile, steam the chard leaves in their own water until wilted. Cool to room temperature, squeeze dry, and dice finely. Melt the butter in a skillet over low heat and sauté the chard for 5 minutes, stirring frequently. Cool to room temperature and set aside.

°Pecorino sardo is a semicooked sheep's milk cheese with small air holes. Three types are available throughout Italy: dolce, a sweet version, aged up to 3 months; semi-dolce, aged up to 9 months for a slightly piquant flavor; and stagionato, a hard, spicy cheese aged for more than a year. Stagionato is the appropriate cheese for this recipe, but other types of hard pecorino can also be substituted.

3 Beat the ricotta with the eggs in a large bowl until creamy. Add the grated cheese, saffron, and nutmeg. Season with salt and pepper and mix until well blended. Stir in the chard, cover, and set aside.

4 Divide the dough into two equal sections. Roll each section into a rectangle about 10 x 20 x 1/8 inches. Place walnut-size dollops of filling 4 inches apart on half of each rectangle. Carefully fold the top over the bottom and press down all around the mounds to seal. Using a ravioli cutter or a butter knife, cut the dough into individual ravioli, making sure each is completely sealed around the edges. Transfer the ravioli to a floured surface and dry for 45 minutes.

5 To make the sauce, heat the oil in a skillet over low heat and sauté the garlic, parsley, and basil for 5 minutes. Add the tomatoes, salt, and pepper, and cook for 30 minutes.

6 Bring 4 quarts salted water to a boil over medium heat. Add the ravioli, one at a time, cover the pot, and cook until the water returns to a boil. Remove the cover and cook for 3 minutes longer. The ravioli are cooked when they float to the surface. Remove with a slotted spoon, carefully draining the water, and arrange one layer in a serving bowl. Top with the sauce and a generous dusting of grated pecorino. Add another layer of ravioli and continue layering, ending with a final layer of sauce and cheese. Serve immediately.

Make Ahead Both ravioli and sauce can be made up to 2 or 3 days in advance and refrigerated or frozen for up to 3 weeks. Immerse frozen ravioli directly in the boiling water and stir to separate.

How to Serve Four or five cullurzones make a fine first course. Accompanied with a bowl of greens sautéed in garlic and oil, they can be a one-course meal.

Wine Suggestion Medium- or Full-bodied Red

1 pound fresh sheep's or cow's milk ricotta

3 large eggs

1/2 cup freshly grated pecorino cheese

1/8 teaspoon saffron

1/8 teaspoon freshly ground nutmeg

Salt to taste

Freshly ground black pepper to taste

SAUCE

3/4 cup extra virgin olive oil

2 cloves garlic, finely minced

2 tablespoons freshly chopped Italian parsley

2 tablespoons freshly chopped basil

2 cups ripe Italian plum tomatoes, peeled, seeded, and roughly chopped

Salt to taste

Freshly ground black pepper to taste

4 quarts water to cook the pasta

3/4 cup freshly grated pecorino sardo*

CASCASA CARLOFORTINA

Couscous with Chick Peas

108

❦ Sicilia ❦

SOMETIME AROUND THE END OF MAY, TAORMINA CELEBRATES IL RADUNO DEL Costume e del Carretto Siciliano—*The Festival of Costumes and Sicilian Carts. The streets of this picturesque coastal resort are filled with traditional handpainted carts, the designs of which illustrate the ancestral diversity for which Sicily is known. Motifs are drawn from the various periods during which the island was dominated by various rulers and includes the Knights of the Round Table, the Paladins of Charlemagne, Aladdin and the Forty Thieves, and I Pupi, the classical Sicilian puppets, whose legend dates back to Greece's Golden Age.*

One of the many extraordinary foods associated with this multicultural festival is this Arab-inspired couscous (tiny kernels of semolina grain) prepared with chick peas and savoy cabbage.

serves 4

Time: 2 hours

Level of Difficulty: Moderate

1/2 cup dried chick peas, soaked for 24 hours, drained, rinsed, and drained again

6 tablespoons extra virgin olive oil

1 small onion, minced

1 small carrot, diced

1 celery stalk, strings removed and diced

8 ounces pork loin, diced

Salt to taste

1 Place the chick peas in a heavy-gauge pot with enough water to cover by 2 inches. Cover and cook over medium-low heat for 2 hours.

2 Meanwhile, heat 3 tablespoons oil in a skillet over low heat and sauté the onion, carrot, and celery for 8 minutes, stirring constantly. Stir in the pork and continue to sauté until the meat is cooked, about 4 to 5 minutes. Season with salt and pepper and keep warm.

3 Steam the cabbage over boiling water for 4 minutes, or until wilted. Transfer to a bowl and keep warm.

4 Cook the couscous in boiling salted water for
3 to 5 minutes, or until tender. Drain and place in a
bowl. Drain and add the chick peas with the meat
mixture and the cabbage. Toss well to blend all
ingredients and serve immediately.

Make Ahead The chick peas can be cooked up to a
day in advance, refrigerated in a sealed container,
and reheated just before using.

How to Serve As a one-dish meal accompanied by
sautéed greens or a mixed green salad.

Wine Suggestion **Medium-Sweet White**

Freshly ground black pepper
   to taste

$^{1}/_{2}$ **pound savoy cabbage, cored
   and roughly chopped**

8 ounces pork loin, diced

1 cup couscous, rinsed and
   drained

2 cups salted water for cooking

$^{1}/_{4}$ packed cup freshly chopped
   Italian parsley

CIALSÓNS CIARGNEI

Egg Dumplings with Smoked Ricotta and Dark Chocolate

❧ Friuli-Venezia-Giuli ❧

A SMALL HILLSIDE VILLAGE NEAR UDINE WITH COBBLESTONE STREETS AND ANCIENT, *narrow overpasses, Fagagna is every inch a photographer's dream. Never more so, however, than on the first Sunday of September, when it serves as the host of an event charming enough to rival Siena's famous Palio—except that here the combatants are all donkeys. The judges, all Fagagnese, are appointed for life, after which the mantle passes to their sons (never the daughters, mind you) in a ritual dating back to 1891. The donkeys (*asini*) race through the streets of the village, stopping (as donkeys are wont to do) whenever they so choose—a turn of events never failing to both stymie the driver and thrill the crowd, who take it upon themselves to offer numerous encouragements. The* Palio degli Asini, *a three-hour event, also encompasses numerous bands and, of course, concludes with a great celebratory meal.*

The following is a specialty of the area, Friuli-style dumplings filled with an unusual blend of cheese, candied fruit, chocolate, spinach, and sugar.

serves 4

Time: 1 hour

Level of Difficulty: Advanced

⚶

DOUGH

4 cups unbleached all-purpose flour, sifted

Salt to taste

3 large eggs

2 tablespoons whole milk

FILLING

1/2 pound fresh spinach, stemmed, or one 8-ounce package frozen spinach

1 To make the dough, heap the flour onto a work surface, add the salt, and make a well in the center. Add the eggs and milk to the well. Using a fork, beat the eggs clockwise, incorporating a little of the flour wall each time until the flour is all used. Knead for 10 minutes, or until a smooth, elastic dough has formed. Roll the dough into two large, 1/8-inch-thick rectangles, cover, and let rest for 20 minutes.

2 Meanwhile, make the filling. Blanch the spinach until wilted, then squeeze it dry and dice finely. Using an electric mixer, beat the egg whites with 1/2 teaspoon salt until foamy. Add the cream of tartar and beat into stiff peaks.

3 Place the yolks and the sugar in the bowl of a food processor and blend until smooth. Transfer to a large bowl. Add the breadcrumbs, grated chocolate, diced spinach, parsley, candied citron, raisins, and grated ricotta. Mix until all ingredients are well blended. Gently fold in the egg whites, a little at a time.

4 Cut the dough into 4-inch-round circles and fill the bottom half of each circle with a walnut-size dollop of filling. Fold the top half almost all the way over the bottom, leaving about 1/2-inch lip of the bottom sticking out. Fold this lip over the top as if making a rolled pie crust and press to seal.

5 To make the sauce, melt the butter over low heat in a small saucepan and stir in the grated cheeses. Cook for a few minutes until the cheeses have melted and the sauce is thick and creamy. Keep warm.

6 Bring 4 quarts salted water to a boil over medium heat. Add the dumplings, cover, and cook until the water returns to a boil. Remove the cover, cook for 4 minutes, and remove the dumplings with a slotted spoon. Place them in a serving bowl, top with sauce, toss carefully, and serve immediately.

Make Ahead The dough can be made earlier in the day and wrapped tightly in plastic until ready to use.

How to Serve Paired with garlic-and-oil sautéed spinach.

Wine Suggestion Dry or Medium-Sweet White

3 large eggs, separated

Salt to taste

1/2 teaspoon cream of tartar

2 tablespoons sugar

1/4 cup unflavored breadcrumbs

2 ounces bittersweet chocolate, grated

1 tablespoon freshly chopped parsley

2 tablespoons candied citron

2 tablespoons raisins

8 ounces smoked ricotta salata, grated, or smoked mozzarella and a pinch of salt

SAUCE

4 tablespoons unsalted butter

2 ounces smoked ricotta salata, grated, or smoked mozzarella and a pinch of salt

2 ounces fontina cheese, grated

4 quarts salted water for cooking

MACCHERONI ALLA PASTORA

Shepherd's Pasta with Fresh Ricotta

❦ Molise ❦

ALTHOUGH THE PEOPLE OF CAMPOMARINO IN MOLISE REFER TO THIS EVENT AS La Sagra del Grano—*the Grain Festival (held generally on the last weekend of June)—the food that is served reaches beyond grain-based dishes to include such traditional preparations as tripe, roast lamb, and various cold fish appetizers. But my favorite dish of all was this wonderfully simple dish of maccheroni tossed with ricotta. Maccheroni is a generic term used throughout southern Italy to mean pasta; in this case, the pasta is rigatoni—thick, ridged tubes.*

serves 4

Time: 30 minutes

Level of Difficulty: Easy

6 ounces luganiça-type sausage,
    removed from casing
    and crumbled

8 ounces fresh sheep's milk ricotta
    or fresh cow's or goat's
    milk ricotta

Salt to taste

Freshly ground white pepper
    to taste

4 quarts salted water for cooking

1 pound rigatoni

6 tablespoons freshly grated
    pecorino cheese

4 sprigs fresh parsley, stems
    removed, for garnish

1 Place the crumbled sausage in a skillet with 3 tablespoons cold water. Cover and cook over low heat for 20 minutes, or until the sausage grease has been completely rendered. Remove the sausage with a slotted spoon and reserve for another use.

2 Pour the remaining grease through a fine sieve into a serving bowl. Add the ricotta, season with salt and pepper, and mix well.

3 Bring 4 quarts salted water to a boil over medium heat and cook the rigatoni for 8 minutes, or until al dente. Drain and add to the bowl. Dust with the grated cheese and stir until all ingredients are well blended. Serve immediately, garnished with the parsley.

How to Serve With panfried broccoli florets.

Wine Suggestion Dry White or Medium-bodied Red

SPAGHETTI A CACIO E PEPE

Spaghetti with Black Pepper and Pecorino Cheese

❦ Lazio ❦

IN 1166, TWO FIELDWORKERS FROM ACQUAPENDENTE IN NORTHERN LAZIO SAT IN A *corner of a fruit orchard plotting to overcome the imperial forces that had dominated the area for decades. Their musing was suddenly interrupted by the spontaneous blossoming of a cherry tree that had been dead for over four years. Since the tree stood alongside a small chapel dedicated to the Madonna, they decided to ask Pope Alexander III for help with their rebellion; the success of the endeavor resulted in* La Festa della Madonna di Mezzo Maggio *(The Festival of the Mid-May Madonna), a wonderful freedom celebration held the third Sunday of every May.*

Following is a typical festival dish, a quick and easy spaghetti dusted simply with cacio—*the local name for pecorino—and black pepper. Heavenly!*

serves 4

Time: 15 minutes

Level of Difficulty: Easy

⚶

1 pound Italian spaghetti*
4 quarts salted water for cooking
5 ounces freshly grated pecorino
    romano cheese
Freshly ground black pepper
    to taste

1 Bring 4 quarts salted water to a boil over medium heat. Cook the spaghetti for 8 to 9 minutes, or until al dente. Drain and reserve 1 cup cooking water. Place the spaghetti in a serving bowl.

2 Dust the spaghetti with the grated cheese and plenty of freshly ground pepper and stir until the spaghetti is completely coated. Add a few tablespoons cooking water as needed to keep the pasta from drying out.

How to Serve With a mixed green salad.

Wine Suggestion Dry or Medium-Sweet White

While one could argue that it is always a good idea to buy the best brand of pasta, it is especially important in sauce-free recipes, such as the above. To my mind, De Cecco and Barilla are the two best brands available in American markets. Both absorb approximately three times their weight in cooking water and, hence, take much longer to cook than softer varieties. When finally placed in the serving bowl and covered simply with cheese and black pepper, they tend to retain far more of their moisture than other brands and will not fall apart if reheated.

MALFATTI AL MASCARPONE

Pasta Dumplings with Mascarpone

❧ Lombardy ❧

ON MAY 29, 1176, THE LOMBARDY LEAGUE DEFEATED THE ARMIES OF EMPEROR *Frederick Barbarossa and restored autonomy to the Nations of Padania, which included Milan. Two hundred years later, Milanese officials drew up a document declaring May 29 to be an official and everlasting day of celebration. Today, this Liberation Festival begins with a procession in Milan's Piazza Mercanti and proceeds to the Basilica of San Simpliciano accompanied by drummers, warriors, soldiers, knights, and damsels on horseback (all dressed in medieval splendor) and led by four young men bearing the Cross of Ariberto di Intimiano, symbol of the Lombardy League's glorious victory.*

The following recipe, one of many created by restaurants along the parade route especially for this occasion, lacks somewhat in authenticity since no one in 1176 ever tasted mascarpone, a fairly new invention and one that has quickly come to symbolize Milanese cuisine. One taste however and it more than justifies its existence. Malfatti means "badly made," a reference to the erratic shape of the finished dumplings.

serves 4

Time: 40 minutes

Level of Difficulty: Moderate

5 tablespoons unsalted butter
1 medium onion, minced
1 pound fresh spinach, stemmed,
    or one 8-ounce box frozen
    spinach

1 Heat 2 tablespoons of the butter in a skillet over low heat and sauté the onion for 5 minutes, or until translucent. Blanch the spinach until wilted, then squeeze it dry and dice finely. Add the spinach, mascarpone, flour, 1 tablespoon of grated cheese, nutmeg, salt, and pepper and mix until all ingredients are well blended. Remove from the heat and cool to room temperature. Stir the eggs into the cooled spinach mixture.

2 Bring 4 quarts salted water to a boil over medium heat. Add the dumplings, 1 tablespoon at a time, and cook for 5 minutes. Using a slotted spoon, remove the dumplings and place them in a serving bowl. Melt the remaining butter and pour over the dumplings. Sprinkle with the remaining cheese and serve.

How to Serve With garlic-sautéed spinach.

Wine Suggestion **Dry White**

2 ounces mascarpone

4 tablespoons unbleached all-purpose flour, sifted

5 tablespoons freshly grated grana padana or Parmigiano-Reggiano

1/8 teaspoon freshly grated nutmeg

Salt to taste

Freshly ground black pepper to taste

2 large eggs, lightly beaten

4 quarts salted water for cooking

PISARÉI CON CECI E CIME DI RAPA

Gnocchetti with Chick Peas and Broccoli Rabe*

❧ Lombardy ❧

A MORE TYPICAL DISH FOR CELEBRATING THE MAY 29 VICTORY OF THE LOMBARDY *League is this traditional dish of pisaréi, which are small dumplings made with flour and breadcrumbs. While it is possible to find already made pisaréi in various specialty stores, they are also fairly simple and very enjoyable to make from scratch. The following sauce is made with chick peas, broccoli rabe, grated pecorino, and tomatoes; equally delicious is one made with dried cranberry beans and fresh tomatoes.*

serves 6

Time: About 75 to 85 minutes

Level of Difficulty: Moderate

GNOCCHETTI
1/4 cup plain breadcrumbs
4 cups unbleached all-purpose
    flour, sifted
Salt to taste

SAUCE
2 cups salted water for cooking
2 pounds broccoli rabe, stemmed
    and rinsed
7 tablespoons extra virgin olive oil
2 cloves garlic, crushed
Salt to taste
Freshly ground black pepper
    to taste
8 ounces canned Italian plum
    tomatoes, liquid reserved
    for another use

1 To make the dumplings, place the bread-crumbs, flour, and a pinch of salt in a large bowl. Add hot water, starting with 1/2 cup and then 1 tablespoon at a time, kneading with floured hands, until a dense, elastic dough is formed, about 5 min-utes. Pinch off a golf ball-size piece of dough and, working on a floured work surface, roll it into a 1-inch-wide rope. Cut the rope into 1-inch-long segments and, using a butter knife, make a cut down the length of each segment that goes almost through to the other side. Transfer the finished dumplings to a floured surface and cover with a clean cloth.

2 Bring the salted water to a boil over medium heat. Put the broccoli rabe in the water and cook until wilted, about 5 minutes. Remove from the water and when it is cool enough to handle, squeeze it dry and dice it. Reserve the cooking water.

3 Heat 4 tablespoons oil in a skillet and sauté one of the garlic cloves over low heat for 3 minutes. Remove with a slotted spoon and discard. Increase

---

Potato gnocchetti or gnocchi can be substituted for pisaréi.

heat to medium, add the broccoli rabe, and cook for
5 minutes, stirring frequently. Season with salt and
pepper and set aside.

4 Heat the remaining oil in another skillet and
sauté the remaining clove of garlic for 3 minutes
over low heat. Remove with a slotted spoon and
discard. Using your hands, shred the tomatoes into
the hot oil, add the oregano, bay leaf, and chili,
and cook for 10 minutes over low heat, stirring
frequently. Add the chick peas and continue to cook
for 5 minutes longer. Season with salt and pepper.

5 Place the reserved broccoli rabe water in a
pasta pot and add 2 quarts additional water. Bring
to a boil and add the dumplings, a few at a time.
Cook for 15 minutes, drain, reserving 2 cups
cooking water, and transfer to the skillet with the
tomatoes. Add the broccoli rabe and cook for
5 minutes over high heat, stirring constantly until
all ingredients are well blended. If necessary, add
some of the cooking water from the pisaréi.
Remove the bay leaf, dust with grated cheese, and
serve immediately.

Make Ahead The dough can be made earlier in the
day, wrapped in plastic wrap, and set aside until
ready to use. Steps 3 and 4 can be prepared up to
1 day in advance, each preparation stored in an
individual sealed container and refrigerated until
needed.

How to Serve As a one-dish meal or as part of a
party buffet.

Wine Suggestion **Dry White or Medium-bodied Red**

1 tablespoon freshly chopped
    oregano
1 bay leaf
1 dried chili, seeded and crushed
8 ounces canned chick peas,
    drained and rinsed
2 tablespoons freshly grated
    pecorino

SPAGHETTI ALLA CARRETTIERA

Spaghetti with Tuna and Porcini Mushrooms

❧ Lazio ❧

THE MID-MAY FESTIVAL OF THE MADONNA IN ACQUAPENDENTE (PAGE 113) IS *also known as* I Pugnaloni, *its more colloquial moniker. The name comes from the huge rectangular panels of beautifully arranged flower petals depicting elaborate scenes from the lives of farmers and fieldworkers. The morning of the festival, the panels (held above the crowd on nine-foot-long poles) are carried from Acquapendente's Piazza Communale in a procession that weaves through the entire town before returning to its point of origin where the pugnaloni are left on display for the remainder of the afternoon.*

The following is another popular festival dish and one that is highly characteristic of the Lazio region at large. Invented by a man named Checco (diminuitive for Francesco) who lived in the 1800s and worked as a carrettiere—*a wagoner—the dish can also be made with fresh tuna.*

serves 4

Time: 20 minutes

Level of Difficulty: Easy

⚶

6 ounces fresh porcini mushroom
    caps or other wild
    mushrooms

2 tablespoons extra virgin olive oil

1 clove garlic, crushed

1 ounce pancetta

Salt to taste

1 Clean the mushroom caps using a damp cloth (do not place under running water) and cut into thin slices. Heat the oil in a skillet and sauté the garlic and pancetta over low heat for 4 minutes, or until the garlic turns golden. Remove the garlic and discard. Increase the heat to medium, add the mushrooms, season with salt and pepper, and cook for 5 minutes, stirring constantly.

2 Crumble the tuna into the skillet and cook for 10 minutes until all ingredients are well blended.

Many versions of this dish substitute tomato sauce flavored with meat.

3 Meanwhile, bring 10 cups salted water to a boil over medium heat. Cook the spaghetti for 7 minutes, or until al dente. Drain the spaghetti and place in a serving bowl. Add the tuna mixture and the heated tomato sauce, mixing well. Dust with the cheese and serve immediately.

How to Serve With thick slices of rustic bread and a platter of marinated vegetables.

Wine Suggestion Medium- or Full-bodied Red

Freshly ground black pepper
   to taste

One 4-ounce can Italian
   oil-packed tuna

10 cups salted water for cooking

1 pound Italian spaghetti

4 tablespoons tomato sauce,
   heated until warm*

6 tablespoons freshly grated
   pecorino cheese

119

BIGOLI IN SALSA DI ANATRA

Spaghetti Tubes with Duck Sauce

❧ Veneto ❧

THROUGHOUT THE VENETO, OCTOBER 7 WAS ORIGINALLY KNOWN AS THE FEAST *of the Virgin Mary, but its name was changed in 1573 by Pope Gregory XII to the Feast of the Sacred Rosary. The decision served as a concession to the growing number of Rosarians, a Dominican sect that once pulled the strings behind a great many papal chairs. The feast day has since been celebrated in every village and town in this northwestern region of Italy and the following has always served as its traditional dish.*

At one time, the bigoli (thick, round spaghetti) were made with duck eggs, which are larger than those of chickens and serve as a better binding agent. The finished pasta was then cooked in duck broth and served with boiled duck. Because duck eggs today are largely unavailable, I have only ever tasted my adapted version, the recipe for which is given here, but I am prepared to swear that it is a more than an adequate compensation.

serves 4

Time: 1 hour

Level of Difficulty: Advanced

BIGOLI

3 cups unbleached all-purpose
    flour, plus additional flour
    for kneading

3 large eggs, lightly beaten

2 tablespoons unsalted butter,
    melted

About 1/4 cup whole milk

Salt to taste

1 To make the pasta, heap the flour on a work surface and make a well in the center. Add the eggs, butter, milk, and salt to the well. Using a fork, begin beating the egg mixture clockwise, incorporating a little of the flour each time until a soft, smooth dough has formed; some flour may remain. Pinch off a marble-size piece of dough and, on a lightly floured surface, roll with the palms of your hands into a long rope about 1/4 inch thick. Cut the rope into 12-inch-long pieces and continue rolling and cutting until all the dough is used. Dry the bigoli on a floured surface for 20 minutes.

2 Meanwhile, make the sauce. Heat the butter and oil in a skillet over medium heat and sauté the duck for 4 minutes per side. Remove with tongs, cool slightly, and cut into thin slivers. Return to the pan, add the tomato sauce, season with salt, and sauté for 10 minutes over low heat, stirring constantly.

3 Bring 4 quarts salted water to a boil over medium heat and cook the pasta for 8 to 10 minutes, or until al dente. Drain the pasta and put in the skillet with the duck, stirring to blend all ingredients. Transfer to a serving bowl, sprinkle with parsley, and serve.

Make Ahead The bigoli can be made earlier in the day and left to dry until needed. The duck sauce can be made up to 1 day in advance and refrigerated in a sealed container until ready to use.

How to Serve With rustic-style bread and a mixed green salad.

Wine Suggestion Full-bodied Red

SAUCE

3 tablespoons unsalted butter

4 tablespoons extra virgin olive oil

1 boneless, skinless duck breast
    (about 1 pound)

1 tablespoon tomato sauce

Salt to taste

4 quarts salted water for cooking

3 tablespoons freshly chopped
    Italian parsley

121

SPAGHETTI AL NERO DI SEPPIA

Spaghetti with Squid and Squid Ink

❧ Sicily ❧

SICILIAN CHILDREN BELIEVE THAT ON THE NIGHT BETWEEN NOVEMBER 1 AND 2 *(The Feast Days of the Dead and the Saints, respectively) their dead ancestors leave their graves after dark and wander through the village, robbing from food markets, pastry shops, and toy stores to gather gifts for them. Church bells ring throughout the night and the hours before bedtime are spent listening to stories about their dead grandparents. Before going to bed, Sicilian children recite this prayer:*

> *Armi santi, armi santi*
> *Io sugnu unu e vuatri siti tanti:*
> *Mentri sugnu 'ntra stu munnu di guai*
> *Cosi di morti mittitiminni assai.*

> Holy spirits, holy spirits
> I am only one and you are many:
> Having been confined to this world of woes,
> At least bring me many gifts from the dead.

In the morning, they race out of bed with the first rays of dawn and search the house for gifts (called I doni dei morti—*gifts from the dead) hidden by their parents in shoes and behind wardrobes. Later, everyone sits down to a celebratory meal, each food element carrying a specific significance. Fava beans, for example, are a sacred symbol of the life-death cycle; raisins, a sign of aging. The traditional dessert is a formless type of cookie, called* ossa dei morti—*bones of the dead. The pasta course is more often than not Spaghetti with Squid Ink, the blackness of the ink signifying the darkness of the afterlife.*

serves 4

*Squid ink can be purchased at many fish stores or specialty food shops. It can also be ordered from the Mail-Order Sources listed on page 476.

**In many cases, fish stores will clean the squid for you.

1 To clean the squid**, hold the body with one hand and pull away the tentacles with the other. Cut the tentacles just above the eyes and remove the little beak inside the detached tentacles. Discard the head. Pull out the long piece of cartilage from inside the body cavity and rinse the body under running water, pulling out any matter that remains inside. Wash and peel away any gray, speckled skin on the wings and discard. Cut the body into 1/4-inch-thick rings.

2 Heat the oil in a skillet over low heat and sauté the garlic and 4 tablespoons of the parsley for 4 minutes, stirring constantly. Add the squid and a hefty dose of black pepper, cover, and cook for 10 minutes, adding salt after 5 minutes of cooking and stirring occasionally.

3 Add the wine and then the tomato paste, diluting the paste in the cooking liquid. Cover and cook for 10 minutes more. Add a few tablespoons of water as needed to produce a liquidy sauce.

4 Add the squid ink to the skillet, stir to blend, cook for 5 minutes, remove from the heat, and place in a serving bowl.

5 Meanwhile, bring 4 quarts salted water to a boil over medium heat and cook the spaghetti for 8 to 10 minutes, or until al dente.

6 Drain the spaghetti, place in a serving bowl, and toss with the squid sauce. Sprinkle the pasta with the remaining parsley and serve immediately.

Make Ahead The sauce can be made a few hours in advance and reheated when needed.

How to Serve Round out with a salad of baby greens.

Wine Suggestion Medium-bodied Red

Time: 2 hours

Level of Difficulty: Moderate

123

1 pound squid, soaked for
    30 minutes in cold water
    and drained
4 tablespoons extra virgin olive oil
2 cloves garlic, minced
5 tablespoons finely chopped
    fresh Italian parsley
Freshly ground black pepper
    to taste
Salt to taste
1/2 cup dry white wine
2 tablespoons tomato paste
1 tablespoon squid ink*
4 quarts salted water for cooking
1 pound Italian spaghetti

PASTICCHIO DI MACCHERONI

Oven-baked Pasta Pie Filled with Porcini Mushrooms and Truffles

❦ Lazio ❦

LE PASSATE IS THE COLLOQUIAL NAME GIVEN TO THE FEAST DAY OF THE MADONNA del Monte, May 14 in Marta, a tiny village on Lake Bolsena in the Lazio. Throughout the day, representatives from the various trades (wood carvers, fishermen, grain harvesters) pass in and out of church (hence, passate), bearing gifts for the Madonna. Outside the church, workers demonstrate their trades using ancient tools made mainly of wood and bamboo canes. Among the varied and wonderful foods associated with this feast day is this extraordinary baked pasta pie layered with béchamel sauce and the earthy flavors of both dried porcini and black truffles.

serves 4 to 6

Time: 90 minutes

Level of Difficulty: Advanced

FILLING

7 tablespoons unsalted butter

1/2 cup cleaned and chopped
   chicken livers

1 ounce dried porcini mushrooms,
   soaked in warm water for
   20 minutes, drained (liquid
   reserved) and finely chopped

2 tablespoons Marsala

1 1/2 cups canned Italian plum
   tomatoes, chopped (liquid
   reserved)

Salt to taste

Freshly ground black pepper
   to taste

1 Heat 3 tablespoons butter in a skillet over low heat and sauté the chopped livers for 5 minutes. Add the mushrooms, Marsala, tomatoes, salt, and pepper and cook for 20 to 25 minutes, stirring frequently.

2 Meanwhile, make the pastry dough. Heap the flour on a work surface and make a well in the center. Add the sugar, butter, two-thirds of the beaten eggs, lemon zest, and salt to the well. Using a fork, begin beating the mixture, incorporating a little of the flour wall each time until a solid ball is formed. Wrap in plastic wrap and refrigerate for 30 minutes.

3 To make the béchamel sauce, melt the butter in a skillet over low heat and whisk in the flour. Pour in the milk, continuing to whisk for 10 minutes, or until the mixture is thick and creamy. Season with the salt, pepper, and nutmeg. Remove from the heat and keep warm.

4 Using a slotted spoon, remove the solids from the chicken liver–mushroom sauce. Add the chicken liver mixture and the truffles to the béchamel. Reserve the remaining mushroom–chicken liver sauce.

5 Preheat the oven to 400°F. Butter a 10-inch-round glass or ceramic pie pan.

6 Bring 4 quarts salted water to a boil over medium heat and cook the pasta for 8 to 10 minutes, or until al dente. Drain and dress with the reserved sauce and grated cheese, tossing until well coated. Cool to room temperature.

7 Divide the pastry dough into two pieces, one slightly larger than the other. Roll out the larger piece into a 12-inch-round circle and place it in the pie pan, letting the excess hang over the sides. Put the pasta into the pan and top with the béchamel sauce. Roll out the smaller piece of dough into a 10-inch-round circle and place on top of the pasta. Roll the edges and press to seal, brush the top with the remaining egg, and bake for 30 minutes, or until golden brown. Remove from the heat, cut into thick slices, and serve immediately.

Make Ahead The dough can be made earlier in the day, wrapped tightly in plastic wrap, and refrigerated until ready to use.

How to Serve Place a slice on each plate with a few spears of steamed broccoli drizzled with oil and lemon.

Wine Suggestion Medium-bodied Red

CRUST

2 cups unbleached all-purpose flour, sifted

3 tablespoons sugar

8 tablespoons unsalted butter, at room temperature

3 large eggs, lightly beaten

1 tablespoon lemon zest

Salt to taste

BÉCHAMEL SAUCE

3 tablespoons unsalted butter

2 tablespoons unbleached all-purpose flour

2 cups whole milk

Salt to taste

Freshly ground white pepper to taste

1/8 teaspoon freshly grated nutmeg

2 ounces black truffles, thinly sliced (optional)

4 quarts salted water for cooking

1 pound penne

2 tablespoons freshly grated Parmigiano-Reggiano

PIZZOCHERI

Buckwheat Pasta with Potatoes and Cabbage

❧ Val d'Aosta ❧

FIOCCA IS LOCAL DIALECT FOR "WHIPPED CREAM," A FOOD ADORED BY THE
*inhabitants of Béileun in Val d'Aosta. Which is why they decided to turn their Alpine village into a
Mecca for like-minded gastronomes by creating the* Sagra della Fiocca, *held the third weekend of every
June since 1972. Béileun is accessible only via a narrow winding road that at one point crosses a
stunningly beautiful forest. This wooded wonderland is the setting for the first event of the sagra: a
six-mile foot race known as* La Martse della Fiocca. *Afterward, runners and spectators sit down at
long tables for an open-air meal consisting of* pizzocheri, *an Alpine pasta made with buckwheat,* soca
*(vegetable stew), and grilled meats. In late afternoon, everyone repairs to a natural grotto (cave) where
the temperature is always a fixed fifty-five degrees for a demonstration in whipping heavy cream. The
cream is then given out in huge quantities to everyone present and seconds are always available.*

serves 4

Time: 90 minutes

Level of Difficulty: Advanced

PASTA

1 1/2 cups unbleached
    all-purpose flour, sifted
1 cup buckwheat flour, sifted
3 large eggs, lightly beaten
Salt to taste

SAUCE

8 small new red potatoes, peeled
    and cut into 1-inch cubes
1 small head savoy cabbage
    (about 1/2 pound), cored
    and julienned

1 To make the pasta, heap both flours on a
work surface and make a well in the center. Add the
eggs, a pinch of salt, and 2 tablespoons cold water to
the well. Using a fork, begin beating the egg mixture
clockwise, incorporating a little of the flour each
time and adding water as necessary to create a thick,
smooth dough; some flour may remain. Knead for
10 minutes, cover with a clean cloth, and let rest for
30 minutes.

2 Meanwhile, put the potatoes and cabbage in a
pasta pot with the salted water and cook for about
20 minutes over medium heat.

3 Meanwhile, divide the dough into two pieces.
On a lightly floured surface, roll out each piece into
two large rectangles, 1/4 inch thick. Cut each into

1-inch-wide strips and put into the pot with the vegetables. Cook the pasta and vegetables for 3 minutes over medium heat. Drain, place in a bowl, and set aside. If you cannot make the times coincide, turn off the vegetables after 15 minutes and return to a boil when ready to add the pasta.

4 Heat half the butter in a skillet over low heat and sauté the onion and garlic for 7 minutes. Toss with the pasta and vegetables and keep warm.

5 Melt the remaining butter in a skillet over low heat and sauté the sage for 5 minutes. Remove the sage and discard.

6 To serve the pizzocheri, arrange a layer of pasta and vegetables in the bottom of a serving bowl. Top with a drizzle of sage-flavored butter, a layer of fontina, and a dusting of grated cheese. Continue layering until all ingredients are used up. Serve immediately.

Make Ahead The pasta can be made earlier in the day, covered with a clean cloth, and set aside until ready to use. It can also be dusted with flour and frozen for up to 3 weeks. Immerse in boiling water without thawing.

How to Serve Round out this one-dish meal with a green salad.

Wine Suggestion Medium-Sweet White

127

10 cups salted water for cooking

4 tablespoons unsalted butter

1 medium onion, thinly sliced

1 clove garlic, thinly sliced

5 leaves fresh sage

8 ounces fontina cheese, thinly sliced*

1/4 cup freshly grated grana padana or Parmigiano-Reggiano

Fontina is Val d'Aosta's most highly prized cheese; in 1955, it was awarded a denomination of origin (D.O.C.), which means that it can only be made in certain regions and according to certain specified methods. This full-fat cow's milk cheese, made within two hours of milking, is a "live" (or unpasteurized) cheese with a thin rind, pale yellow color, and sweet, creamy flavor.

TAGLIATELLE AL PROSCIUTTO

Wide Ribbon Noodles with Prosciutto

❦ Emilia-Romagna ❧

ONCE UPON A TIME, THERE WERE TWO TINY VILLAGES LOCATED ONE MILE FROM *each other and sharing a long history of both friendship and enmity. From this relationship grew the double festival held the Wednesday before Lent (Martedi Grasso or Mardi Gras) when Tossignano hosts La Sagra della Polenta and Borgo di Tossignano, La Sagra dei Maccheroni. The story dates back to 1901 when the reigning baron of Tossignano threw a grand ball in the main salon of the royal palace. Among the guests were two young men from Borgo who, after drinking much too much wine, began hurling themselves around the dance floor and eventually fell against a young girl from Tossignano, completely ripping her gown. "Muli" (mules), she cried, launching into a round of partisan accusations. Wounded both personally and on behalf of their town, the young men decided to boycott Tossignano's famous polenta sagra that year and start one of their own. With the passage of time, this rivalry has transformed itself into a joint effort that results in two wonderful festivals.*

The polenta distributed in Tossignano is served with sausage and Parmigiano-Reggiano and Borgo's maccheroni, a catch-all phrase meaning "pasta" in this case, tagliatelle—wide ribbon noodles— served with the following prosciutto ragù.

serves 4

Time: 1 hour

Level of Difficulty: Moderate

⚵

PASTA*
4 cups unbleached all-purpose
    flour
2 large eggs, lightly beaten
Salt to taste

1 To make the pasta, heap the flour on a flat work surface and make a well in the center. Add the eggs, salt, and 2 tablespoons warm water to the well. Using a fork, begin beating the egg mixture, incorporating a little of the flour each time and adding water as necessary to create a thick, smooth dough; some flour may remain. Knead for 10 minutes.

2 On a lightly floured surface, roll out the dough into two large rectangles 1/8 inch thick or run the dough through a pasta machine (see page 461 for directions) until very thin. Cover with a clean cloth and let rest for 10 minutes.

*Purchased tagliatelle can be substituted.

3 Roll the rectangle widthwise into a tight cylinder. Cut into 1-inch-wide segments, unroll immediately, and transfer to a floured surface to dry.

4 Meanwhile, make the sauce. Using a sharp knife, remove the fat from the prosciutto; finely dice the lean part. Heat the butter and prosciutto fat in a skillet over low heat and sauté the onion for 5 minutes. Add the diced prosciutto and sauté for 3 minutes longer. Pour in the wine and cook until evaporated. Add the tomatoes, season with salt and pepper, stir until all ingredients are well blended, and cook for 10 minutes more, or until the flavors have melded.

5 Bring 4 quarts salted water to a boil over medium heat. Add the tagliatelle and cover. Bring the the water to a boil again and cook the pasta for 3 minutes, drain, and place in a serving bowl. Top with sauce, dust with cheese and a hefty sprinkling of black pepper, toss, and serve.

Make Ahead The noodles can be made earlier in the day, covered with a clean cloth, and set aside until needed. They can also be dusted with flour and frozen for up to 3 weeks. When ready to use, immerse directly into the boiling water without first thawing. Stir well to avoid clumping. The sauce can be made up to a day in advance and refrigerated in a sealed container.

How to Serve With a mixed green salad.

Wine Suggestion Medium-bodied Red

SAUCE

4 ounces prosciutto

6 tablespoons unsalted butter

1 small onion, thinly sliced

1/2 cup dry white wine

4 very ripe Italian plum tomatoes, peeled, seeded, and roughly chopped

Salt to taste

Freshly ground black pepper to taste

4 quarts salted water

4 tablespoons freshly grated Parmigiano-Reggiano

RAVIOLI DOLCE

Oven-baked Sweet Ravioli Filled with Quince

❧ Emilia-Romagna ❧

AT PRECISELY 4 P.M. EVERY THIRD SUNDAY OF MARCH, THOUSANDS OF PEOPLE CRAM *into Casalfiumanese's central piazza and turn their gaze to the middle tower of the castle dominating the square. And suddenly, there he is, Conte Raviolone, an elegantly attired masked figure throwing plastic sacks filled with sweet ravioli out over the assembled hordes. An hour later, 80,000 ravioli will have been distributed, but those who fail to catch the flying manna need not fear. At the entrance to this offbeat winter celebration—La Sagra del Raviolo Dolce (Sweet Ravioli)—attendees are given their own guaranteed bagful of the following delight.*

makes approximately 20 ravioli

Time: 1 hour

Level of Difficulty: Moderate

DOUGH

1/4 teaspoon active dry yeast

1/2 cup warm water

3 cups unbleached all-purpose flour, plus flour for kneading

2 tablespoons sugar

Salt to taste

1 cup whole milk

3 tablespoons unsalted butter, melted

2 tablespoons coarsely ground cornmeal

1 Combine the yeast with 1/2 cup warm water in a small mixing bowl. Place the bowl in a container of hot water to reach two-thirds of the way up the sides. Let rest until the surface of the yeast is foamy.

2 Put the flour, sugar, and a pinch of salt in the container of a food processor and, with the motor running, pour the yeast through the feed tube and immediately pour in the milk and melted butter. Process until the mixture forms a thick ball. Transfer to a floured work surface and knead with floured hands until smooth and elastic, adding additional flour if necessary.

3 Preheat the oven to 400°F. Sprinkle the cornmeal on a large baking sheet.

Canned quince can be found at specialty stores or mail ordered from one of the sources on page 476.

4 Roll the dough into two large rectangles $1/8$ inch thick. Using the floured rim of an 8-ounce water glass or a ravioli cutter, cut the rectangles into circles approximately 3 inches in diameter. Fill one half of each circle with a dollop of quince. Fold over and press the edges shut to seal. Put the ravioli on the baking sheet and bake for 20 minutes. Alternatively, fry the ravioli in olive oil until golden. Cool to room temperature and serve.

Make Ahead The dough can be made earlier in the day, wrapped tightly in plastic, and refrigerated until ready to use. Return to room temperature before rolling out.

How to Serve With roasted vegetables.

Wine Suggestion Medium-Sweet White

FILLING

About 1 cup canned pureed quince* or other thick fruit puree or marmalade

131

TIMBALLO DI MACCHERONI

Eggplant Timballo

❧ Sicilia ❧

MY FAVORITE OF ALL THE ST. JOHN THE BAPTIST'S CELEBRATIONS ON JUNE 24 IS *that held in Mondello, just west of Palermo. Known locally as* Muzzuni, *a reference to the Baptist's decapitation (*mozzato*), the festival begins after sundown, when a woman beating a large drum enters the main piazza. Her entrance marks the beginning of a wildly frenetic ritual of songs, dances, chants, encounters, and exhibitions of sorcery, all with unmistakably pagan overtones. Afterward comes an orgy of eating and drinking that includes the following* timballo, *a labor-intensive preparation, but one that is well worth the effort.*

serves 6

Time: 90 minutes

Level of Difficulty: Moderate

3 large eggplants, cut into thin
    lengthwise strips
2 tablespoons extra virgin olive oil
1 medium onion, diced
8 ounces ground veal
1 cup fresh or frozen peas
2 pounds ripe Italian plum
    tomatoes (about 10 to 12),
    peeled, seeded, and diced
2 chicken kidneys, cleaned and
    diced
1/2 small dried chili, crumbled
4 quarts salted water for cooking
1 pound rigatoni

1 Place the eggplant in a colander, sprinkling the slices with salt. Top with a heavy weight and set aside for 1 hour.

2 Meanwhile, heat 2 tablespoons oil in a skillet over low heat and sauté the onion for 8 minutes, stirring constantly. Add the veal, peas, and tomatoes and cook for 20 minutes, stirring frequently. Stir in the kidneys and chili and set aside.

3 Bring the 4 quarts salted water to a boil over medium heat and cook the rigatoni for 8 minutes, or until al dente. Drain and place in a bowl with the tomato mixture, caciocavallo, and basil. Toss until well blended.

4 Dry the eggplant on paper towels and dredge each slice with flour. Heat 2 inches of olive oil in a skillet to 375°F* and fry the eggplant until golden on both sides. Remove and drain on paper towels.

5 Preheat the oven to 350°F. Butter a
2¹/2-quart-round baking dish with sides at least
4 inches high.

6 Line the dish with overlapping eggplant slices
in a star pattern and lap the slices over the rim of
the dish. Fill the dish with the pasta mixture and top
with the mozzarella. Fold the overlapping eggplant
over the filling in a star pattern to seal the top.

7 Bake for 20 minutes. Unmold onto a serving
platter and cut into wedges to serve.

Make Ahead The sauce through Step 2 can be
made up to a day in advance and refrigerated in a
sealed container until ready to use.

How to Serve With garlic-sautéed broccoli rabe.

Wine Suggestion Medium-bodied Red

2 ounces caciocavallo cheese or
    provolone, cut into thin
    strips
8 leaves fresh basil, chopped
Flour for dredging
Olive oil for frying
Butter for greasing
1 medium bufala or cow's milk
    mozzarella (about 1 pound),
    cut into thin strips

133

To test the temperature of the oil, you can put a cube of bread into the skillet. When it sizzles around the edges and turns golden almost immediately, the oil is the right temperature.

MILLECOSEDDE

Winter Pasta with Chick Peas, Lentils, and White Beans

❧ Calabria ❧

LOCATED IN THE CALABRIAN TOE, GAMBARIE IS A SMALL TOWN WITH ANCIENT *traditions, one of which takes place on December 31. Groups of men and women bearing torches parade through the dark, narrow streets acccompanied by the sounds of trumpets playing and church bells ringing. The leader is an old woman whose face is shrouded with a white sheet—*La Pupa. *Whenever she spies small children in the crowd of spectators, she reaches into one of the many burlap sacks hanging around her waist and pulls out a beautifully wrapped bundle containing cookies called* turtiglioni.

Later many generations of families will sit around large tables eating, among other things, the following multigrain pasta and drinking homemade wine until the old year turns into the new. Millecosedde *means "a million little things," and refers to the tradition of emptying out the legume bins on December 31 to make room for new supplies.*

serves 4

Time: 4 hours, 15 minutes

Level of Difficulty: Easy

⚶

1/2 cup dried chick peas, soaked for 24 hours, drained, and rinsed

1/2 cup dried fava beans, soaked for 24 hours, drained, and rinsed*

1/2 cup dried cannelini (white beans) soaked for 12 hours, drained, and rinsed

1 Put the chick peas, fava beans, cannelini beans, oil, onion, celery, cabbage, mushrooms and mushroom liquid, and 1 1/2 quarts water in a large soup pot, preferably terra-cotta, and cook over very low heat for 4 hours. Add the lentils, salt, and pepper after 2 hours.

2 When the beans are almost ready, bring the 4 quarts salted water to a boil over medium heat and cook the rigatoni for 8 to 10 minutes, or until al dente. Drain and place in a serving bowl. Toss with the legumes, dust with cheese, and serve immediately.

*The chick peas and fava beans can be soaked together.

Make Ahead The legumes can be cooked up to
2 days in advance and kept refrigerated until
ready to use.

How to Serve With bowls of marinated vegetables,
such as onions, eggplant, and peppers.

Wine Suggestion Medium-bodied Red

1 cup extra virgin olive oil

1 medium onion, minced

1 celery stalk, minced

1/2 small head savoy cabbage,
cored and thinly sliced

3 ounces dried porcini
mushrooms, soaked in
warm water for 20 minutes,
drained (liquid reserved),
and chopped

1 1/2 quarts water plus 4 quarts
salted water

1/4 cup lentils

Salt to taste

Freshly ground black pepper
to taste

1 pound rigatoni

4 tablespoons freshly grated
pecorino cheese

BUCATINI AL CAVOLFIORE

Hollow Spaghetti with Cauliflower

◈ Puglia ◈

PUGLIAN TRADITION SPECIFIES THAT ON THE LAST SUNDAY OF CARNIVAL
(the Sunday before Ash Wednesday) a turkey (symbol of tyranny) must be sacrificed to expiate all the sins of the previous year. In Turi, a village in the center of the region and near the boot, the animal is carted on an extravagant float to the central piazza, where eight regally dressed men carry it to the steps of the church. As trumpets play, a town crier announces that before being condemned, the turkey has dictated a last testament. One of Turi's young men, wearing a top hat and large glasses and acting as clerk, then reads a long list of the various peccadillos committed by local residents over the course of the previous year. No one is offended because it is well known that during Carnival, anything goes. In olden days, the turkey would then be slaughtered while everyone watched. Today, it is taken away and replaced by a cooked turkey, which is served as the main course following this wonderful pasta, tossed with cauliflower, and sautéed in garlic, oil, and tomatoes.

serves 4

Time: 50 minutes

Level of Difficulty: Easy

⅂⅃

1/2 cup extra virgin olive oil

1 clove garlic, crushed

2 pounds ripe Italian plum
    tomatoes (about 10 to 12),
    peeled and passed through
    a food mill

1 small head cauliflower, washed
    and cut into florets

Salt to taste

1 Heat the oil in a large skillet over low heat and cook the garlic for 3 minutes. Remove the garlic with a slotted spoon and discard. Add the crushed tomatoes, the cauliflower florets, and a ladleful of water. Season with salt and pepper, cover, and cook for 40 minutes, or until the florets are very tender and the sauce has thickened somewhat.

2 Bring the 4 quarts salted water to a boil over medium heat and cook the pasta for 8 to 10 minutes, or until al dente. Drain and place in a serving bowl. Toss with the cauliflower mixture, the parsley, and a dusting of cheese.

*Bucatini are thick, round, hollow spaghetti

Make Ahead The cauliflower sauce can be made a day in advance and refrigerated in a sealed container until ready to use.

How to Serve With slices of fried butternut squash.

Wine Suggestion Medium-bodied Red

Freshly ground black pepper
   to taste
1 pound bucatini* or spaghetti
4 quarts salted water for cooking
3 tablespoons freshly chopped
   Italian parsley
6 tablespoons freshly grated
   Parmigiano-Reggiano

137

TRENETTE COL PESTO

Trenette with Pesto Sauce

❧ Liguria ❧

THERE IS NO ONE FOOD MORE CLOSELY ASSOCIATED WITH AN ITALIAN REGION THAN *pesto is with Liguria. No one quite knows why, since basil is grown and adored in every one of the country's eighteen regions. In Pontedassio, in the Ligurian province of Imperia, this love affair is authenticated with a festival devoted exclusively to basil—La Sagra del Basilico—held on the first Sunday in June. One of the chief foods served by the village's very competent cooks is the following dish of trenette with pesto. Trenette is a type of linguine that is almost always cooked in the same water as the potatoes and green beans, which gives it its unique flavor.*

serves 4

Time: 35 minutes

Level of Difficulty: Moderate

꽃

4 quarts salted water

2 medium boiling potatoes,
    peeled and cut into
    1-inch cubes

4 ounces baby green beans,
    stems removed

15 to 20 fresh basil leaves*

1/2 teaspoon coarse salt**

1 clove garlic

1 pound trenette or linguine

4 tablespoons freshly grated
    Parmigiano-Reggiano

1 Bring the 4 quarts salted water to a boil over medium heat and add the potatoes and beans. Cook for 20 minutes.

2 Meanwhile, make the pesto. Place the basil leaves, salt, and garlic in a mortar and, using a pestle, pound the mixture to form a thick paste.†

3 For the last 10 minutes of cooking for the potatoes and beans, add the trenette and cook for 8 to 10 minutes, or until al dente. Drain, reserving 1/2 cup cooking water, and place in a serving bowl. Toss with the pesto and cheese and serve immediately.

*Store-bought pesto can be substituted

**The salt helps keep the basil green.

Make Ahead Pesto can be made up to 2 weeks in advance, topped with a layer of oil, and refrigerated until needed. Leave out the garlic and add at the last minute.

How to Serve With a salad of mixed greens and tomato wedges.

Wine Suggestion Medium-Sweet White or Medium-bodied Red

139

†*The pesto can also be made in a food processor although everyone should, at least once, try sampling it the way Ligurians have made it for centuries.*

VINCISGRASSI

Stuffed Lasagne

140

❧ Le Marche ❧

EACH YEAR ON THE SECOND SUNDAY IN FEBRUARY, CAGLI, IN CENTRAL MARCHE, *holds its Sagra dell Vincisgrassi, paying tribute to one of the region's most characteristic foods. Vincisgrassi's origin can be traced back to an Austrian general, the Prince of Windisch-Graetz, who came to Le Marche during the Napoleonic Wars and brought with him the chef credited with this complex stuffed lasagne. While this may seem daunting, keep in mind that this dish is just as wonderful (if not better) the next day and that made in large quantities, it freezes particularly well.*

serves 6 to 8

Time: About 4 1/2 hours, excluding the 6-hour resting period

Level of Difficulty: Advanced

SAUCE

4 tablespoons unsalted butter

1/4 cup diced prosciutto fat

1 small onion, minced

1 small carrot, diced

1/2 cup chicken livers, cleaned and diced

1/2 cup dry white wine

1 tablespoon tomato paste

1/2 cup Basic Meat Broth (page 460), warmed, or good-quality canned broth

Salt to taste

Freshly ground black pepper to taste

8 ounces chopped veal

1 Heat the butter in a skillet over low heat and sauté the prosciutto fat and onion for 8 minutes. Add the carrot and chicken livers; sauté for another 5 minutes, stirring constantly. Pour in the wine and cook until it evaporates, about 4 minutes. Dilute the tomato paste in the broth and add to the skillet. Season with salt and pepper, cover, and cook for 1 1/2 hours, adding water as needed.

2 After 1 1/2 hours, stir in the veal, mushrooms, milk, and cinnamon. Cover and cook for another 30 minutes.

3 To make the pasta, heap the flour and semolina on a work surface and make a well in the center. Add the eggs, a pinch of salt, and the vin santo to the well. Using a fork, begin beating the egg mixture, incorporating a little of the flour each time and adding water as needed to create a smooth, elastic dough; some flour may remain. Knead for 10 minutes.

4 Using a rolling pin on a floured surface or pasta machine (see page 461 for instructions), roll the dough into 3 or 4 sheets 1/8 inch thick. Cut into 3-inch-wide strips the length of a lasagne pan. Dry the strips on a floured surface for 20 minutes.

5 Heat the butter in a skillet over low heat. Whisk in the flour and a pinch of salt. Pour in the milk, whisking constantly for 10 to 15 minutes, or until sauce is smooth. Remove from heat, stir in the nutmeg, and keep warm.

6 Bring salted water and 1 tablespoon oil to a boil over medium heat. Add pasta strips, a few at a time, and cook. When they float to the surface, remove with a slotted spoon. Place in a bowl of cold water and set aside.

7 Butter an 8 x 10-inch lasagne pan. Remove several pasta strips from the water and arrange in one layer on the bottom of the pan. Reserve 1/2 cup sauce. Cover with several tablespoons béchamel and sauce, spreading both over the pasta. Sprinkle with grated cheese and diced truffle, and repeat the layering until all ingredients have been used. Spread the top layer with sauce, grated cheese, and dots of butter. Wrap in foil and refrigerate for 6 hours or overnight before baking.

8 Preheat oven to 400°F. Remove the foil and bake lasagne for 30 to 40 minutes, or until the top is golden brown and crusty. Meanwhile, heat the reserved sauce. Cut the lasagne into wedges, drizzle with the sauce, and serve hot.

Make Ahead This dish can be made the day before and reheated. It can also be frozen for up to 3 weeks. Frozen lasagne should be wrapped in foil and baked in a 350°F oven for 20 minutes, then unwrapped and baked another 40 minutes.

How to Serve This can also be served with sautéed greens.

Wine Suggestion Full-bodied Red

2 ounces dried porcini mushrooms, soaked in warm water for 20 minutes, drained, and diced (reserving soaking liquid for another use)

1/2 cup whole milk

1/8 teaspoon ground cinnamon

PASTA

2 cups unbleached all-purpose flour

1 cup semolina

2 tablespoons unsalted butter

4 large eggs, lightly beaten

Salt to taste

1/4 cup vin santo or Marsala

BÉCHAMEL

2 tablespoons unsalted butter

4 tablespoons unbleached all-purpose flour

Salt to taste

2 cups whole milk

1/8 teaspoon freshly grated nutmeg

4 quarts salted water for cooking

1 tablespoon extra virgin olive oil

1/2 cup freshly grated Parmigiano-Reggiano

3 ounces black truffles, diced (optional)

2 tablespoons unsalted butter

STRANGOLAPRETI ALLA TRENTINA

Green Gnocchi with Butter and Sage Sauce

❧ Trentino-Alto Adige ☙

EVERY APRIL 30, BOLZANO'S PIAZZA WALTHER BECOMES TRANSFORMED INTO ONE *immense flower garden—a fitting metamorphosis for a piazza known as the city's parlor. The festival dates back to the late 1800s, when the piazza was still known by the name of its creator, King Maximilian of Bavaria. Soon after, it became known as Johannesplatz, afer Archduke Johann of Austria. Its present name honors Walther von der Vogelweide, the great German poet of the Middle Ages. The festival consists of flower exhibitions and judgings (more often than not, first prize always goes to some type of geranium—that lovely and ubiquitous mainstay rendering characteristic charm to most of Bolzano's balconies and terraces), music and dance performances, and plenty of open-air food offerings, among which the following stands out as a crowd-pleasing favorite. The literal translation of its name is "priest-stranglers"—a reference to the dense, doughy consistency of these delicious gnocchi which, theoretically, would choke a priest.*

serves 4

Time: 1 hour

Level of Difficulty: Moderate

⚜

¹/₂ cup salted water plus 4 quarts
    salted water for cooking

1 pound chard, stemmed, cleaned,
    and roughly chopped

2 cups cubed day-old bread

¹/₂ cup whole milk

2 large eggs, lightly beaten

Salt to taste

About 2 cups unbleached
    all-purpose flour, sifted

1 Bring ¹/₂ cup salted water to a boil over medium heat, add the chard, and cook until wilted. Drain and cool to room temperature.

2 Put the bread and milk in a bowl. Stir until the bread is wet, cover, and let sit for 25 minutes.

3 Squeeze the cooled chard dry and put in a large bowl. Squeeze the bread dry and add the bread and beaten eggs to the bowl. Season with salt and mix well. Pass the chard mixture through a food mill* and transfer the resulting mash to a floured work surface. Knead for 5 minutes, adding just enough flour to create a smooth, semisoft dough.**

*Do not use a food processor, which would add air and, hence, volume, to the mixture. A food mill or ricer will create the thick, dense mixture necessary for making gnocchi.

4 Using a rolling pin, roll the dough into 1-inch-thick ropes and cut the ropes into 1-inch-long pieces. Transfer the pieces to a floured board.

5 To make the sauce, melt the butter in a skillet and add the sage, cooking over very low heat for 5 minutes. Keep warm.

6 Bring the 4 quarts salted water to a boil over medium heat. Add the gnocchi, a few dozen at a time, cover, and bring to a boil again. When the gnocchi float to the surface, remove them with a slotted spoon. Layer the gnocchi in a serving bowl, alternating with a layer of sauce. Shake the bowl gently to coat the gnocchi, dust with cheese, and serve immediately.

6 tablespoons unsalted butter

6 leaves fresh sage

4 tablespoons freshly grated grana padana or Parmigiano-Reggiano

143

Make Ahead The gnocchi dough can be made earlier in the day, covered with a clean cloth, and set aside until needed. Uncooked gnocchi can also be frozen (initially in one layer to avoid sticking; when completely frozen, the gnocchi can be tossed in a freezer bag) for up to 3 weeks. When ready to use, place directly in the boiling water.

How to Serve With sautéed spinach or chard.

Wine Suggestion Dry White

"The secret to making good, soft gnocchi is to add just enough flour to hold the mixture together, but not enough to toughen the dough.

GNOCCHI DI ZUCCA

Butternut Squash Gnocchi

❧ Veneto ❧

I MET SIGNORA ADELE NISTRI THE DAY BEFORE THE FEAST OF THE SACRED ROSARY *(see page 120) in Teolo, a small town west of Padova. After we had chatted for a few minutes about food and festivals and the overwhelming importance of taking one's time while eating, she told me that, in addition to the town-wide festivities and related food stands, she also held her own celebration in the front garden of her house. "I make a huge pot of gnocchi di zucca (which, she told me, is even more appropriate for the event than Bigoli with Duck Sauce, since October is harvest time for yellow squash) and I open my door to everyone and anyone who wants to wander by." Come, she said, and so I did. And, make no doubt about it, I took my blessed time sitting at a long metal table in her flower-filled garden, eating and drinking and taking part in the feverish fray that passes for mealtime conversation anywhere on Italian soil.*

serves 4

Time: 75 minutes

Level of Difficulty: Advanced

🜉

7 tablespoons unsalted butter

1 medium onion, thinly sliced

2 pounds small butternut squash, peeled, seeded, and cubed

Salt to taste

1/2 cup water plus 4 quarts salted water for cooking

1/2 cup semolina or Cream of Wheat

1 large egg yolk, lightly beaten

About 1/2 cup unbleached all-purpose flour

1 Heat 3 tablespoons butter in a large skillet over low heat. Sauté the onion for 5 minutes, stirring constantly. Add the squash, season with salt, cover, and cook for 30 minutes, stirring occasionally.

2 Transfer the cooked onions and squash to the container of a food processor and puree. Pour the mixture into a large saucepan, add the 1/2 cup water, and heat to boiling. Pour the the semolina in steadily and cook, whisking constantly, for 3 minutes, or until the mixture thickens. Remove from the heat. Pour the mixture into a wet baking pan and cool completely. Stir the egg yolk into the cooled squash mixture and transfer to a floured surface. Knead the dough for 5 minutes, adding flour as needed to create a smooth, dense dough.

3 Pinch off a walnut-size piece of dough and roll into a 1-inch-wide rope. Cut the rope into 1-inch-long pieces, roll each piece gently against the tines of a fork to create a ridged surface*, and transfer to a floured board. Continue pinching off and rolling dough until all the dough has been used.

4 Bring the 4 quarts salted water to a boil over medium heat. Add the gnocchi, a few dozen at a time, cover, and bring to a boil again. When the gnocchi float to the surface, remove them with a slotted spoon. Layer the gnocchi in a serving bowl, dust with cheese, and serve immediately.

Make Ahead The gnocchi dough can be made earlier in the day, covered with a clean cloth, and set aside until needed. Uncooked gnocchi can also be frozen (initially in one layer to avoid sticking; when completely frozen, the gnocchi can be tossed in a freezer bag) for up to 3 weeks. When ready to use, place directly in the boiling water.

How to Serve With sautéed broccoli rabe.

Wine Suggestion **Dry White**

8 tablespoons freshly grated taleggio or montasio cheese, or other soft, sharp-tasting grated cheese

145

Instead of using the tines of a fork, you can also use a box grater or a gnocchi-ridger—a wooden implement specially created for this purpose. Inexpensive and ingeniously low-tech in design, gnocchi makers are simply hand-held rectangles of wood, about 4 inches long and ridged on both sides. They are sold in select specialty stores.

GNOCCHI DI SEMOLINO

Baked Semolina Gnocchi

146

❧ Tuscany ❧

MAY IS FESTIVAL MONTH IN SCARPERIA, A SMALL TOWN JUST NORTH OF FLORENCE. *Every weekend for the entire month, the town celebrates* La Sagra della Ricotta, *a madcap, colorful, fun-filled tribute to those soft, smooth, angelically white curds I remember eating as a child spread on thick slices of bread and sprinkled with sugar. The ricotta in question is sheep's milk ricotta for which, I am convinced, there is no real substitute, although some goat's milk ricotta comes close. The variety of dishes served at this sagra demonstrate perfectly the absolute versatility of ricotta, featured in the following recipe for creamy oven-baked gnocchi made with semolina, otherwise known to Americans as Cream of Wheat.*

serves 4

Time: 45 minutes

Level of Difficulty: Moderate

1 cup whole milk

Salt to taste

1/4 cup finely ground semolina
    or Cream of Wheat

2 tablespoons unsalted butter

3 ounces fresh sheep's milk
    ricotta* or cow's or goat's
    milk ricotta

1 large egg, lightly beaten

1/3 cup freshly grated
    Parmigiano-Reggiano

1 Put the milk and a pinch of salt in a large saucepan and bring to a boil over medium heat. Pour the semolina in steadily, and cook, whisking constantly, for 3 minutes, or until the mixture thickens. Remove from the heat.

2 Transfer the mixture to a bowl and cool slightly. Stir in 1 tablespoon butter, the ricotta, the egg, and half the grated cheese. Stir to blend all ingredients and pour onto a wet, nonporous work surface or onto a wet baking sheet. Using a spatula, smooth until 1/2 inch thick.

3 Preheat the oven to 400°F. Butter a 10 x 12-inch baking dish.

Sheep's milk ricotta is generally imported into the United States from Tuscany or the Lazio and can be found in specialty cheese shops. If unavailable, use either goat's milk or cow's milk ricotta, but, in either case, the product should be purchased fresh from a cheese shop.

4 Cut the semolina into about 3 x 2-inch pieces. Arrange in overlapping fashion in a buttered baking dish. Dot with the remaining butter, sprinkle with the remaining cheese, and bake for 15 minutes, or until lightly browned. Serve immediately.

Make Ahead The gnocchi can be prepared in the baking dish earlier in the day, wrapped in foil, and refrigerated until ready to bake.

How to Serve With a platter of steamed and lemon-drizzled vegetables.

Wine Suggestion Dry or Medium-Sweet White

GNOCCHI DI ASPARAGI

Baked Gnocchi Made with Asparagus, Taleggio, and Asiago

❧ Toscana ❧

FOLLOWING IS ANOTHER TYPE OF GNOCCHI FEATURED AT SCARPERIA'S RICOTTA *festival (see page146). This variety derives its flavor from asparagus, which is both added to the dough as well as sautéed with prosciutto and various types of cheeses to make the sauce.*

serves 6

Time: 90 minutes

Level of Difficulty: Advanced

SAUCE

1 pound fresh or frozen asparagus

4 tablespoons unsalted butter

2 tablespoons extra virgin olive oil

2 ounces prosciutto, diced

1 tablespoon freshly chopped
    Italian parsley

2 ounces goat's milk cheese

5 ounces taleggio cheese or other
    full-fat soft cow's milk cheese

2 ounces soft, young Asiago

GNOCCHI

12 ounces frozen asparagus tips

2 tablespoons unsalted butter

1 medium shallot, diced

8 ounces fresh ricotta

1 To make the sauce, cook the asparagus spears in salted water for 15 minutes. Drain, reserving the cooking liquid, and dice. Heat 2 tablespoons butter and the oil in a skillet and sauté the prosciutto over low heat for 8 minutes, stirring constantly. Stir in half the diced asparagus and the parsley, remove from the heat, and cover to keep warm.

2 Put the remaining diced asparagus with the goat's milk cheese, taleggio, half the Asiago, and a ladleful of the reserved cooking liquid in the container of a food processor. Process until smooth. Stir the puree into the cooked asparagus mixture and keep warm.

3 To make the gnocchi, cook the frozen asparagus in salted water for 8 minutes. Drain and dice. Heat the butter in a skillet and sauté the shallot for 5 minutes over low heat. Add the asparagus and cook for 5 more minutes, stirring constantly.

4 Place the ricotta in a bowl with the cheese, salt, the asparagus-shallot mixture, and the parsley. Add the flour, 1/4 cup at a time, mixing with floured

hands to form a smooth ball of slightly dry dough.
Pinch off a walnut-size piece of dough and, on a
floured surface, gently roll into a 1-inch-wide rope.
Cut the rope into 1-inch-long sections and place
each on a lightly floured surface. Continue pinching
off and rolling dough until all the dough has been
used.

5 Preheat the oven to 400°F. Bring the 4 quarts
salted water to a boil over medium heat. Put the
gnocchi, a few dozen at a time, into the water, cover,
and cook until the water has returned to a boil.
When the gnocchi float to the surface, remove them
with a slotted spoon. Place in a baking dish and top
with the asparagus sauce. Dot with the remaining
butter, sprinkle with the remaining cheese, and bake
for 15 minutes. Serve immediately.

Make Ahead The gnocchi dough can be made
earlier in the day, covered with a clean cloth, and set
aside until needed. Uncooked gnocchi can also be
frozen (initially in one layer to avoid sticking; when
completely frozen, the gnocchi can be tossed in a
freezer bag) for up to 3 weeks. When ready to use,
place directly in boiling water.

How to Serve With gratinéed fennel. To make,
parboil thinly sliced fennel until slightly soft, about
5 minutes, toss with olive oil and grated cheese,
arrange in a baking pan, and bake at 350°F for
20 minutes, or until the top is bubbly and browned.

Wine Suggestion Dry White

2 tablespoons freshly grated
    Parmigiano-Reggiano
Salt to taste
2 tablespoons freshly chopped
    Italian parsley
About 2 cups unbleached
    all-purpose flour
4 quarts salted water for cooking

149

GNOCCHI ALLA GORGONZOLA

Potato Gnocchi with Gorgonzola Sauce

❧ Lombardia ❧

PIAZZA SAN ZENO IN THE HEART OF VERONA IS THE SITE FOR THE *BACANAL DEL Gnoco (also called* Venerdì Gnocolar*) held on the last Friday before Lent. At the height of the festivities, the spirited Veronese elect a* Papà del gnoco, *who parades around in an all-white suit fitted with a stomach pouch crammed to the brim with gnocchi. There's plenty of music and dancing and a big stand set up at the perimeter of the piazza where volunteers hand out plates of gnocchi and copious glasses of wine. The tradition dates back to 1531, when the local government imposed a stiff tax on bread, causing bakers to rebel and cease baking. What seemed a noble cause soon turned ugly, however, as a starving populace began attacking the bakers. With the situation worsening by the minute, a local medic, Tomaso da Vico, decided to give food away and chose gnocchi, the easiest, cheapest, and tastiest of foods. Thus, da Vico became the first* Papà del gnoco *and the festival was born.*

serves 4

Time: 1 hour

Level of Difficulty: Advanced

⚷

8 medium boiling potatoes

About 2 cups unbleached
all-purpose flour, sifted

1 large egg, lightly beaten

Salt to taste

3 tablespoons unsalted butter

3 ounces gorgonzola dolce, rind
removed and crumbled**

4 tablespoons freshly grated
grana padana or
Parmigiano-Reggiano

4 quarts salted water for cooking

1 Put the potatoes in a large pot of water, cover, and cook over medium heat for 30 minutes. Drain, peel the potatoes while still hot, and pass through a food mill.

2 To make the gnocchi, heap the flour on a flat work surface and make a well in the center. Add the mashed potatoes, egg, and a pinch of salt to the well. Using floured hands, blend the ingredients together, adding just enough flour and kneading to form a soft, smooth dough.

3 Pinch off a walnut-size piece of dough and, on a floured surface, gently roll into a 1-inch-wide rope. Cut the rope into 1-inch-long sections and roll each piece gently against the tines of a fork to create a ridged surface, and transfer to a floured board. Continue pinching off and rolling dough until all the dough has been used.

4 To make the sauce, heat the butter in a skillet and add the crumbled gorgonzola. Cook over very low heat, stirring constantly, until the sauce is thick and creamy. Keep warm.

5 Bring the 4 quarts salted water to a boil over medium heat. Put the gnocchi, a few dozen at a time, into the water, cover, and cook until the water has returned to a boil. When the gnocchi float to the surface, remove them with a slotted spoon. Put into a serving dish. Pour the sauce over the gnocchi, stir gently to blend, dust with the grated cheese, and serve immediately.

Make Ahead The gnocchi dough can be made earlier in the day, covered with a clean cloth, and set aside until needed. Uncooked gnocchi can also be frozen (initially in one layer to avoid sticking; when completely frozen, the gnocchi can be tossed in a freezer bag) for up to 3 weeks. When ready to use, place directly in the boiling water.

How to Serve With steamed asparagus.

Wine Suggestion Medium-Sweet White

"Gorgonzola is Lombardy's incredibly delicious blue-veined cheese. A full-fat, whole milk cheese, gorgonzola is made from stracchino and layered to create the blue mold that gives it its flavor. Young, it is known as dolce—sweet, creamy, and mild. Aged gorgonzola is known as piccante—spicy—and is much fuller and sharper. Both types are good for eating as well as for making pasta and gnocchi sauces.

Vegetables

CARDI ALLA PARMIGIANA
Gratinéed Cardoons

VERDURE STUFATE ALL'ACETO BALSAMICO
Cauliflower, Artichokes, Leeks, and Broccoli Rabe Braised in Balsamic Vinegar and Dusted with Anise

TERRINA DI MELANZANE CON PEPERONI E PROSCIUTTO
Eggplant, Red Pepper, and Prosciutto Terrine

CASTAGNE STUFATE
Wine-braised Chestnuts

ZUCCA GIALLA DI CHIOGGIA MARINATA
Marinated Butternut Squash, Chioggia-style

FRITELLE DI BORAGINE
Borage Fritters

FRITELLE DI CAVOLFIORE DI TUSCANIA
Cauliflower Fritters

FAGIOLI CON LE COTICHE
Cannelini Beans Braised with Prosciutto and Herbs

CARCIOFI CON PISELLI
Baby Peas Sautéed with Spring Artichokes

POMODORI RIPIENI DI RISO
Tomatoes Stuffed with Rice and Baked with Fresh Herbs

SCAROLA AI CAPPERI E OLIVE
Braised Escarole with Capers and Black Olives

CIANFOTTA
Eggplant, Red Pepper, Potato and Black Olive Stew

COTOLETTE DI FUNGHI PORCINI
Pan-fried Porcini Mushroom Cutlets

CIPOLLE ALLA MARSALA
Sweet Onions Cooked with Marsala Wine

VERZOLINI DELLA VIGILIA
Twelfth Night Stuffed Savoy Cabbage

PEPERONATA AL FORNO
Red Peppers Roasted with Olives, Capers, and Fresh Oregano

PATATE, SALSICCIA E FAVE
Fava Bean, Sausage, and Potato Winter Stew

PATATE E MAMMOLE
Potato and Artichoke Tart

TUSCANY
Ancient Ruins and Modern Permutations

MAREMMA IS THE UNOFFICIAL NAME GIVEN TO SOUTHERN TUSCANY—to a sleepy backwater region that, until recently, was known mainly for its insalubrious swamps, stagnant waters, and malaria-carrying mosquitos. The Etruscans were the first to "discover" the Maremma or Moorlands; they were also the first to drain it. The Romans conquered the area in 100 B.C. and when they fell from power, the drainage courses silted up again and the region reverted to wilderness.

The Maremma's modern-day reclamation began under the nineteenth-century grand dukes of Tuscany and reached its zenith in the 1920s and 1930s under Mussolini, who redrained the swamps, built new houses, and offered lucrative incentives to farmers to move there. Ortobello, a coastal resort on the Argentario peninsula, still, in fact, bears fascist symbols on the railings of its public park.

Today, the Maremma is prosperous but still relatively undiscovered. Its charms include the mighty Amiata plateau, with mountains blanketed with chestnut and beech forests; gentle inland hills dotted with ancient villages and medieval fortresses; a long, beautiful coastline on the Tyrrhenian Sea with white sand beaches and sheltered marinas; and an offshore group of islands—called the Tuscan archipelago—that includes Gorgona, Montecristo, Giglio, Giannutri, and Elba.

More important than scenic charm, however, is the legacy bequeathed to the region by its most famous inhabitants, the Etruscans who lived, prospered, and died in a period of cosmic time equivalent to the batting of an eye. Emerging from the mists of antiquity during the first millennium before Christ, their entire civilization was abruptly returned to obscurity only a few hundred years later by the rise of the Roman Republic. In spite of the legions of archaeologists who have labored for hundreds of investigative years, we know very little about these mysterious ancients, save for a few select images gleaned from the likes of pottery shards and sarcophagi. From these, we have deduced an amalgam of fuzzy descriptors, among them, "highly evolved," "fun-loving," "free-spirited," "handsome," "fashionable," and "aristocratic."

What we *do* know is that between the eighth and fourth centuries B.C., Etruria Propria flourished as a confederation of twelve city-states in an an area roughly equivalent in acreage to the modern-day Tuscan province of Grosseto. The Etruscans founded cities and settlements, ploughed the land, drained the swamps, and mined the ores and minerals of the wooded *colline metallifere,* or metal-bearing hills.

Objects excavated from Etruscan tombs also tell us they were true epicures who gave enormous importance to the preparation and serving of food as well as being bon vivants extremely fond of dancing and partying. Sexual libertines with respect to both tolerance and experimentation, they also appear to have been relatively free of gender bias. In fact, Etruscan women are often depicted in funerary art attending banquets without their husbands, riding covered wagons to their personal landholdings, and playing flutes and lyres at funerals.

But in the end, their intelligence and competence fell prey to naked power. Over the next two hundred years, the Etruscans were attacked continuously by armies of the developing Roman state and by the first century B.C., all that remained of these remarkable people were their tombs. Their romantic legend continues to flourish, however, as evidenced by this observation by D. H. Lawrence: "Because a fool kills a nightingale with a stone, is he, therefore, greater than the nightingale? Not he! Rome fell and the Roman phenomenon with it. But Italy today is far more Etruscan in its bones than Roman and always will be."

"We *are* Etruscans!" Flavia Buschetti insists as she and I sip from steaming cups of *latte macchiato* in one of Sovana's tonier cafes. The outburst served as a response to my reading of both the passage from Lawrence as well as a subsequent one from H. V. Morton, describing the sensation of emerging from an Etruscan museum only to recognize the same faces on the street as those painted on the ancient urns and tombs—"the same full dark eyes, the same long inquisitive noses, the same Mona Lisa smiles echoing each other in flesh and carved stone over the distance of more than two millennia."

"Do we not live on the same soil?" Flavia elaborates. "Drink from the same springs, eat the same *umidos* of wild boar, gaze at the same panorama of forested hills? Why, the other day, I paused beside those *tufa* tombs just outside town to contemplate what to wear to Aldo's party the following evening." (*Tufa* is a porous, yellow-red volcanic stone from which the Etruscans carved their tombs; the Maremma is dotted with hundreds of perfectly preserved specimens.) She frames her face with upturned palms. "And later, I thought to myself, young Etruscan women probably spent just as much time as I do contemplating what to wear to important soirées."

Flavia is, of course, correct. Position most modern-day Tuscans alongside an ancient Etruscan vase and you will see not only the same proud noses, the same air of aristocracy, the identical shroud of mystery drawn about their countenances, but also the same love of eating and drinking and partying.

Flavia is equally correct when she posits her opinions on cultural differences between Etruscans and Romans, always, of course, concluding with the supremacy of "our" (meaning Etruscan) civilization over "theirs."

"Let me start with a comparison of architectural skills," she is presently opining to the two elderly men at the next table. (For the past forty-five minutes, not a word has passed between these two village stalwarts, so attentive have they been to every one of our utterances.)

"The Romans were technicians," she states in what is obviously not a complimentary tone. The two men nod their heads in agreement. "Their only achievement was in the construction of long, straight roads that sliced intrusively through the landscape without regard for either beauty or integrity." She signals the waiter for another macchiato. "Their towns and villages were just as odious," she continues. "Commonplace forms with regular street grids oriented on the four cardinal points of the compass."

The heavier of the two men raises the ante. "We, on the other hand, built beautiful hilltop towns, each one a unique pattern threaded by a maze of gloriously winding streets. And then there were those incomparable burial sites—most of which are still with us today. "The Founders of Cities," the Romans called the Etruscans, "experts at building cities of the living as well as cities of the dead."

The next half hour is spent listening to Flavia and her compatriot exchange condemnatory views on such topics as Roman art ("Cold. Frightfully cold. Not at all like the sensuality of the Etruscans, whose artistic achievements laid the foundation for the Renaissance"); Roman character ("Those hotheaded imperialists; conquer and control is all they knew"); and—moving up a few centuries—the number of immigrants who left Rome for the Americas during the twenties and thirties ("Obviously an easy place to leave. Not like Tuscany which, as everyone knows, never experienced mass emigration").

Again and again, Flavia and the elderly gentleman, Beppe, return to the same phrase: *Siamo Etruschi*—We are Etruscans—spoken in an assertive manner that testifies as much to what they are not as to what they are. Listening to their diatribe about Rome's centralized bureaucracy, its insensitivity to regional viewpoints, and the widespread corruption plaguing almost every single government minister elected in the last twenty years, one would think these two self-professed renegades regretted Tuscany's ever having decided to join a united Italy—even though the region at large voted overwhelmingly to do so in the referendum of 1860.

Much as I hate to be a spoilsport, I remind Flavia that we have to be going. She and I have scheduled ourselves for an intensive day of work, pleasure, and finally, a little lending of brute energy on behalf of our friends, the Aniellos, who are hosting an end-of-summer *sagra* in Saturnia. First on the list is a long-deferred peek at some exciting research she recently unearthed, documenting the continuing efforts on the part of university scholars to break the code of the Etruscan language—which, she says, is still as mysterious as the culture's origins. "Although the alphabet is borrowed from the Greek, the language is part of no known linguistic group and defies interpretation."

A journalist for the last twenty years, Flavia is working on an important article about the creation of a computerized database of Etruscan words. The hope is that the database will eventually divulge a contextual pattern. "It is not so much the letters themselves," she explains. "As of now, scholars understand the letters and can even articulate the script. But they have not yet found the Rosetta Stone that would enable them to make sense of what they are reading."

But there is also another problem, she says, one that goes beyond the science of understanding languages. "My friend, one of the scholars working on the database, has recently come to realize that many people do not actually want him to succeed; that in fact, the unintelligibility of the Etruscan language is part of a glamorous myth they are unwilling to surrender. He terms the phenomenon an 'ingrained resistance among many Tuscans to hypotheses that do not conform to their idealized impressions.'"

She explains, "Two years ago, Paolo and his team worked for seven months trying to decipher the writing on a pair of silver goblets found in an old tomb. Their undersides were inscribed with a number of symbols that matched those on various objects in local museums: MI, MA, and ME. Single letters were also scattered, apparently at random, over the bowls and stems." She hands me the galleys for her article-in-progress. "From this and other findings," she tells me, "Paolo's team hypothesized that the word fragments were subtle methods of enticing young Etruscans to learn their letters."

But then, she says, the team published their findings in an academic journal complete with a description of which objects had been studied and where they were located. "Excerpts were picked up by the local paper under the headline 'Scholars Make Light of Our Heritage.' The objects, it seems, had previously formed part of a museum exhibit whose curator had promulgated her own speculations. According to that woman, the goblets belonged to Larthia, an Etruscan noblewoman, and the writing alluded to the rites she wished performed at her burial ceremony."

Flavia shakes her head in the despairing manner of someone bewildered by the forces of human unpredictability. "It is not so much whether the curator was right or wrong, or for that matter, whether Paolo was right or wrong. The point is, the public wants to believe what they want to believe and if the truth doesn't fit a certain image of beauty and poetry and drama, then we'll just have to find another truth."

Our academic sides satiated, we proceed to the next priority on our agenda: pleasure. This afternoon, Flavia and I are treating ourselves to a soak in the thermal waters of *Le Terme di Saturnia*. Well, not in the waters of the actual *Terme*, which is a modern and rather luxurious spa the clients of which consist mainly of tourists and wealthy older women. But we will bathe in Saturnia Falls, just to the east of the resort and light years away from that establishment's formal strictures.

Among its many incomparable assets and contrary to the steep tariff imposed by the two-hundred-year-old spa, Saturnia Falls is completely, joyously, and liberatingly free. Not only that, but by virtue of its being a natural phenomenon, accessibility is guaranteed twenty-four hours a day, seven days a week—no closing for every one of the hundreds of feast days routinely celebrated by Tuscans; open during lunchtime, when it is otherwise impossible even to get a loaf of bread anywhere in the region.

The Etruscans were apparently very fond of "taking the waters" to cure themselves of ills both physical and psychological, and today we two are every inch their progeny. The warm waters of this natural pool cascade over a mountain of rocks stained blue-green with mineral deposits; the air is hazy with condensed heat steaming from the surface of the water like a willowy princess rising from her royal sleep. Flavia and I choose a spot high on the rocky summit and stretch out in the pools between the boulders, the sun massaging our naked bodies. Before us lies a bucolic wildflower meadow strewn with the occasional meandering cow.

"There's something I want you to know before we get to Francesca and Davide's house this evening," she says, innocently drizzling some water over my outstretched arm.

Her words are still hovering outside the cortex of my brain, but my body has already begun its reactive tensing.

"What is it?" I ask, struggling to maintain a decided air of nonchalance. My past experiences with Flavia do not serve me well. This is the woman with whom I traveled to India in 1974 only to find upon arrival at Delhi airport that she had brought absolutely no money, having spent it all the previous week on a diamond bracelet she simply "could not resist." It is also the woman who once paired me with a so-called good friend who just happened to be a notorious womanizer; who borrowed my car, drove around southern Italy for an entire summer and only later told me her license had been revoked; who insisted on our skiing into a "bellisima" remote area far from Cortina's trails only to admit, as the sun was waning over the horizon, that she had nary a clue as to where we had wandered.

"I know how you are about these things and I just wanted to warn you in advance so that you have ample time to prepare a response in case one is needed."

I turn my face toward the sun in an effort to appear calm. "Tell me, *cara*, what is it?"

"Well, Francesca may just decide to bring out her Etruscan vase."

I wait. So far it seems benign.

"It's a rather stunning vase, with paintings of Etruscan men and women preparing what looks like a type of bread. The colors are dark and earthy and both base and rim are encircled by a band of rather exuberant designs."

"Hmmm, hmm."

"The vase is in wonderful condition, with both side handles intact and very few pock-marks in the actual clay."

"Sounds wonderful," I comment although what I really want to ask is why she thinks a beautiful vase might make me hysterical. Just wait, I tell myself. All things come to she who waits.

"It is an Etruscan vase," Flavia repeats. "One they found as part of the archaeological excavation going on around their house." She looks me straight in the eyes. "And they kept it."

Ecco!

"I know what you are thinking," she says hurriedly. "I know you're going to say that what they have done constitutes thievery of the first order. That they have no right to hoard what belongs to everyone. That antiquity must, by its very nature, be treated with transcendance and magnanimity."

Actually, I had no intention of saying any of those things. The reality is that I have become overly accustomed to Tuscans trotting out their ill-gotten Etruscan artifacts at chic dinner parties. I don't like it. I think it's wrong. But I am no longer either surprised or moved to voice my unfavorable sentiments for the record.

The fact is, Tuscans—especially the Maremmani—apparently feel no guilt about stealing Etruscan treasures from local tombs. A family's illegally acquired urns are treasured ancestral relics, valued far above Roman coins. Everyone, it seems, knows of at least one farmer pretending to grow vegetables under cover while furtively digging up ancient treasures. Most middle-class residents of the area have at least one item and a few conceal collections worthy of a museum exhibit.

Among trusted friends at dinner parties, in fact, bronze figurines and funerary urns are routinely brought out for admiration. Pots are caressed with love, jewelry is examined under a magnifying glass, and the minute images of deities and animals praised and luxuriously enjoyed as if they were grandchildren. As my friend Loredanna maintains, "The orgy of sensual indulgence generated by these beautiful artifacts is one the Etruscans would have loved."

An ordinance of 1934 allows Italians to keep antiquities they owned prior to that date; in theory, everything discovered since belongs to the state. But it is difficult to prove precisely when an item was acquired. If challenged, the proud owner of an ancient brooch will argue that art is meant to be enjoyed, not forgotten in the ground or locked away in a museum. Besides, "It is our heritage; we are Etruscan."

"When did Francesca and Davide acquire the vase?" I ask, although Flavia's concern for my reaction has already communicated the answer.

"About two or three months ago," she says, giggling. "It actually is a very funny story. One that started with their desire to add another room onto the back of the house. But three days after construction began, the excavators discovered the ruins of an Etruscan tomb beneath the proposed foundation. Well, as you know, under Italian law, the government has the right to claim, without compensation, not only the tomb itself, but the land around it in a fifty-foot radius, as well as everything sitting on top of the land which, of course, included their house."

I had known there was a type of law governing the discovery of artifacts on one's private property, but I had not known it to be so comprehensive.

"So what did they do?"

"What *could* they do? They had to temporarily move. Fortunately for them, Davide's brother owned a house on the other side of the town which he used for summer rentals. I have to tell you though, the experience did not make them feel especially friendly toward the Italian government. At this point, they feel they have more than a right to keep the vase, which, by the way, they found directly outside their back door. In a way, I agree with them."

Her look has question marks written all over it. "Don't you feel the same way?" it asks.

In truth, I am not sure how I feel. Using my American brain, I reason through the filter of the professional looters who routinely raid the burial sites of Native Americans. Does it make any difference whether they do it for personal acquisition or resale value? But my Italian logic introduces factors having to do with both widespread government corruption and a historical framework that encompasses hundreds of years during which poor people were institutionally raped by a totalitarian aristocracy.

Not to mention the overwhelming amount of antiquity contained within the borders of the Italian state. Sometimes it seems that wherever one travels in Tuscany—the tiniest village in the most remote, rural region—there are at least three or four resident artworks dating back several hundred, if not thousands of years. Can one blame Tuscans for approaching art, on the one hand, with total nonchalance, and on the other, as their quintessential, and personal, birthright?

"You don't have to worry," I tell Flavia, by way of reassurance. "I will behave myself in the manner to which you have become accustomed."

As it turned out, we never made it to join Francesca and Davide for what they had termed "an American Fourth of July dinner" (they were planning to prepare chicken on the grill). Davide sprained an ankle stepping out of his car and Francesca deemed his subsequent laments inappropriate for public consumption.

Which was just as well, since we would have been far too late to be of any help to our friend Michele in his great hour of need. Michele Aniello is the owner of Saturnia's most famous restaurant, *I Due Cippi*. Located as it is on the idyllic central piazza of a little town that claims nothing less than to be the first city ever founded in Italy—by Saturn himself, in fact—*I Due Cippi* has become known throughout Tuscany for blending traditional home cooking with both *nuova cucina* and Etruscan influences. Not an easy accomplishment!

Michele runs the restaurant while his wife, Bianca, runs the kitchen. Together the Aniellos oversee the sagra that fills the piazza in midsummer. In addition to a bounty of grilled meats and vegetables, the Aniellos arrange for decorations, entertainment, people to cook and serve and clean, and, of course, publicity. This last of their undertakings—the publicizing of the sagra—is not always appreciated by local residents. There have been many complaints of late about high prices for food and the reality of tourists overrunning what is traditionally an insider event.

"I have given up trying to come out a winner," Michele moans as Flavia and I work alongside him setting up tables and chairs. "This is the last year I am going to subject myself to this type of scrutiny."

"You have said that every year for as long as I can remember," yells his wife, Bianca, from her position behind the large portable table where she is making one of the restaurant's most desired dishes: *ravioli con rucola*—ravioli with arugula.

To no one's surprise, the sagra is an enormous success. The food, the aura created by the tiny lights strung around a cobblestone piazza dating back many centuries, the food, the glow of the late summer sun setting over the Val d'Albegna, the food. . . .

Chief among my favorite foods are the cured meats, the *finocchiata* (pork tenderloin cured with black pepper and wild fennel seeds), *prosciutto di cinghiale* (wild boar prosciutto), *rigatino* (pork belly cured with black pepper) and, of course, *prosciutto di Toscana* (Tuscan ham). This last, Tuscan ham, is a type of prosciutto characterized by the length and method of curing—it is a *salato* (seasoned and aged) as opposed to a *dolce* (sweet and young) prosciutto. Made from the hind legs of cereal-raised pigs, the meat is initially rubbed with a mixture of salt, garlic, and spices and left to cure in open-air attics for six to nine months before eating. To my mind, it is the best of all Italy's prosciuttos.

Also high on my list are the *fagioli al fiasco*, flask-cooked beans, with culinary origins dating back several hundred years. One of a great many extraordinary bean dishes served throughout this region (Tuscans are known thoughout Italy as *mangiafagioli*—bean-eaters), the recipe is basically this: dried white beans are placed in a large, bulbous flask (*fiasco*) with sage and olive oil and simmered for seven or eight hours in the embers of an olive-wood fire. Paired with thick slices of rustic bread and a carafe of red wine, the beans are pure perfection.

Naturally, there is an embarrassment of riches in the choice of wines. From the extraordinary D.O.C. vintages (Brunello di Montalcino, Carmignano, Chianti, Morellino,

Pomino, Rosso di Montepulciano, Bolgheri) to the so-called "Super Toscani"—that great assemblage of red and white wines produced outside the areas identified by the Italian government as D.O.C. (Ornellaia, Solaia, Tignanello, Fontanelle)—Tuscany is unquestionably Italy's foremost wine region.

I have to admit, however, that in the end, I enjoy the people almost as much as the food. Specifically, the democratic bent that comes from living in a region where culture is defined in such broad terms and where the gap between the academically cultured and the experientially cultured is smaller than anywhere else in the world. Perhaps it is the fact of being totally and continuously surrounded by art that makes everyone think himself to be highly cultured. Perhaps it is the hubris of a people whose collective ancestry encompasses Dante, Botticelli, Petrarch, Da Vinci, and De' Medici (as Luigi Barzini once noted, "Tuscan virtues are many, but modesty is not one of them"). Perhaps simply the legacy of a heritage shrouded with enough mystery to simplify the process of self-creation.

Whatever the reason, the people I meet at the sagra all seem to have one thing in common: a perception of themselves as direct descendants of the Etruscans and, as such, more intrinsically cultured than any other group of people on earth. Like the producer of fine wines and olive oils, like the quarryman from Carrara who compared his work to that of Michelangelo, like the seamstress who makes gorgeous costumes for the local palio or the pork butcher who invited me to his home to witness this winter's kill, like the weaver and salesclerk and bread baker and house painter—all consider themselves (when they consider it at all) to be as worthy of cultural consideration as any sculptor or portraitist.

Curzio Malaparte, that eminent chronicler of Tuscan psyches, once noted that Tuscan culture had, as its foundation, a very democratic core. "It does not surprise me that a chemist from the small village of Pitigliano has written a two-volume work on the history of the region dating back to the ancient Etruscans. In this sense, even more than in the strictly artistic sense, Tuscans at large are undoubtedly the world's most cultured people."

To cap off this long, complex day, Flavia and I repair to a nearby dance club with some new friends made at the sagra. Between dances, the talk is more or less what I might have expected—lighthearted discussions about food, movies, music, art. But the general flavor of the evening is best summed up by a stunningly beautiful woman who just happens to turn out to be both a distant cousin of Flavia's as well as one of the Italian fashion industry's most up and coming models. "When I strut down the runway," she says at one point, only half in jest, "I feel myself to be the direct heir of a cultural tradition stretching back to the Renaissance and beyond to the dawn of Etruscan civilization."

Amen.

CARDI ALLA PARMIGIANA

Gratinéed Cardoons

❦ Emilia-Romagna ❦

THE WINNING CHEF FOR THE 1995 *LE VALLI IN TAVOLA* CONTEST DESCRIBED ON *page 206 comes from one of my favorite restaurants in Emilia-Romagna, La Capanna, located in Codigoro in the province of Ferrara. Eraclio Soncini had this to say of his unexpected victory, "The event takes place over the course of two weeks during which chefs are constantly eliminated in a round-robin kind of competition. Each night, after you've finished cooking and the dessert course has just begun, all the chefs are expected to circulate among the guests and judges, smiling and answering questions about themselves and their sources of inspiration. It's a very nerve-rattling time, because guests clamor for the attention of the chef whose food they liked and the other poor guys are left standing on the perimeter of the room alone. The final night is the worst because the stakes are so high. When my name was announced, I started to cry and the guests jumped to their feet and began yelling 'Bravo! Bravo!' It was the most moving experience of my life."*

That night, Soncini accompanied his arrista di maiale tartufato *(truffled pork roast) with this succulent, simple dish of baked cardoons.*

serves 4

Time: 75 minutes

Level of Difficulty: Easy

⚜

3 pounds cardoons
1 lemon
3 quarts salted water for cooking
Salt to taste
8 tablespoons (1 stick) unsalted
   butter
1/2 cup freshly grated
   grana padana or
   Parmigiano-Reggiano

1 Separate the cardoons into individual stalks. Discard the outer, damaged, and hollow stalks. Peel those that remain, cut into 6-inch-long segments, and place in a bowl of water mixed with the juice of half a lemon.

2 Bring the 3 quarts salted water to a boil in a large soup pot over medium heat. Drain the cardoons and place them and the remaining lemon juice in the pot. Cook for 30 minutes and drain.

3 Preheat the oven to 350°F. Butter an 8 x 10-inch ovenproof baking dish with 1 tablespoon butter. Layer the cardoons, dotting each layer with butter and dusting with cheese. Continue layering until all the ingredients are used up.

4 Bake for 30 minutes, remove from the oven, and serve immediately.

Make Ahead The cardoons can be prepared through Step 2 up to 2 days in advance. Keep refrigerated in a sealed container until ready to use.

How to Serve As an appetizer, a vegetable side dish accompanying the aforementioned pork roast, or grilled chicken, or as an entrée paired with sautéed greens or roasted red peppers.

Wine Suggestion Medium-Sweet White (In truth, cardoons—as a member of the artichoke family—do not go well with most wines although, in this case, the butter and cheese required by the recipe contribute enough softening of flavor to make a wine pairing work fairly well.)

VERDURE STUFATE ALL'ACETO BALSAMICO

Cauliflower, Artichokes, Leeks, and Broccoli Rabe Braised in Balsamic Vinegar and Dusted with Anise

❧ Emilia-Romagna ❧

THIS WONDERFUL PLATTER OF CAULIFLOWER, BROCCOLI RABE, ARTICHOKES, AND *leeks braised in balsamic vinegar did not win first place in the* Vallei in Tavola *festival (see page 206). I'm still not sure why because I was absolutely enthralled with both its appearance and flavor. When all the awards had been announced, I hastened to find losing chef, Sergio Ferrarini of San Mauro a Mares' Hotel Capitol (Ferrarini took first prize in 1991) to ask for the recipe, which I have since added to my repertoire of mainstays. Obviously, in this, the heart of balsamic vinegar country, the vinegar used in the recipe was of the very highest quality. Is it worth it to spend a lot of money for an ounce or two of ten-year-old balsamic vinegar? Chef Ferrarini, "Yes, yes, and yes again."*

serves 4

Time: 35 minutes

Level of Difficulty: Easy

1 small head cauliflower, cored

4 small artichokes

Juice of 1 lemon

4 tablespoons extra virgin olive oil

4 ounces smoked pancetta, diced

2 leeks, cleaned and roughly chopped (white parts only)

8 ounces broccoli rabe, tough stems removed and roughly chopped

1/4 cup Basic Vegetable Broth (page 459) or canned broth

Salt to taste

1 Parboil the cauliflower in salted water for 5 minutes. Drain, divide into individual florets, and set aside.

2 Peel the artichoke stems and remove the tough outer leaves. Trim the spiny stems, cut the artichokes in half, and remove the chokes. Cut each half into 4 or 5 thin slices and immediately place in water with lemon juice.

3 Heat the oil in a skillet over low heat and sauté the pancetta for 5 minutes. Increase the heat to high, add the cauliflower, drained artichokes, leeks, and broccoli rabe and sauté for 5 minutes, stirring constantly. Pour in the broth, season with salt and pepper, and cook for 3 to 4 minutes, or until the broth has been completely absorbed.

4 Drizzle with the vinegar, dust with the crushed anise, and cook for 5 more minutes, stirring constantly. Transfer to a serving platter and serve hot.

Make Ahead The entire dish can be prepared up to a day in advance, refrigerated in a sealed container, and reheated just before serving.

How to Serve As an appetizer, a side dish to grilled fish, or a topping for pasta or rice.

Wine Suggestion Medium-Sweet White

Freshly ground black pepper
    to taste
2 tablespoons balsamic vinegar
1/4 teaspoon anise seeds, toasted
    and crushed

165

TERRINA DI MELANZANE
CON PEPERONI E PROSCIUTTO

Eggplant, Red Pepper, and Prosciutto Terrine

❧ Calabria ❧

ON THE THIRD SUNDAY OF EVERY AUGUST, MARINA DI GIOIOSA CELEBRATES *the feast of the Madonna del Carmine with a procession with origins that date back only about sixty years. The centerpiece is a colorful statue of the Madonna, which depicts her floating pacifically above the clouds surrounded by angels and holding the baby Jesus in the palm of one uplifted hand. In early morning, the statue is paraded through the streets of the village; later that day, it is placed prominently on the prow of a regally decorated sailing ship that tours the gulf accompanied by dozens of other vessels. Village residents are utterly devoted to this Madonna and she, apparently, to them—at least according to the enthusiastic accounts of miracles performed through her intercession, the most recent having taken place in 1957 on the actual day of the festival.*

In the words of Gigi Guerzoni, who hosted my stay in Marina di Gioiosa: "The sea was very agitated that morning and Don Chicchi (the church pastor) had forbidden the statue's journey. But none of us wanted to give up seeing the Madonna triumph over the waves. So naturally, we all gathered on the sand to beseech her intercession when, suddenly, a great calm came over the waters turning the sea into a lake."

The following recipe—wonderful in both flavor and appearance—comes from Gigi's wife, Sofia, who makes it specifically for this local and very picturesque festival.

serves 6 to 8

Time: 1¹/2 hours

Level of Difficulty: Moderate

⚥

1 medium eggplant
(about 1¹/2 pounds)
4 red peppers

1 Cut the eggplant lengthwise into ¹/8-inch-thick slices. Arrange the eggplant slices in one layer in a colander, sprinkle with salt, cover with a weight, and let drain for 1 hour.

2 Using tongs, hold the peppers over an open flame until the skins are completely charred.* Place in a paper bag, seal, and let rest for 10 minutes. Remove the peppers, peel away the charred skin, cut in half, remove the seeds, and slice into thin strips.

3 Gently squeeze the eggplant slices to remove as much water as possible, baste with oil, and grill over high heat on a stovetop grill pan or broil in the oven.

4 Preheat the oven to 400°F. Oil and line an 8 x 4-inch-wide loaf pan, preferably glass or terracotta, with eggplant slices, letting the slices overlap the sides.

5 Fill the terrine with the remaining eggplant, and before layering the remaining ingredients, season each layer with salt, pepper, cheese, and a drizzle of oil. Place in the prosciutto, the peppers, the eggs, and the basil. Fold the overlapping eggplant slices toward the center over the filling.

6 Bake for 25 minutes. Line a serving platter with the greens, unmold the terrine, and garnish with a ring of tomato halves arranged lengthwise over the top.

Make Ahead The terrine can be prepared through Step 4 up to 1 day in advance, wrapped in foil, and refrigerated. Just before serving, heat for 15 minutes, or just until hot all the way through, and proceed to unmold and garnish.

How to Serve As an appetizer followed by spaghetti with parsley and garlic, or as an entrée paired with a green salad.

Wine Suggestion Medium- or Full-bodied Red

Salt to taste

Freshly ground black pepper to taste

8 ounces freshly grated pecorino

1/2 cup extra virgin olive oil

4 ounces prosciutto cotto, thinly sliced

3 hard-boiled eggs, peeled and cut into thin rounds

15 to 20 fresh basil leaves

Mixed greens for garnish

8 cherry tomatoes, halved

Alternately, the peppers can be placed in a roasting pan and broiled—turning when necessary—until the skins are charred on all sides.

CASTAGNE STUFATE

Wine-braised Chestnuts

❦ Trentino-Alto Adige ❧

BEING ENAMORED OF ANYTHING HAVING TO DO WITH CHESTNUTS, I CAN PROUDLY *say that I sampled every one of the seventeen dishes offered at Roncegno's* Festa della Castagna *held in late October (that's not mentioning the two paper cones filled with roasted chestnuts devoured between dances). But my favorite was this dish of perfectly stewed chestnuts served with crisply roasted pork and sautéed chard. For added flavor, I substituted beef broth for the water used in the original recipe.*

serves 4 to 6

Time: 45 minutes

Level of Difficulty: Easy

⚜

50 large chestnuts (marroni),
    peeled
1 cup dry white wine
1 teaspoon tomato paste diluted
    in 2 tablespoons water
1/2 cup Basic Meat Broth
    (page 460)
Salt to taste

1 Blanch the chestnuts in boiling water for 2 to 3 minutes and peel away the velvety skin.

2 Put the chestnuts, wine, tomato paste, 2 tablespoons broth, and a pinch of salt in a large saucepan. Cook over high heat for 30 minutes, stirring constantly and adding broth as needed to keep the chestnuts from sticking or breaking. The finished chestnuts should be tender and somewhat dry.

Make Ahead The chestnuts can be parboiled and peeled earlier in the day.

How to Serve As a side dish accompanying meats, poultry, or full-flavored fish.

Wine Suggestion Chestnuts can take a wide variety of wines ranging from Dry White to Full-bodied Red. Use as the determining factor the food with which they are paired.

ZUCCA GIALLA DI CHIOGGIA MARINATA

*Marinated Butternut Squash, Chioggia-style**

❧ Veneto ❧

VENICE'S FIRST REGATTA (SEE PAGE 214) WAS HELD IN 1464 AS A TRIBUTE TO VENETIAN *noblewoman, Caterina Cornaro, on the day that she married Giacomo II, king of Cyprus. Giacomo died in 1473, leaving Caterina pregnant and her financial future in the hands of the Venetian Doge who—in an unprecedented act of nationalism—seized her inheritance and, in exchange, offered her a small annuity and dominion over Asolo, thirty miles to the north. There she retired to live out her days, surrounded by a small but elegant court that included the Venetian painter, Pietro Bembo.*

serves 4 to 6

Time: 40 minutes plus 12 hours marinating time

Level of Difficulty: Easy

⚶

2 medium butternut squash (about 3 pounds total), peeled, seeded, and cut into thin strips

2 tablespoons extra virgin olive oil

Salt to taste

1 cup good-quality red wine vinegar

1 medium red onion, thinly sliced

Freshly ground black pepper to taste

1 large bunch fresh basil

1 Preheat the oven to 350°F.

2 Toss the squash with the oil and a pinch of salt and transfer to a baking pan. Bake for 30 minutes.

3 Meanwhile, place the vinegar, onion, salt, and pepper in a saucepan. Bring to a boil and remove from heat.

4 Transfer the squash to a small glass or plastic terrine with a tight-fitting cover. Arrange the strips in layers, each layer topped with a few basil leaves and a drizzle of the vinegar mixture. Continue in this manner until all ingredients have been used. Refrigerate for at least 12 hours before serving.

Make Ahead The entire dish can be made up to 2 months in advance and refrigerated in a sealed container.

How to Serve As a side dish paired with roasted meats.

Wine Suggestion Medium- or Full-bodied Red

*Chioggia is a small town south of Venice that has, today, become famous for its high-quality produce such as squash, beets, radicchio, and potatoes.

FRITELLE DI BORAGINE

Borage Fritters

❧ Liguria ❧

AROUND CARNIVAL TIME (FEBRUARY) MANY NORTHERN ITALIAN CITIES HOST balli mascherati—*masked balls, generally held in royal palaces or town piazzas. Zignago, a small seaside town in the Ligurian province of La Spezia, erects a grand outdoor stage in Piazza Vittorio Veneto upon which sit twenty members of the regional symphony. On the night of the ball, thousands of people crowd into the square, dressed extravagantly as Renaissance barons and contessas.*

One of the many dishes served is this unique fritter, made with borage, a crisp, nutritious herb that tastes like cucumber. Borage can now be found at many farmer's markets in the United States, and should only be used fresh. The leaves are used raw, steamed, or sautéed like spinach. The stems are peeled, chopped, and used like celery. Toss borage flowers in salads or use as garnishes. In candied form, borage flowers make splendid decorations for pastries and dessert trays.

makes about 20 fritters

Time: 30 minutes

Level of Difficulty: Easy

1/2 cup unbleached all-purpose
    flour, sifted

1 large egg, lightly beaten

Salt to taste

1/2 cup cold water

8 ounces fresh borage, or burnet
    or celery leaves (about
    1/3 cup), stemmed and
    thinly sliced

Olive oil for frying

2 to 3 borage leaves for garnish

1 Put the flour, egg, a pinch of salt, and the 1/2 cup cold water in a large bowl. Beat with a fork, adding water as needed for a well-mixed and semiliquid batter.

2 Heat 1 inch of oil in a heavy skillet to 375°F.* Stir the borage into the batter and place it 1 tablespoon at a time into the hot oil. Fry until golden, remove with a slotted spoon, and drain on paper towels. Serve, garnished with the borage leaves.

How to Serve As an appetizer or a side dish paired with sauced meats or sauced poultry.

Wine Suggestion Dry White

*To test the temperature of the oil, you can put a cube of bread into the skillet. When it sizzles around the edges and turns golden almost immediately, the oil is the right temperature.

FRITELLE DI CAVOLFIORE DI TUSCANIA

Cauliflower Fritters

❧ Lazio ❧

IT IS A DATE THAT PEOPLE FROM ALL OVER LAZIO AND SURROUNDING REGIONS MARK ON *their calendars: the annual* Sagra della Fritella di Tuscania, *held the Sunday after January 17 in Tuscania, a stunningly picturesque Etruscan city in northern Lazio. After a morning devoted to processions (including* butteri *[cowboys], marching bands, and assorted cattle), the ever-larger crowds assemble in front of the massive frying pans erected in the historic piazza just inside the city's walls. For the remainder of the afternoon, the fragrance of frying cauliflower fills the air as the fritters—both sweet and salty—are distributed gratis.*

makes about 20 fritters

Time: About 1 hour

Level of Difficulty: Moderate

❀

5 tablespoons unbleached
    all-purpose flour

1 egg yolk

1 cup whole milk

Salt to taste plus 1/4 teaspoon salt

1 large head cauliflower, cored
    and cut into florets

2 large egg whites

1/4 teaspoon cream of tartar

Olive oil for frying

1 Put the flour, egg yolk, milk, and a pinch of salt in a large bowl and beat with a fork until well mixed and smooth. Cover and let rest for 30 minutes.

2 Meanwhile, boil the cauliflower florets in salted water for 10 minutes, or until fork tender. Drain and air dry.

3 Beat the egg whites with the 1/4 teaspoon salt until foamy. Add the cream of tartar and beat until they form stiff peaks. Gently fold into the flour batter.

4 Heat 1 inch of oil in a heavy skillet to 375°F.* Dip the florets in the batter and fry, a few at a time, until crisp. Remove with a slotted spoon, drain on paper towels, and serve immediately.

How to Serve As an appetizer dusted with powdered sugar or a side dish (spritzed with lemon) accompanying braised poultry or fish.

Wine Suggestion Medium-Sweet or Dry White

To test the temperature of the oil, you can put a cube of bread into the skillet. When it sizzles around the edges and turns golden almost immediately, the oil is the right temperature.

FAGIOLI CON LE COTICHE

Cannelini Beans Braised with Prosciutto and Herbs

❧ Lazio ❧

GOD ONLY KNOWS HOW MANY RELIGIOUS PROCESSIONS I HAVE SEEN IN MY DAY, BUT *one of the ones that unquestionably stands out in memory is that honoring Santa Rosa, patron saint of Viterbo, which is an Etruscan city thirty-five miles north of Rome. What makes this festival so unique is the size of the saint carried through the streets. Santa Rosa sits in a huge obelisk that is thirty-five feet high and weighs over five tons. One hundred and fifty men are required to transport her through narrow cobblestone passageways on which all semblance of light has been extinguished, save for the thousands of candles mounted on the obelisk itself. More than once, I am told, the saint has rammed against a house, sheering off a window or door. The festival takes place on the night of September 3 and the procession begins and ends at the Church of San Sisto, near Porto Romana. The accompanying food is all as deliciously rustic as this hearty dish of braised beans.*

serves 4

Time: 2 hours, excluding the overnight soaking of the beans

Level of Difficulty: Moderate

1 pound dried cannelini beans, soaked for 12 hours in warm water, drained, and rinsed

5 quarts water

1 tablespoon freshly chopped rosemary

1 clove garlic, peeled and halved plus 1 clove garlic, minced

1 Put the beans, 3 quarts water, the rosemary, and halved garlic clove in a heavy-gauge soup pot. Cover and cook over low heat for 1 hour. Drain, reserving 1 cup bean broth.

2 Meanwhile, place the prosciutto or pork rind in 2 quarts water in a large soup pot, cover, and cook for 15 minutes over medium heat. Drain and repeat three times—each time, boiling the rind in water and draining to remove as much fat as possible. After the third boil, cut the rind into thin strips, place them in a large saucepan with 2 cups salted water, cover, and cook for 15 minutes. Drain and set aside.

Since every Italian grocery store or supermarket stocks prosciutto, Italians tend to flavor many dishes, especially soups, with the rind, called cotiche. If you have ever tasted anything prepared this way, you will undoubtedly agree there is no substitute. I have always had great success asking for a piece of prosciutto rind in Italian specialty stores. Pork rind is a very distant substitute, but cured or smoked pork rind comes a little closer.

3 Heat the oil in a large skillet over low heat and sauté the basil, parsley, garlic, onion, and prosciutto for 8 minutes, stirring constantly. Stir in the tomatoes, season with salt and pepper, and cook for 15 minutes.

4 Add the prosciutto rind, drained beans, and reserved bean broth to the skillet. Season with salt and pepper and cook for 20 minutes. Serve immediately.

Make Ahead The entire dish can be made up to 2 days in advance, covered, refrigerated, and reheated just before serving.

How to Serve As a first course followed by roast chicken, or as a one-course meal paired with a mixed green salad or sautéed greens.

Wine Suggestion Medium- or Full-bodied Red

8 ounces prosciutto rind or cured or smoked pork rind

2 tablespoons extra virgin olive oil

4 tablespoons freshly chopped basil

3 tablespoons freshly chopped Italian parsley

1 medium onion, minced

2 ounces prosciutto, diced

1 pound ripe Italian plum tomatoes, peeled, seeded, and roughly chopped (about 2^{1}/$_{2}$ to 3 cups)

Salt to taste

Freshly ground black pepper to taste

173

CARCIOFI CON PISELLI

Baby Peas Sautéed with Spring Artichokes

174

❧ Lazio ❧

THE PROCESSION DETAILED ON PAGE 172 IS ONLY ONE PART OF THE COLORFUL *three-day celebration attending Santa Rosa's feast day. Two days before on September 1, the 150 men who will carry her through the streets go through a sort of gymnastic gearing up. Dressed all in white with red scarves around their waists, they meet at the Priori Palace and proceed through a series of ritualistic movements dating back to 1664, when the first procession was held. Afterward, they pray together, eat together, and spend the rest of the night together in the church housing the saint's embalmed body. The morning before the procession, they appear together at the altar, where they receive the final benediction. Turning to face the crowd of thousands, the leader of the group then pronounces the words, "Santa Rosa, avanti," (Let's go, Saint Rose), which signals the official beginning of the music, dancing, and eating that characterizes this great festival.*

serves 4

Time: 40 to 45 minutes

Level of Difficulty: Moderate

8 baby artichokes*, stems trimmed
2 lemons
4 tablespoons extra virgin olive oil
1 medium onion, minced
Salt to taste
2 cups fresh or frozen baby peas
Freshly ground black pepper
    to taste
Fresh parsley for garnish

1 Remove and discard the artichokes' tough outer leaves and slice off the spiny tips. Peel the stems† and cut the artichokes into quarters. Immediately immerse in a bowl of water with the juice of 1 lemon.

2 Heat the oil in a large skillet. Sauté the onion over low heat for 8 minutes. Drain the artichokes and add to the skillet, seasoning with salt and stirring to blend the flavors. Cook for 15 minutes.

3 Cut the remaining lemon into halves. Thinly slice one half. Add the peas to the skillet, cover, and cook for 5 minutes**. Dust with pepper, drizzle with the juice of the half a lemon and transfer to a serving bowl. Garnish with the parsley and lemon slices.

Sometimes even artichokes designated "babies" have chokes. If so, remove them along with as many outer leaves as is necessary to reach the lighter-colored inner leaves.

Make Ahead The artichokes can be prepared through Step 2 up to 1 day in advance, wrapped in plastic wrap, and refrigerated until ready to use.

How to Serve As an appetizer or a side dish paired with roasted meats or poultry or grilled fish. Also works well as a topping for pasta or rice.

Wine Suggestion None, since artichokes do not go well with any type of wine.

175

*If the peas are older and larger, cook for an additional 5 to 8 minutes, or until tender.

†There are many varieties of artichokes and some come with long stems (which, to me, are the best part). If the ones you buy have stems, peel them in the same way as you would peel carrots or asparagus.

POMODORI RIPIENI DI RISO

Tomatoes Stuffed with Rice and Baked with Fresh Herbs

❦ Lazio ❦

IN MARCH 1283, A PLOWMAN WORKING THE FIELDS NEAR VITERBO BECAME *infuriated when the oxen pulling his cart simply folded their legs beneath their massive bodies and refused to move another inch. In the process of attempting to change the animals' minds, the plowman noticed the cart had become stuck on a large mound which, when excavated, revealed a stone box. Prying open the lid, he pulled out an illuminated triptych depicting Christ the Savior (Il Salvatore), flanked by the Madonna and John the Baptist. As he later discovered, the triptych had been buried forty years earlier when Frederick II ordered Lazio's rural churches looted and the booty given his soldiers in lieu of pay. Today, the triptych resides in the Chuch of Santa Maria Nuova 364 days a year. On the third Saturday of September, it is paraded through the streets of Viterbo's Salvatore quarter as part of a charming, unassuming festival attended mainly by local residents. Tables are set up outside peoples' homes and food served to both family members and whoever wanders by.*

I happened upon La Festa del Salvatore *by chance and was taken in by Franco Muzzio and his family, who fed me an endless series of wonderful dishes, including the following dish of tomatoes stuffed with an unlikely combination of rice and potatoes.*

serves 4

Time: 1 hour

Level of Difficulty: Moderate

⚶

8 medium ripe tomatoes
Salt to taste
4 small boiling potatoes,
    peeled
8 tablespoons Arborio rice
4 cloves garlic

1 Make a horizontal slit across the stem end of the tomatoes, as if cutting off a small slice, but do not cut all the way through; this creates a hinged lid. Using a teaspoon, carefully hollow out the tomatoes and finely chop the extracted pulp. Transfer the pulp to a bowl and set aside. Salt the insides of the tomatoes and place them upside down, hinge open, to drain.

2 Cut the potatoes into matchsticks 1 x 1 x 4 inches. Salt the potatoes and set aside.

3 Preheat the oven to 350°F. Oil a baking pan.

4 Place the rice, garlic, parsley, basil, oregano, mint, and olive oil in a bowl. Add the reserved tomato pulp, mix well, and season with salt and pepper. Stuff the tomatoes, leaving ³/4 inch at the top, and press down on the lid. Arrange the stuffed tomatoes on the baking pan. Place the potato matchsticks standing up between the tomatoes.

5 Bake for 45 minutes, remove from the oven, and serve hot or lukewarm, garnished with the fresh mint.

Make Ahead The entire dish can be made earlier in the day and served lukewarm or reheated just before serving.

How to Serve As an appetizer, a side dish paired with grilled meats or fish, or even as an entrée served with a green salad.

Wine Suggestion Medium-bodied Red

3 tablespoons freshly chopped
    Italian parsley
2 tablespoons freshly
    chopped basil
¹/8 teaspoon dried oregano
2 tablespoons freshly
    chopped mint
4 tablespoons extra virgin olive oil
Freshly ground black pepper
    to taste
Mint leaves for garnish

177

SCAROLA AI CAPPERI E OLIVE

Braised Escarole with Capers and Black Olives

❧ Campania ❧

LA SAGRA DEI GIGLI (THE LILY FESTIVAL) TAKES PLACE EVERY JUNE 22 IN HONOR *of an event dating back to the fifth century, when the Vandals conquered the city of Nola in Campania. Many Nolese were taken to Africa to serve as slaves, among them, the son of a poor widow who subsequently turned to the bishop for help. Having already spent all the church's money buying back hundreds of prisoners, however, there was nothing the poor bishop could do except offer himself to the king of the Vandals in exchange—a trade that was readily accepted. And so Nola's Bishop Paolino served as a slave for many years until he gained the sympathy of the Vandal king and was sent back home. Upon his return, Nola's residents raced to the beach to greet his ship; along the way, they gathered thousands of lilies to make a carpet for his path. Today, the lilies have, somehow, been symbolically transformed into eight 75-foot bell towers, weighing thousands of pounds each. The towers are carried throughout the city and are accompanied by a carriage containing actors playing the parts of both Bishop Paolino and the* turco—*the black African—who accompanied him home.*

Afterward there is much eating, drinking, and dancing in the city's main piazza and, as the grand finale, a general benediction by the bishop.

serves 4

Time: 45 minutes

Level of Difficulty: Easy

⚶

2 large heads escarole (about
    2 pounds total)
6 tablespoons extra virgin olive oil
3 cloves garlic, minced

1 Divide the escarole into individual leaves and separate the tough outer leaves from the tenderer inner ones. Wash both well, dry, and roughly chop.

2 Heat the oil in a large skillet over low heat and sauté the garlic for 4 minutes. Add the tough outer escarole leaves, cover, and cook for 10 minutes. Add the tenderer leaves, replace the cover, and cook for another 10 minutes.

3 Place the capers and olives in the skillet and stir to blend the flavors. Season with salt, cover, and cook for 10 minutes. Add the anchovies, mashing them into the liquid with a wooden spoon. Cook for 5 minutes, transfer to a heated platter, and serve immediately.

Make Ahead The entire dish can be made earlier in the day and served lukewarm or reheated just before serving.

How to Serve As a side dish accompanying grilled or roasted poultry or broiled fish, or as a pasta topping.

Wine Suggestion Dry or Medium-Sweet White

2 ounces salt-packed capers, drained and rinsed

4 ounces gaeta or other black olives, pitted

Salt to taste

3 salt-packed anchovies, filleted (see page 25 for directions)

179

CIANFOTTA

Eggplant, Red Pepper, Potato, and Black Olive Stew

❧ Campania ☙

ANOTHER OF THE WONDERFUL VEGETABLE DISHES SERVED AT NOLA'S *SAGRA DEI GIGLI* *celebrates the flavors of summer—the red peppers, eggplant, and new potatoes that characterize the cuisine of this area during what is now referred to as "tourist season." According to legend, this delicious summer stew was originally created by one of Naples' well-known madames as an inexpensive way to put food on the table of her brothel. Hence its name, which is a dialectal shortening of "ciana" (slut) and "fotta" (made).*

serves 4

Time: 75 minutes

Level of Difficulty: Moderate

⚷

3 small eggplants (8-ounces each), cut into 1-inch cubes

Salt to taste

2 large red peppers

1 pound ripe Italian plum tomatoes (about 6 or 7), peeled

8 tablespoons extra virgin olive oil

2 large red onions, thinly sliced

1 clove garlic, minced

1 pound new red potatoes, peeled and cut into 1-inch cubes

Freshly ground black pepper to taste

4 ounces gaeta or other black olives, pitted

2 tablespoons freshly chopped Italian parsley

1 Toss the eggplant cubes with salt and place in one layer on a platter or cutting board set at a 3-inch angle to allow the juices to drain. Weight down the eggplant and set aside for 1 hour.

2 Using tongs, hold the peppers over an open flame until the skins are completely charred.* Place in a paper bag, seal, and let rest for 10 minutes. Remove the peppers, peel away the charred skin, cut in half, remove the seeds, and slice into thin strips.

3 Pass the tomatoes through a food mill, transfer the pulp to a bowl, and set aside.

4 Heat the oil in a large skillet over low heat and sauté the onion and garlic for 8 minutes. Pour in the tomato pulp, raise the heat to medium, and bring to a boil, stirring frequently. Add the potatoes and drained eggplant, season with pepper and cook over low heat for 8 minutes, adding water if necessary.

*Alternately, the peppers can be placed in a roasting pan and broiled—turning when necessary—until the skins are charred on all sides.

5 Add the peppers, olives, and half the parsley, and stir until well blended. Cook for 8 to 10 minutes, or until the potatoes are tender. Stir in the remaining parsley and cool to room temperature before serving.

Make Ahead The peppers can be prepared up to 1 day in advance, wrapped tightly in plastic wrap, and refrigerated until ready to use. The entire dish can be prepared earlier in the day and reheated just before serving.

How to Serve As an appetizer, served lukewarm and drizzled with lemon, or as an entrée paired with a green salad and crusty bread. Also makes a wonderful topping for pasta, polenta, gnocchi, or rice.

Wine Suggestion Medium-bodied Red

COTOLETTE DI FUNGHI PORCINI

Pan-fried Porcini Mushroom Cutlets

❧ Friuli-Venezia-Giulia ❧

THE FIRST TWO WEEKS OF SEPTEMBER ARE A HEADY TIME FOR RESIDENTS OF *Budoia. Teenagers as well as grandparents leave their beds at 3:00 A.M. to tramp through the surrounding forests in hope of finding mushrooms grand enough to exhibit at the annual* Festa dei Funghi. *One year (noted for an overabundance of mushroom-producing rain showers) over 350 edible varieties were displayed, poisonous mushrooms having been removed from classification since 1991, when four foragers died after sampling their find. With food stands, mushroom conviviums, and a host of judges entrusted with deciding the best, the biggest, and the most unusual, the city is one big festival. Budoia's restaurants do their part by planning menus exclusively offering exquisite mushroom dishes such as the following.*

serves 4

Time: About 15 to 20 minutes

Level of Difficulty: Easy

⚶

8 porcini caps*, cleaned with a
    vegetable brush
2 large eggs, lightly beaten
1/2 cup unbleached all purpose
    flour, sifted
1 cup unflavored breadcrumbs
2 tablespoons unsalted butter
6 tablespoons extra virgin olive oil
Salt to taste

1 Dip the mushroom caps first in the beaten egg, then quickly in flour, and then in the breadcrumbs. Pat the breadcrumbs onto the mushrooms.

2 Heat the butter in a skillet over medium heat. Add the olive oil and when hot, fry the mushroom caps until golden brown on both sides. Remove with a slotted spoon, drain on paper towels, sprinkle with salt, and serve.

How to Serve As an appetizer served with lemon wedges or an entrée paired with sautéed greens and a mixed salad. Leftover mushrooms can be sliced, reheated, and used as a pasta topping.

Wine Suggestion Dry or Medium-Sweet White. Porcini can also be paired with Medium- or Full-bodied Reds.

Portobello caps, which are as large as porcini, can be substituted although their flavor is significantly milder.

CIPOLLE ALLA MARSALA

Sweet Onions Cooked with Marsala Wine

❦ Sicilia ❧

ANOTHER FOOD ASSOCIATED WITH THE FEAST OF ST. ROSALIE (SEE PAGE 416)
*is this wonderful casserole of onions cooked in Sicily's famous Marsala wine. Produced south of
Palermo, in the town that bears its name, Marsala is fortified with grape brandy, sweetened with
grape must, and widely used as a thick, sweet cooking wine.*

serves 6

Time: 90 minutes

Level of Difficulty: Easy

12 large sweet onions, peeled
24 whole cloves
3 sprigs fresh thyme
Salt to taste
1/2 cup Marsala
1 tablespoon capers, drained
    and minced

1 Preheat the oven to 350°F.

2 Pierce each onion with 2 whole cloves. Arrange in one layer in a deep baking pan, cover with water, seal with aluminum foil, and bake for 1 hour, or until the onions are tender and the pan is relatively dry.

3 Uncover the pan, pour the Marsala over the onions, and bake for another 20 minutes, or until the wine has been completely absorbed.

4 Remove and discard the cloves. Arrange the onions on a serving platter, sprinkle with the capers, and serve.

Make Ahead The entire dish can be made earlier in the day and reheated just before serving.

How to Serve As an appetizer or side dish accompanying roasted, grilled, or broiled meats or fish. Also makes a wonderful topping for pasta or rice.

Wine Suggestion Dry White

VERZOLINI DELLA VIGILIA

Twelfth Night Stuffed Savoy Cabbage

184

❧ Emilia-Romagna ❧

ELEVEN NIGHTS AFTER CHRISTMAS, ITALIANS EVERYWHERE CELEBRATE WITH LARGE, *festive dinners, consisting of specific foods (such as this Romagnolo version of traditional stuffed cabbage) served after midnight. In Faenza, thirty miles east of Bologna, the festivities reach yet another height, attached, as they are, to* La Nott de'Biso', *a festival of music, fireworks, and the drinking of* biso, *hot, mulled wine. The name* biso *is Romagnolo dialect for "bevete su" or "drink up."*

Sometime around 10:00 P.M., *the huge vat of spiced Sangiovese wine begins to boil and thousands flock to the Piazza del Popolo to stand in line with their* gott—*ceramic containers decorated for the occasion by Faenza's ceramic artists. Two hours later, just after midnight, there is the ritualistic burning of* Il Niballo, *a thirty-foot-tall straw man hung by his neck on a scaffolding erected directly in front of the loggias.* Il Niballo *is dialect for "Annibale," the historical mercenary who helped the Moors invade Rome. Obviously, the people of Faenza have never forgotten that flagrancy.*

serves 4

Time: 2 hours

Level of Difficulty: Moderate

CABBAGE

2 slices stale country-style bread

1/2 cup whole milk

30 to 35 large leaves savoy cabbage

1/4 cup plain breadcrumbs

1/4 cup freshly grated grana padana or Parmigiano-Reggiano

1 Place the bread in a bowl and cover with milk. Let rest for 10 minutes.

2 Boil the cabbage leaves in salted water for 8 minutes. Drain. Choose the 24 largest and set aside. Finely dice the others.

3 Squeeze the bread dry and place in a bowl with the diced cabbage, breadcrumbs, cheese, eggs, and salt. Mix by hand until all ingredients are well blended. Place a dollop of stuffing in the center of each of the 24 cabbage leaves. Fold like an envelope, fasten with a toothpick, and set aside.

4 To make the sauce, heat the butter in a large skillet over low heat. Add the oil and sauté the onion for 8 minutes. Dilute the tomato paste in the broth and pour into the skillet. Season with salt and cook, stirring constantly, for 5 minutes. Add the cabbage packets in one layer, cover, and cook for 1 hour. Transfer to a heated platter and serve, garnished with parsley.

Make Ahead The entire dish can be made up to 2 days in advance, refrigerated in a sealed container, and reheated just before serving. Many people actually prefer this dish as a leftover.

How to Serve As an appetizer or an entrée paired with roasted potatoes and a mixed green salad.

Wine Suggestion Medium- or Full-bodied Red

2 large eggs, lightly beaten
Salt to taste

185

SAUCE
2 tablespoons unsalted butter
6 tablespoons extra virgin
 olive oil
1 medium onion, minced
2 tablespoons tomato paste
1 cup Basic Vegetable or Meat
 Broth (page 459, 460)
5 to 6 sprigs fresh parsley
 for garnish

PEPERONATA AL FORNO

Red Peppers Roasted with Olives, Capers, and Fresh Oregano

❦ Abruzzo ❦

AT THE END OF THE SUMMER, ABRUZZO'S SHEPHERDS ABANDON THEIR GREEN *mountain meadows and descend toward the plains. Campo Catino's September 29 festival*—La Festa di San Michele Arcangelo *(St. Michael the Archangel) celebrates just this transition from one season to the next. At one of the food stalls set up in the main piazza, I found a copy of this verse written by one of Italy's greatest poets, Gabriele D'Annunzio:*

Settembre, andiamo. È tempo di migrare.
Ora in terra d'Abruzzi I miei pastori
lascian gli stazzi e vanno verso il mare;
scendono all'Adriatico selvaggio
che verde è come I pascoli dei monti.
Han bevuto profondamente ai fonti
alpestri, che sapor d'acqua natía
rimanga ne'cuori esuli a conforto,
che lungo illuda la lor sete in vita.
Rinnovato hanno verga d'avellano.
Ah perche non son io co' miei pastori?

September, let's go. It is time to migrate.
Now in the land of the Abruzzo, my shepherds
Leave their stations and journey toward the sea;
Climbing down toward the wild Adriatic
Green as mountain meadows.
My shepherds have sipped profoundly from alpine fountains
And the fragrance of native waters
Will remain in those exiled hearts as a comfort
To satiate their thirst along the way
Renewed, they are now as strong as the boughs of the hazelnut
Oh why am I not like my shepherds?

serves 6

1 Preheat the oven to 400°F.

2 Using a sharp paring knife, remove the stems of the peppers and hollow out the interiors, removing the seeds and stringy fibers. Place in a round or oval baking dish, arranging the peppers, stem side up, in a star pattern around the perimeter.

3 Cut the onions into thick slices and pile in center of the circle of peppers.

4 Sprinkle the olives and capers evenly over the surface, drizzle with oil, season with salt, and bake for 45 minutes. Dust with fresh oregano and serve immediately.

Make Ahead The entire dish can be made up to 2 days in advance, wrapped in plastic wrap, refrigerated, and reheated just before serving.

How to Serve As an appetizer, a side dish paired with grilled, roasted, or broiled chicken or fish, or as an entrée served with roast potatoes and a green salad.

Wine Suggestion Dry White

Time: 1 hour

Level of Difficulty: Easy

12 red peppers,
 washed and dried
8 small onions,
 peeled and cored
20 green olives, pitted
3 tablespoons capers, drained
6 tablespoons extra virgin
 olive oil
Salt to taste
2 tablespoons freshly
 chopped oregano

PATATE, SALSICCIA E FAVE

Fava Bean, Sausage, and Potato Winter Stew

188

❧ Toscana ❧

TUSCANY IS FAMOUS FOR ITS OPEN-AIR NATIVITY SCENES, SOME INSTALLED ACROSS *the span of an entire hillside, others consisting of living characters, still others performed in fifteen or twenty rooms of a house, each room a spontaneous dramatic performance into which spectators are drawn. One of my favorites takes place in the tiny village of Gioviano in Lucca province. The village itself is a maze of narrow cobbled streets sculpted out of the summit of a mountain.*

No cars are allowed in the village and there is only one main pathway that winds its way up and down the mountain, under stone archways capped with someone's living room, over bridges connecting one minuscule piazza to another. The nativity follows this half-mile trail, with figures facetiously peeping out of fountains and hidden in the nooks and crannies of rock outcroppings. At night, the entire village is lit with candles illuminating La Via del Presepio—*The Path of the Nativity. Food stalls are scattered along the journey.*

serves 6

Time: 50 minutes

Level of Difficulty: Easy

⚜

1 cup dried fava beans, soaked for
    12 hours and drained

8 cups water

1¹/2 pounds boiling potatoes,
    peeled and cut into
    1-inch cubes

1 Cook the fava beans in salted water over medium heat for 20 minutes. Drain, peel, and place the beans in a large, heavy-gauge saucepan. Add the potatoes, shallots, sausage, chili, oil, broth, salt, and wine. Cover and cook over medium heat for 30 minutes.

2 Sprinkle with parsley and serve immediately.

Make Ahead The entire dish can be prepared earlier in the day and reheated just before serving.

How to Serve As a one-dish meal paired with a mixed green salad or as a topping for rice or pasta.

Wine Suggestion Medium-bodied Red

3 shallots, peeled and halved

4 ounces fennel sausage, removed from casing and roughly crumbled

$1/2$ dried chili, crumbled

3 tablespoons extra virgin olive oil

$1/4$ cup Basic Vegetable Broth (page 459) or canned broth

Salt to taste

$1/3$ cup dry white wine

2 tablespoons freshly chopped Italian parsley

PATATE E MAMMOLE

Potato and Artichoke Tart

§ Lazio §

SOMETIMES IT SEEMS THAT EVERY REGION IN ITALY GROWS ITS OWN VARIETY OF *artichoke. There's the compact Ligurian spinoso; the spiny Sardinian Sardo; the squat, spineless Apulian Pugliese; the deep purple Toscano; and the largest of all—the Romano. It was this giant of the artichoke world—beautifully layered with potatoes and shaped into a delicious tart—that was heaped onto my plate by Signora Violeta Muzzio at Viterbo's* Festa del Salvatore *(see page 176). Facilissimo, the Signora said when I asked for the recipe. Extremely easy.*

serves 6

Time: 75 minutes

Level of Difficulty: Moderate

⚖

2 pounds boiling potatoes, peeled
    and sliced into thin rounds
1 tablespoon white vinegar
4 tablespoons unsalted butter
1/4 cup extra virgin olive oil
3 large globe artichokes
Juice of 1 1/2 lemons
1/4 cup water
Salt to taste
Freshly ground black pepper
    to taste
1/4 cup freshly grated
    Parmigiano-Reggiano

1 Boil the potato rounds for 2 minutes in salted water with the vinegar. Drain and pat the potatoes dry with paper towels.

2 Heat the butter and 3 tablespoons oil in a large, heavy skillet over medium heat. Fry the potatoes, a few pieces at a time, until both sides are light golden. Remove with a slotted spatula and drain on paper towels.

3 To prepare the artichokes, peel the stems, if any, and remove the tough outer leaves. Cut off the spiny tips, slice the artichoke in half lengthwise, and, using a paring knife or melon baller, remove the central chokes. Cut each half into 5 or 6 thin slices and soak in water with the juice of half a lemon.

4 Heat the remaining oil in a skillet over low heat. Add the artichokes, the remaining lemon juice, 1/4 cup water, salt, and pepper. Cook for 20 minutes, or until the artichokes are tender and the liquid almost totally evaporated.

5 Preheat the oven to 350°F. Butter a 2-quart round baking dish.

6 Place a layer of potatoes first in an overlapping circle, seasoning the layer with salt, pepper, and grated cheese. Place a layer of artichokes next, seasoning with salt, pepper, grated cheese, and continue alternating and seasoning layers of potatoes and artichokes until all the ingredients are used up. Wrap the dish in aluminum foil and bake for 30 minutes. Unmold onto a platter or serve directly from the baking dish.

Make Ahead The entire dish can be made up to 1 day in advance through Step 5, wrapped in plastic wrap, and refrigerated until ready to bake.

How to Serve As an appetizer; a side dish paired with grilled or roasted meats, poultry, or fish; or as an entrée paired with bread and a green salad.

Wine Suggestion Although I never recommend pairing artichokes with wine, the potatoes and cheese used in this recipe soften the flavor of the dish enough to make it work well with a medium-sweet white wine.

Soups, Breads, Focaccias, and Pizzas

Soups

MINESTRONE COL IL PESTO
Summer Vegetable and Pasta Soup with Pesto Cream

FONDUTA ALLA VALDOSTANA
Thick and Creamy Alpine Cheese Soup

ZUPPA DI FARRO
Farro Soup

PASTARASA
Chicken Broth with Grated Pasta

MINESTRONE D'ORZO ALLA TRENTINA
Barley, Chestnut, and White Bean Minestrone

MINESTRA DI TENERUMI
Zucchini Leaf and Fresh Tomato Soup

PALLOTTOLINE IN BRODO
Beef Broth with Tiny Meatballs

MACCU E FINOCCHIETTO
Cold Soup of Dried Favas and Wild Fennel

PASSATO DI ZUCCA
Cream of Butternut Squash Soup

ZUPPA SARDA
Sardinian Bread and Mozzarella Soup

FAVATA
Sausage and Fava Bean Soup

LE VIRTÚ
The Virtues (Many Vegetable Soup)

ZUPPA DI COZZE
Soup Made with Mussels and Fresh Tomatoes

Breads, Focaccias, and Pizzas

CRISPEDDI
Deep-fried Anchovy Rolls

TARALLI CON IL PEPE
Braided Pepper Biscuits

TORTA DI PROSCIUTTO
Prosciutto and Black Pepper Pizza

SCHIACCIATA AL ROSMARINO
Rosemary Focaccia

FITASCETTA
Onion and Mozzarella Ring Bread

PIADINA ROMAGNOLA
Toasted Flat Bread

CULLURELLI
Fried Potato Pizzette

SFINCIONE DI SAN VITO
St. Vito's Day Pizza

FANTASIA DI PIZZETTE
Four Variations of Pizza Tartlets

FOCACCIA AL FORMAGGIO
Cheese-stuffed Focaccia

FOCACCIA CON LE OLIVE VERDI
Focaccia with Green Olives

PANE CON LA ZUCCA
Butternut Squash Bread

SARDINIA
Sacred Rites and Profane Pleasures

FURAT CHI DE SU MARE VENIT IS THE LATIN TITLE of Sardinian writer Elia Riui's most recent book. In English, *Those From the Sea Come to Rob*. The jacket copy displays a stern picture of Riui with a cigarette dangling from his lips. Underneath, in large black letters, this declaration: "The entire story of Sardinian history encapsulated in six simple words."

The sentiment is not new to anyone who has spent time traveling through Sardinia. In fact, the six simple words often seem to be everywhere—burnished onto wooden plaques, embroidered on satin banners, even graffitied on road signs over the names of seaside villages. It is a peculiar conviction for a land surrounded by water, especially one that was first settled by peaceloving, seafaring Phoenicians. And yet, until a few decades ago, the overwhelming majority of Sardinians lived not on the coast, but in the rocky, mountainous interior where, by their reckoning, they were undeniably safe.

The fear apparently began with the fall of the Roman Empire, when anarchy replaced order and Sardinia fell into the hands of an ongoing series of marauders, including Arab pirates, ruthless Vandals, Moors, Pisans, and the newly united Spanish. Coupled with the malaria endemic to coastal wetlands, the raids resulted in the virtual transformation of Sardinians from a seagoing people almost completely dependent on fish as a source of sustenance, to an agricultural one whose main foods consisted of meat, cheese, and grains.

"I'm looking forward to spending plenty of time at the beach and eating lots of scrumptious fish," I had declared to my friend Francesca when I first visited her in Sardinia years ago.

"Then you'll be missing out on the best we have to offer," she had answered. "Not only on our most genuine traditions, but also on our most delicious foods."

This last visit, I knew better. And so I was thrilled when soon after my arrival Francesca said we were traveling to a nearby mountain village for a thoroughly carnivorous lunch with shepherd friends of her mother. The village was approximately 35 miles away and we stopped numerous times along the road to inspect the various *nuraghi*—cone-shaped constructions built over 3,000 years ago from huge stones and devoid of mortar. "Did people live in them?" I had asked Francesca the first time we spotted some along the road.

"No one is exactly sure whether they were just houses or also used for worship," she had answered.

Later I had looked through some of her archaeology books and found that the *nuraghi* often had several floors and were sometimes joined one to the other with walls forming a sort of castle. "In the Middle Ages, *our* castles were already archaeological treasures," Francesca had teased. They also were invariably constructed in positions allowing for complete surveillance and control of wide areas of territory.

When we arrive at the shepherds' for lunch, I am hungry and chilled by the brisk February winds and eager to simply spend the rest of the day sitting in a warm house, eating. I am not to be disappointed. The shepherds, Eliseo and Pasqualino, have a wood fire blazing out in front of the house and are spit-roasting everything from homemade sausages, to hunks of veal, to huge slabs of lamb. Instead of placing the meat on a dish, they serve it on layers of *pane carasau* (music paper)—a poetic and appropriate name for this traditional Sardinian bread, which is made in round paper-thin sheets that crackle, or "sing," when eaten.

Also on the table are plates of roasted yellow peppers, artichokes that have been boiled in vinegar and seasoned with herbs, and a large bowl of tomato-and-red-onion salad. The cheeses range from *caprino*, a soft, young goat's milk cheese with a mild, slightly oily consistency, to *fiore sardo*, a fresh ewe's milk cheese curdled without cooking, using lamb rennet, and then smoke-dried. There is also, of course, the superb *pecorino sardo*, a hard, light-yellow D.O.C. cheese made from the milk of Sardinian ewes.

To wash it all down, we delight in *cannonau*, an intense, garnet-colored D.O.C. wine with a 13.5-percent alcohol level that makes it the perfect accompaniment to the strong flavors of Sardinian food. The best known of all Sardinia's wines, *cannonau* is similar in flavor to *canonazo* of Seville, *granaxa* of Aragon, and *grenache* of France. Its legendary appeal was memorialized by Gabriele D'Annunzio, Italy's great poet, while on a trip through the Sardinian interior.

"To you, an island wine," he joked, "I consecrate my body and spirit. May you flow without ceasing from decanter to glass and from glass to throat. Until my final breath, may I know the joy of your aroma and have a nose that is your same vermillion color."

There are nine of us seated around the table that day including the two shepherds and their wives. For my part, I am thrilled to be in the midst of a food tradition dating back hundreds of years. For Francesca, a passionate archaelogist, the event's importance also lies in its ancient roots, although on a level somewhat removed from the carnal pleasures about to be introduced.

It being February, we sit inside, in a brick-ceilinged room warmed by a huge stone fire-place. The only sound, besides that of our voices commingled in Italian-style, everyone-speak-ing-at-once conversation, is the crackling of olive logs and the consistent chime of forks and knives tapping against porcelain. But just as Pasqualino's wife is about to serve dessert, the heavenly pastoral silence is interrupted by loud buzzing: a powerful motorcycle advancing up the hill.

"Roberto!" cries Eliseo's wife, Angela, as a good-looking teenage boy comes bursting through the doorway. "I thought you said you were having lunch with Don Fausto at the rectory."

"I thought so, too," he answers crossly. "But I was told to come home and begin studying my texts."

As Francesca and I finish the last of our wine, Angela hurriedly clears away the remains of the lunch and begins bustling around the room, warming the bread and setting a place for her son. "Eliseo," she bellows at one point, waving her arms in front of her husband, who has just that minute poured himself another glass of *mirto* (myrtle liqueuer). "*Vai e prenderni un cucino.*" Hurry and get a pillow for your son.

Uttering not one word of greeting to anyone in the room including his parents, a scowling Roberto struts toward the table, still wearing his helmet. His mind seems far away as he positions himself in front of his mother who, to my amazement, reaches up to unhook the strap and gently lifts the helmet from his head. Clearly glowing with adoration, she pulls a cloth from the waistband of her apron, mops his sweaty brow and carefully rearranges his hair. Finally she removes his jacket and caresses his face, all the while cooing a stream of dialectal endearments.

During all of this, Roberto remains still as a statue, his gaze fixed on the faraway hills visible through the window, his expression blank. His only movements are involuntary ones—the slight mechanical surrenders necessary to allow his jacket to be taken, his brow to be dried. He utters not a word and cedes no semblance of acknowledgment.

"I don't believe what I'm seeing," I think to myself. "Even in this land of total *mammismo,* where sons are so incredibly coddled as to render them handicapped but for the care and devotion of a besotted mother—even here, this behavior seems extreme."

"What's going on," I query Francesca in English, hoping no one will understand.

"I'll tell you later," she growls in a clipped, urgent tone of voice. "But don't do or say anything that would be in the slightest bit judgmental." The firmness of her words is accompanied by a *very* serious stare. "There's a perfectly good explanation for everything that's taking place although I know it's hard for you to believe right this minute."

The next few hours go by quickly, Eliseo and Pasqualino serving as ideal hosts. When we finish dessert—a trio of traditional local sweets that include *mustazzolus* (diamond-shaped cookies made with concentrated grape must, flour, yeast, and sugar), *sebadas* (fried cakes filled with cheese, bran, and grated citrus and topped with bitter [arbutus] honey), and *pirichittus* (snowball-like flour dumplings iced with lemon sugar), the two amiable shepherds cart out a bottle of arbutus liqueur and enage us in a game of *scopa*—an Italian card game similar to rummy.

The fragrance of the liqueur is addictive and reminds me of my first encounter with arbutus; then, it had been the actual plant which, in winter, is covered with small, round berries ranging in color from yellow to orange to fiery red. After tasting the berries and finding them very sweet, I had brought some home to Francesca and we had spent the afternoon making jam. That afternoon, Francesca had also introduced me to arbutus honey, which in contrast to the sweetness of the jam, was very bitter and smelled somewhat like unroasted coffee beans.

"Stop staring," Francesca admonishes me again and again as the card game progresses. "Pay attention to what's in your hand and forget about what's going on over there."

But no matter how hard I try, it is impossible not to notice Angela waiting on Roberto hand and foot. Literally! At one point, she even removes his shoes and socks and, using a soft cloth that looks like sheepskin, scrubs his feet with perfumed water.

"What the hell was that all about?" I ask as soon as Francesca and I have settled into her car for the return.

"It's a very long story and I truly hope you can suspend your American judgments long enough to hear it through."

Roberto, it seems, has been chosen to be "The Androgynous One" in a Carnival celebration that is to take place the next day—*martedi grasso* (Fat Tuesday)—in Oristano. "We call it *La Sartiglia*," Francesca explains, "and its aristocratic origin dates back to the days when Sardinia was ruled by Spain, hence the name whose Castilian version means 'ring.'

"Its main focus is a high-speed joust," she continues. "Six horsemen riding at full gallop, trying to snare a ring suspended over the main piazza on a ribbon of gold thread. The horsemen represent the Sardinian people and the ring is a metaphor for the hope that, after the retrenchment of Lent, there will be an abundant harvest. Everyone is dressed in period costumes, especially the leader, who rides on a white stallion and is called *L'Androgino*—the Androgynous One. This *Androgino* is always a teenage boy chosen by representatives of the various trade unions after a long and difficult selection process."

"That's all well and good," I interrupt, "but what does it have to do with the way Angela was slaving over her son's every desire?"

"This year Roberto has been chosen to be *L'Androgino*," she explains with forced patience. "And that being the case, he has now been transformed into a quasi-saintly figure. At least until Carnival is over. Contrary to your feeling that his mother was debased by her actions, the reality is that she was elevated by having such an important role to play." My friend is silent for a moment, her face taking on the worried expression of someone attempting to explain the inexplicable.

Francesca is not exactly what I would call a religious person but she is very traditional and very tied to the earth. Like many Sards, her spiritual practice blends traditional Catholicism with a firm belief in a variety of pagan deities. "Probably the best way for me to make you understand is to outline what Roberto will undergo tomorrow before the joust," she says, settling back against her seat. She checks to make sure I'm willing to listen, adjusts her rear-view mirror, and begins.

"Around noon, he will be transported to a dark underground room completely draped in branches, leaves, and flowers so as to resemble a womblike cave. The room has only one entrance and its location is kept secret from everyone except those directly involved in the ritual. In this symbolic 'uterus,' he is entrusted to the care of eight young girls—*massaieddas*—working under the direction of an older woman known as *sa massaia manna* or Great Earth Mother. Acting as priestesses, these nine females will direct Roberto to a chair placed on top of a table. From that moment on, his feet are not allowed to come into contact with the ground.

"The purpose," she adds quickly, anticipating my question, "is to prevent the energy acquired during the subsequent dressing ceremony from dispersing itself in the earth. *La Sartiglia* is the last great output of bacchanalian energy before the retrenchment of Lent sets in."

By now, I am completely enthralled. "Go on," I urge when she stops to make sure I'm still listening.

"At this point, Roberto is wearing only high leather boots and a pair of heavy velvet trousers. The girls clothe him in silence, placing a white buttonless shirt over his head and then they sew the shirt tight with colored threads. When the sewing is complete, they mask his face in white gauze.

"At that point the Earth Mother takes over, placing on Roberto's head a decidedly feminine mask designed to represent Everywoman. The mask—an extremely beautiful construction—is made with plaster of paris and painted creamy white with sensuous wine-colored lips. A bridal veil completes the costume—a long drape of white lace cascading over his shoulders and topped with an ornate black crown. The crown dates back to the Spanish occupation, when it was forbidden for men to wear the traditional Sardinian red caps."

"Why couldn't they wear their red caps?" I ask.

"Because they were a sign of national pride. Pride has always been our strongest attribute, so much so that every occupying power has always targeted our attachment to tradition as the first thing that had to go. But the harder they tried to humble us, the harder we held on."

"So, if that's the case, why wasn't there a return to the red caps once the Spanish had been cast out?" I query.

"Because," she says, with a hint of facetiousness. "Because by then *not* wearing them had become our tradition and changing back would have seemed too revolutionary."

Sounds perfectly plausible.

"Once dressed," Francesca continues as she exits the autostrada at Oristano, "Roberto will have been transformed into a completely androgynous figure—feminine in *la parte superiore* [from the waist up] and masculine in *la parte inferiore* [from the waist down.] The women will then lace their hands together to create a throne and, on that throne, transport Roberto to an adjacent room where they will place him—backward—astride a beautiful white stallion. And there he will stay, in that awkward position, until it is time for him to exit the so-called 'womb.'"

"And then?"

"The girls will place in his hands a bouquet of violets and periwinkles, referred to as *sa pippia de maiu*—the Child of May—and he will ride through the crowd, 'blessing' everyone by making signs of the cross over their heads with the bouquet. In return, the crowd will yell and scream and shower him with kernels of grain as they root for him to win the joust and, thus, insure the fecundity of the soil for the coming season." She turns to look at me and laughs naughtily.

"What?"

"*Sa pippia de maiu?* In polite circles, we say it means 'Child of May.' But the true meaning is closer to the vulgar terms for 'vagina,' and 'penis.' In fact, according to my grandfather, the festival was at one time much more overtly sexual, especially because it was originally tied exclusively to ancient pagan rituals celebrating nature. Now apparently, it has been taken over by the Church and cleaned up."

This is a story I have heard again and again as I traveled throughout Italy in search of festivals. Pagan rituals subsumed by the Catholic Church. At first, the Church tried positioning a Christian festival on the same day as the pagan one, hoping people would embrace one and forget the other. But when people continued to hold fast to their revered traditions concerning the Sun or the Moon or the gods and goddesses governing the earth, the Church dug in its heels and adjusted the stories, backing up religious feast days to incorporate long-held pagan beliefs.

One of my favorite examples is the feast of St. John the Baptist, which replaces the pagan festival of midsummer solstice. Instead of people lighting huge bonfires to stave off the gradual waning of the sun's powers and thus extend the growing season, we now have St. John's Day with all its religious processionry, but accompanied by enormous firework displays and people begging the saint's intercession on behalf of a bountiful harvest.

The next day I hurry out of bed to get a good spot for *La Sartiglia*. "Why didn't you tell me about this Carnival earlier," I had demanded after Francesca's tale of androgynous characters and equestrian jousts. "You know I'm here to work on a book about festival food."

"Because I'm perfectly happy to not have you include us. The last thing we need is a half-million Americans flooding Oristano for what is essentially a very personal celebration."

"But you said we should go early because there would be big crowds."

"Yes. People do come from all over the island. It's still, however, a distinctly Sardinian festival."

Her description of the events turned out to severely underestimate their beauty and power. Not that she had failed to convey each of the details in glowing terms. Only that it would be impossible to verbally do justice to a celebration of such breathtaking magnitude. The costumes, the horses, the drama, the devotion. From the first minute Roberto appeared on his magnificent white stallion, signing his blessing over the boisterous crowds, to the clanging of the church bells drowning out the drums and trumpets and *launeddas* (traditional Sardinian flutes), to the final joust and the excitement of enormous horses performing at full gallop, to the nougat sellers and meat roasters and wine bottlers and *maccarones* cookers and *zippulas* (dough fritters) fryers—all of it swirled around me in a kaleidoscope of colors and smells and sounds and uniquely unbelievable sensations. I embraced it all, even the swarming mobs whose insistence led to my brand-new sunglasses being reduced to a heap of plastic crumbs.

But it was the people, their belief in the sanctity of the Carnival tradition, their acceptance of the fact that, for the next forty days, there would be no more feasting and carousing. What I realized as I stood enraptured on the sidelines was that this was not a spectacle held for passive viewers, for tranquil Sards out for a little afternoon entertainment. This was a watershed event affirming their continued acceptance of the never-ending paradox between birth and death, between sacrifice and celebration. I had no doubt that most of the people around me would be penitent and vegetarian starting the next morning.

Francesca is not much of a "picker" when it comes to the consumption of festival food. Not for her the pork sandwich stalls and makeshift tables selling Signora Malvidia's lamb croquettes. Her idea of eating is to sit down at a fine restaurant and order from stem to stern. So to thank her for her patient company as I shuffled past every one of the food purveyors associated with *La Sartiglia*, I had promised her dinner at Il Portico, one of Oristano's finest restaurants. Located on Piazza Roma right off the Corso Umberto, the restaurant sits opposite the thirteenth-century Tower of Mariano II, once a fortified entrance to this ancient city.

In true carnival spirit, we order much more than we can ever consider eating. To start with, *cullurgjonis (*chard and mint ravioli) and *fregula* (small pellet-size pasta topped with oil, saffron, and pecorino cheese); as an entrée, a double order of spit-roasted lamb with fried potatoes and sautéed beet greens; for dessert, *aranzada* (moist pastries filled with honeyed orange peel, dried apples, and almonds) and *casadinas (*soft disks of dough filled with grated ewe's milk cheese aromatized with saffron, sugar, and grated orange peel).

"Sardinian cooking reflects our history," Francesca says when I comment on the tremendous complexity of flavors. "Each ingredient can be traced back to one or another of those who dominated the island over the centuries. In fact, Sardinia's culinary logo—the one imprinted on products labeled 'typical foods'—speaks to this diversity by having each letter of Sardinia printed in a different typeface."

In addition to sampling a great many local wines that day, we also treat ourselves to a smattering of local liqueurs. At Francesca's suggestion, I try three distillations made, respectively, from cactus pears, thistle bitters, and anise. We also try a somewhat hardier liquor called *filu e ferru.*

"It's a funny story," Francesca says when I inquire about the origins of the name (which means "metal wire"). "Toward the end of the last century, the government levied heavy taxes on the production of distilled beverages. So everyone began brewing in secret. My grandfather was especially fond of this particular liquor so he, like others, started making it in containers placed in a hole in the ground. He covered the hole with a trapdoor which, itself, was covered with dirt and then leveled. The only sign left to reveal its presence was a piece of wire tied to the still and sticking out just enough to show my grandfather where he could find his precious brew."

The dinner has been wonderful but I continue to be confused by menus featuring meat to the almost total exclusion of fish. "Again no seafood on the menu," I had commented when we were first presented with the choices.

"When are you going to accept the fact that Sardinians are simply not seafarers?" she said then.

"But it's so strange," I tell her now. "Here you are, completely surrounded by water. It's not as if we still live in an age where pirates are going to come raping and plundering."

"Oh no? Then you obviously haven't spent any time driving along the coast."

"What do you mean?" I look to see if she is joking, but her face is tight and somber.

"Haven't you seen the new, twenty-first-century marauders?" she says with barely concealed hostility. "The contractors and sun-worshippers and Rolex-wearing VIPs who are quickly 'cementifying' every inch of our shoreline?"

In truth, I had noticed that large sections of scenic coastline were now in the hands of foreign speculators. What was not already sold and developed had signs announcing availability; two-lane roads once used for a minimum number of vehicles were now clogged with everything from zooming Mercedes to barn-size campers. Even John Kennedy Jr. now has a house on the Costa Smeralda, Sardinia's glitzy northeast resort.

"Isn't the government doing anything to halt the development?" I suddenly sense a wisp of fear taking root in my stomach.

"Some, but it's hard to claim these newcomers are pushing out residents because most people have always lived in the interior. The only thing we can do is mount a campaign to preserve our green spaces, which is exactly the course the government is pursuing."

"But they obviously are not moving fast enough!" The anxiety in my voice is now unmistakable. "These people have to be stopped or they will completely take over!"

"Ohhhh!" Francesca laughs. "*Now* you understand." She holds up her key chain to which is attached a large leather oval inscribed with the words "*Furat chi de su mare veni.*"

"It's like I always told you," she says, signaling for the waiter to bring the check. "Invaders from the sea are once again coming to rob."

MINESTRONE COL IL PESTO

Summer Vegetable and Pasta Soup Perfumed with Pesto Cream

❦ Liguria ❦

SESTRI LEVANTE IS A GORGEOUS SEASIDE VILLAGE ON LIGURIA'S RIVIERA. *In summer, the beach is blanketed with bikini-clad bodies who have fled Genoa's dark, steamy streets for a holiday consisting of nothing more than reveling in the stunning backdrop of green rolling hills. On any given day, hundreds of languorous sailboats cruise the warm waters of the Mediterranean and the most urgent event on anyone's calendar is the necessity of remembering to buy another tube of suntan cream.*

But on the second weekend in August, this tiny slice of paradise is also the setting for La Sagra del Minestrone—*a rollicking vegetable soup festival, featuring this light summer soup served with a heap of bright green pesto cream. People sit at long tables slurping soup and drinking wine and afterward repair to the dance floor to swing to the music of a traditional orchestra while the stars shine down on the close of yet another perfect day.*

serves 4

Time: About 2 hours

Level of Difficulty: Easy

☩

SOUP

1 medium onion

1 clove garlic

1 celery stalk

5 to 6 sprigs fresh Italian parsley

4 tablespoons extra virgin olive oil

4 quarts salted water for cooking

1 Place the onion, garlic, celery, and parsley on a cutting board and mince finely. Heat the oil in a large, heavy-gauge soup pot over medium heat and sauté the vegetables for 8 minutes, stirring constantly.

2 Pour in 4 quarts salted water and bring to a boil. Add the cabbage, chard, potatoes, peas, beans, tomatoes, and salt and cook for 1 1/2 hours over medium heat.

3 Remove the potatoes with a slotted spoon, crumble, and return to the soup.

4 Add the pasta to the boiling soup and cook for 5 to 7 minutes, or until tender.

5 Meanwhile, put the oil, basil, garlic, and salt in a food processor and blend until just pureed but not foamy. Transfer to a bowl and stir in the cheese.

6 Distribute the soup among four large bowls. Place a dollop of pesto cream in the center and serve.

Make Ahead The soup can be made a day in advance through Step 3 and reheated just before using.

How to Serve As a one-dish meal paired with a mixed green salad.

Wine Suggestion **Dry White**

1/2 small head savoy cabbage, cored and roughly chopped

1 cup freshly chopped chard leaves, stems discarded or reserved

3 medium boiling potatoes, peeled

1 cup fresh or frozen shelled peas

1/2 cup freshly shelled cranberry or other beans

3 ripe Italian plum tomatoes, peeled, seeded, and cut into thin fillets

Salt to taste

8 ounces small pasta (ditalini, pennette, or elbows)

PESTO

2 tablespoons extra virgin olive oil

20 leaves fresh basil

1 clove garlic

1/4 teaspoon salt

1/4 cup freshly grated Parmigiano-Reggiano

203

FONDUTA ALLA VALDOSTANA

Thick and Creamy Alpine Cheese Soup

❧ Val d'Aosta ❧

IN THE ALPINE VILLAGE OF PERLOZ, THE NEXT-TO-LAST SUNDAY IN JULY IS *reserved for the* Festa du Pan Ner—*The Black Bread Festival. The village contains a 600-year-old outdoor oven, which today is used only for this festival. Local women prepare the dense, dark dough the night before; on the appointed day, the air is thick with the fragrance of baking bread, which is then served with—among other things—this wonderful soup that testifies to the region's pastoral origins.*

serves 4

Time: About 45 minutes

Level of Difficulty: Moderate

🌼

1 pound fontina cheese or other
   full-fat cow's milk cheese,
   at room temperature and
   cut into 1-inch cubes

1 tablespoon cornstarch

1 cup whole milk

2 large egg yolks, lightly beaten

4 thick slices dark, country-style
   bread, cut in half

1 Put the cheese and cornstarch in a heavy-gauge soup pot, add the milk, and stir to blend the ingredients. Cover and let rest for 30 minutes.

2 Cook the soup over very low heat, stirring constantly, taking care not to boil. When the cheese is completely melted, whisk in the eggs and continue to cook until the soup is thick and creamy, about 4 minutes.

3 Distribute among four bowls and serve immediately, each bowl flanked by 2 slices bread.

How to Serve As a one-dish meal paired with sautéed greens. Also works well when served as a fondue.

Wine Suggestion Dry or Medium-Sweet White

ZUPPA DI FARRO

Farro Soup

❧ Toscana ❧

ONE OF ITALY'S MORE ESOTERIC FESTIVALS MUST SURELY BE *LA FESTA DELL CIPRESSO*— *The Cypress Tree Festival—held in Silliano in mid-October. Cypresses are considered cemetary trees everywhere in Italy except for Tuscany, where they are prized as both a symbol of fertility (due to their phallic appearance) and—because of their long life and evergreen leaves—as a sign of immortality. In fact, cypress wood was used for Eros's arrows, Zeus's scepter, and Hercules's staff.*

This small local festival combines a spirit of thanksgiving for an abundant harvest with a sincere appreciation for the tall, slender trees that have come to define the beauty of the Tuscan landscape. In Silliano, a tiny village in the heart of the Garfagnana, an abundant harvest means only one thing: farro, a barleylike grain grown on terraced slopes throughout the area and used in everything from desserts to stews to casseroles to thick, hearty soups.

serves 4

Time: About 1 hour

Level of Difficulty: Easy

8 tablespoons extra virgin olive oil

1 medium onion, minced

1 small carrot, diced

1 celery stalk, diced

2 ounces pancetta, diced (optional)

1/2 cup farro*, soaked for 2 hours and drained

2 quarts Basic Vegetable Broth (page 459) or canned broth

1 1/2 cups canned Italian plum tomatoes

Salt to taste

Freshly ground black pepper to taste

Extra virgin olive oil

1 Heat half the oil in a large, heavy-gauge soup pot over medium-low heat and sauté the onion, carrot, celery, and pancetta for 8 minutes, stirring constantly.

2 Add the farro, broth, and tomatoes; cover, and cook for 45 minutes, or until the farro is tender. Add more water if necessary, but note that this is a very thick soup. Season with salt and pepper and serve drizzled with very good oil.

Make Ahead The soup can be prepared earlier and reheated (add more broth, if necessary) or made up to 3 days in advance, refrigerated, and reheated when ready to serve.

How to Serve As a one-dish meal paired with bread and a mixed green salad.

Wine Suggestion Dry White or Medium-bodied Red

Farro can be purchased in specialty food stores or ordered by mail from Toscana Saporita at 476. Do not confuse it with spelt, which is a softer look-alike that will have much too mushy a texture for this salad.

PASTARASA

Chicken Broth with Grated Pasta

❦ Emilia-Romagna ❧

ALTHOUGH NOT A FESTIVAL WITH EITHER ANCIENT TRADITIONS OR ANCIENT ORIGINS, Le Valli in Tavola *is a food-lover's dream. Professional chefs come from all over northern Italy to compete with each other over who can produce the best dish made strictly from local products. Held over the course of two weeks straddling May and June in one of Italy's most scenic natural reserves—Valli di Ostellato near Ferrara—the competition is judged by members of the general public, who pay aproximately $35 per person to partake of five-course meals accompanied by wines from the Po Delta region.*

The following quick, easy, and delicious soup recipe comes from Lino Rossi, chef of Francesco Rossi Restaurant in Bologna and the winner of the 1993 competition.

serves 4

Time: 45 minutes, excluding the two 2-hour resting periods

Level of Difficulty: Easy

⚖

1/4 cup unbleached all-purpose flour, sifted

3 large eggs, lightly beaten

3 tablespoons unflavored breadcrumbs

1/8 teaspoon freshly grated nutmeg

Salt to taste

1 quart chicken broth

6 tablespoons freshly grated Parmigiano-Reggiano

1 Put the flour, eggs, breadcrumbs, nutmeg, and a pinch of salt in a large bowl. Using floured hands, mix the ingredients until a solid ball forms. Cover and let rest for 30 minutes.

2 Grate the ball, using the fine end of a mandoline or the wide blade on a box grater, dust the pasta curls lightly with flour, cover, and dry for 2 hours.

3 Put the broth in a large soup pot. Bring to a boil and pour in the grated pasta. Cook over medium heat for 5 minutes. Remove from the heat and let sit for 2 hours.

4 Bring the cooled pasta once again to a boil and immediately remove from the heat. Stir in the grated cheese and serve.

Make Ahead The pasta ball can be made up to
2 days in advance, wrapped tightly in plastic, and
refrigerated until ready to grate.

How to Serve As a first course followed by grilled
chicken breasts with roasted root vegetables.

Wine Suggestion Medium-Sweet White

MINESTRONE D'ORZO ALLA TRENTINA

Barley, Chestnut, and White Bean Minestrone

208

❧ Trentino-Alto Adige ❧

WHEN OCTOBER COMES TO NORTHERN ITALY AND CHESTNUT TREES BEGIN *dropping those spiky green balls, there is not a region anywhere from the Alps to the Apuans—from the Po to the Serchio—that does not contain at least three dozen villages holding chestnut festivals. What makes Roncegno's special is the combination of events included in that festival. In addition to the variety of wonderful chestnut-based dishes, the live bands and dancing, this Sud-Tirolean village also includes both a demonstration of ancient tools and an event similar to American debutante balls, but without the gowns and crystal chandeliers. Unmarried men and women from seventeen to about twenty-five parade through the streets in their best clothes and accompanied by traditional music. Afterward, they are seated at specially set tables and served before anyone else. Said fifty-eight-year-old Martina Schmidt when I asked about the event's origins, "I can still remember the days when I marched in the parade and so does my mother." One of the cooks for Roncegno's chestnut festival, Frau Schmidt, is responsible for this wonderfully hearty and complex soup.*

serves 4

Time: 3 hours

Level of Difficulty: Easy

⚜

1/4 cup dried chestnuts, soaked for 2 hours in warm water, drained, and rinsed

1/4 cup dried cannelini beans, soaked for 12 hours in warm water, drained, and rinsed

1/4 cup pearl barley, rinsed and drained

3 quarts Basic Vegetable Broth (page 459) or canned vegetable broth

1 Place the chestnuts, cannelini beans, and barley in a heavy-gauge soup pot with the broth, cover, and cook over low heat for 2 hours, adding water if necessary.

2 Add the potatoes, carrots, and pig's foot or pancetta. Cover and cook for another hour, adding additional water if the soup becomes too dry. The consistency of the finished soup should be quite dense.

3 Fifteen minutes before serving, remove the pig's foot, scrape off any meat, and return to the pot. Season the soup with salt and plenty of pepper and add the parsley.

Make Ahead The soup through returning the pig's foot meat to the pot in Step 3 can be made up to 2 days in advance and reheated when ready to serve. Add water if the consistency is too dense.

How to Serve Can be a one-dish meal, if rounded out with a mixed green salad.

Wine Suggestion Dry or Medium-Sweet White

2 russet potatoes, peeled and cut into 1-inch cubes

2 medium carrots, peeled and cut into rounds

1 smoked pig's foot or 3 ounces smoked pancetta, cubed

Salt to taste

Freshly ground black pepper to taste

3 tablespoons freshly chopped Italian parsley

MINESTRA DI TENERUMI

Zucchini Leaf and Fresh Tomato Soup

❦ Sicilia ❦

MANY OF TODAY'S CHRISTIAN FESTIVALS WERE CREATED IN AN ATTEMPT TO *eradicate the memory of pagan ones. Few more clearly evoke this effort than the Holy Thursday and Good Friday ritual, held in San Fratello, a village in the province of Messina. The protagonists, called* abballu di li giudei, *are dressed in shirts and trousers made of red muslin adorned with black stripes and a long, black tail. Their faces are covered by masks, also made of red muslin, with a long patent-leather tongue hanging from the front. Their "helpers" carry chains made of fabric, which they whip against unsuspecting spectators.*

All day Thursday and Friday, these diabolical creatures race through the streets of San Fratello, in and out of dark alleys, yelling and screaming and scaring everyone who happens upon them. The Christian interpretation is that they represent Christ's murderers. In reality, their significance has more to do with the change of season, with the demons and other wordly spirits who were said to exert their influence during times of transition.

The following is a traditional Sicilian soup made during Holy Week. The unique, slightly bitter flavor created by the use of fresh zucchini leaves is perfectly counterbalanced by the sweetness of the tomatoes and sautéed onion.

serves 4

Time: 55 minutes

Level of Difficulty: Easy

❦

4 tablespoons extra virgin olive oil
1 small onion, thinly sliced
4 fresh basil leaves
4 quarts salted water for cooking

1 Heat the oil in a skillet over low heat and sauté the onion and basil for 4 minutes. Remove from the heat and set aside.

2 Meanwhile, bring the 4 quarts salted water to a boil over medium heat and cook the zucchini leaves for 20 minutes. Add the crushed tomatoes and, after 10 minutes, the taglierini. Cook for 8 minutes, stirring frequently.

3 Just before serving, add the onion and basil mixture and sprinkle with black pepper. Divide among four bowls and serve hot or lukewarm.

How to Serve For a one-dish meal, round out with a green salad and rustic bread.

Wine Suggestion Dry or Medium-Sweet White

1 pound fresh zucchini leaves or escarole, roughly chopped

1 pound ripe Italian plum tomatoes (about 6 or 7), sieved through a food mill

8 ounces taglierini, vermicelli, or angel hair pasta

Freshly ground black pepper to taste

211

PALLOTTOLINE IN BRODO

Beef Broth with Tiny Meatballs

❧ Sicilia ❧

THE HOLY THURSDAY AND GOOD FRIDAY RITUALS MENTIONED ON PAGE 210 HAVE *many counterparts throughout Sicily. In Adrana, in the province of Catania, on a stage divided into two sections, heaven and hell, five devils and their leader, Lucifer, argue the existence of Easter with a figure representing death, one representing the soul, and an angel played by a young boy, who eventually routs Lucifer simply by repeating the chant, "Viva Maria." Chaos and terror reign in the streets during the subsequent game of tag between the forces of Christ and the remaining devils. Very bizarre, which is probably why this simple and serene soup is needed afterward.*

serves 4

Time: 20 minutes

Level of Difficulty: Easy

8 ounces chopped sirloin

1 large egg

4 tablespoons freshly grated
    Parmigiano-Reggiano

2 tablespoons plain breadcrumbs

Salt to taste

Freshly ground black pepper
    to taste

4 tablespoons freshly chopped
    Italian parsley, divided

1 clove garlic, minced

1 quart Basic Meat Broth (page
    460) (or canned beef broth)

1¹/2 cups orzo

1 Place the chopped sirloin, egg, cheese, bread-crumbs, salt, pepper, 3 tablespoons parsley, and the garlic in a bowl. Using your hands, mix the ingredients until well blended. Form meatballs the size of walnuts and place on a platter.

2 Heat the broth to boiling over medium heat, add the meatballs, a few at a time, and cook for 5 minutes. Add the orzo and cook for 5 more minutes, or until the orzo is tender. Sprinkle with the remaining parsley and serve hot.

Make Ahead The meatballs, or simply the meatball mixture, can be made the day before, wrapped in plastic, and refrigerated until ready to use.

How to Serve As a first course followed by a platter of boiled meats and vegetables with parsley sauce.

Wine Suggestion Dry White

MACCU E FINOCCHIETTO

Cold Soup of Dried Favas and Wild Fennel

❦ Sicilia ❦

THROUGHOUT THE AGES, SICILIANS HAVE LOOKED UPON FAVA BEANS AS REPRESENTING *pagan deities. When Christianity conquered the island, nature-based gods and goddesses assumed a place of lesser importance, but the fava bean continued to be a major source of spiritual belief. They were appropriated by the Catholic Church and attached to St. Anthony of Padova, who was said to favor them as a symbol of Christ's purity. Anthony's feast, celebrated on June 13 throughout Sicily but most raucously in the villages around Ragusa, is cause for many-course feasts consisting of fava beans—or, in Sicilian,* maccu.

serves 4 to 6

Time: 2 hours

Level of Difficulty: Easy

⚶

2 cups dried fava beans, soaked in warm water for 24 hours, drained, and rinsed

3 quarts salted water for cooking

8 ounces wild or cultivated fennel (about 3/4 packed cup), finely chopped

4 tablespoons extra virgin olive oil

1 medium onion, minced

1 pound very ripe Italian plum tomatoes, peeled and diced (about 2 cups)

Salt to taste

Freshly ground black pepper to taste

8 ounces ditalini*

Ditalini, which means "small fingers," are a type of elbow macaroni; other types of small, cut pasta can be substituted.

1 Place the fava beans and 3 quarts salted water in a pot. Cover and cook for 1 1/2 hours over low heat. Add the fennel halfway through the cooking period.

2 Heat the oil in a skillet over low heat and sauté the onion for 8 minutes, or until translucent. Add the tomatoes, season with salt and pepper, and cook for 20 minutes, stirring occasionally.

3 Add the tomato mixture and the ditalini to the cooked fava beans, stirring to blend all ingredients. Cook for 8 minutes, or until the pasta is al dente. Transfer to a soup tureen, cool to room temperature, and serve.

Make Ahead The fava beans can be cooked the day before and refrigerated until needed. The tomato sauce can also be made the day before, sealed in an airtight container, and refrigerated until ready to use.

How to Serve As a one-dish meal with a mixed green salad.

Wine Suggestion Medium-bodied Red

PASSATO DI ZUCCA

Cream of Butternut Squash Soup

214

❧ Veneto ❧

VENICE'S VERSION OF A PALIO (THE SPLENDID MEDIEVAL HORSE/DONKEY RACES *held in many Italian cities) is the* Regata Storica, *which has taken place the first Sunday of every September since 1274. The Grand Canal's balconies and belvederes are draped with gorgeous antique tapestries in expectation of a cortege numbering dozens of exquisitely decorated gondolas, among which the* Bucintoro *stands out as the most spectacular. A gold-plated gondola with twenty oars, the* Bucintoro *was originally assigned to carry the doge, who, upon approaching the Rialto Bridge, would throw his ring into the water, thereby signifying his dominion over the city.*

Today, the regatta concludes with a two-oared gondola race; at one time, the participants consisted of gondolas powered by forty or fifty oars. The race begins in Castello quarter and terminates at Santa Chiara at the end of the Grand Canal—after which everyone partake of grand dinners that, invariable include this smooth, velvety soup made with butternut squash and Cream of Wheat.

serves 4

Time: 75 minutes

Level of Difficulty: Moderate

2 small butternut squash,
    peeled, seeded, and cut
    into 1-inch cubes
5 tablespoons unsalted butter
3 tablespoons semolina or
    Cream of Wheat
1 large egg, lightly beaten
Salt to taste

1 Put the squash in a medium saucepan, cover with water, and cook over medium heat for 30 minutes. Drain and pat dry, then pass through a food mill or crush with a hand masher.

2 Heat 3 tablespoons butter in a skillet and sauté the mashed squash for 4 minutes over medium heat, stirring constantly. Add the semolina, pouring in a steady stream and whisking until the mixture attains a pastelike consistency. Add the egg and continue to whisk until the ingredients are well blended. Season with salt and transfer to a soup pot.

3 Cook the squash mixture over low heat until heated through. Add the broth in a slow, steady stream and cook for 30 minutes, stirring constantly for the first 10 minutes and then occasionally.

4 Meanwhile, heat the remaining butter in a skillet and panfry the bread, tossing with a spatula until all sides are toasted.

5 To serve, divide the soup among four bowls, add a few croutons to each bowl, and sprinkle with parsley.

Make Ahead The squash can be prepared through Step 2 the day before, sealed in an airtight container, and refrigerated until necessary. The croutons can be made up to 3 days in advance, wrapped tightly in plastic, and refrigerated. When ready to use, they can be placed on a baking sheet and reheated in a 350°F oven for 10 minutes. The entire soup can be made a few days in advance and reheated just before serving. It can also be frozen for up to 3 weeks.

How to Serve As a first course followed by roast chicken and panfried potatoes with rosemary.

Wine Suggestion Medium-Sweet White

1 quart Basic Meat Broth
  (page 460) or canned
  beef broth
Four 3/4-inch-thick slices rustic
  bread, cut into 1-inch cubes
2 tablespoons chopped fresh
  Italian parsley

215

ZUPPA SARDA

Sardinian Bread and Mozzarella Soup

❧ S a r d i n i a ❧

ITALY FEATURES A GREAT MANY PROCESSIONS WHERE SAINTS ARE CARRIED THROUGH *the streets of various villages, but the longest distance traveled by any saint takes place in Arbus in southern Sardinia on the feast day of St. Anthony of Santadi. Held every year for three days in the middle of June,* La Sagra di S. Antonio di Santadi *begins in Arbus's central piazza and journeys twenty-three miles to the outskirts of Santadi. The procession leads off with an ox-drawn cart carrying the saint followed by seventy elegantly dressed horsemen, the local faithful, hundreds (sometimes thousands) of tourists, and about fifty traditional bands.*

Having reached Santadi, everyone sits down to a well-deserved meal whose first course consists of this very simple and unexpectedly delicious oven-baked soup.

serves 4

Time: 3¹/₂ hours

Level of Difficulty: Moderate

⚶

STOCK**
1 small chicken, washed
    and giblets removed
About 1 pound beef bones†
About 1 pound lamb bones†
About 1 pound veal bones or
    veal ribs†
1 onion, halved
1 carrot, scraped
1 celery stalk

1 Put all the ingredients for the stock in a large soup pot with 2 quarts salted water and cook for 2 to 3 hours. Remove the chicken and slice into individual pieces for a second course entrée. Strain the stock, discarding the bones and vegetables. Return the stock to the soup pot and maintain at a slow boil.

2 Preheat the oven to 400°F.

3 Arrange a layer of bread on the bottom of an ovenproof baking pan. Top with a layer of mozzarella and, using a fork, pierce a few holes in each slice. Continue layering in this manner until the bread and cheese have all been used.

In Val d'Aosta, this soup is made with fontina cheese instead of mozzarella and cinnamon-flavored melted butter is poured over the bread before baking. This alpine version forms the focus of Val d'Aosta's Festa della Seupa a la Vapelenentse *held in Valpelline in July on the Sunday preceding or following the July 27 feast of San Pantaleone.*

4 Pour the boiling stock over the layers and bake for 20 minutes. The finished soup should be quite dry since the bread will have absorbed most of the liquid. Ladle into individual bowls and serve immediately.

Make Ahead The broth can be made up to 3 days in advance and refrigerated in a sealed container. It can also be frozen for up to 3 weeks.

How to Serve As the first course followed by the boiled chicken that was used to make the broth. Cut the chicken into individual pieces and serve with marinated vegetables.

Wine Suggestion Medium-Sweet White

7 to 8 sprigs fresh Italian parsley
2 quarts salted water for cooking

SOUP

1 pound stale country-style bread, cut into 3/4-inch-thick slices
1 pound fresh mozzarella or other soft cheese, cut into 1/2-inch slices

---

Canned broth can be substituted for homemade stock, but the flavors will be quite different, since this particular soup is almost totally flavored by the stock. If using canned meat broth, boil the broth until it has reduced by half to condense the flavor.

†*A broth is as good as the ingredients that were used to make it. That having been said however, any of these types of bones can be eliminated and a double quantity of another type substituted. In terms of which kind of bone, any type will work to create a rich, flavorful broth. You can also make a double quantity and reserve the remaining half or freeze it for another use.*

FAVATA

Sausage and Fava Bean Soup

❧ Sardinia ❧

THE MENU FOR ARBUS'S *SAN ANTONIO SAGRA* GENERALLY FEATURES TWO OR THREE *selections for each course, decided according to the whims of the cooks, who generally hold their positions for twenty or thirty years. This succulent, meaty soup is the "whim" of Renzo Cannas, whose family holdings in southern Sardinia date back to the eighteenth century, when the island was ruled by the Aragons.*

serves 4

Time: 3¹/2 hours

Level of Difficulty: Moderate

¹/2 cup extra virgin olive oil

12 ounces spareribs

1 pound fennel sausage, removed from casing and crumbled

2 cups dried fava beans, soaked in warm water for 12 hours, drained, and rinsed

One 8-ounce piece lean pancetta

¹/2 small head savoy cabbage, cored and thinly sliced

2 to 3 stalks wild fennel, finely diced, or 2 to 3 finely diced fennel fronds

2 medium onions, thinly sliced

1 Heat the oil in a skillet over medium heat and sauté the spareribs and sausage for 10 to 12 minutes, turning frequently until the meat is lightly browned on all sides.

2 Add the fava beans and enough water to cover the meat and beans. Cover and cook over low heat for 1 hour.

3 Add the pancetta, cabbage, fennel, onions, and tomatoes. Season with salt and pepper, stir to blend all ingredients, cover, and cook for 2 hours, adding water as necessary to maintain a thick, soupy consistency.

4 Using a slotted spoon, remove the spareribs and cut into individual segments. Remove the pancetta and cut into a fine dice. Return both to the soup and heat through.

218

5 Toast the bread on both sides and divide among four bowls. Pour in the soup, arranging a few ribs in each bowl, dust with grated cheese, and serve.

Make Ahead The entire soup can be prepared through Step 4 a day or two in advance and reheated just before serving.

How to Serve As a one-dish meal paired with a green salad.

Wine Suggestion Medium-bodied Red

2 Italian plum tomatoes,
   peeled and diced
Salt to taste
Freshly ground black pepper
   to taste
Four 3/4-inch-thick slices
   country-style bread
4 tablespoons freshly grated
   Parmigiano-Reggiano

LE VIRTÚ

The Virtues (Many Vegetable Soup)

❧ Abruzzo ❧

EVERY CITY IN SOUTHERN ITALY HAS ITS MAY 1 RITUALS CELEBRATING THE ARRIVAL *of* la bella stagione—*the beautiful season. In the Abruzzo—especially in Teramano—those celebrations always include the following soup, whose ingredients include both dried legumes left over from winter and the first fresh spring vegetables. The name indicates the high esteem in which Italians hold vegetables. In some cities, the soup is called* Le Sette Virtú—*The Seven Virtues—for the seven ingredients included. Teramano's is obviously a much more virtuous creation.*

serves 6

Time: About 5 hours

Level of Difficulty: Moderate

⚶

1/4 cup dried fava beans, soaked
    for 24 hours in warm water,
    drained, and rinsed

1/4 cup dried chick peas, soaked
    with the fava beans, drained,
    and rinsed

1/4 cup dried cannelini beans,
    soaked for 12 hours in warm
    water, drained, and rinsed

1/4 cup dried lentils

1/4 cup dried split peas, soaked
    with the cannelini, drained,
    and rinsed

1 prosciutto bone or smoked ham
    bone, soaked for 12 hours

1 pig's foot, washed in running
    water and soaked with the
    prosciutto bone

1 Put the fava beans and chick peas in a large, heavy-gauge soup pot with enough water to cover by 2 inches. Cover and cook over medium heat for 1 1/2 hours. Add the cannelini, lentils, peas, and another 1 quart of water, and continue to cook for 1 hour.

2 Put the prosciutto bone and pig's foot in another heavy-gauge pot with enough water to cover by 2 inches. Cover and cook for 2 1/2 hours over medium heat.

3 Heat the oil in a skillet over low heat and sauté the pancetta, onion, and garlic for 8 minutes, stirring constantly. Add the tomatoes and cook for 5 minutes longer.

4 Using a slotted spoon, remove the cooked meats, reserving the broth. Cut any meat away from the prosciutto bone and pig's foot. Dice and return to the pot with the meat broth. Discard the bones.

Drain the cooked legumes and add to the meat broth along with the chard, endive, carrot, and the pancetta mixture. Season with salt and pepper, stir to blend all ingredients, cover, and cook for 2 hours over low heat.

5 Stir in the pasta and cook for 4 minutes. Add the marjoram, parsley, and mint and cook for 5 more minutes. Stir in the grated cheese, cool for 30 minutes, and serve.

Make Ahead The soup can be prepared through Step 4 up to a day or two in advance and refrigerated in a sealed container until needed.

How to Serve As a hearty one-dish meal or following an appetizer of marinated vegetables.

Wine Suggestion Medium-bodied Red

3 tablespoons extra virgin olive oil

2 ounces pancetta, diced

1 medium onion, diced

2 cloves garlic, minced

4 ripe Italian plum tomatoes, peeled, seeded, and diced

8 ribs fresh chard, stems removed and roughly chopped

12 leaves curly endive, cored and roughly chopped

1 medium carrot, peeled and thinly sliced

Salt to taste

Freshly ground black pepper to taste

8 ounces mixed small-cut pasta, such as ditalini, fusilli, rotelle, or farfalle or 8 ounces other small pasta

3 tablespoons chopped fresh marjoram

3 tablespoons chopped fresh Italian parsley

1 tablespoon chopped fresh mint

3 tablespoons freshly grated pecorino

ZUPPA DI COZZE

Soup Made with Mussels and Fresh Tomatoes

222

❦ Sicilia ❦

BECAUSE EVEN PARTICIPANTS AT BREAD FESTIVALS SUCH AS AGRIGENTO'S *Sagra del Grano (Wheat Festival) cannot live by bread alone, designated cooks have taken to accompanying the traditional anchovy rolls described on page 224 with this wonderful fish soup. One of the most popular of wheat festivals, Agrigento's coincides very nicely with St. Calogero's feast day, St. Calogero being the saint most often associated with grain since he spent most of his life walking through the Sicilian countryside handing out rolls of bread to the poor.*

While Sicilian mussels tend to be much larger and fresher than those in most other parts of the country, the soup will taste equally delectable even if smaller specimens are used.

serves 4

Time: About 30 minutes

Level of Difficulty: Easy

3 tablespoons extra virgin olive oil

1 garlic clove, crushed

1/2 small dried chili

1 pound ripe Italian plum tomatoes, peeled, seeded, and diced

Salt to taste

2 pounds blue mussels, scraped, bearded, and thoroughly washed

1 cup dry white wine

1 Heat the oil in a large skillet over low heat. Sauté the garlic and chili until the garlic turns golden, about 3 minutes. Remove and discard both the garlic and chili. Increase the heat to medium, add the tomatoes, and cook for 10 minutes, stirring constantly. Season with salt.

2 Increase the heat to high and add the mussels. Cover and cook for 5 to 7 minutes, shaking the pan every minute, until the mussels have all opened. Discard any unopened mussels.

3 Pour the wine over the mussels and cook until the wine evaporates, about 3 to 4 minutes. Add the minced garlic and parsley, stir to blend all ingredients, and heat through.

4 Distribute the croutons among four bowls, top with soup, and serve immediately.

How to Serve As a first course followed by grilled or poached fish with parsley sauce and sautéed zucchini.

Wine Suggestion **Dry White**

1 clove garlic, minced

2 tablespoons freshly chopped Italian parsley

4 slices country-style bread, cut into croutons and fried in olive oil

CRISPEDDI

Deep-fried Anchovy Rolls

❦ Sicilia ❧

THERE ARE MANY THINGS ABOUT AGRIGENTO'S WHEAT FESTIVAL (SEE PAGE 222) *that will remain in my mind. One that I'm sure I won't forget is the early morning procession in honor of San Caló (as he is affectionately referred to by locals) and the number of men, women, and children who would break out from behind the barricades to wipe the saint's plaster of paris brow with their handkerchiefs. According to local legend (and no one could tell me its origin), Caló sweats profusely on his feast day and, thus, requires frequent ministrations of this sort. The other fond memory I retain is of these wonderfully crisp rolls, hand-crafted by the women of Agrigento and fried on the spot in huge vats of oil set up all over the city.*

makes about 20 rolls

Time: About 1 hour plus 3 hours rising

Level of Difficulty: Moderate

4 cups unbleached all-purpose flour, sifted

1/2 teaspoon active dry yeast, dissolved in 1/4 cup warm water until foamy

2 tablespoons extra virgin olive oil

7 salt-packed anchovies, filleted (see page 25)

Olive oil for frying

1 Put 1 cup flour in a large bowl, add the yeast, and, with floured hands, work the dough into a ball. Cover with a clean cloth and let rise for 1 hour.

2 Transfer the dough to a floured work surface. Add the remaining flour and the oil and knead for 10 minutes, adding water as needed to create a smooth, soft dough. Place in a floured bowl, cover, and let rise for 2 hours.

3 Put the dough on a floured surface, knead for 5 minutes, and pinch off walnut-size pieces of dough. Roll each into 3-inch-long oval rolls. Place a piece of anchovy fillet on each and enclose it by pressing together the long sides of dough.

Olive oil is hot enough for frying when it sizzles around a test piece of bread.

4 Heat 3 inches of oil in a deep skillet until the temperature reaches 375°F.* Fry the crispeddi, a few at a time, for 7 to 9 minutes, or until golden brown on all sides. Drain on paper towels and serve.

Make Ahead The dough can be made earlier in the day, wrapped tightly in plastic wrap, and refrigerated until ready to use. It can also be frozen for up to 3 weeks and thawed when necessary.

How to Serve With soups, salads, or as a snack

Wine Suggestion Depends on the dishes with which it is paired.

TARALLI CON IL PEPE

Braided Pepper Biscuits

❧ Campania ❧

THE LARGEST PROCESSION IN ITALY TAKES PLACE SEPTEMBER 7, TEN MILES OUTSIDE *the city of Avellino, just east of Naples. More than a million people come each year to climb the 3,600-foot mountain blanketed with beech trees and crowned at the summit by the sanctuary of La Madonna di Montevergine. The pilgrimage begins in the middle of the night and includes sojourns at many places of historical and architectural importance, including—at 1,200 feet—the Loreto Monastery, a twelfth-century palace (rebuilt after the earthquake of 1769) that once served as the vernal seat of Montevergine's abbot. Along the way, pilgrims stop to sleep, eat, drink, sing, dance, chant, pray, play the drums—all outdoors and all with true festival spirit. At one time, it was characteristic to bring along the following hard biscuits, which were consumed with various types of salumi and homemade red wine.*

makes about 40 taralli

Time: 1¹/2 hours plus 1¹/2 hours for rising

Level of Difficulty: Moderate

꽃

1¹/2 cups unbleached all purpose flour, sifted

Salt to taste

¹/2 teaspoon freshly ground black pepper

¹/2 teaspoon active dry yeast, dissolved in ¹/2 cup warm water until foamy

3 tablespoons unsalted butter, melted

2 tablespoons coarsely ground polenta

1 Heap the flour on a work surface and make a well in the center. Add a pinch of salt, the pepper, yeast, and butter. Stir with a fork, incorporating a little flour each time and adding more water as needed to form a solid ball; some flour may remain. Knead for 15 minutes, or until the dough is smooth and soft.

2 Pinch off a walnut-size piece of dough and roll into an 8-inch rope. Holding each end of the rope in separate hands, twist the ends a few times in opposite directions—right hand twisting forward, left hand twisting back—as if forming a rolled cord. Seal the two ends together to create a circle and place on a floured board. Continue until all the dough is used up. Cover the dough with a clean cloth and let rise for 1¹/2 hours.

3 Preheat the oven to 350°F. Sprinkle a baking pan with polenta.

4 Transfer the dough to the baking pan. Bake for 1 hour. Remove from the oven and cool completely before serving.

Make Ahead The biscuits can be made up to a week in advance and kept in a sealed container until needed.

How to Serve Makes a wonderful snack when heated and paired with red wine. Can also form part of a mealtime bread basket, or be served with soups and salads.

Wine Suggestion Full-bodied Red

TORTA DI PROSCIUTTO

Prosciutto and Black Pepper Pizza

228

❧ Campania ❧

THE TWELFTH-CENTURY PALACE MENTIONED ON PAGE 226 ACTUALLY REPLACED A *pavillion erected to the goddess Diana, whose followers can still be found journeying to the summit alongside unsuspecting Christian pilgrims. Pagan, Christian, or undecided, Montevergine is worth the trip, if only for the stunning panoramic view of the Irpinia valley. For sustenance, you might want to do like many of the pilgrims and take along a slice or two of this buttery prosciutto pizza. In olden days, pork fatback was used in place of the butter.*

serves 4

Time: 1 hour plus 1 hour rising

Level of Difficulty: Moderate

4 cups unbleached all-purpose flour, sifted

1/2 teaspoon active dry yeast, dissolved in 1/2 cup warm water until foamy

4 tablespoons unsalted butter at room temperature

Salt to taste

Freshly ground black pepper to taste

1 Heap the flour on a work surface and make a well in the center. Add the the yeast, 2 tablespoons of the butter, salt, pepper, and 1 cup warm water. Beat with a fork, incorporating a little flour at a time until a solid ball has formed. Knead for 10 to 15 minutes, or until smooth and elastic. Butter a bowl and put the dough inside. Cover with a clean cloth and let rise for 1 hour.

2 Meanwhile, put the diced eggs, prosciutto, and the remaining 2 tablespoons butter in a bowl and set aside.

3 Preheat the oven to 500°F.

4 Butter a 10-inch-round baking pan with sides at least 2 inches high. Using your hands, shape the dough into a large, rough circle. Baste with half the melted butter and fold in half. Reshape roughly into the original circle and dust the surface with black pepper. Knead for 5 minutes, or until all ingredients are well incorporated, and shape into a 12-inch circle. Arrange in the pan and press the excess dough against the sides.

5 Top the dough with the egg, prosciutto, and butter mixture and work the overlapping edges into a rolled crust. Baste with half the remaining butter and bake for 20 minutes, basting the surface two or three times with the rest of the butter. Cut into wedges and serve hot or cold.

Make Ahead The dough can be made earlier in the day, wrapped tightly in plastic wrap, and refrigerated until ready to use. It can also be frozen for up to 3 weeks and thawed when necessary.

How to Serve As an appetizer, an accompaniment to soups or salads, or as an entrée paired with sautéed greens or a green salad.

Wine Suggestion Medium-bodied Red

1 cup warm water

4 large eggs, hard-boiled, peeled, and diced

One 12-ounce slab prosciutto, diced

8 tablespoons (1 stick) unsalted butter, melted

229

SCHIACCIATA AL ROSMARINO

Rosemary Focaccia

❦ Umbria ❦

ON GOOD FRIDAY, GUBBIO IN CENTRAL UMBRIA HOSTS A CHORAL PROCESSION *whose vocal magnificence sends shivers up my spine. Two choruses parade side by side, their voices battling with each other to create an atmosphere of incredible spiritual tension. For aficionados of liturgical music, this event is a must. This is a traditional Umbrian schiacciata, which means "pressed flat."*

serves 4

Time: About 45 minutes plus 1 hour rising

Level of Difficulty: Moderate

1 recipe Basic Pizza Dough (page 463)

Unbleached all-purpose flour for sprinkling

3 tablespoons extra virgin olive oil

1 tablespoon coarsely ground cornmeal

3 tablespoons chopped fresh rosemary

Salt to taste

1 Put the bread dough on a floured work surface and make a large hole in the center without breaking through the underside. Pour in the oil. Knead for 5 minutes, or until the oil is completely incorporated. Transfer to an oiled bowl, cover with a clean cloth, and let rise for 1 hour.

2 Preheat the oven to 500°F. Sprinkle a 12-inch-square baking pan with cornmeal.˙

3 Using a rolling pin, roll the dough on a floured surface into a 12-inch circle. Transfer to the baking pan. Distribute the rosemary over the surface of the dough, pressing the needles down into the dough with your fingers. Salt and bake for 15 minutes, or until golden. Remove from the oven and serve hot or cold.

˙*If using a pizza stone or tiles instead, preheat the tiles for 15 minutes. Sprinkle some cornmeal on a wooden or metal peel, top with the schiacciata, and slide onto the stone.*

Make Ahead The dough can be made earlier in the day, wrapped tightly in plastic wrap, and refrigerated until ready to use. It can also be frozen for up to 3 weeks and thawed when necessary.

How to Serve With soups, salads, or as an accompaniment to a vegetable entrée. Sliced into thin wedges, can also form part of a mealtime bread basket.

Wine Suggestion Depends on the dishes with which it is paired.

FITASCETTA

Onion and Mozzarella Ring Bread

232

❦ Lombardia ❦

A *PALIO* IS A CONTEST BETWEEN A TOWN'S HISTORICAL RIVAL FACTIONS.
*Throughout Italy, palios are fought between riders on horses, riders on donkeys, and even riderless
pigs. But Gessate's* Palio del Pane *is fought between people armed with buckets of water, salt, flour, and
yeast—in other words, all the ingredients necessary for a bread bakeoff. Elegantly dressed in seventeenth-century costumes, the factions "battle" in the huge courtyard of one of Gessate's most beautiful
villas. The subsequent "peace" expresses itself in the various loaves of bread offered to the spectators,
among them, this wonderfully light ring topped with sautéed onions and rounds of fresh mozzarella.*

serves 4

Time: About 1 hour plus 1¹/₂
hours rising

Level of Difficulty: Moderate

⅊

1 recipe Basic Pizza Dough
    (page 463)
Unbleached all-purpose flour
    for sprinkling
3 tablespoons extra virgin olive oil
4 tablespoons unsalted butter
3 large red onions, thinly sliced
Salt to taste
¹/₂ teaspoon sugar
1 tablespoon coarsely ground
    cornmeal
8 ounces fresh mozzarella,
    cut into thin strips

1 Put the bread dough on a floured work
surface and make a large hole in the center without
breaking through the underside. Pour in the oil.
Knead for 5 minutes, or until the oil is completely
incorporated. Transfer to an oiled bowl, cover with
a clean cloth, and let rise for 1 hour.

2 Heat the butter in a skillet over low heat and
sauté the onions for 8 minutes, stirring frequently.
Season with salt and the sugar.

3 Sprinkle a 10 x 12-inch baking pan with
cornmeal. Form the dough into a long, thick sausage
shape. Roll into a ring and press the ends together
to seal. Transfer to a baking pan spread with the
cornmeal. Cover and let rise for 30 minutes.

4 Preheat the oven to 350°F.

5 Create a large hollow on the surface of the dough and fill with the sautéed onions. Top with the mozzarella strips and bake for 30 minutes. Remove from the oven, and serve hot or cold, cut into wedges.

Make Ahead The dough can be made earlier in the day, wrapped tightly in plastic wrap, and refrigerated until ready to use. It can also be frozen for up to 3 weeks and thawed when necessary.

How to Serve With soups, salads, as a snack, or as an accompaniment to a vegetable entrée. Sliced into thick wedges, can also form part of a mealtime bread basket.

Wine Suggestion Depends on the dishes with which it is paired.

PIADINA ROMAGNOLA

Toasted Flat Bread

❧ Emilia-Romagna ❧

PIADINA, PIDA, PIADA, PIÉ—ALL NAMES FOR THIS SIMPLE, FLAT FOCACCIA BAKED *between wrought-iron plates over an open fire. Long associated with Emilia-Romagna, where in ancient times it was prized as both a bread and a dinner plate upon which meats and cheeses could be placed, piadina has as many different methods of preparation as there are fish in the sea. But in Milano Marittima, in the Romagnola province of Ravenna, there is ultimately only one way to make piadina, and that way is decided after a long elimination involving bakeoffs and popular referendums and a panel of judges chosen by the area's restaurateurs. The event is known as* Piadina d'Autore, *held in Viale Romagna sometime during the month of June. Eight finalists come together to prepare and present their piadina recipe and the results are presented to the crowd who cheer more or less enthusiastically for each contestant. At the end of the evening, the winner is crowned and leads off the first dance.*

makes 12 piadini

Time: About 45 minutes plus
1 hour rising

Level of Difficulty: Moderate

6 cups unbleached all-purpose
   flour, sifted

Salt to taste

3 tablespoons unsalted butter,
   melted

$1/2$ teaspoon active dry yeast,
   dissolved in $1/2$ cup warm
   water until foamy

1 cup water

1 Heap the flour on a flat work surface and make a well in the center. Add the salt, butter, yeast, and half the water. Beat with a fork, incorporating a little of the flour at a time and adding water as needed for a slightly dense dough; some flour may remain. Knead for 15 minutes, or until smooth and elastic. Butter a bowl and put the dough in, cover with a clean cloth, then transfer to a greased bowl. Let rise for 1 hour.

2 Knead the dough for another 5 minutes and then divide into 12 walnut-size pieces. Roll each piece into a 6- to 8-inch circle that is $1/8$ inch thick.

3 Heat an 8-inch nonstick skillet over medium heat and cook the piadini one at a time for 4 to 6 minutes per side. The finished bread will have some charring on its surface.

Make Ahead The dough can be made earlier in the day, wrapped tightly in plastic wrap, and refrigerated until ready to use. It can also be frozen for up to 3 weeks and thawed when necessary.

How to Serve With soups, salads, as a snack, or as an accompaniment to a vegetable entrée. Sliced into thick wedges, can also form part of a mealtime bread basket.

Wine Suggestion Depends on the dishes with which it is served.

CULLURELLI

Fried Potato Pizzette

✣ Calabria ✣

CULLURELLI ARE SMALL FRIED PIZZAS ASSOCIATED WITH THE TRADITIONAL *meatless meals served on Christmas Eve. In Soverato, a small coastal village on the instep of the boot, these delicious pizzas are made outdoors in huge community frying pans placed over wood-burning fires. When I was there two years ago, Signora Imelda D'Onoria gave me a lesson in tossing large pizzas up in the air in the way usually associated with Neapolitans. Try as I might, I was never able to catch the pizza without putting my fist through the dough. "Next time you come back," she said, "you'll be older and it will be easier." Before that moment comes to pass, I use a rolling pin.*

makes about 40 small pizzas

Time: About 45 minutes plus
1 hour rising

Level of Difficulty: Moderate

1/2 teaspoon active dry yeast

1 cup warm water

4 cups unbleached all-purpose
    flour, sifted

1 tablespoon extra virgin olive oil

2 medium boiling potatoes,
    boiled, peeled, and put
    through a food mill

Salt to taste

Olive oil for frying

Confectioner's sugar for dusting

1 Stir the yeast into 1/2 cup warm water. Place the cup in a saucepan with enough very hot water to come halfway up the sides of the cup. Let rest for 15 minutes, or until foamy.

2 Put 3 cups flour and a pinch of salt in the bowl of a food processor and, with the motor running, pour the yeast mixture through the feed tube. Add the tablespoon oil and the remaining 1/2 cup warm water and process until a thick ball has formed. Put the dough on a floured work surface and knead until smooth and feels slightly wet. Oil a bowl, put in the dough, cover with a clean cloth, and let rise for 1 hour.

3 Put the dough on a floured work surface and top with the mashed potatoes and a pinch of salt. Knead the mixture until smooth and elastic, adding more water as needed.

To test the temperature of the oil, you can put a cube of bread into the skillet. When it sizzles around the edges and turns golden almost immediately, the oil is the right temperature.

4 Pinch off a walnut-size piece of dough and roll into a 2-inch round. Put the round on a lightly floured surface and continue rolling until all the dough has been used.

5 Heat 2 inches of oil in a heavy skillet to 375°F.* Fry the pizza rounds, two or three at a time, until golden on both sides. Remove with a slotted spoon, drain on paper towels, dust with powdered sugar, and serve immediately.

How to Serve **With soups, salads, or as a snack.**

Wine Suggestion **Dry White**

SFINCIONE DI SAN VITO

Saint Vito's Day Pizza

❧ Sicilia ❧

IT TOOK A GREAT DEAL OF PERSONAL DISCIPLINE TO WITNESS ALL THE EVENTS *included in the St. Vito's Day Festival (*'U fistinu di Santu Vitu*) celebrated by residents of Mazaro del Vallo, a port city in southern Sicily in the third week of August. The heart of the festival takes place on Thursday, with a colorful procession led by fishermen carrying the martyred saint's relics and starting at 4:00 A.M.!!! At 5:00 A.M., it's time for fireworks on the beach (*socu di focu a diunu*). Then, after a civilized break for breakfast and a shower, there's a second procession, this one consisting of "living floats"—floats containing actors and actresses portraying scenes from the life of St. Vito. Throughout Mazaro, residents erect food stalls selling fresh fish, cookies and candies, and the following pizza made solely on this day.*

serves 4

Time: About 1 hour

Level of Difficulty: Moderate

8 tablespoons extra virgin olive oil

1 clove garlic, minced

1 pound ripe Italian plum
    tomatoes, peeled, seeded,
    and roughly chopped
    (about 3 cups)

Salt to taste

Freshly ground black pepper
    to taste

12 fresh sardines, heads removed
    and filleted (see directions,
    page 372)

1 Heat 4 tablespoons oil in a skillet over low heat and sauté the garlic for 5 minutes, stirring constantly. Add the tomatoes, season with salt and pepper, and cook for 30 minutes.

2 Preheat the oven to 350°F. Sprinkle a 10-inch round pizza pan with cornmeal.*

3 Add half the sardine fillets to the sauce and cook for 10 minutes, stirring frequently.

4 Put the dough on a floured surface and roll into a 10-inch circle, and place in the pizza pan. Brush with olive oil and spread with half the tomato sauce. Top with the caciocavallo and bake for 20 minutes.

If using a pizza stone or tiles instead, preheat the tiles for 15 minutes. Sprinkle some cornmeal on a wooden or metal peel, top with the pizza, and slide onto the stone.

5 Bake for 20 minutes. Remove from the oven, top with the remaining sauce and the remaining sardines. Drizzle with the remaining oil and bake for 10 more minutes. Remove from the oven, cut into wedges, and serve immediately.

How to Serve As a one-dish meal paired with a mixed green salad.

Wine Suggestion Medium- or Full-bodied Red

1 recipe Basic Pizza Dough (page 463)

1 tablespoon coarsely ground cornmeal

3 ounces caciocavallo or provolone, cut into 1/2-inch cubes

239

FANTASIA DI PIZZETTE

Four Variations of Pizza Tartlets

❧ Sicilia ❧

Throughout Italy, there are as many toppings for pizza as for pasta. Just about any combination of ingredients can be transformed into a crispy baked delicacy. Pizza tartlets are a common festival food among Sicilians and the following varieties are just four of the many possibilities that confounded my decision-making powers as I stood in front of Antonietta DeBenedetto's food stall at Marzaro's fistinu di Santu Vitu *(see page 238).*

serves 4

Time: About 2 hours plus rising

Level of Difficulty: Advanced

Equipment: Twelve 3-inch-round individual tart pans

⚜

1 small red pepper
1 small yellow pepper
Approximately 1/2 cup extra
    virgin olive oil
1 small eggplant, peeled and cut
    into 1/2-inch cubes
Salt to taste
Freshly ground black pepper
    to taste
1 large onion, thinly sliced
5 tablespoons water
5 small zucchini
4 ripe Italian plum tomatoes,
    halved
1 teaspoon finely chopped
    fresh mint

1 Using tongs, hold the peppers over an open flame until the skins are completely charred.* Place in a paper bag, seal, and let rest for 10 minutes. Remove the peppers, peel away the charred skin, cut in half, remove the seeds, and slice into thin strips.

2 Heat 3 tablespoons oil in a skillet over medium heat and sauté the eggplant for 7 to 9 minutes, stirring constantly. Season with salt and pepper, transfer to a bowl, and set aside.

3 Heat 2 tablespoons oil in the same skillet over medium heat. Sauté the onion, adding 5 tablespoons water, and cook for 8 minutes, or until completely wilted. Transfer to another bowl and set aside.

4 Parboil the zucchini in salted water for 5 minutes. Drain, cut into thin slices, and set aside.

5 Heat 2 tablespoons oil in the same skillet over high heat. Sauté the tomatoes for 8 minutes, stirring constantly. Transfer to a bowl, toss with the mint, and set aside.

*Alternately, the peppers place the peppers in a roasting pan and broil—turning when necessary—until the skins are charred on all sides.

6 Heat 3 tablespoons oil in a skillet over medium heat. Sauté the mushrooms for 4 minutes, stirring constantly. Season with salt and pepper, transfer to a bowl, and set aside.

7 Blanch the arugula in boiling salted water for 2 minutes. Drain and squeeze dry. Heat 3 tablespoons oil in a skillet over low heat and sauté the garlic for 4 minutes. Add the arugula, season with salt and pepper, and sauté for 6 minutes, stirring constantly. Set aside.

8 Preheat the oven to 450°F. Oil the tart pans.

9 Put the dough on a floured surface and roll into a large rectangle about 1/8 inch thick. Cut into twelve 3-inch circles and arrange in the tart pans, pressing the edges against the sides. Cover the surface of each tart with waxed or parchment paper and weight down with 15 to 20 beans or commercial pie weights.

10 Bake the tarts for 10 minutes. Remove the beans and paper. Increase the oven temperature to 500°F. Top three pizzettes with zucchini, tomatoes, and scamorza; three with peppers, mushrooms, and fontina; three with eggplant, tuna, mozzarella, and olives; and three with arugula and paprika. Drizzle the 12 pizzettes with the remaining oil and bake for 10 minutes. Remove from the tart pans and serve immediately.

How to Serve As an appetizer or as part of a party buffet. Three large (9- or 10-inch) pizzas can be made instead of twelve individual ones. Simply roll the dough into three circles, place in baking pans or on a pizza stone or tiles, top with the appropriate combinations, and bake for 15 to 20 minutes, or until the undersides of the crusts are golden.

Wine Suggestion Medium-bodied Red

8 ounces mixed wild mushrooms, such as shiitake, porcini, and chanterelles, finely minced

4 cups packed arugula, stemmed

1 clove garlic, minced

1 recipe Basic Pizza Dough (page 463)

1 pound dried beans for weighting

2 ounces smoked scamorza or smoked mozzarella, cut into 1/2-inch cubes

2 ounces fontina, shaved

2 ounces bufala or cow's milk mozzarella, cut into 1/2-inch cubes

2 ounces oil-packed tuna, drained

12 black olives, pitted and chopped

1/2 teaspoon paprika

FOCACCIA AL FORMAGGIO

Cheese-stuffed Focaccia

242

❧ Liguria ❧

AS SOON AS THE FOCACCIAS ARE PULLED OUT OF THE OVEN, THEY'RE IMMEDIATELY *consumed by the thousands of spectators come to celebrate Recco's* Festa della Focaccia *every third Sunday of May. The queen of the festival is this cheese-stuffed focaccia, served exclusively in the late afternoon. Since 1990, when festival organizers built an oven large enough to house a focaccia twelve feet in diameter, they have thrilled the crowds by tearing wedges right from the pan and handing them out to anyone lucky enough to be in the front lines.*

serves 4

Time: 1 hour plus 2 hours rising

Level of Difficulty: Moderate

⚶

¹/₂ teaspoon active dry yeast

2 cups warm water

4 cups unbleached all-purpose
    flour, sifted

Salt to taste

7 tablespoons extra virgin olive oil

2 tablespoons coarsely ground
    cornmeal

8 ounces taleggio or other creamy
    cheese, thinly sliced

1 Stir the yeast into 1 cup warm water. Place the cup in a saucepan with enough very hot water to come halfway up the sides of the cup. Let rest until foamy.

2 Put the flour and a pinch salt in the bowl of a food processor and, with the motor running, pour the yeast through the feed tube. Add 1 cup warm water and 4 tablespoons oil and process until a ball has formed. Put the dough on a floured surface and knead until smooth. Oil a bowl, put in the dough, cover with a clean cloth, and let rise for 1 hour.

3 Divide the dough into two unequal portions. Roll one portion into an 8 x 10-inch rectangle; roll the other potion into a 9 x 11-inch rectangle.

*If using a pizza stone or tiles instead, preheat the tiles for 15 minutes, then sprinkle with cornmeal. Place the focaccia on a wooden or metal peel and slide onto the stone.

4 Sprinkle an 8 x 10-inch baking sheet with cornmeal. Transfer the larger rectangle to the pan; press the edges up the sides of the pan. Distribute the cheese slices evenly across the surface and top with the smaller rectangle. Seal the edges by rolling the edges of the larger rectangle over the smaller rectangle, cover with a clean towel, and let rise for 1 hour.

5 Preheat the oven to 350°F.

6 Brush the focaccia with the remaining oil and bake for 30 minutes, or until lightly browned. Remove from the oven, cut into wedges, and serve immediately.

Make Ahead The dough can be made earlier in the day, wrapped tightly in plastic wrap, and refrigerated until ready to use. It can also be made up to 3 weeks in advance and frozen in a tightly sealed container. Thaw before using.

How to Serve As an appetizer, a snack, a party buffet item, or as an entrée paired with various vegetables or a green salad.

Wine Suggestion **Dry White**

FOCACCIA CON LE OLIVE VERDI

Focaccia with Green Olives

244

❧ Liguria ❧

WHEN RECCO'S FESTIVAL ORGANIZERS DECIDED TO BUILD AN OVEN LARGE ENOUGH *to hold the "World's Largest Focaccia" (see page 242), they took their cue from another of Liguria's gorgeous seaside villages—Camogli—located just up the road. Camogli has long been the site for the "World's Largest Fish Fry" held the second Sunday in May. Recco's festival is now the more picturesque of the two, not having been quite as "discovered" by tourists as its neighbor. Also, the food is better, with afternoons devoted to the succulent cheese-stuffed focaccia on page 242 and mornings reserved for this traditional, unyeasted, olive-studded variety that can also be found any other day at any* panificio *throughout Liguria.*

serves 4

Time: About 45 minutes plus 1 hour rising

Level of Difficulty: Moderate

⚜

1/2 teaspoon active dry yeast

2 cups warm water

4 cups unbleached all-purpose flour, sifted

Salt to taste

8 tablespoons extra-virgin olive oil

1 cup green olives, pitted

2 tablespoons coarsely ground cornmeal

1 Stir the yeast into 1 cup warm water. Place the cup in a saucepan with enough very hot water to come halfway up the sides of the cup. Let rest until foamy.

2 Put the flour and a pinch salt in the bowl of a food processor and, with the motor running, pour the yeast through the feed tube. Add 1 cup warm water and 4 tablespoons oil and process until a ball has formed. Put the dough on a floured surface, add 3/4 cup olives, and knead until smooth. Oil a bowl, put in the dough and coat well with the oil, cover with a clean cloth, and let rise for 1 hour.

3 Preheat the oven to 400°F. Sprinkle a 10-inch-round baking pan with cornmeal.*

*If using a pizza stone or tiles instead, preheat the tiles for 15 minutes. Sprinkle some cornmeal on a wooden or metal peel, top with the focaccia, and slide onto the stone.

4 Put the dough on a floured surface and roll it into a 10-inch round. Transfer to the pan. Brush the focaccia with the remaining oil, season with salt, and press the remaining olives into the surface, cut side down and evenly distributed.

5 Bake for 20 to 25 minutes, or until lightly browned. Remove from the oven, cut into wedges, and serve hot or lukewarm.

How to Serve As an appetizer, snack, party buffet item, or, cut into thin wedges, part of a mealtime bread basket.

Wine Suggestion **Dry White**

PANE CON LA ZUCCA

Butternut Squash Bread

❦ Friuli-Venezia Giulia ❧

THROUGHOUT FRIULI, CHRISTMAS NIGHT IS SEEN AS A TIME WHEN MAGICAL THINGS *happen. Valentino Ostermann, a writer who achieved fame chronicling traditional Friuli life, recounted in one of his books this legend born in the Natisone Valley: "Flowers bloom under the snow, the water in fountains turns to wine, animals talk and are understood, the souls of those who die float directly to heaven, and those standing in life's crossroads can read in the clouds everything that will come to pass in the new year."*

Many are the foods associated with this enchanted night, but one of my favorites is boiled lentils (their small, moneylike shapes said to be a harbinger of financial fortune) combined with these unique, slightly sweet rolls made with butternut squash.

makes 8 rolls

Time: About 2¹/2 hours plus 5 hours rising

Level of Difficulty: Advanced

⚷

1¹/2 cups whole milk
1 teaspoon sugar
Salt to taste
¹/2 teaspoon active dry yeast
About 6 cups unbleached
    all-purpose flour
Butter and olive oil for oiling

1 Heat the milk until warm. Pour 1 cup of milk into a bowl and stir in the sugar, a pinch of salt, and the yeast. Set aside the remaining ¹/2 cup milk. When the yeast mixture is slightly foamy, add 1 cup flour, or as much as is needed to completely absorb the milk and form a dense, solid dough. Put the dough on a floured surface and knead until smooth. Using a butter knife, cut a cross into the surface of the dough, cover with a clean cloth, and let rise for 2 hours in a warm place.

2 Preheat the oven to 350°F. Oil a baking sheet.

3 Put the squash on the baking sheet and bake for 30 minutes. Pass the squash through a food mill, transfer the puree to a bowl, add the raisins and the risen dough, and stir until well combined.

4 Heap the remaining flour on a flat work surface and make a well in the center. Add the squash and dough mixture and begin to knead, taking in a little flour at a time. Knead vigorously for 15 minutes, adding 1 to 2 tablespoons of the reserved milk as necessary to create a smooth, elastic dough. Cut a cross into the surface, place in a bowl, cover with a clean cloth, and let rise in a warm place for 2 hours.

5 Butter a baking sheet. Divide the dough into 8 pieces. Form each into a slightly flat circle and arrange the circles about 2 to 3 inches apart on the baking sheet. Cover with a clean cloth and let rise for 1 hour.

6 Preheat the oven to 400°F.

7 Bake the rolls for 15 minutes, then reduce the temperature to 325°F and bake for 1 hour. Remove from the oven and cool to room temperature before serving.

How to Serve Works equally well as a breakfast bread, a snack, or a not-too-sweet dessert.

Wine Suggestion Dry White

1 pound butternut squash, peeled, seeded, and cut into small cubes

1/2 cup golden raisins, soaked in warm water for 20 minutes, drained, and squeezed dry

247

Eggs, Cheeses, and Savory Tarts

Uova in Cocotte
Oven-poached Eggs with Prosciutto and Fontina

Asparagi con le Uova
Asparagus with Fried Eggs

Frittata al Riso
Sliced Frittata Rounds Made with Rice and Thyme-scented, Oven-dried Tomatoes

Frittata di Carciofi
Artichoke Frittata

Frittata di Pane
Light, Golden Bread Frittata

Frittata al Tartufo
White Truffle Frittata

Sfogliata con Olive e Acciughe
Olive and Anchovy Savory Pie

Torta di Verdura
Escarole, Curly Endive, Capers, and Black Olive Tart

'Mpanata con Pomodori Secchi
Stuffed Pizza Made with Chard and Sundried Tomatoes

Torta Rustica
Country-style and Prosciutto Pie

Erbazzone
Savory Spinach Pie

Timballo di San Giovanni
St. John's Day Cheese Timballo

Torta Pasqualina
Chard and Ricotta Tart

Panzerotto alla Caponata
Eggplant, Red Pepper, and Black Olive Calzone

Frittelle di Ricotta
Sweet Ricotta Fritters

Tramezzini
Fried Bread Squares Stuffed with Mozzarella and Olive Paste

Fritelle di Mozzarella
Fried Mozzarella Rounds

Frico
Fried Cheese Wedges

Spiedini di Scamorze e Caciocavallo
Baked Kebabs Made with Scamorze and Caciocavallo Cheeses

Caciocavallo al Fumo
Lightly Smoked Caciocavallo

Timballo di Scamorze e Caciocavallo
Scamorze, Caciocavallo, and Potato Terrine

Provolone all'Aceto
Smoked Provolone Panfried with Oregano and Balsamic Vinegar Sauce

CAMPANIA
The Drawbacks of Being Boring

THE FOUR FACES OF NAPOLI ARE REVEALED in four of its most popular proverbs:

Vedi Napoli e poi muori—Visit Naples and then you can die.

Napoletano, largo di bocca e stretto di mano—Neapolitan, wide of mouth,
but tight of hand.

I Napoletani ingannano anche il Diavolo—Neapolitans will cheat even the Devil.

*Tre cose sono dificile a fare: cuocere un uovo, fare il letto ad un cane, ed insegnare a un
Napoletano qualcosa che non gia sa*—Three things are hard to do: cook an egg,
keep a dog's bed neat, and teach a Neapolitan something he does not already know.

One of my earliest memories is of sitting at the piano with my uncle Aldo, the two of us
locked inside his study in Viareggio, tinkling away beneath the dozens of framed librettos
lining the ocher walls. Aldo, a journalist, author, and composer, always let me "help" when he
was working on a new composition, my ideas the stuff of what he graciously referred to as
"holidays from the rigors of reason."

It was during just one of these sessions that I first heard him play a song later made famous by Lara St. Paul called *Ti fai desidera* ("You Make Yourself Desired"). By the time he played it for me, it had gone through various revisions and was one or two bars away from the recording studio. He played it first on trumpet, then on piano, singing the words which he had written in Neapolitan dialect. It was my first introduction to the extravagantly passionate style of Neapolitan music—*bel canto*—and I was completely mesmerized.

"*Bel canto* is the music of another time," Aldo had said. "A mask through which we view a world that vanished along with the elegance of aristocracy."

But what I have since learned is that he was wrong, because in Naples that world is still there, still intact, still relevant and very much alive in the chant of the fish seller, bundling his calamari in paper cones to sell for 5,000 lire each; in the person of the *pazzariello* wandering through the back alleys playing his trumpet to the rhythm of the *tarantella*; in the freshness of the laundry, draped across alleys so narrow as to prohibit passage; in the fragrance of the braided garlic festooning the stands at the mile-long outdoor markets; in the ingenuity of the *ramarielli*—brokers who lend money to engaged couples so they can pay for a wedding and set up house.

It is all still there, in a Naples that is at once modern enough to host eleven heads of state arriving for week-long congresses on international finance, but still tied collectively to Sunday afternoon dinners where fifteen people sit for five hours eating pasta, drinking Lacryma Christi, and singing spirited renditions of "*O Sole Mio.*"

I have come to Naples both to visit my friend Luigi, whose family lived for years in my Tuscan town of Massarosa, and to attend the September 19 San Gennaro festival ("*La madre delle feste*" as one tourist brochure described it—the mother of all festivals).

When I announced my intention to make the trip, every Tuscan aware of my plans had the same reaction: "*sei pazza*"—you're crazy. At first I thought their sentiments were based on an aversion to crowds and noise and the overall sense of uncontrolled bedlam generated by festivals of this magnitude. But no, it was simply the old North-South prejudices once again coming to the fore, the old why-would-anyone-want-to-spend-even-a-minute-in-such-a-classless-place conviction.

I have written much in other books about the Tuscan attitude toward Southerners and I will not here add fuel to that fire. Suffice to say that the entire compendium of stories and dispositions can be summed up in the one descriptive term most often employed by Tuscans when talking about anyone south of Rome (although Romans are more often than not also included): *cafone*, defined by my thesaurus as peasant, rustic boor, vulgar fellow.

"Yes, but do you know what we say about *them*?" asked Luigi on my first night in Naples.

I can't imagine anything that would be worse.

"*Noiosi*," he says.

"That's all?" *Noiosi* only means "boring."

"In Naples, there is nothing as personally damning as being thought boring. And boring is exactly what Northerners are, with all their rigid sophistication and absurd judgments that extend even to whether or not one uses a spoon when twirling pasta. In the long run, who cares?"

I have been in these types of discussions before and always find myself agreeing with the "live and let live" frame of mind. But in the very next moment, there is a little voice whispering in my ear. "*You* care" it says, "even if you don't feel comfortable admitting it right now." And then I get angry. Angry at my mother. Angry at my uncles and cousins. Angry at anyone in Tuscany I have ever known or spoken to. Because in those moments, I know that, being Tuscan, I have absorbed all those anti-Southern prejudices and, try as I might, there they are.

"Well, what would you answer to all those Northerners who say the South is nothing but a financial black hole—that all the money earned by hardworking Northerners and sent down here for legitimate urban projects winds up in the pockets of crooked politicians?"

He laughs.

"What would you say about the fact that the North produces more goods and that its people enjoy a higher standard of living?" I am trying very hard to keep that certain edge out of my voice, but I can feel it creeping in. "What about the crime rate, which is much higher in the South? Or the level of social services—the schools and hospitals?"

Enough, Anna, I tell myself. You have demonstrated your point more than adequately.

"Do you really want an answer," he says, still smiling. "Or shall I just save my breath?"

"No. Tell me what you think."

"What I think is that it's all part of a Northern scheme for marginalizing the South, for making people think that, down here, we do nothing other than lie in the sun and eat garlic." He leans forward in his chair. "What I think is that Northerners and Southerners are different in the most fundamental of things which is what they believe to be important."

I must have achieved a certain level of success in keeping my face passive because he continues.

"Do you really believe Northerners have a higher standard of living?" he says, the sarcasm oozing through his words. "That they have more *things,* I can grant. But not that they love their families more or derive more pleasure in spending time with them. In fact, every time I go North, I am amazed at the speed with which family traditions are fading away, especially in Lombardy."

I have to admit that's a very good point.

"Let's go even further. Let's take the fact that southern Lombardy and certain sections of the other Northern regions are now completely covered with concrete. Or let's talk about the industrial smog that makes living in Milan an absurdity. Or the pace of life which leaves no time for playing cards in the local caffè after dinner. Or how about the bankers and financiers who embezzle great sums of money and buy their way out of jail—are they better than the pickpockets and petty thieves we have here?"

He is right. There is no question but that he is right. So why do I feel that given the same options afforded Northerners as they "progressed" their way toward the type of life he is describing, that he—and most all of southern Italy—would likewise succumb?

"So are you saying this is a deliberate choice on the part of the South? As opposed to even taking the reigns of control enough to be in the *position* of choosing?"

Luigi leans forward in his chair. "*Esatto!*" he says, banging the table with his fist. "Now we've gotten to the point. It's all about control, is it not? Northerners have fallen so much in love with control that they want to control us, too. And it irks them to no end that, no matter what they try with respect to yanking us into line, they fail." He heaves a great sigh and relaxes back against the cushions. "It all goes back to what I said before. The North and the South are different. Why can't we all just leave it at that?"

The next day, Thursday, I am scheduled to have lunch with Luigi's family. But first, we're going to take in what Luigi calls the quintessential Neapolitan experience: watching his uncle Beniamino make pizza. Actually, Beniamino is less important to the equation than the act of pizza-making itself (although it is true that Luigi considers his uncle to be "the best *pizzaiuolo* in Spaccanapoli"—Naples's historic district).

"Pizza *is* Napoli," Luigi claims. "The two are joined together in a symbiotic relationship that helps each of them achieve unparalleled brilliance. The fact is, pizza is best when consumed against the flambuoyant backdrop that is Naples and Naples is best when consumed while chewing a flamboyant slice of pizza."

He pauses to make sure I have understood. "Imagine eating pizza on the streets of Milan," he says by way of further explanation. "*Certo,* you can do it and the pizza might even be somewhat acceptable. But compare the satisfaction of that stale, lifeless slice with one consumed, say, in the middle of this bright, colorful piazza."

He huddles into his jacket and hurries across the square, chewing furiously on an imaginary wedge of pizza. Looking at no one, he moves with the hunched gait of one too burdened to stand straight. "Milan," he says at the end of his little performance. "Cold, linear, busy, and impersonal. Not at all a good city for street food. If for nothing else, pizza is too sloppy to eat unless you have the attention to devote to it."

His next vignette is, obviously, quite different. Chest puffed, head turning from side to side, he ambles across the piazza, taking long luxurious bites from another imaginary slice and waving expansively to one phantom figure after another. "You cannot walk around Naples without immersing yourself in the events of the street," he says. "And the streets are a perfect metaphor for pizza—complex, colorful, and involved.

Uncle Beniamino greets me with a warm hug and a direct question: "*Come la vuole?*" What type would you like? This is my kind of man, I tell myself. Someone who wastes no time getting to the point. When I hesitate, he opens the gate leading to the food preparation rooms and says, "*vieni con me.*" Come with me.

In the back, his three pizza makers are preparing more types of pizza than I can even imagine. There is *Margherita* (originally made for Italy's first queen to simulate the colors of the Italian flag) with tomatoes, basil, and mozzarella; *alla vongole* with clams; *marinara* (so named because its simplicity established it as the favorite of mariners or sailors) with tomatoes, raw garlic, and parsley; *ai frutti di mare* with a shellfish mixture; *ai funghi e cipolle* with fresh mushrooms and onions; *ai muscoli* with mussels; *con caperi e acchiughe* with capers and anchovies; and *ai quarti* which means divided into four sections, each topped with something different.

"Neapolitans were eating pizza even before the tomato arrived here in the 1600s," he tells me. "And not only the *contadini* (peasants) but the Bourbons, too." He narrates a story about how Ferdinand IV preferred his pizza cooked in the wood-fired kilns belonging to Capodimonte, the porcelain statue maker whose ceramic flowers have graced the houses of aristocrats for 500 years.

In Naples, pizza is eaten sandwich-style—two slices folded over onto each other. "This way, you get twice as much in your stomach for the same amount of chewing," Beniamino declares in sly Neapolitan style. His statement brings to mind the stories my uncle Aldo would tell about the Neapolitans who came to Tuscany in the mid-1960s to help build the autostrada.

"You couldn't help but admire their desire to have it all for the least amount of effort," Aldo would chuckle. "But they would spend enormous amounts of time and energy figuring how to avoid doing the least little thing. Droves arrived and droves departed, each group of workers lasting approximately four or five weeks before giving up and returning home. It mattered not one lira to them that they had no money and desperately needed the job. In their view, the job was not worth doing if it cut into their personal pleasure."

"I'll have half a slice of each," I say to the delight of both Luigi and his uncle who refers to me from then on his *inamorata*—his beloved.

As he hurries to prepare my plate, Beniamino tells Luigi that he has decided to close the pizzeria early and take me to Battipaglia. "Someone who loves pizza as much as this wise and wonderful gastronome should have a personal introduction to the buffalos."

That's buffalos as in water buffalos. As in the ones the milk of which leads to the mozzarella that elevates Neapolitan pizza several stratospheres above its competitors. There is no question but that the pizza in Naples is better than any pizza anywhere. But why should that be so? Yes, things are always better when made with the proprietary passion of one whose life's work reaches its apex in the perfect toss of a circle of dough. Yes, it's true that the South grows better tomatoes than just about anywhere else on the face of the earth—as Luigi would say, "Tomatoes and the South go together like pasta and parmigiano." One might even say that Neapolitan pizza is better because Naples is such a fertile training ground for prospective pizza chefs (in 1979, 87 percent of New York's pizzerias employed pizza makers who came from Naples). But more important than any of these factors is undoubtedly the fact that Neapolitan pizza always uses *bufala* mozzarella.

Battipaglia (whose name means "beat the hay") turns out to be little more than a long road connecting one water buffalo farm to another. The buffalos themselves are comic characters, turning to gaze at visitors with an expression belying the best of Neapolitan attitude. "Yeeees?" Their languid eyes grace your presence. "What can you do for me?"

"*I bufali* are very difficult to take care of," Beniamino tells me. "They need more space than cows and the females yield far less milk. Each water buffalo, for example, produces five gallons daily as opposed to seven or eight from a similar-size cow. When you consider that a gallon of milk yields little more than a pound of mozzarella, you can see why it is very difficult to find pure buffalo mozzarella. Most mozzarellas—even if they say *bufala*—are, today, made from a mixture of cow's and water buffalo's milk."

But sometimes it is worth holding out for the real thing, Luigi adds. "For one thing, buffalo mozzarella has more than three times as much fat, which I know you Americans think of in the same terms as a plague, but using low-fat mozzarella is worse than not using any at all."

In the next two hours, we watch as the mozzarella is made from the curds of the fresh, unpasteurized milk. First the curds are laced with natural rennet and, after a short period of coagulation and acidification, torn apart by hand, placed in wooden sieves and cooked in boiling water. The cheese is turned continuously with a long wooden stick, a process that allows the excess whey to drain off. Once the balls reach the desired texture and consistency, workers pull them apart and form small rounds that are placed immediately in brine. At this point, they are ready to eat. And eat them we do.

"Hurry," Beniamino says between bites. "Buffalo mozzarella begins to lose its elasticity almost immediately. Even the ones you buy fresh in the best *latticino* (creamery) are more rubbery than the one that is melting in your mouth right now."

I'm not sure about the ones in the *latticino*, but the one in my mouth is absolute heaven.

Battipaglia behind us, Beniamino decides against reopening the pizzeria. "A beautiful afternoon and a beautiful woman—what better excuse for a holiday," he says, convincing Luigi that we should instead go for a tour of San Lorenzo's historic center. "Naples is like a gigantic version of Pompeii," he tells me. "Very little has changed since the days it was known as Neapolis (from the Greek for "New City")—not even the chaos. We Neapolitans thrive on chaos."

As we walk through the Piazza Sannazzaro, we pause in front of a crowded *gelato* stand to watch street performers whose talents range from miming to magic to reinterpreting the music of Roy Orbison. But our decided favorite is a very funny comedian spoofing the cleverness with which Neapolitans manage to continuously thwart the law. *Fatta la lege, trovato l'inganno,* says the comedian, capping a story about the legendary T-shirt airbrushed to look as though the owner were wearing a seat belt. Law passed, loophole found.

In the middle of the performance, Luigi whispers into my hair. "Just for the record, this is the very spot where Nero, his myopic eye hidden by an emerald monocle, delivered falsetto speeches to the applause of Egyptian slaves. It's like Beniamino told you, nothing has changed."

A few hours later, we wind up in the studio of Lello Esposito, a self-taught Neapolitan artist whose expressive sculptures are now housed in many of the world's finest museums. "Lello is best known for his masks of Pulcinella," Luigi tells me, and then, noticing my confusion, hastens to add. "Pulcinella is a puppet character who, in the universality of the situations he encounters, represents the heart and soul of all that we are as Neapolitans."

We are greeted by Lello himself, a small impish-looking man who, upon seeing Luigi, immediately dons one of the many white ceramic masks hanging against the far wall. "You have brought this woman to meet Pulcinella," he orates in the round exaggerated tones of a theatrical diva. "Well done, *carissimo*. Pulcinella greets you and your handsome *cavalieri* with one universal embrace." He throws his arms wide and lunges to encompass our little group, but halfway through the gesture, pretends to fall helplessly on his side, rolling comically across the marble floor and finishing up in a crumpled heap on the other side of the room. "Enough said about Pulcinella's embrace," he jokes, removing the mask and motioning us to sit down.

"So that's the heart and soul of Neapolitans?" I tease Luigi. "Not very flattering, I must say.

"Not to you Northerners," he tosses back. "*Your* heart and soul are frozen into the cold marble statues of the Uffizi." He laughs at his own brilliance as Lello motions his assistant to bring a pot of espresso.

"By contrast," he continues, "Pulcinella, or Punch, expresses all the contradictions, oppositions, and contrasts of life as it truly is—at least here. When Pulcinella scores a victory, he turns out to be the loser. When he loses, he wins. Smarter than anyone, he often behaves like a fool. Both miser and spendthrift, chaste and licentious, he is always questioning the why of everything but nobody ever provides him with any answers."

"Pulcinella hatched from an egg, like a chick," Beniamino adds. "That's where his name comes from (*pulcino*). White and round as a hen, he has a big, beak-shaped black nose." By way of example, he points to a full-scale sculpture of the character on one of the side tables. "His appearance is always the same—a large egg balancing on a pair of thin legs encased in the baggy trousers of a miller. The expression on his face evokes the sufferings of the world but, at the same time, there is an element of surprise—as if he is dreaming of white sand beaches."

Lello takes one of the larger masks down from the wall. "Look at the eyes," he says, holding it in front of me. "Pulcinello's eyes are marked by every one of the world's hungers and all in brilliant contrast. His line of sight straddles the border between life and death, black and white, light and darkness, sunshine and shadow, knowledge and ignorance, identity and nonidentity, constancy and metamorphosis. He is constantly cheeping "why," but his lips are as full and dreamy as those of a glutton."

"What better metaphor for Naples?" Luigi laughs.

Friday is the Feast of Saint Gennaro, which is the true reason I have come to Naples. It will not be my first experience with this festival since, in New York, I live on the border between Soho and Little Italy, one block away from the northern tip of what is billed as "the largest San Gennaro festival outside Naples." According to Luigi, that claim is about as valid as stating that New York's Metropolitan Museum has the largest collection of Renaissance paintings outside Italy. There is simply no comparison.

"The devotion, the lights, the people, the noise, the passion, the geographic area encompassed." He shakes his head in definitive dismissal. "Let's do this. I will personally guide you through every facet of the experience and afterward you will tell me that I was right."

As a prelude to the festival, Luigi takes me to his mother's house for lunch, which he calls "the quintessential tourist experience." "You cannot come to Naples and eat only in restaurants," he maintains. "The best of what we have to offer can be found only by sitting around the table with a big bowl of pasta and the entire family in attendance."

There is no question that, if not the entire family, then a very large percentage of Luigi's relatives are, in fact, sitting around his mother's table this balmy Thursday afternoon. The table itself is made up of three planks of wood resting on metal sawhorses set up on the sidewalk outside a three-story stone house in the heart of the Mergellina district. Down the block, other tables are similarly erected and there is much running between the tables with sampler plates of food. "Just a typical Thursday," Luigi had answered when I wondered whether this was some sort of holiday. "Few things are more important to Neapolitans than sitting down at lunchtime with family and friends. No rushing is allowed."

The menu is a model of simplicity: *caprese* (salad of buffalo mozzarella interspersed with slices of fresh tomato and topped with slivered basil and extra virgin olive oil), spaghetti with a fiery tomato sauce, grilled sausages and spareribs served with sautéed greens, plenty of good crusty bread, infinite carafes of red wine, and, for dessert, a *zuppa inglese*, Italy's version of an English trifle, made with layers of sponge cake soaked in coffee liqueur and topped with creamy custard.

But there is something incomplete and unfair about reciting the menu's ingredients in the way I just did. To Americans, for whom pasta with tomato sauce has become what one makes in lieu of having the time to make something more sophisticated, the idea of a another bowl of pasta is, at best, unimaginative. *Peccato.* A shame.

Like most of the world's poverty-based cusines, Neapolitan home cooking is labor-intensive, manually ingenious, and creative in a way that can only result from combining the few available ingredients with a passionate love and desire for extraordinary food. "What my mother does with simple dried pasta, tomatoes, and a few herbs," Luigi says, dipping his bread into the sauce left on his plate. "*Fa le gambe alle mosche.*" She can even put legs on flies.

Luigi's love for his mother's cooking expresses itself in a wide range of colorful flatteries, among my favorite, the use of death as a metaphor to describe a certain state of culinary ecstasy. "*E la su morte,*" he might say about pairing cooked fava beans with sautéed chicory. It is its death. I'm not sure whether he means that the perfect union of the two renders them an inseparable pair until death do them part, or whether the expression reveals a perverse definition of death as the ultimate and, hence, most perfect pairing.

"You know, sometimes you should give your brain a rest," he says, when I confront him with my musings. "Just eat the food and enjoy it."

"THE BLOOD, WHERE IS THE BLOOD? Has San Gennaro's blood been brought out yet?"

For fifteen centuries, huge crowds of people have assembled on this piazza outside Naples' Duomo to commemorate San Gennaro's beheading, which took place on September 19, 305, in nearby Pozzuoli. According to legend, holy women gathered up every drop of the miraculous red liquid that had squirted on the surrounding grass that day and placed it in twin vials. Those same vials now spend 363 days inside the cathedral to be placed on display only twice a year, once in May and once in September, at which times the coagulated blood "miraculously" liquefies while the frenzied crowd looks on.

"How many of these people do you think actually believe in the miracle of the liquefaction?" I ask as we stand surrounded by hordes of faithful worshippers.

"Just about every Neapolitan here," Luigi answers casually.

"That can't be true," I counter. "Even the Vatican itself takes a dim view of this so-called miracle."

"And that proves what?"

"I'm not saying it proves anything, but how could anyone believe that this happens all by itself? It's a gimmick, a trick, a scam. Can't you see that?"

"It doesn't matter whether or not I can see it. The fact is, I won't. Why should I?"

"Because it would tie you more securely to reality."

"The same reality that is more and more turning us into miserable cynics? No, I really think I am much happier with the belief system I have right now." He pats my shoulder consolingly. " I know it doesn't seem rational to you but reason is not the great power you think it to be."

My tendency would be to continue this discussion until Luigi had accepted the wisdom of my point of view. But then I realize that, the more I argue, the more I lose, since my argument is based purely on reason and his, purely on belief.

"It is another of those North-South differences," he says noticing my consternation. "If Northerners can't see or touch it, it is not real. They have become too attached to material things. Here in this historic land of poverty, all we have is our beliefs."

The twin vial and the clot of solidified blood are finally visible. Millions of eyes are riveted on the sacred objects. A collective sigh rises from countless praying lips. The speed with which the miracle occurs is an omen for the fortunes of the city: If the liquefaction is fast, the future is assured; if slow, it augers a curse that will blight the city for months to come.

"It runs! The blood runs!" A shout rages through the crowd. Everyone stretches their necks to see, to witness, to corroborate, to make sure. As the priest hoists the vials above his head, there is an eruption of emotion. People weep, they pray, they cheer, they chant, men hoist their children up toward the sun. "Gennaro's blood runs!"

"Naples is safe," Luigi yells to me above the noise of the crowd. "For six more months, our lives can go on as normal."

"Does Naples ever lead a 'normal' life?" I yell back to him, not altogether teasingly. "Are Neapolitans not always outside the barrier?"

His answer is tinged with precisely the same duplicity. "If we were inside the barrier, we would be boring," he says, "and there is nothing—absolutely nothing—worse than being boring."

UOVA IN COCOTTE

Oven-poached Eggs with Prosciutto and Fontina

❧ Piemonte ❧

CHIVASSO'S *FESTA DELLE UOVA* (EGG FESTIVAL) OFFERS A BOUNTY OF EGG-RELATED *dishes from soufflés and frittatas to eggs scrambled with truffles and rice-filled tomatoes topped with fried eggs. Held usually on the second weekend of April, the festival is mainly a local event and all the food is prepared by town residents. The following recipe comes from Signora Giulia Montenero, with whom I spent three wonderful days learning to cook Piemontese style.*

serves 4

Time: 30 minutes

Level of Difficulty: Moderate

Equipment: 4 oven-proof ramekins or egg cups

⚶

2 tablespoons unsalted butter
2 ounces fontina, cut into
   1/2-inch cubes
2 ounces prosciutto cotto (ham),
   preferably in one piece,
   cut into 1/2-inch cubes
4 large eggs
Salt to taste
4 sprigs fresh Italian parsley

1 Preheat the oven to 350°F. Butter four ramekins or egg cups.

2 Distribute the fontina and prosciutto cubes among the ramekins. Bake for 5 minutes, or until the cheese is completely melted. Break 1 egg into each ramekin, salt the yolks, pepper the whites, and dot with butter. Place the ramekins in a pan filled with enough boiling water to reach halfway up the sides. Bake for 10 minutes. Remove from the oven, garnish with sprigs of fresh parsley, and serve immediately.

How to Serve Makes a wonderful lunch when the ramekins are centered on a larger plate, surrounded with broccoli rabe sautéed in garlic and oil, and accompanied by fresh bread.

Wine Suggestion **Dry White**

ASPARAGI CON LE UOVA

Asparagus with Fried Eggs

❦ Trentino-Alto Adige ❦

DURING APRIL AND MAY, TERLANO'S GASTRONOMIC FOCUS TURNS ALMOST *exclusively to asparagus, which is served in all possible variations (I had the following recipe for breakfast one morning at the local cafe) and accompanied by a white wine bottled specifically for the occasion,* Vino degli asparagi di Terlano. *For eight weekends, this charming Alpine village transforms itself into one big party with open-air musical offerings, cooking demonstrations, and food stalls. Terlano (Terlan in German) is located twenty miles northeast of Bolzano in Alto Adige and its residents speak mainly German.*

serves 4

Time: 25 to 35 minutes

Level of Difficulty: Easy

3 pounds fresh asparagus,
    trimmed and peeled
2 tablespoons unsalted butter
4 large eggs
Salt to taste
Freshly ground black pepper
    to taste
4 tablespoons freshly grated
    grana padana or
    Parmigiano-Reggiano

1 Tie the asparagus with kitchen string into bundles of about 8 or 10. Stand the asparagus in enough salted water to reach halfway up the stalks and bring to a boil over medium heat. Cook for 8 to 10 minutes, or until tender. Drain, remove the string, and distribute the asparagus among four plates. Dot with half the butter and keep warm.

2 Heat the remaining butter in a skillet over medium heat and fry the eggs until the whites are set. Using a spatula, carefully lift the eggs from the pan, keeping the yolks intact, and place one on top of each bundle of asparagus. Salt the yolks, pepper the whites, and dust the whole with grated cheese. Serve immediately.

How to Serve For breakfast or as a light lunch entrée. Accompany with diamond-shaped toast wedges.

Wine Suggestion **Dry White**

FRITTATA AL RISO

Sliced Frittata Rounds Made with Rice and Thyme-scented Oven-dried Tomatoes

❦ Piemonte ❦

THIS IS ANOTHER OF SIGNORA MONTENERO'S WONDERFUL EGG DISHES—A BASIC *frittata layered with rice and thyme-scented, oven-dried tomatoes, then rolled and sliced into decorative rounds. The Signora dries her own tomatoes and, although I have tried the recipe with a packaged sundried variety, drying your own works infinitely better. To make the effort worthwhile, dry a few dozen tomatoes and seal in plastic containers for future use.*

serves 4

Time: 3 hours

Level of Difficulty: Moderate

6 ripe tomatoes, peeled,
    halved, and seeded
Salt to taste
2 tablespoons chopped fresh
    thyme
1/2 cup Arborio rice
1 cup water
1/4 teaspoon sugar
1 tablespoon red wine vinegar
4 large eggs
1/4 cup whole milk
2 tablespoons unsalted butter
3 to 4 sprigs fresh thyme

1 Preheat the oven to 250°F. Line a baking pan with aluminum.

2 Place the tomatoes cut side up in the baking pan. Sprinkle with salt and thyme and bake for 2 hours, or until completely dry.

3 Meanwhile, boil the rice in 1 cup water until the liquid is almost absorbed. Without draining, pour the rice into a bowl and toss with a pinch of salt, the sugar, and vinegar. Transfer to a sheet of aluminum foil and spread into a 1/4-inch-thick rectangle. Cool to room temperature.

4 Beat the eggs with the milk and a pinch of salt. Heat the butter in a slope-sided nonstick 8-inch skillet over medium heat. Add the egg mixture and cook for 7 minutes, or until the underside is set. Slide onto a plate, cover with another plate, turn upside down, and slide the frittata back into the skillet. Cook for 5 minutes, or until both sides are a light golden color.

5 Cool the frittata for 3 minutes, then slide onto the layer of rice. Cut the rice so that it is the same size and shape. Cover with a large piece of plastic wrap and turn the rice and frittata upside down. Remove the foil and arrange the tomatoes over the rice. Carefully roll the frittata into a tight cylinder and wrap in plastic wrap. Let rest at room temperature for 30 to 45 minutes.

6 Remove the plastic wrap and cut the roll into slices about 3/4 inch thick. Arrange on a serving platter in a circular pattern, overlapping the slices. Fill the center with fresh thyme.

Make Ahead The tomatoes and rice can be prepared earlier in the day.

How to Serve Works well as an appetizer or a lunch entrée when served on a bed of mixed greens dressed with olive oil and balsamic vinegar.

Wine Suggestion Dry White

FRITTATA DI CARCIOFI

Artichoke Frittata

❧ Lazio ❧

THE TURKS WERE CAST OUT OF ROME ON OCTOBER 7, 1571, IN A GLORIOUS SEA *battle whose victory was attributed by Pius V to the intercession of the Virgin Mary. Four centuries later, the residents of Marino, just south of Rome, continue to celebrate this event with a combination wine and harvest festival held on the first Sunday of October. The festival opens with a historic parade that features gold-painted chariots, actors and actresses dressed in sumptuous velvet costumes, and musicians playing ancient instruments. At 4 P.M., the city's fountains cease spouting water in favor of a deluge of new red wine free for the taking. The grand finale takes place around 7 A.M., a cortege of horse-drawn carts parading through the city giving out grapes and plates of food to the thousands of Romans who have fled their city for the day. The festival is preceded, on Saturday, by the awarding of the Leone Cipreli prizes for music and poetry.*

serves 4 to 6

Time: 40 minutes

Level of Difficulty: Moderate

4 large globe artichokes
1 lemon
3 tablespoons extra virgin
    olive oil
1 tablespoon finely chopped
    Italian parsley
Salt to taste
1/2 cup dry white wine
4 large eggs, whisked for
    3 minutes with a pinch
    of salt

1 Remove the tough outer leaves of the artichokes, cut 1 1/2 inches off the tops, and peel the stems. Slice the artichokes in half and, using a melon baller or paring knife, remove the choke. Soak in water with the lemon juice.

2 Heat the oil in an 8-inch slope-sided nonstick skillet over low heat. Drain the artichokes, dry on paper towels, and slice thinly. Add to the skillet and cook for 10 minutes, stirring occasionally. Stir in the parsley and a pinch of salt and cook for 4 minutes more.

3 Pour the wine over the artichokes and cook until it evaporates, about 4 minutes. Continue to cook for 20 minutes, stirring occasionally, until the artichokes are fork tender.

4 Add the eggs, pouring in a slow, steady stream over the entire surface of the artichokes. Cook for 7 minutes, or until the bottom is browned. Slide onto a plate, cover with another plate, turn upside down, and slide the frittata back into the skillet. Cook for 5 to 7 minutes, or until browned on the underside. Cut into wedges and serve hot or lukewarm.

Make Ahead The artichokes can be prepared the day before through Step 3, refrigerated, and heated through when ready to use.

How to Serve As a lunch entrée accompanied by a mixed green salad and rustic-style bread.

Wine Suggestion Dry or Medium-Sweet White

FRITTATA DI PANE

Light, Golden Bread Frittata

264

❧ Lazio ❧

AS I WATCHED THE PROCESSION OF FOOD CARTS PARADING THROUGH THE CROWDED *streets of Marino (see page 262), one of the girls riding aboard the bread cart leaned over and handed me a slice of this unique omelet. I thanked her and, as I took my first bite, an old man dressed in a white apron and cook's hat said "Questa c'e l'avete voialtri?" Do you have this where you come from? I wasn't sure how he knew I wasn't from the Lazio. He gave me the following directions, which turned out to not exactly correspond with the bread omelet I had eaten, but is exquisitely delicious nonetheless.*

serves 4

Time: 25 to 30 minutes

Level of Difficulty: Moderate

⚶

4 tablespoons extra virgin
    olive oil

1 medium onion,
    thinly sliced

Six 3/4-inch-thick slices stale
    country-style bread,
    crusts removed

3 tablespoons freshly chopped
    Italian parsley

6 large eggs, beaten
    until frothy

8 sprigs fresh parsley
    for garnish

1 Heat the oil in a nonstick 8-inch skillet over low heat. Sauté the onion for 8 minutes, stirring constantly. Arrange the bread slices in one layer on top of the onions, sprinkle with parsley, and cook for 3 minutes. Turn with a spatula and cook for 3 minutes more.

2 Pour the eggs over the bread, distributing the mixture evenly across the surface of the skillet and cook for 6 to 8 minutes, or until the underside is set. Slide onto a large plate, cover with another plate, turn upside down, and slide the omelet back into the skillet. Cook for 4 to 5 minutes, or until the underside is golden brown. Transfer to a serving platter, cut into wedges, and serve garnished with parsley.

How to Serve Works equally well as a breakfast, brunch, or lunch entrée. Follow with a bowl of cooked fruit drizzled with a little raspberry vinegar.

Wine Suggestion Dry or Medium-Sweet White

FRITTATA AL TARTUFO

White Truffle Frittata

❦ Lombardia ❦

DURING OCTOBER AND NOVEMBER, THERE ARE LITERALLY HUNDREDS OF TRUFFLE *festivals throughout Lombardy, Piedmont, Emilia-Romagna, Umbria, and Tuscany. The most famous is Alba's* Festa del Tartufo, *held the first Sunday in October. Equally popular, however, is the one held in Milan's Via Ripamonti three weeks later, on the last Sunday of October. Both attract millions of visitors, both offer lavish quantities of foods prepared with the area's famous white truffles, and both feature a donkey* palio *(race) to help take one's mind away from how many dishes have yet to be sampled.*

serves 4

Time: 20 minutes

Level of Difficulty: Easy

6 large eggs, lightly beaten

4 tablespoons freshly grated grana padana or Parmigiano-Reggiano

2 ounces white truffle, cleaned with a brush and thinly sliced (preferably with a truffle slicer)

Salt to taste

Freshly ground black pepper to taste

3 tablespoons unsalted butter

1 Crack the eggs into a bowl and whisk with the cheese until frothy. Add all but 4 slices of the truffles, salt, and pepper.

2 Heat the butter in a slope-sided, 8-inch nonstick skillet over medium heat and pour in the frittata batter. Cook for 4 to 6 minutes, or until lightly browned on the underside. Slide onto a large plate, cover with another plate, turn upside down, and slide the frittata back into the skillet. Cook for 3 minutes, or until the underside is lightly browned. Serve immediately, garnished with the remaining truffles.

How to Serve As an appetizer followed by a radicchio and truffle risotto, or as a main course with roasted potatoes and panfried chicory.

Wine Suggestion Medium- or Full-bodied Red

SFOGLIATA CON OLIVE E ACCIUGHE

Olive and Anchovy Savory Pie

❦ Apulia ❦

RESIDENTS OF TARANTO IN SOUTHERN APULIA CELEBRATE HOLY THURSDAY BY *participating in a number of liturgical rituals among which the most fascinating is the placing of barley grains in open dishes exposed on window sills. The grains, which are drizzled frequently with water, sprout just in time for Easter, signifying the rebirth or resurrection. Foods eaten during this period include a variety of savory pies, such as the following.*

serves 4 to 6

Time: About 2 hours

Level of Difficulty: Advanced

CRUST

**1¹/₂ cups unbleached
    all-purpose flour, sifted**

**4 tablespoons extra virgin
    olive oil**

¹/₂ teaspoon active dry yeast

Salt to taste

FILLING

**6 salt-packed anchovies, filleted
    (see page 25) and diced**

5 ounces picholine olives, pitted

**4 tablespoons extra virgin
    olive oil**

1 Heap the flour on a work surface and make a well in the center. Place half the oil, the yeast, and a pinch of salt in the well and beat with a fork, incorporating the flour a little at a time and adding warm water, 1 tablespoon at a time as needed to form a smooth, slightly wet dough. Divide into 5 portions, cover with a clean cloth, and let rise for 45 minutes, or until doubled in bulk.

2 Preheat the oven to 350°F. Oil an 8-inch springform pan.

3 Put the dough on a floured surface. Using a rolling pin, roll the first piece of dough into a 10-inch circle. Transfer to the springform pan and let the edges hang over the sides.

4 Separate the anchovies and olives into four equal parts. Distribute one part evenly over the surface of the dough and drizzle with oil. Roll the second piece of dough into an 8-inch circle and arrange in the pan on top of the first. Top this with anchovies and olives and drizzle with oil. Continue until the ingredients have all been used, ending with a top layer of dough. Pull up the excess dough from the first layer and press together with the edges of the top circle to seal tightly.

5 Brush the top with oil, pierce with a fork in a few places, and bake for 40 minutes. Remove from the oven, cut into wedges, and serve hot or cold.

Variations Other traditional fillings include thinly sliced red onions, olives, anchovies, diced caciocavallo (a southern Italian pecorinolike cheese), raisins, and tomatoes; or sardines, pine nuts, almonds, and raisins.

Make Ahead The dough can be prepared up to 2 days in advance, wrapped in plastic wrap, and refrigerated, or frozen for up to 3 weeks. In either case, return to room temperature before using.

How to Serve As a first course followed by broiled snapper (or other white fish) served with steamed asparagus or as a light lunch entrée accompanied by a green salad.

Wine Suggestion **Dry or Medium-Sweet White**

TORTA DI VERDURA

Escarole, Curley Endive, Capers, and Black Olive Tart

❧ Apulia ❧

ANOTHER OF THE BREADS AND PIES CREATED BY RESIDENTS OF TARANTO TO *commemorate Holy Thursday is this wonderful tart, blending a host of diverse flavors and colors. The Tarantini, naturally, cook their pizzas over wood fires, but a simple hot oven and a pizza stone will work almost as well. In lieu of a pizza stone, you can use simple unglazed terra-cotta building tiles, but make sure to purchase only American-made tiles which, unlike their imported counterparts, are lead-free.*

serves 6

Time: 45 minutes

Level of Difficulty: Moderate

6 tablespoons extra virgin
    olive oil
1 large head curly endive,
    washed, trimmed, and
    roughly chopped
1 large head escarole, washed,
    trimmed, and roughly
    chopped
1 clove garlic, crushed
Salt to taste
Freshly ground black pepper
    to taste

1 Heat 4 tablespoons oil in a heavy-gauge saucepan over low heat. Add the endive, escarole, garlic, salt, and pepper, cover, and cook for 8 to 10 minutes, or until the greens are completely wilted. Cool to room temperature. Remove and discard the garlic.

2 Preheat the oven to 500°F. Sprinkle a 10-inch-round pizza pan with cornmeal.*

3 Put the dough on a floured work surface. Divide the dough in half. Roll one half into a 10-inch circle and place in the pizza pan. Top with the greens, capers, and olives, leaving a 1-inch border around the edges.

If using a pizza stone or tiles instead, preheat the tiles for 15 minutes, then sprinkle with cornmeal. Place the torta on a wooden or metal peel and slide onto the stone.

4 Roll out the remaining dough into another 10-inch circle and carefully place it on top of the first. Press the edges of the circles closed to seal. Brush the surface with the remaining oil and bake for 15 to 20 minutes, or until crispy and golden brown. Remove from the oven, cut into slices and serve hot.

Make Ahead The topping can be made earlier in the day and kept in a covered container at room temperature.

How to Serve As a light lunch accompanied by a mixed green salad; or as a first course followed by broiled chicken breasts served with lemon wedges and fresh-cooked fava beans that have been lightly drizzled with oil.

Wine Suggestion Dry or Medium-bodied White

Cornmeal for sprinkling
2 recipes Basic Pizza Dough
    (page 463)
2 tablespoons capers, drained
2 ounces gaeta or other black
    olives, pitted and roughly
    chopped

269

'MPANATA CON POMODORI SECCHI

Stuffed Pizza Made with Chard and Sundried Tomatoes

270

❧ Sicilia ❧

ANOTHER TYPE OF PIZZA ASSOCIATED WITH ST. VITO'S DAY (SEE PAGE 238) IS THIS *semolina-crust tart, stuffed with a spicy mixture of chard, sundried tomatoes, and crushed chilies. More a home-cooked pizza than one sold in festival stalls, 'mpanata is generally consumed as an afternoon snack, after the procession featuring the "living floats." When I visited Mazara del Vallo, I was fortunate enough to meet the family of Franco Messina, an actor portraying the character of Captain Valeriano, who ordered the arrest and torture of St. Vito after the martyr was repudiated by his father. "Guarda che figliolo bello," Franco's mother said as we watched her son be struck dumb by an angel sent by God to save Vito's life. Look what a beautiful son.*

Later, after the procession was over and Franco had returned home, Signora Messina brought out this pizza and gave me the recipe. Its name, which comes from the Spanish empanadillas, underscores the multicultural history of Sicilian domination.

serves 4

Time: 2 1/2 hours

Level of Difficulty: Advanced

DOUGH

1/2 teaspoon active dry yeast

1 1/2 cups warm water

2 cups semolina flour

2 cups unbleached all-purpose flour

Salt to taste

1/2 cup extra virgin olive oil

Flour for sprinkling

1 teaspoon baking soda

1 To make the dough, stir the yeast into 1/2 cup warm water. Place the cup in a saucepan with enough very hot water to come halfway up the sides of the cup. Let rest 15 minutes, or until foamy.

2 Place both flours and a pinch of salt in the bowl of a food processor and, with the motor running, pour the yeast through the feed tube. Add 1 cup warm water and process until a ball has formed, adding more water as needed.

3 Put the dough on a floured work surface and knead for 5 minutes, or until smooth and elastic. Oil a bowl and put the dough in the bowl. Roll the dough around to cover with oil. Cover with a clean cloth and let rise for 1 hour.

4 Preheat the oven to 450°F. Oil and flour a 10-inch springform pan.

5 Put the dough on a floured work surface, add the baking soda, and knead. Add all but 1 tablespoon of the remaining oil, a little at a time, until it has been completely incorporated. Divide the dough in half. Roll one half into a 12-inch circle and place the circle in the springform pan. Roll out the remaining doung into a 10-inch circle and set aside.

6 To make the filling, put the chard, chopped tomatoes, crushed chili, salt, pepper, and oil in a bowl. Mix until well blended. Top the 12-inch circle evenly with the filling. Carefully place the 10-inch circle over the filling. Press the edges of the circles closed to seal. Pierce the surface in two or three places with the tines of a fork. Brush with the remaining 1 tablespoon oil.

7 Bake for 30 minutes, or until the crust is golden brown. Remove from the oven and cool for 20 minutes. Remove from the pan, cut into wedges, and serve.

Make Ahead The dough can be made up to 2 days in advance, wrapped tightly in plastic, and refrigerated until ready to use. It can also be frozen for up to 3 weeks. In either case, return to room temperature before using.

How to Serve Can be an appetizer, part of a party buffet, or a lunch or dinner entrée when paired with a green salad.

Wine Suggestion Medium-bodied Red

FILLING

2 pounds chard, stemmed and roughly chopped

1/2 cup oil-packed sundried tomatoes

1 dried chili, crushed

Salt to taste

Freshly ground black pepper to taste

2 tablespoons extra virgin olive oil

271

TORTA RUSTICA

Country-style Cheese and Prosciutto Pie

❦ Apulia ❦

NOVOLI IN THE APULIAN PROVINCE OF LECCE CELEBRATES ST. ANTHONY'S DAY, *January 17, with a huge bonfire in the main piazza. Residents begin collecting wood and depositing it on the assigned site in early December. According to legend, the fire must reach at least as high as the bell tower on the Duomo (and when I saw it, it almost had). An orange bough always serves as the crown (known in dialect as* la marangia de papa Peppu—*Father Peppu's orange—because, at one time, it was cut from a tree in the garden of a priest by that name). Late on the afternoon of January 16, there is a procession (*l'intorciata*) accompanied by dark-suited men who somberly collect the offerings, mainly consisting of gold watches (no kidding). Afterward, there is a huge food festival in the church hall that is open to everyone. Don't miss it.*

serves 6

Time: 1 hour, 45 minutes

Level of Difficulty: Moderate

FILLING

1 tablespoon extra virgin olive oil

8 ounces prosciutto cotto, cut into 1/2-inch cubes

8 ounces fresh bufala or fresh cow's milk mozzarella, cut into 1/2-inch cubes

8 ounces fresh sheep's milk, goat's milk, or very fresh cow's milk ricotta

8 ounces caciocavallo or young pecorino or provolone, cut into 1/2-inch cubes

1 To make the filling, heat the oil in a skillet over low heat and sauté the prosciutto cotto for 8 minutes. Put in a bowl and cool to room temperature. Add the mozzarella, ricotta, caciocavallo, eggs, and a pinch of salt and mix until well blended. Set aside.

2 To make the dough, heap the flour on a work surface and make a well in the center. Add the oil, wine, and a pinch of salt and stir with a fork, incorporating a little flour each time and eventually forming a ball; some flour may remain. Knead for 15 minutes, or until the dough is smooth and solid.

3 Preheat the oven to 350°F. Oil and flour a 10-inch springform pan.

4 Divide the dough into two uneven portions, one portion equaling three-quarters of the dough. Put the larger portion on a floured surface and roll into
a 12-inch circle that is 1/2 inch thick and place the circle into the springform pan, patting the crust against the sides. Set aside 2 to 3 tablespoons filling and top the circle evenly with the remainder.

5 Roll out the remaining dough into a 10-inch square that is 1/2 inch thick. Cut the dough into 1-inch-wide strips and arrange as latticework on the filling. Top the pie evenly with the remaining filling and sprinkle with the sugar.

6 Bake for 45 minutes, or until the crust is golden brown. Remove from the oven, cut into wedges, and serve hot or cold.

Make Ahead The dough can be made up to 2 days in advance, wrapped tightly in plastic wrap, and refrigerated until ready to use. It can also be frozen for up to 3 weeks, but in either case, should be returned to room temperature before using.

How to Serve As part of a party buffet, an appetizer followed by roast loin of pork with sautéed greens, or as a lunch or dinner entrée paired with broccoli rabe sautéed in garlic and oil.

Wine Suggestion Medium- or Full-bodied Red

2 large eggs, lightly beaten
Salt to taste

DOUGH
4 cups unbleached all-purpose
    flour, sifted
4 tablespoons extra virgin
    olive oil
1/2 cup dry white wine
Salt to taste
1 teaspoon sugar

ERBAZZONE

Savory Spinach Pie

274

Emilia-Romagna

IN OLDEN TIMES THROUGHOUT EMILIA-ROMAGNA, GROUPS OF YOUNG PEOPLE *would venture together into the woods on the night of April 30 to cut down the largest possible tree. This would then be installed in their village's central piazza as a sign of the fecundity of spring. In Gualdo Tadino, a small village in the province of Perugia, the ritual continues, followed by a May 1 festival with associated foods that evoke the bounty and freshness of May.*

The following recipe comes from Signora Malva Fotticini, whose spinach tarts have achieved legendary status with the residents of Gualdo Tadino.

serves 6

Time: 1 hour

Level of Difficulty: Moderate

4 pounds fresh spinach, washed
    and left wet

4 tablespoons unsalted butter

2 ounces pancetta, finely chopped

1 clove garlic, minced

6 spring onions or large scallions,
    finely diced (both white and
    green parts)

Salt to taste

Freshly ground black pepper
    to taste

1¹/₂ cups unbleached
    all-purpose flour

1 Put the spinach in a large pot. Cover and cook in its own water over medium heat for 3 minutes, or until wilted. Drain, cool, and form into three or four balls, squeezing each ball until dry. Chop the spinach balls and set aside.

2 Heat 2 tablespoons butter in a skillet over low heat. Add the pancetta, garlic, and onions and sauté for 8 minutes, stirring constantly. Add the spinach and cook for 5 minutes more, stirring until all ingredients are well blended. Season with salt and pepper and set aside.

3 Sift the flour and a pinch of salt into a large bowl. Cut in the remaining butter and begin to knead, adding cold water, 1 tablespoon at a time as is needed, to form a soft, elastic dough.

4 Preheat the oven to 350°F. Butter and flour an 8-inch springform pan.

5 Divide the dough into two uneven portions, one slightly larger than the other. Put the larger portion on a floured surface and roll into a 10-inch circle that is 1/8 inch thick and place the circle into the springform pan, patting the dough against the sides. Top with the spinach mixture, smoothing the surface with a spatula. Beat the eggs with the cheese and pour over the spinach.

6 Roll out the remaining portion into an 8-inch circle that is 1/8 inch thick. Cover the filling with the smaller circle, pressing the edges of the dough to seal shut. Pierce the top with a fork in three or four places.

7 Bake for 20 minutes, or until the surface of the dough is golden brown. Cool slightly, remove from the pan, slice, and garnish with 2 or 3 cherry tomato halves.

Make Ahead The spinach can be prepared through Step 2 up to 2 days in advance and refrigerated in a sealed container until ready to use. The dough can be made earlier in the day, wrapped in plastic wrap, and refrigerated until needed.

How to Serve Works very well as part of a party buffet, as an appetizer, or as a main course when served with braised leeks or braised celery.

Wine Suggestion Dry White

2 large eggs

1/2 cup freshly grated Parmigiano-Reggiano

9 cherry tomatoes, halved

TIMBALLO DI SAN GIOVANNI

St. John's Day Cheese Timballo

❦ Abruzzo ❧

E domani e San Giovanni
fratel caro; e San Giovanni
Su la Plaia me ne vo gire,
per vedere il capo mozzo
dentro il Sole, all'apparire,
per veder nel piatto d'oro
tutto il sangue ribollire.

Tomorrow is Saint John's Day
Dear Brother; it is Saint John's Day.
I want to go to the beach
To see the head
In the sun, to see it appear,
In the plate of gold
With the blood boiling anew.

AT ONE TIME, THROUGHOUT ITALY, ALMOST EVERY CITY AND VILLAGE CELEBRATED *the feast of St. John the Baptist, which falls on June 24, three days after the summer solstice. Gigantic fires were lit in huge terra-cotta pots filled with pork fat, their purpose to pull the waning sun back into the summit of the heavens. I remember, as a young girl, seeing the fires rise into the sky over St. John's Baptistry in Florence, the flames stretching up to Giotto's campanile and lighting up the palaces of the Signoria. Today, there are few such celebrations left. But in Vasto, on Abruzzo's southern coast, young girls still stand at their windows the night of June 23, waiting to spot the first rays of the sun. According to legend, the first girl to see the decapitated head of St. John in the golden circle of sun rising over the Adriatic (a visualization recalling the golden platter on which Herod offered the Baptist's head to Salome) will marry within the year. This fanciful legend was memorialized by Italian poet, Gabriele D'Annunzio in "Figlia di Iorio," one verse of which is reprinted above.*

serves 6

1 Boil the potatoes in salted water for 15 to 20 minutes, or until soft and easily pierced with a fork. Peel, cool to room temperature, and cut into thin slices.

2 Heat 2 inches of oil to 375°F in a heavy-gauge skillet.** Dredge the potato slices in flour, dip in egg, and fry until golden brown. Drain the potatoes on paper towels and salt.

3 Preheat the oven to 350°F. Butter an 8-inch-round baking pan.

4 Transfer the fried potatoes to the baking pan and top with the cheese. Season with salt and pepper, dot with 2 tablespoons of the butter, and bake for 20 minutes, or until the cheese is completely melted. Remove from the oven, top with prosciutto, and sprinkle with cheese. Melt the remaining butter and pour over the top. Serve immediately.

How to Serve As an appetizer or an entrée served with a mixed green or simple tomato salad.

Wine Suggestion Medium-bodied Red

Time: 80 to 90 minutes

Level of Difficulty: Moderate

277

1 pound boiling potatoes (about 5 to 7)
Salt to taste
Flour for dredging
2 large eggs, lightly beaten
Olive oil for frying
1 pound scamorza* or mozzarella, thinly sliced
Freshly ground black pepper to taste
4 tablespoons unsalted butter
5 ounces prosciutto, cut into thin strips
3 tablespoons freshly grated Parmigiano-Reggiano

---

*Scamorza is a type of pasta filata cheese popular in southern Italy. Similar to mozzarella, it is made by slicing soft cow's milk cheese into curds, fermenting the curds for a few days, and then boiling them. The curds are then formed into balls that are tied up at one end (or placed in nets) and soaked in brine.

**To test the temperature of the oil, you can put a cube of bread into the skillet. When it sizzles around the edges and turns golden almost immediately, the oil is the right temperature.

TORTA PASQUALINA

Chard and Ricotta Tart

❦ Liguria ❦

LEGEND HAS IT THAT WHEN SAINT ROCCO WAS DYING OF A PESTILENCE PLAGUING *the Ligurian village of Camogli, he went to live in the woods so as not to endanger those who were still well. There he encountered great numbers of animals also affected by the pestilence and each one he blessed spontaneously healed—a miraculous turn of events depicted by Tintoretto on a huge canvas residing in the Church of Saint Rocco in Venice. Thus Camogli honors Saint Rocco, patron saint of all animals, especially dogs, every August 16, his birthday, with a procession beginning at the Monumento ai cani—the Monument to Dogs, and eventually winding up at Rocco's namesake church where everyone—both paraders and their pets—actually enter the church for a communal benediction.*

Then it's time to eat and drink—pets too! The following tart—a tour de force of the Ligurian kitchen and one traditionally reserved for Easter celebrations (hence the name)—has now ascended into the lexicon of essential foods whenever any Ligurian town holds a festival. A scrumptious tower of chard, porcini mushrooms, ricotta, and ten layers of flaky dough, Torta Pasqualina is well worth every one of the 120 minutes it takes to prepare.

serves 6 to 8

Time: About 2 hours

Level of Difficulty: Advanced

⨳

CRUST

6 cups unbleached all-purpose flour

4 tablespoons extra virgin olive oil plus oil for brushing

1 teaspoon salt

2 tablespoons water

1 To make the dough, heap the flour on a work surface and make a well in the center. Add the oil, salt, and 2 tablespoons water and stir with a fork, incorporating a little flour each time and adding water, 1 tablespoon at a time as needed to create a smooth, elastic dough; some flour may remain. Divide the dough into 10 balls, each the size of an egg*, cover with a clean cloth, and set aside.

2 To make the filling, blanch the chard in boiling salted water for 3 to 4 minutes, or until completely wilted. Remove from the heat, cool to room temperature, squeeze dry, and mince.

*A traditional Torta Pasqualina consisted of thirty-three layers, one for each year of Christ's life.

3 Heat the oil in a skillet over medium heat and sauté the onion for 3 to 4 minutes, or until translucent. Strain the mushrooms (reserve the liquid for another use), chop, and add them and the chard to the onions. Sauté for 7 minutes, stirring constantly. Remove from the heat and set aside.

4 Put the ricotta, milk, bread, and salt in a bowl. Mix until the ingredients are well blended.

5 Preheat the oven to 400°F. Butter and flour a 10-inch springform pan.

6 Put the dough on a floured work surface and roll each of the balls into a 10-inch circle. Place the first circle on the bottom of the pan and brush with olive oil. Layer with 4 more circles, brushing each with oil.

7 Spread the fifth layer with chard mixture. Cover with the sixth layer of dough and spread it with ricotta. Make 6 egg-size depressions in the ricotta. Break 1 egg into each depression; sprinkle the cheese over the eggs.

8 Gently layer the remaining dough in the pan, brushing each layer with oil. Pierce the top layer in two or three places with a fork. Brush with oil.

9 Bake for 60 minutes, or until golden brown. Remove from the oven, cool slightly, remove from the pan, slice, and serve, either cold or at room temperature.

Make Ahead The chard can be blanched and diced a day or two in advance and refrigerated in a sealed container. The dough can also be made a day or two in advance, wrapped in plastic wrap, and refrigerated. It can also be frozen for up to 3 weeks, but in either case, should be returned to room temperature before spreading.

How to Serve As part of a party buffet, an appetizer, or an entrée paired with warm, marinated mushrooms.

Wine Suggestion Dry White

FILLING

1 1/2 pounds chard, stemmed

4 tablespoons extra virgin olive oil

1 small onion, diced

2 ounces dried porcini, soaked in warm water for 30 minutes

1 1/2 cups fresh ricotta

1 cup whole milk

2 slices white bread, crusts removed

Salt to taste

6 large eggs

1/2 cup freshly grated Parmigiano-Reggiano

279

PANZEROTTO ALLA CAPONATA

Eggplant, Red Pepper, and Black Olive Calzone

❧ Campania ❧

EVERY YEAR ON OCTOBER 16, MILLIONS OF PILGRIMS JOURNEY TO THE MATERDOMINI *Sanctuary—just above Caposele—to participate in the festival honoring San Gerardo Maiella. At the beginning of the trip, everyone is handed a small bag of wheat seeds blessed specifically for the occasion. When planted, the sacred wheat is said to protect the rest of the crop from harm.*

This wonderful calzone (panzerotto is another name for calzone) is closely associated with the feast of St. Gerard, as are a number of other bread- and cheese-based dishes.

serves 4

Time: 90 minutes

Level of Difficulty: Moderate

🜊

1 medium eggplant (about
    1 pound), peeled and cut
    into 1-inch cubes

Salt to taste

1 small red pepper

1 small yellow pepper

1/2 cup extra virgin olive oil

1/4 cup water

2 medium red onions,
    thinly sliced

1 teaspoon sugar

Freshly ground black pepper
    to taste

2 tablespoons capers, drained

1 Toss the eggplant with salt and place in a colander to drain for 1 hour.

2 Meanwhile, using tongs, hold the peppers over an open flame until the skins are completely charred.* Place in a paper bag, seal, and let rest for 10 minutes. Remove the peppers, peel away the charred skin, cut in half, remove the seeds, and slice into thin strips.

3 Heat 3 tablespoons oil in a skillet over low heat, add 1/4 cup water, and braise the onions for 8 minutes, stirring constantly. Add the sugar, salt, pepper, capers, pine nuts, olives, and peppers and toss until well blended.

4 Rinse the eggplant and dry on paper towels. Heat the remaining oil over medium heat and sauté the cubes for 7 to 8 minutes, stirring constantly. Season with salt and toss with the onion mixture.

*Alternately, the peppers can be placed in a roasting pan and broiled—turning when necessary—until the skins are charred on all sides

5 Preheat the oven to 500°F.

6 Put the dough on a floured work surface and roll into a 20-inch circle that is 1/4-inch thick. Place the vegetables on one half of the circle, fold the dough over the filling, and press the edges together to seal.**

7 Beat the egg, cream, and cheese together in a bowl. Brush the calzone with this mixture to cover all surfaces. Transfer to a 10 x 12 baking sheet.

8 Bake for 25 minutes. Remove from the oven, slice, and serve.

Make Ahead The pizza dough can be made earlier in the day, wrapped tightly in plastic wrap, and refrigerated until needed. It can also be frozen for up to 3 weeks. Return to room temperature in either case before spreading.

How to Serve As an appetizer or an entrée paired with a radicchio and arugula salad.

Wine Suggestion Dry White

1/4 cup pine nuts

12 black olives, pitted and chopped

1 recipe Basic Pizza Dough (page 463)

1 small egg

2 tablespoons heavy cream

2 tablespoons freshly grated grana padana or Parmigiano-Reggiano

"This recipe can be adapted to make four individual calzones. Divide the dough into four pieces and roll each into a 5-inch circle.

FRITTELLE DI RICOTTA

Sweet Ricotta Fritters

❧ Campania ❧

GERARD MAIELLA (SEE PAGE 280) IS A FAIRLY RECENT SAINT, HAVING BEEN BORN IN *1726 to a poor family in Muro Lucano. One night when he was still a child, a white-robed infant appeared to him bearing a wafer of bread. The scene was repeated every night for weeks and finally Gerard asked to receive communion, but was refused because he was too young. After crying for hours before the statue of St. Michael to whom he was devoted, Gerard found that the infant reappeared and placed a sacred host on his tongue. From then on, Gerard understood his vocation and spent the next twenty years of his life as a member of the Order of St. Alfonso. In 1755, he was assigned to a mission in the Sele valley, then plagued with widespread malaria and died that very year. Miracles attributed to him generally involve either farmers or small children.*

These St. Gerard Day ricotta fritters are generally served as a merenda—*midmorning or midafternoon snack. They can also be served as a dessert with vin santo or other dessert wine.*

makes about 20 fritters

Time: About 30 minutes

Level of Difficulty: Moderate

⚚

8 ounces fresh ricotta, preferably
    not prepackaged
2 slices soft, white bread, crusts
    removed
1/2 cup whole milk
1/4 cup sugar
1 large egg yolk, well beaten
Grated zest of 1 small orange

1 Place the ricotta in a large bowl and beat with a wooden spoon or electric mixer until smooth.

2 Soak the bread in the milk, then squeeze dry. Add the bread, sugar, egg yolk, and orange zest to the ricotta, stirring until well blended.

3 Heat 2 inches of oil in a heavy skillet to 375°F.* Pinch off walnut-size pieces of the ricotta mixture, dredge in flour, and then dip in the egg. Fry the fritters, 4 or 5 at a time, until each turns a light golden. Remove with a slotted spatula and drain on paper towels.

*To test the temperature of the oil, you can put a cube of bread into the skillet. When it sizzles around the edges and turns golden almost immediately, the oil is the right temperature.

4 Arrange the fritters on a serving platter, dust with powdered sugar, and serve hot.

How to Serve Works well as part of a salad course when the powdered sugar is eliminated; place three or four fritters on a bed of baby greens and drizzle with vinaigrette. When dusted with the sugar, the fritters can be finger food at parties or a dessert served with vin santo or other dessert wine.

Wine Suggestion If served as part of a salad, dry white; as a dessert, serve with a medium-sweet type of dessert wine.

Olive oil for frying
Flour for dredging
1 large egg, well beaten
Confectioner's sugar for dusting

283

TRAMEZZINI

Fried Bread Squares Stuffed with Mozzarella and Olive Paste

❦ Calabria ❦

IN SANTA SOFIA D'EPIRO, IN THE COSENTINO, THE FIRST SUNDAY OF MAY IS *devoted to the Feast of Saint Athanasius, who was a member of the Albanian Orthodox church. Participants—men and women—are all dressed in traditional Albanian costumes and the songs and chants are all in Albanian. For anyone unfamiliar with Orthodox traditions, this is a wonderful opportunity to participate in a ritualistic celebration not otherwise seen in Italy.*

This quick and easy fried sandwich is served on festival days throughout the Cosentino where it is prepared in huge caldrons of boiling oil.

serves 6

Time: 20 to 30 minutes

Level of Difficulty: Moderate

⚱

12 slices white bread, crusts
    removed
1/3 cup prepared black or
    green olive paste*
12 ounces bufala or fresh cow's
    milk mozzarella, thinly sliced
Flour for dredging
2 large eggs, well beaten
Breadcrumbs for dredging
Olive oil for frying

1 Spread the bread slices with the olive paste. Top half the slices with thin slices of mozzarella cut to fit. Do not let the mozzarella overlap the bread. Cover with the remaining bread slices.

2 Dredge the sandwiches in flour, dip in egg, and roll in breadcrumbs. Heat 2 inches of oil in a heavy skillet to 375°F.** Add half the sandwiches and fry until golden brown. Repeat until all the sandwiches are fried. Drain on paper towels and serve immediately.

How to Serve As an appetizer followed by roast chicken served with panfried artichokes.

Wine Suggestion Medium-bodied Red

Olive paste can be prepared at home. Place 1/2 pound black or green pitted olives, 3 tablespoons extra virgin olive oil, and a pinch of salt in the bowl of a food processor and process to a smooth paste.

***To test the temperature of the oil, you can put a cube of bread into the skillet. When it sizzles around the edges and turns golden almost immediately, the oil is the right temperature.*

FRITTELLE DI MOZZARELLA

Fried Mozzarella Rounds

❧ Calabria ❧

THESE QUICK, EASY, AND SO INCREDIBLY DELICIOUS MOZZARELLA ROUNDS ARE ALSO *associated with the Feast of St. Athanasius (see page 284) and are, in fact, fried in the same oil as the bread squares in recipe on page 284. No matter which food stall I approached, however, there were never any left to sell—they had all been eaten as soon as they emerged from the cauldron. On the one hand, they should not sit around or the mozzarella will solidify; on the other, I was amazed at how the people of the village just popped one after another into their mouths as if eating fritters made of air.*

makes 8 slices or 4 servings

Time: 20 minutes

Level of Difficulty: Moderate

✼

2 large eggs
Salt to taste
2 tablespoons whole milk
1 pound bufala or fresh cow's milk
   mozzarella*, cut into eight
   1/2-inch-thick rounds
1 cup breadcrumbs
Olive oil for frying

1 Beat the eggs, a pinch of salt, and milk together in a bowl until smooth.

2 Dip the mozzarella into the egg and then roll in breadcrumbs. Dip again in egg and roll again in breadcrumbs.

3 Heat 2 inches of oil in a heavy skillet to 375°F.** Fry the mozzarella slices, a few at a time, until golden brown. Remove immediately and drain on paper towels. Serve hot.

How to Serve Works well as an appetizer surrounded with slivers of yellow roasted peppers.

Wine Suggestion Dry White

*Do not use prepackaged mozzarella for this recipe. It is too dry to result in the soft, runny texture required.

**To test the temperature of the oil, you can put a cube of bread into the skillet. When it sizzles around the edges and turns golden almost immediately, the oil is the right temperature.

FRICO

Fried Cheese Wedges

❧ Friuli-Venezia-Giulia ❧

SANTA LUCIA IS CELEBRATED ALL OVER ITALY, BUT IN NO PLACE IS SHE MORE *revered than in Udine, where her bones lie buried. Italian children particularly love this December 12 celebration, since it is another of those days when they receive gifts. In fact, there is a children's song with lyrics that display both a certain aspect of youthful cunning and the traditional identification of the father as the keeper of the purse:*

> *Santa Lucia, Santa Lucia,*
> *Porta bomboni in calza mia*
> *Se la mamma no me le mete*
> *Resta svode le calzete*
> *Ma con la borsa de papá*
> *Santa Lucia porterá.*

> Saint Lucia, Saint Lucia
> Fill my stocking with candies
> If my mother won't do it
> My stocking will stay empty
> But with father's money
> Saint Lucia will prevail.

The following is a traditional Friuli snack and one that is especially associated with Saint Lucia's Day, given that most children everywhere love fried finger food. It can also be made as one large frittatalike circle and cut into wedges.

makes approximately 4 fricos

1 Cut the cheese round into $1/2$-inch-thick slices. Dip each slice in milk and dredge in the polenta.

2 Heat the butter in a nonstick skillet over medium heat and fry the cheese rounds for 2 to 3 minutes per side, or until golden brown. Drain on paper towels and serve hot.

How to Serve Works very well as a breakfast or brunch entrée, especially when topped with freshly fried eggs.

Wine Suggestion **Dry White**

Time: 20 minutes

Level of Difficulty: Easy

287

One 8-ounce round goat or
  cow's milk cheese, such as
  camembert, brie, or chèvre)
$1/2$ cup whole milk
2 ounces coarsely ground polenta
8 tablespoons (1 stick)
  unsalted butter

SPIEDINI DI SCAMORZE E CACIOCAVALLO

Baked Kebabs Made with Scamorze and Caciocavallo Cheeses

❧ Molise ❧

ON THE SECOND WEEKEND OF JULY, FROSOLONE—WEST OF CAMPOBASSO—
celebrates both the Festa della Montagna *and* La Sagra del Caciocavallo *(Mountain Festival and
The Caciocavallo Cheese Fair), two local events that encompass cultural presentations, sporting events,
cheese-making demonstrations, and wonderful, generous cheese-tastings. The festival's guest of honor is,
of course, caciocavallo, a large, pear-shaped cheese made in pairs, tied together, and slung over a piece of
wood known as the* cavallo *or horse (*cacio *means cheese). Like scamorza, caciocavallo is often smoked
before using. The Molisani eat it as a main course, grilled over charcoal (or lightly smoked as per the
following recipe) and served with crusty bread, assorted meats, and heady red wine.*

*Here, it is paired with scamorza, a mozzarellalike cheese that melts perfectly around the harder
caciocavallo to create these delectable oven-baked kebabs.*

serves 4

Time: 45 minutes

Level of Difficulty: Easy

Equipment: 12 wooden skewers

॥

8 ounces scamorza or fresh
    mozzarella, cut into
    1/2-inch-thick squares
4 tablespoons extra virgin olive oil
8 ounces country-style bread,
    crusts removed and cut into
    the same size squares as
    the cheese

1 Preheat the oven to 400°F.

2 Marinate the scamorza squares in
2 tablespoons of the oil for 10 minutes, turning
the squares three or four times.

3 Arrange the bread slices in a baking pan and
toast the bread on both sides in the oven.

4 Thread skewers with 1 slice bread, 1 slice
scamorza, 1 slice caciocavallo, and 1 slice bread.
Continue until all the ingredients are used up and
all the skewers are tightly packed. The last ingredient
at either end of the skewers is bread.

Young cheeses are softer and sweeter than the aged varieties.

5 Oil a baking pan and arrange the skewers so that the ends rest on the edges of the pan and the centers are suspended over the center. Bake for 20 minutes.

6 Meanwhile, heat the remaining oil in a skillet over low heat and cook the anchovies for 5 minutes, stirring constantly until dissolved.

7 Remove the baking pan from the oven and transfer the skewers to a heated platter. Blend the pan juices with the dissolved anchovies to create a thick sauce. Season with salt and pepper. Brush the skewers with the sauce and serve immediately.

How to Serve Makes a wonderful lunch when served with leeks braised in white wine.

Wine Suggestion Dry White, Medium- or Full-bodied Red

8 ounces fresh, young caciocavallo* or young, soft pecorino or provolone, cut to the same size as the scamorza (see note page 293 about provolone)

4 salt-packed anchovies, filleted (see page 25)

Salt to taste

Freshly ground black pepper to taste

CACIOCAVALLO AL FUMO

Lightly Smoked Caciocavallo

❧ Molise ❧

THE MOLISANI SMOKE THEIR CACIOCAVALLO IN HUGE OUTDOOR PITS OVER POTS OF *boiling water; the resulting creation is consumed with thick slices of* mulette *(cured pork shoulder) or* capelomme *(smoked pork tenderloin), wedges of country-style bread, and maybe a bottle or two of* Copertino *(a local D.O.C. wine made from the Negroamaro grape). A Weber-type smoker will work just as well as an open pit, but a wok can also be used. The following recipe is for wok cooking. If using an outdoor smoker, smoke for twenty-five to thirty-five minutes over aromatic wood.*

serves 4

Time: 25 to 35 minutes

Level of Difficulty: Moderate

꒰꒱

1 pound caciocavallo or young
    pecorino or provolone
    (see note on page 293
    about provolone)
3 tablespoons extra virgin olive oil
1 tablespoon dried oregano
3 to 4 tablespoons dried herb
    mixture or oregano, thyme,
    rosemary, and sage
1 tablespoon black tea leaves

1 Cut the cheese into 1/2-inch-thick disks, baste both sides with the oil, and sprinkle with oregano.

2 Line the wok with aluminum foil, folding the foil over the sides. Place the dried herb mixture and the tea leaves on the foil. Arrange the cheese on a rack and place in the wok over the herbs. Cover the wok and seal the overlapping foil over the opening. Cook for 25 to 35 minutes over low heat, or until the cheese is soft. Serve immediately.

How to Serve As a main course, accompanied by thick wedges of cured meats. Precede with a bowl of thick vegetable soup.

Wine Suggestion Full-bodied Red

TIMBALLO DI SCAMORZE E CACIOCAVALLO

Scamorza, Caciocavallo, and Potato Terrine

❦ Molise ❧

THIS IS ANOTHER OF THE UNIQUE DISHES PRESENTED AT THE CACIOCAVALLO FESTIVAL *(see page 288). In the original recipe, the potatoes were dipped in an egg-and-flour batter before frying; I have eliminated this step in favor of adding a final layer of prosciutto and a sprinkling of grated cheese.*

serves 6 to 8

Time: 55 minutes

Level of Difficulty: Easy

⚶

Olive oil for frying

1 pound boiling potatoes
(about 5), peeled and cut
into 1/4-inch rounds

Salt to taste

8 ounces caciocavallo or young
pecorino or provolone,
cut into 1/4-inch rounds

8 ounces scamorza or fresh
mozzarella, cut into
1/4-inch rounds

Freshly ground black pepper
to taste

4 tablespoons unsalted butter

4 ounces prosciutto, cut into
very thin strips

3 tablespoons freshly grated
Parmigiano-Reggiano

1 Heat 2 inches of oil in a heavy skillet to 375°F.* Fry the potatoes until golden. Drain on paper towels and salt to taste.

2 Preheat the oven to 350°F. Butter an 8- or 9-inch-square baking pan, preferably glass or terra-cotta.

3 Place the potatoes in the bottom of the pan. Cover with a layer of caciocavallo, dust with pepper, add a layer of scamorza, dust with pepper. Dot with half the butter and bake for 20 minutes.

4 Remove from the oven. Raise heat to broil. Top the terrine with a layer of prosciutto and a sprinkling of cheese. Melt the remaining butter and pour over the top. Broil for 3 to 5 minutes, or until browned. Remove from the oven, cut into wedges, and serve immediately.

How to Serve Can function as a lunch or dinner entrée when combined with sautéed spinach.

Wine Suggestion Medium-bodied Red

To test the temperature of the oil, you can put a cube of bread into the skillet. When it sizzles around the edges and turns golden almost immediately, the oil is the right temperature.

PROVOLONE ALL'ACETO

Smoked Provolone Panfried with Oregano and Balsamic Vinegar Sauce

❦ Sicilia ❦

AS WITH ANY SICILIAN FESTIVAL, CALTAGIRONE'S *FESTA DI SAN GIACOMO* *(Feast of St. James) stupefies the imagination. On the night of July 24, James's relics are carried through the town along with an extremely heavy throne upon which a statue of the saint teeters precariously. That night and the next, the 142 steps of Santa Maria del Monte Church are lit on both sides with candles enclosed in large colored-paper "flowers." At 9:30 P.M., when the capomastro blows the ceremonial horn, the festival "captain" lights both the two long wicks tying together each set of 142 candles, and another series attached to yet another 3,000 candles surrounding the piazza. With all the city lights dimmed for the occasion, the effect is spectacular—a multicolor blaze of fire illuminating the ancient houses surrounding the square.*

Following is a wonderful recipe for panfried smoked provolone I have taken to serving as a light summer entrée accompanied by a salad of greens and tomatoes, crusty bread, and, of course, plenty of red wine.

serves 4

Time: 25 minutes

Level of Difficulty: Easy

⚶

4 tablespoons extra virgin olive oil

2 cloves garlic, crushed

1 1/2 pounds smoked provolone*, cut into strips about 1 x 1/2 inch

4 tablespoons balsamic vinegar

1 teaspoon freshly chopped oregano

1 Heat the oil in a large, heavy-gauge skillet over low heat and sauté the garlic for 4 minutes, stirring constantly. Remove and discard the garlic and add the cheese strips, arranging them in one layer. Cook for 3 to 4 minutes per side without allowing the cheese to brown.

2 Pour the vinegar over the cheese, sprinkle with the chopped oregano, and cook for 4 minutes longer. Serve immediately.

How to Serve As an appetizer followed by penne
with *arrabiata* (angry) sauce and a green salad.
Arrabiata is tomato sauce spiced up with hot chilies.

Wine Suggestion Medium or Full-bodied Red

*Provolone is a delicious southern Italian cheese made by first boiling cow's milk curds and then soaking them in brine.
Sicilians are blessed with many varieties: dolce, a mild version aged two or three months; piccante, sharp and spicy and
aged for up to a year; and affumicato, lightly smoked for a week and then aged for three to four months. If the smoked
version is unavailable, substitute only very good quality provolone; do not attempt this recipe with the flavorless,
rubbery, prepackaged provolone sold in supermarkets.*

Meats, Game, and Poultry

BRASATO AL BAROLO
*Beef Sirloin
Braised in Barolo*

PITAGGIO
*Veal Sausages with
Artichokes and
Fresh Fava Beans*

AGNELLO BRODETTATO
Lamb Ragù

SCOTTIGLIA
*Chicken, Veal, Pork,
and Guinea Hen Cooked
with Tomatoes and Herbs*

**ANATRA IN
DOLCE E FORTE**
*Duck Cooked in
White Wine and
Chocolate*

**PICCIONI IN
CASSERUOLA**
*Roast Pigeon with
Black Olives*

**CONIGLIO IN
PORCHETTA**
*Oven-roasted Rabbit
Stuffed with Prosciutto*

**CAPRIOLO ALL
GINEPRO**
*Ragù of Venison
with Herbs and
Juniper Berries*

**POLPETTONCINI CON
LA MOZZARELLA**
*Mozzarella-stuffed Meatballs
Braised in Tomatoes*

**SCALOPPINE AI
CAPPERI**
*Veal Scaloppine with
Parsley-Caper Sauce*

**ABBACCHIO ALLA
CACCIATORA**
*Panfried Spring Lamb with
Herbs and Anchovy Sauce*

**VITELLO AL
VINO ROSSO**
Veal in a Red Wine Ragù

**OSSOBUCO CON
GREMOLATA**
*Veal Shanks with Lemon Zest
and Dried Porcini*

LEPRE ALLA BARBERA
Hare with Red Wine Sauce

FAGGIANO TARTUFATO
Truffled Pheasant

POLLO ALLA MARENGO
*Sautéed Chicken with
Poached Shrimp and
Fried Eggs*

**POLLO RIPIENO
ALLE NOCI**
*Chicken Stuffed with
Walnuts*

QUAGLIE IN UMIDO
*Panfried Quail with
Buttered Rice*

**SUPREME DI POLLO
ALLE VERDURE**
*Rolled Chicken Breast
Stuffed with Vegetables
and Braised in White Wine
and Heavy Cream*

CONIGLIO GRATINATO
Gratinéed Rabbit

**TACCHINO ARROSTO
ALLA MELAGRANA**
*Roast Turkey with
Pomegranates*

**CINGHIALE ALLO
SPELLO**
*Wild Boar Braised with
Pine Nuts, Raisins,
Chocolate, and Prunes*

SPIEDINI MISTI
*Chicken, Lamb, and Pork
Kebabs Grilled with Sage
and Pancetta*

**INVOLTLINI DI
MAIALE AL FORNO**
*Grilled Bundles of
Herb-stuffed Pork*

FARAONA ALLA CRETA
*Guinea Hen Cooked
in Terra-cotta*

PUGLIA
Going Once, Going Twice

AN OLD BLUE-HAIRED WOMAN LEANS OUT OF A WINDOW on the fifth floor of the turn-of-the-century tenement building. "Alfredo," she shouts to her son waiting down below. "*Fattene presto.*" She slowly unravels a white laundry cord and lowers the wicker basket that contains that day's shopping list. Thirty minutes later, Alfredo once again stands beneath the window. "*Mamma,*" he yells loud enough for the neighborhood to hear; the old woman retrieves the basket the contents of which now include four tomatoes and a fresh loaf of hot, crusty bread.

Thousands of people line the procession route as the gilded statue of Saint Anthony weaves its way through the narrow streets. Borne on the shoulders of ten men nattily clad in gold cuff links and navy blue suits, the saint's bodice is heavy with the weight of $20 bills.

The storefront windows reveal nothing other than a neatly etched sign, "Society of San Gandolfo." Inside, the room is bare except for a few tables and chairs and, in the corner, an old espresso machine installed above a small, minimally stocked bar. The air is thick with the aroma of DeNobili cigars as the six old men hunch over the table, holding their cards close to their chests.

Such are the images of life in New York's Little Italy—a palette of sights, sounds, and smells as exotic to me, a native Tuscan perfectly fluent in Italian, as to my friends of Scottish, Dutch, or Jewish ancestry. Despite my Italian heritage, I have never had any understanding of such things as the dialectal exchange between the two waiters standing outside Umberto's Restaurant on Mulberry Street, or the hand gestures accompanying an argument over whose vehicle was to blame for the accident involving a garbage truck and a double-parked Lincoln Continental. Tuscany has no stands selling lemon ice, no Tuscan celebrates a religious feast day by leaving a small plate of fruit on the windowsill, and Tuscan bread has no sesame seeds on the outside crust.

But the first time I traveled to southern Italy—especially Puglia—it suddenly all made sense, every bit of it. So much so that I felt instantly at home. Here, live and in brilliant color, were all the nuances and customs that have always defined New York's "Italian Experience"— an experience I observed while growing up part of every year on the border of New York's Little Italy. To me, it had always seemed as though the neighborhood's largely Southern Italian population had fashioned the details of its existence not on heritage, but on a sort of melting-pot experience—which, as immigrants sequestered inside those twenty-odd square blocks for so many years, they had collectively evolved into a distinctly new breed of person, the Italian-American.

I was wrong. What really happened was that New York's Southern Italian immigrants brought with them, intact, their foods, dialects, values, traditions, even their plastic slipcovers and their love of kitschy religious knicknacks!

This was the realization that attended my first visit to Puglia in 1995. I had journeyed to the region to soak up its smells and flavors on behalf of my cooking school in Tuscany, which that spring was sponsoring a week of lessons with Giuseppe Mafeii, one of Bari's most famous chefs. Giuseppe, whose summers have long been spent in the beach cabana near mine in Viareggio—therefore, the friendship—had offered to give me a gastronomic tour spanning five Puglian cities. Included were Lecce, Ostuni, Taranto, Gallipoli, and Alborobello, which is in the heart of the *trulli* district (*trulli* are sixteenth-century cone-shaped stone dwellings built without mortar so they could be quickly razed by their peasant inhabitants whenever the royal inspectors came to assess residential taxes).

My impressions on that initial whirlwind trip were tantamount to those of someone who suddenly discovers a long-lost sister. I felt as if some part of me had been reconciled; as if all the things that had prevented me from unconditionally embracing Millie and Joe and Theresa and Frances and all the other Southern Italians in my New York neighborhood had evaporated. Puglia's gastronomy became secondary, although no one should ever feel that way about such culinary marvels as *orecchiette con cima di rape* (ear-shaped pasta with broccoli rabe) and the heavenly *tortiera di cozze* (baked stuffed mussels).

I returned to Puglia this year, again at Giuseppe's invitation. This time—knowing I was researching this book—he insisted I witness Altamura's *Festa della Madonna del Buoncammino.* "The most authentic religious festival in all of Puglia," he declared.

To get here, I once again drove south—past the Etruscan Maremma in southern Tuscany, through the golden foothills of the Lazio, around the mountain curves of Campania, and finally across the flat, fertile plains of the Pugliese interior to explore what northern Italians refer to as *La terra dei temperamenti vivaci*—The Land of Mercurial Passions. The attribution is not wrongly leveled, although I suspect an undercurrent of meaning other than that the Pugliese simply have a great zeal for life.

I am to meet Giuseppe in Altamura, a small picturesque town that is about twenty-five miles outside Bari and as different from that combustible port city as silk is from sackcloth. A tranquil enclave surrounded by walls dating back to 300 B.C., Altamura is regionally famous for both its thirteenth-century, twin-towered cathedral and a legion of wood-fired ovens churning out the legendary *pane accavallato* (*u sckuanéte* in dialect)—thick, crunchy loaves of bread made from *semolino di grano duro* (semolina flour milled from the heart of the amber-colored durum wheat grain), which weigh from four to ten pounds each.

Giuseppe, bless his soul, consigned me to the care of Altamtura's local priest, in whose house I would spend the next few days. "Don Pierino knows everybody," Giuseppe assured me by phone. "You will undoubtedly have no problem getting a good viewing spot once he picks through his Rolodex and introduces you to the right people."

Getting a good viewing spot for the *Madonna del Buoncammino* festival is not an easy thing, Giuseppe explains. Apparently tens of thousands flock to Altamura to pay tribute to this particular Madonna, who is fêted for three tumultuous days, climaxing in a Sunday-night procession that involves four white oxen, hundreds of horses, a flower-bedecked float bearing legions of white-robed children, and a never-ending column of costumed faithful. The procession begins in late afternoon at the Buoncammino Sanctuary five miles outside town and journeys at snaillike pace along a dirt road that eventually, around 10:00 P.M., arrives at Porta Bari, the arched entry into the city's historic center.

While the Madonna is still hours away from arrival, however, another event asserts its prominence and it is this event that has Don Pierino in a completely agitated state when Giuseppe and I first arrive on his doorstep. "Mario Lamantia is planning to bid on the banner," he whispers to Giuseppe as soon as we are seated in his office.

"*Bene,*" Giuseppe says with an enthusiasm that belies his lack of comprehension. Great.

"*Bene?*" booms Don Pierino, his eyes bulging from their widened sockets. "What are you talking about, *bene*? Mario's motives have absolutely nothing to do with religious devotion."

"Then what?" Giuseppe asks, chastened.

"Publicity!" As spoken by Don Pierino, the word assumes a sudden aura of red lights and dark, illicit transactions.

"*Ma che dici?*" says a shocked Giuseppe. And then they notice my confusion.

The banner, Giuseppe pauses to explain, is the satin standard of Altamura's patron, the Madonna dell Buoncammino. "Every year, the church auctions it off to the highest bidder, who wins the right to keep it in his possession for the next twelve months." Generally, he says, the banner goes for about $12,000.

"Purely and simply a demonstration of faith," he explains, when I ask why anyone would offer so much money just for the sake of a satin banner. "People know the money goes toward continuing this beautiful tradition and they're happy to do their part. Bidding represents nothing more than basic devotion to a very deserving Madonna."

"The problem," adds don Pierino, returning to the situation at hand, "is that Mario sees the banner as a vehicle for publicizing that fancy restuarant he opened last year on the outskirts of Altamura."

Mario, they add, has recently moved back to Altamura after eleven years in Los Angeles, where he worked as an advertising copywriter. "Ever since his return, he has driven people in this town crazy with his constant talk about the value of publicity," says don Pierino. "A few months ago, he wanted me to begin placing weekly notices in the local paper announcing the theme for the following Sunday's sermon. 'Reminds people you're here,' he offered by way of motivation. 'Nobody needs to be reminded of where we are,' I told him, but I knew as soon as I had spoken that I might as well have saved my breath."

Giuseppe shakes his head in disbelief. "At first, he tried to start an advertising company like the one he worked for in America," he says, sadly. But after talking to every business owner in town, he evidently failed to convince even one that his services were needed." He reaches across Don Pierino's desk and picks up a well-designed flyer announcing the upcoming festival. "Some people never learn though."

"His mother came in yesterday," Don Pierino adds. "Poor woman was almost in a state of shock after Mario told her his plans. 'Do something,' she begged me. But what am I supposed to do?"

"Who else is planning to bid?" Guiseppe asks.

"Antonio Bernardi and Vincenzo Tresca that I know of. But I'm sure there are at least ten or twelve others."

"Well, perhaps Mario will simply be outbid."

"Perhaps," says Don Pierino unconvincingly. "But just in case, I think I will ask the good Madonna to stretch forth her influential hand."

Giuseppe was right: Don Pierino does, in fact, know everyone. Before my bag was even unpacked, he had entrusted me to the *commandante* of Altamura's police whose job it would be to introduce me to the local dignitaries. Moreover, he had arranged for me to view the procession from a balcony belonging to Giacomo Carissimo, doctor and sometime journalist who lives directly across from the *cattedrale,* the eventual endpoint of the Madonna's journey.

But first, this well-connected man-about-town decided to give me a personally guided tour of the city's gastronomic strongholds. The first stop is Pastificio Le Mure, known throughout the area for its unique, artisan-made pasta. Contrary to northern Italy's fresh, egg-based pasta, dressed with an endless array of complex sauces, the country's impoverished south has traditionally subsisted on dried pasta—*pastasciutta*—flavored mainly with simple tomato-based sauces.

The Pugliese, it seems, consume more pasta per capita than any other Italians; perhaps, Don Pierino ventures, because of its topography. One of the few regions in Italy not dominated by the Appenines, Puglia is mainly composed of flat, fertile fields—many devoted to the cultivation of the high-quality, hard durum wheat used to make an endless quantity of dried shapes. From *recchietelle* (shells) to *minuicchi* (tiny dumplings) to *laganelle* (small-cut lasagne) to *bucatini* (thick, hollow spaghetti) to *orecchiette* (shaped like ears), to *frciid* (finger-length batons) Pugliese pasta consists of nothing more than flour and water.

"We make it here," says Tomasso—Le Mure's owner and chief pasta maker—pointing to a room filled with bags of ground flour. "But then we dry it in the sun, sometimes for five or six hours. The result is a very hard pasta that can take as long as twenty minutes to cook."

As prearranged by Don Pierino, Tomasso guided us to a table set with a ready-to-eat bowl of homemade minuicchi dressed simply and deliciously with fresh, uncooked tomatoes, arugula, basil, and olive oil. "*Mangiate,*" he says and pours us each a large glass of dark, viscous wine.

"Santo Stefano?" asks Don Pierino, holding the wine up to the light.

"*Sì,*" says Tomasso. "Unfortunately, I only have three bottles left of the '94."

As we eat, Tomasso explains that Santo Stefano is one of Puglia's finest red wines. "Although," he concedes, "that is a very difficult assessment to make since so many towns produce excellent local vintages." In fact, he says, Puglia is one of Italy's foremost—albeit, undiscovered—wine regions. When I ask him to be more specific with respect to individual vintages, he names Sansevero del Tavoliere (a very pale and dry white wine), Torre Quatro del Cerignola (a hearty red that, after five or six years, reaches 14-percent grade), and Primitivo del Castel del Monte (a ruby-red wine from the Gioia del Colle region) as his favorites. He also cites the many excellent red wines originating from the area around Brindisi. "Ergo, the term, *fare un brindisi* (make a toast)."

"Tell her about our oil," Don Pierino prompts.

"But Anna is from Tuscany," Tomasso says. "No matter what I say, she is going to insist on the superiority of Tuscan olive oil—even if most of their oil has to be blended with ours in order to be any good!" He jokingly holds up his hands in fear of a potential attack.

"It's true," Don Pierino says. "But then, so much of what we Southerners produce is shipped to the North and sold for five times as much under their own private label." He looks at me and smirks.

I'm not sure we agree on the actual amount of food exported, but I am sure that what Tomasso says about olive oil is true. Puglia is just now beginning to realize the value of their olives. Even so, a great deal of their heavily fragrant, green-veined oil is still shipped to the North to even out lesser quality blends. The region's best oil comes from the areas around Bitonto, Adria, Barletta, and Molfetta, where the olives seem infused with the heady fragrance of fresh almonds—Puglia's most important food product.

"It's not only a question of quality," Tomasso says, "although quality is certainly important when talking about olive oil. But it always makes me mad that Tuscany is known throughout the world as the land of olive trees when the truth is, you probably only have one tree for every ten planted here!"

No truer words were ever spoken. The number of olive trees in Puglia is probably only exceeded by the number of mussels fished every year from its fecund waters. The land is flat and the region vast (Puglia has a longer coastline than any of Italy's other regions), and as you drive from Bari in the north to Lecce in the south, you see endless panoramas blanketed with dusty green *ulivi*.

By now we have finished the last of the *minuicchi al pomodoro fresco* and, as if on cue, Tomasso reappears at our table bearing an assortment of beautiful terra-cotta bowls, each containing an individual vegetable preserved *sott'olio*—in olive oil. "The tradition of bottling vegetables in oil dates back to the days before houses had refrigerators," he explains, "when women laid the vegetables out in the sun to dry and then packed them in jars of oil."

The perfect solution for dealing with summer abundance, oil-marinated vegetables eventually came to define the South so much so that it is now commonplace to serve a complete course consisting of nothing other than thick-skinned plum tomatoes, strips of white or purple eggplant, red and yellow peppers, tender fava beans, porcini mushrooms, and sweet summer onions—all served with their oil marinades and consumed with *friselle*.

"Do you know what *friselle* are?" Tomasso asks when we have sampled a little of each vegetable. When I shake my head no, he produces a bowl of water and a basket of very hard bread rounds. "Another example of our genius," he declares, immersing the bread for only a split second. "It is so hot here in Puglia that fresh bread goes stale very quickly. So the ancient *massaie* took to baking bread in thin rounds, splitting the rounds in half and then baking them again until they were hard as rocks. When ready to eat, they were simply reconstituted with water, piled with chopped tomatoes or marinated vegetables, and drizzled with oil." He tops one with slivers of roasted yellow peppers and places it on my plate. "Delicious with a glass of red wine," he urges.

When the meal and tour are over, Don Pierino and I speed to the southern end of Corso Vittorio Emanuele, where the auction for the banner has already begun. "I have so much to do today," he grumbles, as we make our way through Altamura's narrow back streets. "But I promised Mario's mother I would at least try one more time to make him change his mind.

It is clear to me as soon as I lay eyes on Mario La Mantia that nothing Don Pierino can say is going to make even the slightest bit of difference. There he stands, directly behind the auction officials, his face glowing with the thrill of anticipated victory. In truth, the other bidders look equally determined, but there is a ferocious edge about Mario that separates him from the joyous, almost naive, quality of the dozen or so other contenders.

"The man with the megaphone is Nicola Olivieri," Don Pierino explains. "President of the Madonna dell Buocammino Society for the last twenty-six years. During the next hour or so, he will walk up this street, a few steps at a time, pausing every third or fourth step to announce a new amount. Those men you see standing behind him are all bidders. When the procession finally arrives at the large cobblestones in front of the Piazza Madonna dei Martiri"—Pierino points in the direction of Altamura's walls—"Olivieri will take one last step onto the stones, bring the bidding to a close, and the winner will take possession of the banner."

"*Prima candela,*" Olivieri booms into his megaphone, just as Don Pierino completes his explanation—Going once—"Mario La Mantia, five million lire" ($3,500). There is silence for a moment, and then the ragtag group of octogenarian musicians making up the front line breaks into a rather pathetic version of "*Funicoli, funicola.*" The crowd applauds and Mario stands a little straighter in his tailored navy-blue suit.

Everyone takes another step. "*Prima candela,*" Olivieri begins again, "Carlo Morettini, five-and-a-half million lire." Again, the silence, again the band, again the applause. "*Bravo, Carlo,*" a voice from the crowd yells out.

Another step. "*Prima candela,* Bernardo Scarzantonio, six million lire." At this point, the procession stops so that journalists and photographers can appropriately record the event. Don Pierini nudges me forward and introduces me to Olivieri who, in turn, introduces us to two dark-suited men standing directly alongside him. The men, it turns out—George and Nicholas Lucarello—emigrated from Altamura to North Bergen, New Jersey, in 1951 along with a large group of other Altamurans; they have since returned as often as they could, specifically for this festival. When they find out I am from New York, they beg me to come to North Bergen on Labor Day weekend. "Our neighborhood holds a Buoncammino festival almost exactly like this one," they tell me.

The auction continues. At one point, a verbal fight breaks out among the bidders. Olivieri has apparently attributed what is now an 18-million lira bid to Bernardo Scarzantonio and Vincenzo Tresca is saying it was his. Different men take sides and the procession comes to a twenty-minute halt until the matter can be properly straightened out.

By 5:00 P.M., the procession is about ten feet away from the cobblestones that will define its termination and the bidding has reached 24 million lire. "Let's move a little closer to the endpoint," Don Pierino urges me. "When the final amount is announced, the crowd crushes in on the bidders and everyone surges toward the walls." I heed his warning, especially since the crowd is now at least 50,000 people strong.

"*Prima candela,*" Olivieri continues, wiping away the sweat with a rumpled white handkerchief, "Mario La Mantia, 25 million lire." The crowd breaks into booming applause. Mario's face is tight. He cannot be stopped, I think to myself. But then I remember that, as the afternoon has progressed, Don Pierino has seemed less and less worried. Has he just given up, I ask myself. Is this his way of dealing with the inevitable?

"*Prima candela,* Vincenzo Tresca, 25.5 million lire."

"Who is this man, Vincenzo Tresca," I ask Don Pierino. In the past fifteen minutes, it seems the bidding has narrowed to a contest between him and Mario.

"Truck driver," Pierino answers. "Bidding on behalf of himself and his partner, Tomasso Marinelli. Very appropriate it would be if the two of them win. The Madonna is the patron saint of drivers you know. Very nice men, those two. Very nice."

"*Prima candela,* Mario La Mantia, 25.750 million lire."

"Seems like he's determined," I say as Don Pierino and I struggle to hold our front line positions.

"The will of God will soon reveal itself," he answers with what I swear is the beginning of a self-satisfied smirk.

"*Prima candela,* Vincenzo Tresca, 25.780 million lire."

The crowd roars.

"*Seconda candela,* Mario La Mantia, 25.790 million lire."

"This is it," Don Pierino screams above the growing exhortations. "Olivieri is just about on the cobblestones and there's only room for one more bid.

"Mario! Mario! Mario!" The crowd is surging forward and booming its support..

"Vincenzo! Vincenzo! Vincenzo!" My arms are pinned against my sides.

"*Terza candela......* Vincenzo Tresca, 26 million lire!" A roar erupts from the crowd as everyone surges through the walls, Vincenzo and Olivieri leading the pack.

"Anna!" Don Pierino's urgency pierces the din.

"I'm here!" I grab his outstretched hand and the two of us are pulled along into City Hall piazza

Ten minutes later, Vincenzo and a number of festival officials emerge onto the balcony of the ornate government building. There is a ribbon draped across Vincenzo's chest and as he hoists the Buoncammino banner over the crowd, Olivieri leans over the edge, showing off the check for 26 million lire.

"Well, I guess the best man won," I say to Don Pierino, turning to see his expression. But his gaze is turned up toward Vincenzo. And just then, just as I also turn my gaze upward, I think I see Vincenzo staring at Don Pierino and his lips forming the words "*fatto*"—done.

But I am not sure that's what I really saw. And no amount of questioning Don Pierino over the next few days produces anything other than a sort of self-satisfied grin.

BRASATO AL BAROLO

Beef Sirloin Braised in Barolo

304

❦ Piemonte ❦

IMAGINE FOR ONE DAY BEING ABLE TO TRAVEL TO ANY OF OVER 400 VINEYARDS *(many otherwise closed to the public) throughout all of Italy's eighteen regions and having the doors thrown open in greeting. Imagine long baronial tables filled with magnificent platters of food, proprietors hovering at your elbow anxious to pour just one more vintage. Best of all, imagine that it is all free! Fortunately, one need no longer simply imagine; since 1994, the Italian Wine Trade Commission has organized Cantine Aperte, a one-day open-door event involving many of Italy's finest vineyards. The event takes place on one Sunday in mid-May and lasts from 10:00 A.M. to 6:00 P.M.*

The following recipe, a perfect marriage of tender, aged beef and barolo wine, was prepared by chef Paolo Vigniatoro at Monvigliero, one of the many superb barolo producers located southwest of Alba.

serves 4 to 6

Time: 2 1/2 hours, excluding the 24-hour marinating period

Level of Difficulty: Moderate

⚔

2 pounds boneless beef sirloin
1 bottle barolo wine or other
    full-bodied red wine
1 onion, quartered
1 medium carrot, julienned
1 celery stalk, julienned
1 bay leaf
1/4 teaspoon salt

1 Put the meat in a large glass pan with the wine, onion, carrot, celery, bay leaf, salt, and peppercorns. Cover and marinate for 24 hours in the refrigerator, turning the beef five or six times during that period.

2 Using tongs, lift the beef from the marinade, roll into a cylinder, and tie with kitchen string. Heat the butter in a large skillet over medium heat until foamy. Add the prosciutto fat, cook for 3 minutes, stirring constantly, and then add the meat and sear on all sides. Strain the marinade, discarding the solids, and pour the liquid into a saucepan. Cook over medium heat to reduce by half.

3 Reduce the heat to low. Pour the marinade over the meat, cover, and cook for 2 hours. Season with salt toward the end of the cooking time. Transfer the beef to a heated serving platter and degrease the pan juices.* Heat the juices until warm and whisk in the potato starch. Cook for 5 minutes over low heat until thickened.

4 Slice the meat thinly and arrange the slices on a serving platter. Pour a few tablespoons of the marinade over the beef and pass the remaining sauce in a saucebowl.

Note *According to Chef Vigniatoro the beauty of this dish lies in the beef being cooked to such a degree of tenderness that it can be simply eaten with a fork.*

How to Serve Accompany with roasted potatoes and baby green beans cooked until just tender.

Wine Suggestion Full-bodied Red

6 to 8 black peppercorns
4 tablespoons unsalted butter
1 ounce prosciutto fat, diced
1 teaspoon potato starch or other
    sauce thickener

305

Use a degreasing cup or roll up a wad of paper towels, dipping the end into the grease, cutting off the greasy end, and continuing dipping and cutting until the grease has all been removed.

PITAGGIO

Veal Sausages with Artichokes and Fresh Fava Beans

❧ Sicilia ❧

IN MODICA (RAGUSA PROVINCE), HOLY SATURDAY IS CELEBRATED WITH AN *idiosyncratic dramatization of the Virgin Mary playing the part of a sorrowful sleuth. At 10:00 A.M., a statue of Jesus leaves Santa Maria church on the shoulders of eight burly men, who carry it through the streets in a random directional pattern. Half an hour later, a black-clad woman playing the part of Mary exits through the back door of the church and begins searching for her son (trailed by hundreds of spectators screaming, "This way" "Turn left" "Go toward the market"). Somehow, I'm told, the two always manage to meet up around noon (conveniently in time for lunch), at which point Mary throws open her arms and from the folds of her cape, six white doves break into flight. The sky becomes a rainbow of blue and white and purple ribbons weaving around each other as the doves stuggle to free themselves of the silk ribbons attached to their feet. A suddenly joyful Mary approaches the statue of Jesus with tears in her eyes and kisses him (hence the name of the festival,* vasa vasa *which means kiss) and the crowd erupts into thunderous applause.*

Later that night, when the meatless vigil has been broken, Sicilians partake of this wonderful dish, combining four of spring's most cherished foods: baby artichokes, fresh fava beans, tiny peas, and tender spring veal.

serves 4

Time: 30 to 40 minutes

Level of Difficulty: Moderate

3 baby artichokes*
Juice of 1 lemon
6 tablespoons extra virgin olive oil
1¹/2 cups fresh or frozen
    baby peas

1 Remove and discard the artichokes' tough outer leaves and slice off the spiny tips. Remove the chokes and cut the artichokes into quarters. Put in a bowl, cover with water, and add the lemon juice.

2 Heat 3 tablespoons oil in a heavy-gauge saucepan over low heat. Add the peas, fava beans, artichoke quarters, salt, and pepper, cover and cook for 10 minutes, adding a few tablespoons water, if needed, to keep from sticking.

*Some baby artichokes have neither spines nor chokes.

3 Meanwhile, put the veal, cheese, bread, salt, pepper, and egg in a bowl and mix until well blended. Using your hands, form sausages the size of large wine corks. Dredge in flour and brown on all sides in the remaining oil.

4 Add the sausages to the vegetables, stir to blend the flavors, and cook for 10 minutes. Serve hot.

Make Ahead The sausage mixture can be prepared up to a day in advance and refrigerated until ready to use

How to Serve Accompany with *misticanza*—salad made with mixed baby greens

Wine Suggestion Medium-bodied Red

1 cup freshly shelled fava beans, or 1 pound unshelled
Salt to taste
Freshly ground black pepper to taste
12 ounces freshly ground veal
2 tablespoons freshly grated Parmigiano-Reggiano
1 thick slice stale country-style bread, crusts removed, soaked in milk for 20 minutes, and squeezed dry
1 large egg, lightly beaten
Unbleached all-purpose flour for dredging

307

AGNELLO BRODETTATO

Lamb Ragù

❧ Abruzzo ❧

AN ELEVENTH-CENTURY LEGEND TELLS OF SAN DOMENICO ARRIVING IN COCULLO *to find a large crowd racing after a rabid wolf that had just kidnapped a newborn baby. Moved by the parents' tears, the saint ordered the wolf in the name of God to drop the baby and, miraculously, the wolf obeyed. The residents were so enthralled that they begged the saint to donate something of his that they could use to protect themselves in the future. Domenico, the legend continues, ripped out a molar and gave it to them (that molar is today preserved in a golden tabernacle in the Church of San'Egidio) Centuries later, the Coculli's fear of rabid animals broadened to include a fear of snakebites, which led to an extremely bizarre festival called* La Sagra delle Serpi—*The Snake Festival—held the first Thursday of every May. Residents of Cocullo comb the woods searching for snakes, which are then displayed around the necks of specially trained men called* serpari—*snakemen—who strut around the festival grounds holding out the snakes for visitors to pet. The next day, all the snakes are returned to the woods.*

Afterward, at dinner, I have to admit I was a little suspicious of the various meat preparations spread beautifully across the table. But then I tasted this heavenly dish and decided, if it was indeed made with snakes, more power to the cooks.

serves 4

Time: 2¹/₂ hours

Level of Difficulty: Moderate

⚕

2 tablespoons extra virgin olive oil
4 ounces prosciutto, finely diced
1 medium onion, thinly sliced
¹/₈ teaspoon freshly grated
    nutmeg
¹/₈ teaspoon freshly ground

1 Heat the oil in a large, heavy-gauge skillet over low heat and sauté the prosciutto and onion for 8 minutes, stirring frequently. Stir in the nutmeg and pepper.

2 Increase the heat to medium, dredge the lamb in flour, and add to the skillet, cooking until browned on all sides. Increase the heat to high and pour in the broth, cooking 2 to 3 minutes, or until it evaporates. Reduce the heat to low, add the wine, and cook for 2 hours, stirring occasionally. Season with salt after 1 hour.

3 Remove the skillet from the stovetop and, using a slotted spoon, transfer the cooked lamb to a serving platter. Whisk the egg yolk with the lemon juice and pour into the skillet. Cook over medium heat for 1 minute, stirring constantly. Strain the sauce, pour over the lamb, top with lemon zest, and serve immediately.

Make Ahead In a pinch, the lamb can be half-cooked a few hours in advance and left to sit in the sauce. For best flavor, however, make the entire dish in one sitting.

How to Serve Can be arranged over rice or accompanied with garlic-rubbed bread. To make a one-dish meal, add a side dish of perfectly steamed green beans drizzled with extra virgin olive oil.

Wine Suggestion Full-bodied Red

black pepper
2 pounds boneless lamb,
    cut into 1-inch cubes
Unbleached all-purpose flour
    for dredging
1 cup Basic Meat Broth
    (page 460) or canned broth
1 cup dry white wine
Salt to taste
1 large egg yolk
1 tablespoon freshly squeezed
    lemon juice
1 tablespoon lemon zest

SCOTTIGLIA

Chicken, Veal, Pork, and Guinea Hen Cooked with Tomatoes and Herbs

❦ Toscana ❦

WHEN NOVEMBER ARRIVES WITH ITS CHILL WINDS, THE PEOPLE OF THE LUCCHESÍA *say that* I denti della vecchia San Frediano l'aspetta—*old women's teeth rattle on the feast of Saint Frediano, which falls on November 18. Another proverb on the same theme maintains* per San Frediano la neve al monte e al piano—*For the feast of Saint Frediano there is snow on the hills as well as the plains. Before being elevated to sainthood, Frediano was one of Lucca's most popular bishops; in 1455, the people of the Frediano area built a church in his honor which, today, remains one of Tuscany's most beautiful. On the morning of November 18, residents of Frediano hold a winter festival consisting of musical performances, poetry recitals, and ultimately, a grand communal lunch in the church hall where I was very surprised to find a dish I had never before tasted. Being Tuscan, I, of course, assumed I knew everything.*

serves 4

Time: 1 hour, 45 minutes

Level of Difficulty: Easy

5 tablespoons extra virgin olive oil

1 medium onion, minced

2 cloves garlic, minced

2 tablespoons finely chopped
   Italian parsley

2 tablespoons finely chopped
   fresh basil

4 ounces chicken breast, cut into
   1/2-inch cubes

4 ounces veal, cut into 1/2-inch
   cubes

1 Heat the oil in a large skillet over low heat. Sauté the onion, garlic, parsley, and basil for 8 minutes, stirring constantly.

2 Increase the heat to medium, add the four meats and cook, stirring frequently, until lightly browned. Pour in the wine and cook until it evaporates, about 3 minutes.

3 Add the tomatoes, salt, and pepper and when the sauce is somewhat thickened, add the broth, reduce the heat to low, cover, and cook for 1 hour.

4 Toast the bread on both sides and rub with garlic. Divide the meat among four plates, arrange 5 pieces of bread around each rim, garnish with parsley, and serve hot.

Make Ahead The meat can be cooked earlier in the day and reheated just before serving.

How to Serve Makes a wonderful entrée following a bowl of tortellini in chicken broth or simply a bowl of chicken broth cooked with rice or orzo.

Wine Suggestion Full-bodied Red

4 ounces pork loin, cut into 1/2-inch cubes

4 ounces guinea hen, rabbit, pheasant, or beef, cut into 1/2-inch cubes

1 cup dry white wine

1 pound ripe Italian plum tomatoes, peeled, seeded, and passed through a food mill

Salt to taste

Freshly ground black pepper to taste

1 quart Basic Meat Broth (page 460) or canned broth

Twenty 3-inch squares country-style bread

2 cloves garlic, halved

12 leaves fresh Italian parsley for garnish

ANATRA IN DOLCE E FORTE

Duck Cooked in White Wine and Chocolate

❧ Toscana ❧

AS PLEASANTLY SURPRISED AS I WAS TO FIND THE UNFAMILIAR *SCOTTIGLIA* *(see page 310), at last year's San Frediano festival, I was just as surprised to find this old favorite— an absolutely scrumptious dish the name of which—*dolce e forte—*means sweet and strong, a Tuscanization of sweet-and-sour. This blend of pignolis (pine nuts), chocolate, raisins, onions, broth, vinegar, and dry white wine is not common to Tuscan cooking, and yet the recipe for this dish dates back over 400 years. The same preparation can also be used with chicken, rabbit, pheasant, or guinea hen.*

serves 4 to 6

Time: 2³/4 hours, excluding the 3-hour marinating period

Level of Difficulty: Moderate

1 duck, about 5 pounds
2 large onions, minced
2 celery stalks, minced
1¹/2 cups red vinegar
4 tablespoons extra virgin olive oil
1 medium carrot, diced
1 cup dry white wine
Salt to taste
Freshly ground black pepper
    to taste
1¹/2 cups Basic Meat Broth
    (page 460) or canned broth
¹/4 cup pine nuts

1 Put the duck in a large bowl with half the minced onions and celery. Pour in 1 cup of the vinegar and enough water to cover. Soak for about 3 hours.

2 Heat the oil in a Dutch oven or heavy-gauge saucepan over low heat. Sauté the remaining onion, celery, and carrot for 8 minutes, stirring constantly. Increase the heat to medium, remove the duck from the marinade, pat dry with paper towels, and put into the pan. Cook until lightly browned on all sides. Discard the marinade.

3 Pour the wine into the pan, season with salt and pepper, and cook over high heat until reduced, about 5 minutes. Add 1 cup of the broth, reduce the heat to medium, and cook for 1¹/2 hours, or until tender. Add broth, if need, to prevent the duck from sticking.

4 Remove the duck it from the pan, cut into serving pieces, and keep warm. Add two-thirds of the pine nuts, the raisins, chocolate, and sugar to the pan juices, stir up any meat scrapings, and cook, stirring constantly, over low heat for 5 minutes, or until well blended.

5 Return the duck to the pan, pour in the remaining vinegar, and stir gently until the sauce is blended and the duck is well coated. Season with salt and pepper and cook for 5 minutes. Transfer the duck to a serving platter and garnish with the remaining pine nuts. Pour the sauce into a sauce bowl and serve immediately.

Make Ahead As with many other meat recipes requiring a long cooking period, this one works fairly well even if the meat is cooked halfway earlier in the day and left to sit in the juices until finished. For maximum flavor, however, cook the entire dish in one sitting.

How to Serve Accompany with roasted potatoes and some type of sautéed greens. Also works well when preceded by a bowl of pasta tossed with parsley and garlic.

Wine Suggestion Full-bodied Red

1/4 cup sultana raisins, soaked in warm water for 20 minutes, drained, and squeezed dry

1/4 cup grated bittersweet chocolate

1 teaspoon sugar

313

PICCIONI IN CASSERUOLA

Roast Pigeon with Black Olives

❦ Le Marche ❦

IN THE MOUNTAIN VILLAGES SURROUNDING ASCOLI PICENO, THE NIGHT OF *December 9 is devoted to blazing fireworks that, according to ancient tradition, served to illuminate the coming of the Madonna of Loreto, who is the patron saint of aviators. The story behind why this particular Madonna was chosen by aviators is somewhat of a comedy of errors. Originally, the legend maintains, she was moved in statue form from place to place by angels who, although anxious to establish her presence among Christians, were unable to decide on the proper spot. Then, when Moslems occupied Nazareth, the statue was borne "on a carpet of clouds" to the port of Recanati, to a forest owned by a woman named Loreta. But then the forest was found to be inhabited by bandits and so the Madonna once again took flight, this time just down the road, to a farm belonging to the brothers Simone and Stefano Antici. The brothers, however, now possessing such a valuable treasure, began to fight between themselves, resulting in the Madonna being moved to the middle of a public road in Ascoli Piceno where she now resides in a specially created sanctuary. In her honor, many of the surrounding villages throw* porta-aperta *(open-door) parties, where, following the fireworks, people can wander in and out of houses, sampling a vast array of local and traditional foods such as the following.*

serves 4

Time: 45 minutes

Level of Difficulty: Moderate

⊥

1/2 cup extra virgin olive oil

4 pigeons or quail, washed, dried,
    and seasoned with salt
    and pepper

4 thin slices pancetta

1 medium onion,
    thinly sliced

1 Preheat the oven to 350°F.

2 Put 6 tablespoons oil in a roasting pan. Stuff each pigeon with 1 slice pancetta, arrange in the pan, breast side up, and roast for 30 minutes.

3 Meanwhile, heat the remaining oil in a skillet over low heat and sauté the onions for 8 minutes, stirring constantly. Add the flour, stir a few seconds to make a thick paste, add the wine, and cook, stirring constantly, 4 to 6 minutes, or until it evaporates.

4 Add the broth and olives and cook for 10 minutes. Season with salt.

5 Pour the olive sauce over the pigeons, stir to blend the juices, and bake for 5 more minutes. Remove the pigeons and place on individual serving plates. Surround with a pool of sauce, arrange the olives around the perimeter like the numbers on a clock, and serve.

Make Ahead The pigeons can be stuffed earlier in the day and refrigerated until cooked. The sauce can be made the day before and refrigerated in a sealed container until ready to use.

How to Serve Accompany with garlic-roasted potatoes and sautéed broccoli.

Wine Suggestion Medium- or Full-bodied Red

1 tablespoon unbleached all-purpose flour

1 cup dry white wine

1/2 cup Basic Meat Broth (page 460) or canned broth

5 ounces gaeta or other black olives, pitted

315

CONIGLIO IN PORCHETTA

Oven-roasted Rabbit Stuffed with Prosciutto

❦ Le Marche ❧

I SAMPLED THIS AMAZING STUFFED RABBIT IN THE HOME OF LORENA TALERI, *a ninety-two-year-old resident of Colle San Marco, a tiny village east of Ascoli Picena (see page 314). Signora Taleri is known throughout the area as the queen of the* porta-aperta—open-door—*festivities. For the past thirty-eight years, she has blanketed her table with an array of foods that boggle the mind. Last year—I am happy to report—was no exception.*

serves 4

Time: 2 hours

Level of Difficulty: Advanced

2 cloves garlic, crushed

2 stalks wild fennel, roughly
    chopped, or 2 fennel fronds

1 rabbit (about 2 1/2 pounds),
    washed, dried, and seasoned
    with salt and pepper

1 cup water

6 tablespoons extra virgin olive oil

2 ounces prosciutto, diced

2 ounces hard salami, diced

2 ounces pancetta or
    unsmoked bacon, diced

Salt to taste

Freshly ground black pepper
    to taste

1 Put the garlic, fennel, and rabbit in a soup pot. Add 1 cup water, cover, and cook for 20 minutes over low heat.

2 Heat 2 tablespoons oil in a skillet over medium heat. Sauté the prosciutto, salami, and pancetta for 3 minutes, stirring constantly.

3 Using tongs, remove the rabbit from the pot, discarding the garlic, fennel, and any liquid. Put the rabbit in the skillet. Cook the rabbit, turning frequently, until very lightly browned on all sides.

4 Preheat the oven to 350°F.

5 Remove the rabbit from the skillet and stuff the cavity with the sautéed meats. Using kitchen thread, sew up the opening and season with salt and pepper. Pour the remaining oil into a baking pan, add the rabbit, and roast for 30 minutes.

6 Pour the wine and broth over the rabbit and cook for another half hour, basting 4 or 5 times with pan juices.

1 cup dry white wine

About $1/2$ cup Basic Meat Broth (page 460) or canned broth

3 to 4 sprigs fresh Italian parsley for garnish

7 Remove the rabbit from the pan and let sit on a carving board for 10 minutes. Meanwhile, transfer the pan juices and any scrapings to a small saucepan and cook over low heat, stirring constantly, until reduced by half.

8 Using a serving spoon, remove the meats from the cavity of the rabbit. Cut the rabbit into serving pieces and arrange on a platter surrounded by the stuffing. Pour the sauce over the top and garnish with fresh parsley.

Make Ahead The rabbit can be prepared earlier through Step 1. Remove from the liquid and refrigerate until ready to use.

How to Serve This dish pairs well with garlic-sautéed greens such as chard, spinach, or broccoli rabe.

Wine Suggestion Full-bodied Red

CAPRIOLO* ALL GINEPRO

Ragù of Venison with Herbs and Juniper Berries

318

☙ Val d'Aosta ❧

ARNAD'S *SAGRA DEL LARDO* IS A FAIRLY YOUNG FESTIVAL, DATING BACK ONLY TO *1970. But its focus is a food that has been highly prized by every Valtellina family for centuries: lard, a quintessential pork delicacy used to flavor soups, stews, and sautés. Not to be confused with fatback, Val d'Aosta's lardo, or salt pork, comes from privately raised pigs nourished exclusively on vegetables, chestnuts, chick pea flour, and whey. Immediately after butchering season in November, each family seasons its lard with herbs and spices and layers it in chestnut casks (doils) where it ages for six to nine months. The result, sad to say, has no American counterpart and so instead of turning to the dried wedges of fatback sold in American markets, I have substituted butter in this hearty cold weather ragù.*

serves 4

Time: 2³/4 hours, excluding marinating time

Level of Difficulty: Moderate

2 pounds venison, cut into
    1-inch cubes
1 celery stalk, chopped
1 medium carrot, sliced in half
2 cloves garlic
1 medium onion, halved
6 to 8 sprigs fresh Italian parsley
8 juniper berries, crushed
1 bay leaf
5 to 6 sprigs fresh thyme

1 Put the venison in a bowl and toss with the celery, carrot, garlic, onion, parsley, juniper berries, bay leaf, thyme, cloves, cinnamon, and wine. Cover with plastic wrap and marinate in the refrigerator for 24 hours, turning the venison 2 or 3 times.

2 Remove the venison from the marinade and drain well, making sure to remove any traces of herbs or seasoning that might cling to the meat. Heat the butter in a large skillet over low heat and cook the venison until all surfaces are lightly browned. Pour in the grappa and cook 3 to 4 minutes, or until it evaporates. Season with salt and pepper and then add the flour, stirring until blended, and adding 1 to 2 tablespoons of marinade, as needed, to prevent sticking.

Capriolo means roe buck, a smaller, more tender type of deer common to the Valtellina.

3 Reduce the heat to low, stir in the tomato pulp, cover, and cook for 2 hours, stirring occasionally and adding an equal blend of marinade and broth, as needed. The finished product should be heavily sauced and the sauce should be quite thick.

4 Using tongs, remove the venison pieces from the skillet and place on a heated platter. Add the cream to the remaining sauce, season with salt and pepper, and cook over low heat for 5 minutes, stirring constantly. Do not allow to boil. When the sauce is thick and creamy, return the venison to the skillet, add the parsley, toss until all pieces are well coated, and serve immediately.

Make Ahead The venison can be half-cooked earlier in the day and refrigerated in the pan until necessary.

How to Serve Can be served as is accompanied by a green salad and plenty of bread to soak up the sauce, or placed over rice and served with sautéed greens.

Wine Suggestion Full-bodied Red

319

3 whole cloves
1 cinnamon stick
2 cups dry red wine
2 tablespoons unsalted butter
1 cup grappa or cognac
Salt to taste
Freshly ground black pepper
   to taste
2 tablespoons unbleached
   all-purpose flour
1½ cups canned Italian plum
   tomatoes, drained and passed
   through a food mill
About ½ cup Basic Meat Broth
   (page 460) or canned broth
1 cup heavy cream
1 tablespoon freshly chopped
   Italian parsley

POLPETTONCINI CON LA MOZZARELLA

Mozzarella-stuffed Meatballs Braised in Fresh Tomatoes

❧ Campania ❧

THROUGHOUT CAMPANIA, THERE ARE MORE THAN 300 CATHOLIC ORGANIZATIONS *devoted specifically to the Madonna dell'Arco, whose feast day is celebrated on the Monday after Easter. The devotion originated in 1450 on a country road leading from Naples to the village of Ottaviano where someone had painted an image of the Madonna (who takes her name, dell'Arco, from the numerous arches of a nearby aqueduct) on a stone retaining wall. One day, a young man playing* pallamaglio, *an ancient version of golf, fell into a rage after a bad swing and flung his ball against the painted image which began to bleed. A chapel was subsequently constructed on the site and, in 1594, after another series of miracles, followers begged Pope Clement VIII to enlarge the chapel into the sanctuary it is today. On the assigned Monday, pilgrims flock from all over Naples to the outskirts of Ottaviano where they hold elaborate prayer services with dramatizations and musical performances. Afterward, the long fasting days of Lent having ended, they repair to local restaurants for rich, satisfying dishes such as the following.*

serves 4

Time: 90 minutes

Level of Difficulty: Moderate

LOAVES

4 thick slices country-style bread,
 soaked in warm water for 20
 minutes and squeezed dry

3 tablespoons chopped fresh
 Italian parsley

1 pound chopped beef

1/2 cup freshly grated
 Parmigiano-Reggiano

1 To make the loaves, put the bread, parsley, beef, cheese, salt, pepper, and egg in a bowl. Using your hands, mix until the ingredients are well blended and then form into four 3 x 5-inch rectangles, about 1/2 inch thick. Arrange a few mozzarella batons in the center of each rectangle and roll from the long end into tight cylinders. Press the meat slightly to hold the cylinders firm.

2 To make the sauce, heat the oil in a skillet over low heat and sauté the onion, carrot, celery, parsley, and basil for 8 to 10 minutes, stirring constantly, or until soft. Add the tomatoes, season with salt and pepper, cover, and cook for 20 minutes, stirring occasionally.

3 Meanwhile, fry the beef rolls in 1 inch oil in a large skillet over medium heat until browned on all sides. Remove with a slotted spoon and drain on paper towels.

4 Put the rolls in the tomato sauce, replace the cover, and cook for 20 minutes, turning 4 or 5 times during that period and adding broth, if needed, to keep the rolls from sticking. To serve, place one roll on each plate. Surround with a pool of sauce and garnish with basil leaves.

Make Ahead The mozzarella-stuffed meat loaves can be prepared earlier in the day and refrigerated until cooked.

How to Serve Pair with sautéed greens—broccoli rabe works especially well.

Wine Suggestion Medium- or Full-bodied Red

Salt to taste

Freshly ground black pepper to taste

1 large egg, lightly beaten

8 ounces fresh bufala or cow's milk mozzarella, cut into 1 x 2-inch batons

SAUCE

3 tablespoons extra virgin olive oil

1 medium onion, minced

1 small carrot, diced

1 celery stalk, diced

2 tablespoons freshly chopped parsley

4 fresh basil leaves

1 pound ripe Italian plum tomatoes, peeled, seeded, and diced

Salt to taste

Freshly ground black pepper to taste

About 1/2 cup Basic Meat Broth (page 460) or canned broth

Olive oil for frying

8 to 12 basil leaves for garnish

SCALOPPINE AI CAPPERI

Veal Scaloppine with Parsley-Caper Sauce

322

❧ Campania ❧

WHEN I MADE THE CLIMB TO THE MADONNA DELL'ARCO SANCTUARY
(see page 320), I was one of the only people dressed in casual clothes. The bulk of her followers generally don white robes with a blue sash across the chest and a red one wrapped around the waist. According to ancient tradition, they race up the hill as fast as possible, but always remaining a few paces behind the flag bearer, who is generally chosen for his athleticism. Upon arriving, they line up in formation before the Madonna and give a vaguely militaristic salute, right hand raised to forehead, palm outstretched. The day I went, I was very careful to remain in the back, walking alongside Signora Rosanna Pallidi, who is not one of the faithful, but thought I might enjoy the experience. "Andiamo a mangiare," she said, as dozens of older men launched into their devotional chants. Let's go eat. And so we did.

serves 4

Time: 30 minutes

Level of Difficulty: Moderate

⚎

8 wafer-thin veal scaloppine,
    about 3/4 pound total*
Unbleached all-purpose flour
    for dredging
8 tablespoons unsalted butter
1 tablespoon extra virgin olive oil
1/2 cup capers, drained
3 tablespoons chopped fresh
    Italian parsley

1 Dredge the scaloppine in the flour. Heat the butter and the oil in a large, heavy-gauge skillet over medium heat until foamy. Fry the scaloppine until both sides are golden brown. Drain on paper towels and keep warm.

2 Increase the heat to high and put the capers, parsley, salt, and pepper in the skillet. Cook for 5 minutes, gently stirring to blend the ingredients.

3 Pour in the broth, add the vinegar, and cook for 2 more minutes. Add the scaloppine, turning once to coat both sides with the sauce. Serve immediately on a bed of lettuce and garnish with parsley.

If the scaloppine are not thin enough, place between waxed paper and pound gently with a kitchen mallet.

323

How to Serve Works especially well following a bowl of simple meat or mushroom broth.

Wine Suggestion Dry White

Salt to taste
Freshly ground black pepper
   to taste
1/2 cup Basic Meat Broth**
   (page 460) or canned broth
1 tablespoon white wine vinegar
Lettuce leaves for bedding
8 to 12 parsley leaves for garnish

**I also tried this recipe with porcini mushroom broth and very much liked the results.*

ABBACCHIO ALLA CACCIATORA

Panfried Spring Lamb with Herbs and Anchovy Sauce

❧ Lazio ❧

ON DECEMBER 8 IN ROME'S PIAZZA DI SPAGNA (THE SPANISH STEPS), IT IS THE *custom to lay flowers at the base of the ornate column that Pius IX erected in 1854 after proclaiming the doctrine of the Virgin Birth. The Feast of the Immaculate Conception is a national holiday throughout Italy and families gather at large tables for four- to seven-course meals. I spent last December 8 with my friend Count Ugo Pecchioli, who is also the owner of Camporomano, the estate where I have my cooking school in Tuscany. Despite overcast skies and quasi-wintry weather, Ugo dragged me around Rome and together we came upon a large crowd laying flowers and singing hymns as Rome's bishop held a prayer service in the neoclassical Church of Santa Trinita dei Monti. Later, he and I drank some wonderful brunello and cooked this most traditional dish made with new spring lamb.*

serves 4

Time: 40 to 45 minutes

Level of Difficulty: Easy

⚵

5 tablespoons extra virgin olive oil

3 pounds new spring lamb*, hacked into rough chunks

Salt to taste

Freshly ground black pepper to taste

2 tablespoons chopped fresh rosemary

2 cloves garlic, minced

1 tablespoon chopped fresh sage

1 Heat the oil in a large, heavy-gauge skillet over medium heat and cook the lamb until seared on all sides. Season with salt and pepper.

2 Add the rosemary, garlic, and sage and dust with flour. Mix well and when the flavors have thoroughly blended, about 3 minutes, reduce the heat to low, add the vinegar and 1/2 cup water, and cook for 15 minutes, stirring occasionally and adding vinegar and water, if needed, to prevent sticking.

3 Meanwhile, heat 1 to 2 tablespoons of cooking liquid from the lamb in a small skillet over medium heat. Chop the anchovies and add them to the pan, stirring until they disintegrate, about 3 minutes.

New spring lamb is milk fed and available fresh in spring, obviously. The best part is the haunch, which is tender and meaty. Ask your butcher to hack it into pieces.

4 Pour the anchovy sauce over the lamb and cook for 4 minutes, stirring constantly to coat all the pieces. Increase the heat to high and cook for 4 to 6 minutes, stirring constantly, until the lamb is coated with a dark, dense sauce of which there will be very little. Serve immediately, garnished with rosemary.

How to Serve Accompanied with fresh fava beans, boiled, salted, and drizzled with oil. Also works well as a rice or pasta topping.

Wine Suggestion Full-bodied Red

1 tablespoon unbleached all-purpose flour

About 1/2 cup red wine vinegar

1/2 cup water

3 salt-packed anchovies, filleted (see page 25)

4 sprigs fresh rosemary for garnish

325

VITELLO AL VINO ROSSO

Veal in Red Wine Ragù

❧ Sardegna ❧

SARDINIA'S *SAGRA DELLE LAUNEDDAS* IS ONE OF THE FEW SAGRAS IN ALL OF ITALY *focused on something other than food. Held in San Vito, a small village on the island's southeastern coast, this unique event features an ancient wind instrument made from three bamboo canes of various lengths and called* launeddas. *On the third weekend in August two years ago, I laid on my blanket under the stars of San Vito and gave myself up to the beauty of the sound, which seemed created by sea sirens. Every now and then, I wandered over to one of the food tables and grabbed a plate filled with wonders such as this incomparable veal drenched in buttery red wine.*

serves 4

Time: 2¹/₂ hours

Level of Difficulty: Moderate

7 tablespoons unsalted butter

1 medium onion,
    thinly sliced

2 pounds boneless veal,
    cut into 1-inch cubes

Salt to taste

Freshly ground black pepper
    to taste

1 Heat 4 tablespoons butter in a large skillet over medium heat and sauté the onion for 6 minutes, stirring constantly. Add the veal and brown on all sides. Bring the remaining butter to room temperature.

2 Season the veal with salt and pepper and pour in the wine and broth. Wrap the parsley around a bundle made from the garlic, bay leaf, and 1 sprig thyme and fasten it with kitchen string. Reduce the heat to low, place the bundle in the skillet, cover, and cook for 2 hours, adding water as needed to prevent sticking.

3 Using a slotted spoon, remove the veal and put on a heated platter. Discard the bundle of herbs, but reserve the pan juices. Put the remaining butter in a small bowl and add the flour, mixing with a fork until well blended. Add the butter mixture, a little at a time, to the reserved pan juices, stirring until smooth and thick. Pour the sauce over the veal and serve immediately, garnished with rosemary.

Make Ahead Step 1 can be prepared an hour or two in advance, covered, and set aside until needed.

How to Serve With sautéed greens and rustic bread.

Wine Suggestion Full-bodied Red

2 cups dry red wine

1 cup Basic Meat Broth
 (page 460) or canned broth

2 large bunches parsley, washed
 and dried

1 clove garlic, crushed

1 bay leaf

5 to 7 sprigs fresh thyme

1 tablespoon unbleached
 all-purpose flour

327

OSSOBUCO CON GREMOLATA

Veal Shanks with Lemon Zest and Dried Porcini

❧ Lombardia ❧

FERRARA'S PALIO IS HELD IN HONOR OF THE CITY'S PATRON, SAINT GEORGE, ON THE *last Sunday in May. One of Italy's oldest such events, this palio dates back to 1259 when it was held on Saint George's actual feast day, April 23, as a citywide celebration to which everyone was invited. Later it was reserved for the aristocracy and was only returned to the general public in 1930. The palio is really four separate competitions: first, among horses; the second, donkeys; the third, men; and the fourth, women. As with all palios, this one has more than its share of gorgeous costumes and extravagant pageantry. It also has a number of associated food traditions, of which this unique osso buco is my favorite.*

serves 4

Time: 1 hour

Level of Difficulty: Easy

⚖

4 veal shanks, about
    1½ pounds each
Salt to taste
Unbleached all-purpose flour
    for dredging
3 tablespoons extra virgin
    olive oil
5 tablespoons unsalted butter
1 medium onion, minced
1 small carrot, diced
1 celery stalk, diced

1 Season the shanks with salt and dredge in flour. Heat the oil in a large skillet over medium heat and brown the shanks on all sides. Drain on paper towels.

2 Heat the butter in another skillet over medium heat and sauté the onion, carrot, celery, and mushrooms for 10 minutes, stirring constantly. Add the veal shanks and, a few minutes later, pour in the wine. Cook for 20 to 30 minutes, or until the wine completely evaporates. Turn the shanks once or twice during cooking.

3 Shred the tomatoes into the skillet and add the broth. Season with salt and pepper and cook for 10 minutes, stirring frequently to blend the flavors.

4 Transfer the shanks to a serving platter and sprinkle with parsley and lemon zest. Surround with sauce and serve immediately.

Make Ahead Step 1 can be readied an hour or two in advance.

How to Serve Accompany with creamy polenta and perfectly steamed green beans.

Wine Suggestion Full-bodied Red

2 ounces dried porcini, soaked in warm water for 20 minutes, drained, and squeezed dry (reserve the liquid for another use)

2 cups dry red wine

2 cups canned Italian plum tomatoes, drained

1 cup Basic Meat Broth (page 460) or canned broth

Freshly ground black pepper to taste

2 tablespoons chopped fresh Italian parsley

2 tablespoons lemon zest

329

LEPRE ALLA BARBERA

Hare with Red Wine Sauce

330

❦ Piemonte ❦

LA SAGRA DEL MASENG WAS BORN FIFTEEN YEARS AGO AS AN ATTEMPT AT REVIVING *an old country festival dating back to the 1930s. At that time, farmers celebrated the end of a bountiful harvest with a three-day bacchanalia of eating, drinking, and game playing. The revival, slotted for late October, comes very close in spirit; held in a huge poplar-shaded park on the road from Asti to Alba, this sagra encompasses everything from dance contests to bocce competitions, as well as a wonderful menu featuring traditional dishes from every province in the Piedmont.*

This marinated hare was prepared by Signora Francesca Taglierini from a recipe handed down through six generations. When I asked if rabbit could be substituted, she shook her head violently in the uncomprising way that Italian cooks tend to do. She was only partly right; hare is better, if only because of its rich gamey taste. But the rabbit I sometimes use is still magnificent.

serves 4

Time: 3 hours, 15 minutes excluding the 2-day marinating period

Level of Difficulty: Advanced

¾

1/2 cup hare or rabbit blood*
 or red wine
11/2 bottles dry red wine**
Salt to taste
Freshly ground black pepper
 to taste
1 hare or rabbit, about 3 pounds,
 cut into pieces, washed, and
 dried with paper towels

1 Pour the blood into a bowl with a few table-spoons wine, a pinch of salt, and a pinch of pepper. Mix well, cover, and refrigerate. If you are not using blood, eliminate this step.

2 Marinate the hare or rabbit in a large bowl in the remaining wine, cloves, bay leaves, celery, carrot, onion, marjoram, thyme, salt, and the peppercorns. Refrigerate for 2 days, turning the pieces two or three times during that period.

3 On the day of preparation, heat the oil and butter in a large, heavy-gauge casserole, preferably terra-cotta, over low heat. Sauté the prosciutto fat and onion for 8 minutes, stirring constantly.

**Butchers who sell hare can save the blood for you, if notified in advance. If you cannot find or prefer not to use it, marinate the meat in wine.*

***Traditionally, aged barbera wine is used.*

4 Increase the heat to medium. Drain the
rabbit, reserve the marinade, dry with paper towels,
and add to the casserole, cooking until lightly
browned on all sides. Season with salt and add the
marinade ingredients. Cook for 2 hours over
medium heat, stirring occasionally, then add the
blood or wine, and cook for another 30 minutes.

5 Using tongs, remove the meat and place on
a heated platter. Pass the sauce, solids and liquids,
through a food mill and return to the skillet.
Stir in the sugar, return the meat to the stew,
and heat through.

6 Pour in the cognac, stir until well blended,
and serve immediately.

How to Serve The Piemontese have always
accompanied this dish with a hefty dollop of
creamy polenta.

Wine Suggestion Full-bodied Red

3 whole cloves
2 bay leaves
3 celery stalks, diced
3 small carrots, diced
1 large onion, thinly sliced
1/8 teaspoon dried marjoram
1/8 teaspoon dried thyme
4 black peppercorns
3 tablespoons extra virgin
   olive oil
2 tablespoons unsalted butter
2 ounces prosciutto fat or
   mezzina, diced
1 small onion, minced
1 tablespoon sugar
1 cup cognac

331

FAGIANO TARTUFATO

Truffled Pheasant

332

❦ Piemonte ❧

ANOTHER OF THE TRADITIONAL DISHES SERVED AT THE *SAGRA DEL MASENG* WAS *this delicious roasted pheasant, whose incomparable flavor derived both from the earthiness of the white truffles with which it was impregnated for twenty-four hours prior to cooking, and from the slices of lardo or salt pork placed over the pheasant during roasting for moisture retention. The truffles used are white tuber* Magnatum pico, *which come from the Monferrato-Langa area of Piedmont. Three types of truffles grow here, their differences having to do with the variety of trees under the roots of which they grow. The white variety, called* bianconi, *are found near poplar trees; truffles with a gray-hazel color grow near oaks; and the most precious and rare ones—gray with pink spots—which grow near cherry trees.*

serves 4

Time: 1 hour, excluding 1-day refrigeration

Level of Difficulty: Moderate

One 3- to 5-pound pheasant, cleaned and dried

2 to 3 small white truffles, brushed clean and cut into very thin slices

2 ounces mezzina or bacon, finely diced

3 slices mezzina or bacon for larding

Salt to taste

1 The day before cooking, stuff the pheasant with the truffles and diced mezzina. Wrap thoroughly in foil, place in a roasting pan, and refrigerate.

2 On the day of preparation, bring the pheasant to room temperature.* Preheat the oven to 350°F.

3 Arrange the slices of mezzina over the breast, tie the legs together with kitchen string, season with salt, and drizzle with oil. Bake for 45 minutes, or until cooked throughout.

4 Remove from the oven and cut the pheasant into serving pieces, retaining the skin of roasted mezzina. Arrange on a platter surrounded by watercress and serve.

It is a good idea to bring refrigerated meats to room temperature before cooking to ensure that they will cook evenly.

How to Serve Accompany with a platter of roasted vegetables that includes potatoes, onions, carrots, red peppers, fennel, and garlic.

Wine Suggestion Full-bodied Red

3 tablespoons extra virgin
    olive oil
1 bunch fresh watercress
    for garnish

333

POLLO ALLA MARENGO

Sautéed Chicken with Poached Shrimp and Fried Eggs

❦ Piemonte ❦

THIS UNLIKELY COMBINATION OF INGREDIENTS RESULTS IN ONE OF THE PIEDMONT'S *most traditional and delicious meat dishes. At the sagra, I was amazed at the number of fried eggs that seemed to be streaming out of the kitchen, each done to perfection and uniformly round. When I went back to meet the cooks, I saw a very old man leaning on a cane with one hand and flipping dozens of fried eggs with the other. "How do you get them all so perfect?" I asked. His answer made me smile. "I am seventy-one years old. If the eggs are not perfect by now, God will not give me another chance."*

serves 4

Time: 1 hour

Level of Difficulty: Moderate

6 tablespoons extra virgin olive oil

One 3-pound chicken, cut into pieces, washed, and dried

2 cloves garlic, crushed

5 ripe Italian plum tomatoes, peeled, seeded, and diced

1 1/2 cups dry white wine

Salt to taste

Freshly ground black pepper to taste

1 beef bouillon cube

4 large shrimp, unpeeled

1/2 cup chicken broth or any broth

1 tablespoon unsalted butter

1 Heat the oil in a skillet over medium-high heat and sauté the chicken, a few pieces at a time, until lightly browned on all sides. Drain on paper towels.

2 Reduce the heat to low and sauté the garlic in the oil for 5 minutes, then add the tomatoes, 1 cup wine, salt, and pepper and cook for 10 minutes, stirring frequently. Stir in the bouillon cube.

3 Return the chicken to the skillet and cook until tender, about 20 minutes.

4 Meanwhile, heat the remaining wine and the broth over low heat and poach the shrimp for 3 to 5 minutes. Remove from the wine using a slotted spoon; peel and set aside. Heat the butter in a skillet over medium heat and fry the eggs to desired doneness. Arrange each egg on a piece of toast. Top each egg with a poached shrimp.

5 To serve, place the chicken in the center of a platter, sprinkle with parsley, and surround with the egg and shrimp toasts.

How to Serve Precede with a bowl of cream of onion, cauliflower, or leek soup.

Wine Suggestion Full-bodied Red

4 eggs

4 thick slices country-style bread, toasted

2 tablespoons chopped fresh Italian parsley

335

POLLO RIPIENO ALLE NOCI

Chicken Stuffed with Walnuts

336

❦ Trentino-Alto Adige ❧

I DON'T THINK I HAVE EVER SEEN AS MANY CHICKEN DISHES AS AT LEVICO'S *Sagra del Pollo. This tiny town, east of Trento, had signs posted everywhere and each advertised a different chicken recipe followed by the word* Venite!—Come! *This strictly local festival was held in the tree-shaded piazza outside city hall and the food was all prepared by residents. There used to be a prize for the best recipe, one woman told me. "But the new mayor—a socialist—decided that was too competitive."*

serves 4 to 6

Time: 1 hour, 45 minutes

Level of Difficulty: Moderate

2 thick slices country-style bread

1 cup chicken broth

1 cup walnuts, soaked in boiling
water for 4 minutes, drained,
dried, and finely diced

1/2 cup pine nuts, finely diced

One 3-pound chicken, washed
and dried, kidneys reserved
and finely diced

2 tablespoons freshly grated
grana padana or
Parmigiano-Reggiano

1/8 teaspoon freshly grated
nutmeg

1 Tear the bread into small pieces and soak in the broth for 10 minutes. Drain and squeeze dry. Place in a bowl with the walnuts, pine nuts, diced kidneys, cheese, nutmeg, eggs, salt, and pepper. Mix until all ingredients are thoroughly blended.

2 Stuff the chicken with the walnut mixture and tie the chicken like a package, using kitchen string, once around widthwise and once around lengthwise.

3 Heat 5 quarts salted water in a large pot and bring to a boil. Immerse the chicken in the water and boil for 1 hour. Drain, unwrap, remove the stuffing, and cut into individual pieces.

4 Arrange the chicken on a platter, leaving a central area clear. Place the walnut stuffing in the center and serve hot or cold.

Make Ahead The stuffing can be made earlier in the day and refrigerated until needed

How to Serve With a mixed green salad as an entrée following a simple bowl of chicken or vegetable broth served with butter-fried croutons.

Wine Suggestion Dry White or Full-bodied Red

2 large eggs, lightly beaten

Salt to taste

Freshly ground black pepper to taste

5 quarts salted water for cooking

1/2 cup mixed walnuts and pine nuts for garnish

8 to 10 sprigs fresh Italian parsley for garnish

QUAGLIE IN UMIDO

Panfried Quail with Buttered Rice

338

❦ Emilia-Romagna ❦

IL PERDONO DI CANOSSA RECALLS A DAY IN JANUARY 1077 WHEN EMPEROR *Enrico IV of Germany traveled in penitential clothes to beg pardon from Pope Gregory VII, who had excommunicated him for blasphemy. At the time, the pope was staying at the castle home of Contessa Matilde, great noblewoman and even greater gastronome, and was in the middle of a multiday eating festival organized by Matilde for a group of local aristocrats. Poor Enrico had to wait outside the gates of Canossa Castle for three days and, each day, a missive would arrive from the pope, informing the starving Enrico of the nature of the day's menu. The festival—celebrating the eventual pardon—takes place on the first weekend in April in Canossa, southwest of Reggio nell Emilia, and encompasses regally costumed dramatizations, food stalls as far as the eye can see, and a judged competition among the town's food purveyors to see who can create the most appetizing window display, this last event aptly called* vetrine per Matilde—*windows created for Matilde.*

serves 4

Time: 50 minutes

Level of Difficulty: Moderate

8 quail, washed and dried
4 tablespoons unsalted butter
2 ounces prosicutto fat
    or mezzina
1 tablespoon freshly
    chopped thyme
3 bay leaves
Salt to taste

1 Put skewers through both legs of each quail to hold the bird together during cooking.

2 Heat 2 tablespoons butter in a skillet over low heat and sauté the prosciutto fat for 5 minutes. Add the quail, thyme, bay leaves, salt, and pepper and cook until the quail are very lightly browned on all sides.

3 Pour in the wine and cook until evaporated, about 3 minutes. Cover and cook for 20 minutes, add the broth, and cook 20 minutes more, or until the quail are done.

4 During the last 20 minutes of cooking, cook the rice in 4 cups boiling salted water for 15 minutes, or until tender. Drain, toss with the remaining butter and cheese, and transfer to a serving platter. Arrange the quail on top, drizzle with the pan juices, and serve immediately.

Make Ahead The quail can be cleaned and skewered earlier in the day and kept refrigerated until needed.

How to Serve With garlic-roasted potatoes and steamed asparagus.

Wine Suggestion **Dry White or Medium-bodied Red**

Freshly ground black pepper
to taste
1/2 cup dry white wine
1/2 cup Basic Meat Broth (page
460) or canned broth
8 ounces Vialone Nano rice or
other type of Arborio
2 tablespoons freshly grated
Parmigiano-Reggiano

339

SUPREME DI POLLO ALLE VERDURE

Rolled Chicken Breast Stuffed with Vegetables and Braised
in White Wine and Heavy Cream

❧ Toscana ❧

LUCCA IS AN ELEVENTH-CENTURY WALLED CITY AND THE CAPITAL OF THE *westernmost Tuscan province. On the last weekend of every July, the city hosts a folkloric festival in the Piazza Amfiteatro, a completely enclosed ovular piazza with Roman arches at both the entrance and the exit. This is a very sophisticated event, with wonderful musical performances, regal costumes, and surrounding restaurants offering some of the most delicious food I have ever eaten.*

This sliced chicken roll makes an elegant presentation when served on top of a perfectly rounded layer of polenta.

serves 6

Time: 1 hour

Level of Difficulty: Advanced

6 tablespoons extra virgin
  olive oil
1 large leek (white part only),
  cleaned and diced
2 small carrots, diced
1 celery stalk, diced
8 ounces butternut squash,
  seeded and cut into
  1-inch cubes
6 ounces turnip, cut into
  1-inch cubes
8 ounces red radicchio, cored
  and julienned

1 Heat 1 tablespoon oil in a skillet over low heat and sauté the leeks, carrots, and celery for 8 minutes, stirring constantly. Add the squash, turnip, and radicchio and cook for 10 minutes. Season with salt, remove from the heat, and set aside.

2 Place the chicken breasts between sheets of waxed paper and gently pound with a kitchen mallet until wafer thin. Distribute half of the vegetable mixture among the four pieces of chicken, mounding it in the center of each. Roll the breasts into tight cylinders completely enclosing the vegetables and tie with kitchen string. Dredge the four rolls in flour.

3 Heat the remaining oil in a skillet over medium heat and sauté the chicken rolls until lightly browned on all sides. Pour in the wine and cook until evaporated, then add the broth. Season with salt and pepper, cover, and cook for 7 minutes. Reduce the heat to low, add the cream, and cook 5 minutes, or until thickened.

4 Using tongs, remove the rolls and keep warm. Add the cheese to the sauce and cook until melted and smooth. Cut the rolls into 1/2-inch-thick slices and arrange on a serving platter in a circle in overlapping fashion. Mound the remaining vegetables in the center, pour the cheese sauce over the chicken, and serve immediately.

Make Ahead The chicken rolls can be prepared up to Step 2 earlier in the day and kept refrigerated until needed.

Wine Suggestion **Dry White**

Salt to taste

Two 1-pound boneless chicken breasts, cut in half

Unbleached all-purpose flour for dredging

1/2 cup dry white wine

1/2 cup chicken broth

Freshly ground black pepper to taste

2 cups heavy cream

5 ounces fontina, cut into 1-inch cubes

CONIGLIO GRATINATO

Gratinéed Rabbit

342

❦ Toscana ❦

IN RECENT YEARS, THE CULINARY TREND THROUGHOUT TUSCANY IS TO ATTACH THE *term* nostrale *to everything from apricots to pork loin to olives. Literally translated, the word means "ours" but is used in the same way as the American "organic" to convey a sense of basic purity. When I approached a food stall selling this rabbit at Lucca's* Festival del Folclore *(see page 340), the woman hastened to tell me the rabbit was nostrale, which, in this case, means she raised it herself. Trying to refine my understanding, I asked what she fed her rabbits and whether the term could legitimately be applied to personally raised rabbits that had not been fed well. "Why would anyone do that?" she asked, to which I could only reply that sometimes it's cheaper or quicker. "But then they would be poisoning themselves," she shot back. "And what* cretino *would do such a thing?"*

serves 4

Time: 55 minutes

Level of Difficulty: Easy

⚶

One 2¹/2-pound rabbit or
    chicken, cut into
    bite-size pieces
1 large onion, thinly sliced
1¹/2 pounds boiling potatoes,
    peeled and cut into
    ¹/2-inch cubes

1 Preheat the oven to 350°F.

2 Put the rabbit, onion, potatoes, salt, pepper, bay leaves, and oil in a large bowl and toss to combine. Transfer to a glass or terra-cotta baking dish and pour in as much broth as necessary to reach halfway up the sides of the dish.

3 Distribute the cheese evenly over the surface and bake for 45 minutes, or until the crust is golden brown and crispy. Serve immediately.

Make Ahead The rabbit can be tossed with the vegetables an hour or two ahead of time and refrigerated until needed.

How to Serve Wonderful when served with a green salad and following a bowl of pasta tossed with fresh tomatoes.

Wine Suggestion Dry White or Medium-bodied Red

Salt to taste

Freshly ground black pepper to taste

2 bay leaves (preferably fresh), crumbled

4 tablespoons extra virgin olive oil

About 3 cups Basic Meat Broth (page 460) or canned broth

5 ounces Emmental or other yellow melting cheese, cut into thin strips

TACCHINO ARROSTO ALLA MELAGRANA

Roast Turkey with Pomegranates

❧ Veneto ❧

SOMETIME AROUND THE SECOND WEEK OF JUNE, THE RESIDENTS OF COMBAI, A *charming walled village in the Veneto, throw a festival to celebrate the glory of their beloved Verdiso wine. The verdiso grape is a regional varietal used for making both dry, delicate white wines and spumante secco, a type of sparkling wine. Needless to say, there is a copious amount of eating, drinking, and nonstop merriment. A chef in one of the restaurants near the festival site lured me in with his description of this created-expressly-for-the-Verdiso festival turkey delight, roasted with sage and butter and basted to perfection with the juice of six pomegranates. "The bittersweet nature of pomegranates makes the perfect balance to our exceptional wines," he propagandized. He was right.*

serves 6

Time: 2 hours

Level of Difficulty: Moderate

⚷

7 tablespoons unsalted butter
One 4- to 5-pound young
    turkey, kidneys reserved
10 leaves fresh sage
Salt to taste
Freshly ground black pepper
    to taste
10 pomegranates

1 Preheat the oven to 450°F. Butter a roasting pan with 1 tablepoon butter. Wash the turkey inside and out and dry with paper towels. Butter the cavity with 3 tablespoons butter and add the sage, salt, and pepper.

2 Loosely tie the legs together with kitchen string. Rub the skin all over with another 3 tablespoons butter and season with salt and pepper. Place the turkey with the wings tucked under in the roasting pan and roast for 20 minutes. Reduce the heat to 375°F and cook for 30 minutes.

3 Meanwhile, peel the pomegranates, extract the seeds, and juice all but 1 cup in a juicer or food processor. Strain to remove the seeds and pour two-thirds of the juice over the turkey. Cook for another 30 to 45 minutes, or until an instant read thermometer inserted in the inner thigh below the leg joint registers 175 to 180°F.

4 While the turkey is cooking, clean the kidneys, removing the exterior sack without breaking it. Dice the kidneys and cook over high heat for 10 minutes with the remaining pomegranate juice, stirring constantly.

5 Remove the turkey from the oven, transfer to an ovenproof platter, and surround with the remaining pomegranate seeds. Strain the pan juices and stir the sauce into the cooked kidneys. Pour the mixture over the turkey and return the platter to the oven for 10 minutes. Serve hot.

Make Ahead The turkey can be cleaned and seasoned earlier in the day and kept refrigerated until needed.

How to Serve With bitter vegetables such as broccoli rabe, dandelion, or chicory sautéed in garlic and oil.

Wine Suggestion **Dry White (Verdiso is perfect)**

CINGHIALE ALLO SPELLO

Wild Boar Braised with Pine Nuts, Raisins, Chocolate, and Prunes

❧ Umbria ❧

CENTRAL ITALY CELEBRATES THE MID-JUNE FEAST OF *CORPUS DOMINI* WITH *extravagant processions that weave through narrow streets carpeted with hundreds of thousands of flowers. The flowers are arranged to form a vast array of intricate patterns that range from doves to animals to depictions of religious figures. In Spello, in the province of Perugia, the designs are decided many months before the actual June day and assigned to individual quarters of the city—rione. The work begins just after dinner the night before when the entire town takes to the streets to chalk up the pavement with the winning patterns. Just before dawn, the flower placement begins. Men, women, children and teenagers all participate—one sweeping away the excess petals, another bearing a backpacklike watering can with which to keep the flowers fresh, yet another measuring to make sure the designs remain faithful to the master plan. On the actual day of Corpus Domini, the local pastor leads the congregation along the entire length of the carpet (approximately half a mile), the church band bringing up the rear. An hour later, everyone is ready to sit down at the table.*

serves 4 to 6

Time: 2 hours, excluding the 24-hour marinating period

Level of Difficulty: Moderate

2 pounds wild boar (or pork loin), boned, skinned, and fat removed and cut into bite-size chunks

4 cups dry red wine

1 onion, thinly sliced

1 carrot, diced

1 celery stalk, diced

1 bay leaf (preferably fresh), crumbled

1 Put the boar in a large bowl with the wine, onion, carrot, celery, bay leaf, juniper berries, garlic, marjoram, rosemary, and thyme. Marinate for 24 hours in the refrigerator, turning the meat 3 or 4 times during that period.

2 Using a slotted spoon, remove the boar, dry with paper towels, and dredge in flour. Heat the oil in a skillet over medium heat and sauté the boar until lightly browned all over. Strain the marinade, keeping the solids separate from the infused wine.

3 Pour the wine into the skillet and season the meat with salt. Cook for 30 minutes, or until the sauce has significantly thickened.

4 Remove the meat with a slotted spoon and keep warm. Strain the pan juices and return to the skillet. Replace the meat and add the raisins, pine nuts, chocolate, prunes, and vinegar. Cook for 30 minutes, transfer to a serving platter, garnish with the fresh herbs, and serve immediately.

How to Serve Like many meat braises and ragùs, this dish is traditionally served with sautéed greens. It also works very well when arranged over a bed of polenta or tossed with pasta.

Wine Suggestion Full-bodied Red

6 juniper berries, crushed

1 clove garlic, crushed

1 sprig fresh marjoram

1 sprig fresh rosemary

1 sprig fresh thyme

Unbleached all-purpose flour for dredging

6 tablespoons extra virgin olive oil

Salt to taste

1/3 cup sultana raisins, soaked in warm water for 20 minutes, drained, and squeezed dry

1/3 cup pine nuts

1/3 cup bittersweet chocolate, grated

4 dried prunes, pitted and chopped

1/2 cup red wine vinegar

3 to 4 sprigs fresh herbs for garnish

347

SPIEDINI MISTI

Chicken, Lamb, and Pork Kebabs Grilled with Sage and Pancetta

❧ Le Marche ❧

THROUGHOUT THE SPRING AND SUMMER, THE MARCHISANI ARE NOT BIG MEAT *eaters, preferring instead the numerous varieties of fresh fish harvested from the cold waters of the Adriatic. But come autumn, when the weather is still warm enough to eat outdoors but not too hot for more substantial types of foods, the grills are scrubbed clean and the fragrance of roasting meat sears the air from Pesara to San Benedetto. In Numana, just south of Ancona, late September to early October is time for the* Sagra della Carne Grigliata—*The Festival of Grilled Meats. The menu is very simple and just about perfect: grilled meats such as the following and bottles of good red wine.*

serves 4

Time: 20 to 30 minutes, excluding the marinating period

Level of Difficulty: Easy

Equipment: 8 skewers

⚖

1 pound pork loin, cut into
    eight 1-inch cubes

1 pound lamb, cut into
    eight 1-inch cubes

1 pound boneless chicken breast,
    cut into eight 1-inch cubes

12 slices pancetta

16 leaves fresh sage

8 sprigs fresh rosemary

Freshly ground black pepper
    to taste

4 juniper berries, crushed

1/4 cup extra virgin olive oil

Salt to taste

1 Thread eight skewers, alternating cubes of meat with pieces of pancetta, sage, and rosemary. Sprinkle heavily with black pepper and press with juniper berries. Baste with oil and place in a closed container. Marinate in the refrigerator for 5 to 6 hours.

2 Prepare a charcoal grill or preheat the broiler. Coat the grill rack with vegetable oil cooking spray.

3 Grill over hot coals or under the broiler for 5 to 10 minutes, or until the meat is done to taste. Salt and serve.

How to Serve Wonderful when accompanied by a mixed green salad and dense, crusty bread.

Wine Suggestion Full-bodied Red

INVOLTINI DI MAIALE AL FORNO

Grilled Bundles of Herb-stuffed Pork

❧ Sardegna ❧

ON THE FIRST WEEKEND IN AUGUST, VILLANOVAFRANCA IN CAGLIARI PROVINCE HOSTS *a festival in honor of all the Sardinians who have ever emigrated from the island—La Festa dell'Emigrato. Many who moved to the mainland in search of jobs actually return for the event, which also coincides with the feast day of the town's patron, Saint Lorenzo. This is a wonderful opportunity not only to sample local dishes such as these grilled pork bundles, but also to witness a traditional Sardinian festival, with music, dancing, and folkloric costumes.*

serves 6

Time: 30 minutes

Level of Difficulty: Easy

Equipment: 12 skewers

4 ounces pork kidneys, diced

4 ounces pancetta, diced

1 clove garlic, minced

2 tablespoons chopped fresh Italian parsley

1 thick slice country-style bread, soaked in warm water for 20 minutes and squeezed dry

Salt to taste

1 large egg, lightly beaten

2 pounds pork loin, cut into 12 thin slices

Six 2-inch squares of country-style bread

1/4 cup extra virgin olive oil

Freshly ground black pepper to taste

1 Put the kidneys, pancetta, garlic, parsley, bread, salt, and egg in a bowl and mix well.

2 Using a kitchen mallet, gently beat the pork slices between waxed paper until uniformly thin. Spread each slice with a dollop of the pancetta mixture, roll into tight cylinders, and tie with kitchen string.

3 Prepare a charcoal grill or preheat the broiler. Coat the grill rack with vegetable oil cooking spray.

4 Thread each of twelve skewers with two pork bundles separated by a bread square. Arrange the skewers in a baking pan, drizzle with oil, and season with salt and pepper. Grill over hot coals or under the broiler for 10 to 15 minutes, turning the skewers once. Serve immediately.

How to Serve With slices of eggplant, zucchini, and red or golden peppers that have been basted with olive oil and grilled over the same hot coals as the meat.

Wine Suggestion Medium- or Full-bodied Red

FARAONA ALLA CRETA

Guinea Hen Cooked in Terra-cotta

350

❧ Lombardia ❧

A VILLAGE DATING BACK TO THE NINTH CENTURY (WHEN IT WAS USED AS A STATION *for the exchange of horses), Gorgonzola lies just east of Milan and is known mainly for the delicious, creamy cheese that bears its name. On the Sunday nearest November 25, it celebrates the feast of its patron, Saint Catherine, with a festival betraying its peasant origins: all the food leans heavily on pastas, polentas (one laced with aged Gorgonzola cheese), and game.*

Among the menu options was this delicious guinea hen, roasted inside a shell of soft clay molded to fit its contours and sealed with a type of rolled crust. When I made it at home, I used a terra-cotta chicken cooker which worked just as well.

serves 4

Time: 2 hours, 20 minutes

Level of Difficulty: Easy

⚖

3 leaves fresh sage, finely minced

1 tablespoon finely minced fresh rosemary

2 cloves garlic, minced

1 bay leaf

3 juniper berries, crushed

3 whole cloves, crushed

Salt to taste

1 Place the sage, rosemary, garlic, bay leaf, juniper berries, cloves, salt, and pepper in a bowl and mix well. Rub all the mixture into the cavity and on the skin of the guinea hen.

2 Preheat the oven to 350°F.

3 Wrap the hen in the prosciutto slices and place in a terra-cotta baking pan, cover tightly, and cook for 2 hours.*

4 Remove from the oven, transfer to a serving platter, and garnish with the rosemary sprigs.

A cast-iron Dutch oven can be substituted. A roasting pan tightly sealed with aluminum foil can also be used although the meat will lose some of its moisture.

Make Ahead The hen can be seasoned and wrapped in prosciutto earlier in the day and kept refrigerated until cooked.

How to Serve With potatoes panfried in garlic and sage and brussel sprouts boiled until tender and drizzled with fruity olive oil.

Wine Suggestion **Dry White or Full-bodied Red**

Freshly ground black pepper
   to taste

One 2- to 3-pound guinea hen
   or chicken, washed and dried

4 ounces prosciutto, thinly sliced
   (the fatter the better)

2 sprigs fresh rosemary
   for garnish

351

Fish and Seafood

GAMBERI IN POCETO
*Shrimp in Wine
and Parsley*

CASSOLA
*Fish Soup with
Garlic-rubbed Bread*

**MUGGINI ARROSTI
NEL SALE**
Mullet Roasted in Salt

ZUPPA DI VONGOLE
*Fresh Clams in
Tomato-Parsley Broth*

TORTIERA DI COZZE
Baked Stuffed Mussels

ORATA AL FORNO
*Oven-roasted Dourade
Served on a Bed of
Potato Wafers*

SARDE AL FORNO
*Sardines Baked
with Tomatoes and
Parlsey-Garlic Pesto*

CACCIUCCO
Tuscan Fish Soup

SARDE A BECCAFICO
*Gratinéed Sardines Stuffed
with Parsley
and Pignoli Pesto*

**AGGHIOTTA DI
PESCE SPADA**
*Swordfish Steaks Baked
with Tomatoes, Raisins,
and Olives*

**PESCE PERSICO
ALLA PIEMONTESE**
Panfried Royal Perch

TROTA AL ERBE
*Freshwater Trout with
Herbs and Lemon Fragrance*

SARDELLE IN SAOR
*Fried Sardines
Marinated with Onions*

**STORIONE IN UMIDO
CON LA POLENTA**
*Sturgeon Steaks Braised
in White Wine and
Tomatoes and Served
with Creamy Polenta*

CAPPON MAGRO
*Fish and Vegetable
Salad*

**PESCE SPADA
ALLO SPIEDINO**
*Braised Swordfish
Kebabs with Wedges
of Red Onion*

**NASCELLO ALLA
PALERMITANA**
*Roasted Hake with
Anchovies and Rosemary*

RAVIEU DE MA
*Sea Bass Ravioli with
Marjoram Sauce*

**STOCCAFISSO
AL VERDE**
*Poached Codfish and
Potatoes with Parsley Pesto*

COZZE RIPIENE
*Mussels Stuffed with
Sausage and Herbs*

**ACCIUGHINI COL
PROSCIUTTO**
*Fried Sage Sandwiches with
Anchovies and Prosciutto*

ZUPPA DI CERNIA
Spicy Sea Bass Soup

**INSALATA DI
FRUTTI DI MARE**
*Shellfish Salad with
Lemon-Mustard Vinaigrette*

BACCALÀ MANTECATO
*Codfish Salad with
Fried Polenta Wedges*

CALAMARETTI PICANTE
Spiced Baby Shrimp

**TONNO FRESCO
ALLA MARINARA**
*Tuna Steaks Baked
with Olives, Capers,
and Fresh Tomatoes*

CALABRIA
A Belief in Believing

THE FIRST TIME I JOURNEYED TO CALABRIA, I was armed with dozens of booklets and brochures from the Italian Government Tourist Board showing a warm, semitropical peninsula surrounded by crystal-blue seas. The sands were white, the populace sparse, the water clear, the opportunities for doing nothing guaranteed.

I imagined myself ensconced in a tiny undiscovered village located on the crest of a verdant hill overlooking the Ionian Sea. I would journey to the beach each day wearing nothing more than a tiny bikini and a pair of espadrilles and at noon, would repair to the local trattoria for a long, bountiful lunch consisting of pasta with a fiery tomato sauce, lamb charred over an open grill, and a plethora of fresh, marinated vegetables.

Here's what actually came to pass. I drove along the entire Ionian coast on Monday, Tuesday, and Wednesday, switched to the Tyrrhenian Coast for the remainder of the week, and finally gave up after winding my way through dozens of beach towns blanketed with more people than in that famous 1950s photo depicting Coney Island on the Fourth of July.

The food I consumed ranged from good tourist to bad tourist—soggy pasta, rubbery shellfish, warmed-over vegetables, and desserts with a pronounced refrigerator taste.

Worse, what I eventually came to realize was that there are two main reasons for the incredible crowding on Calabrian beaches: (1) Many coastal areas have been usurped for industrial purposes, creating a relative paucity of available beach frontage; and (2) What beaches *do* exist are often backed by a major highway and are smaller than an Italian postage stamp.

But, as the Italians so uncharacteristically say, *tutti salmi reescono in gloria* (roughly equivalent to "every cloud has a silver lining," although with a slightly more cynical undercurrent). Because just as I was ready to give up on Calabria and board the ferry back to Tuscany, I discovered the Calabrian mountains.

As it turns out, ninety percent of Calabria consists of hills and mountains, many replete with unique tree and wildlife species (for example, the loricate pine; the Sila wolf). The Sila plateau, which occupies much of central Calabria, is the largest plateau in Europe and contains thousands of small, picturesque rivers crisscrossing the terrain en route to the sea.

More important for my purposes, however, the mountains are where one discovers the real Calabria, the Calabria where pasta continues to be arranged on long, wooden dowels and laid out in the sun to dry; the Calabria where each family retains a separate closet filled with costumes heralding their Greek, Arbreshe, or Albanian heritage (costumes they don many times each year for ancient festivals celebrating their religious heritage); the Calabria of indigenous folklore and traditional manifestations handed down from generation to generation.

"What were you *thinking*?" said my friend Sandro when I called to moan about my frustrations with the coast. "The beaches are for tourists. Why go all the way to Calabria and then spend your time with the same people you can see here in Tuscany?"

This time, at Sandro's insistence, I decide to head directly for Serre San Bruno, the tiny mountain town that was his home until six years ago and which he has always heralded as "*il polso della Calbria*"—Calabria's true pulse. "*Mettiti nelle mani di don Reggio e lasciati guidare,*" he elaborates. Put yourself in the hands of Don Reggio and let him be your guide. As Sandro explains at great length, Don Reggio is the spiritual leader of Serre San Bruno. "But that doesn't mean he simply says mass and baptizes babies."

Apparently Don Reggio's responsibilities range from making sure no discotheques are opened in residential areas (the only disco in existence is a safe two miles outside town and fronted by a large statue of the Madonna erected by the disco owners as part of their agreement with Don Reggio) to buying lotto tickets in large, discounted blocks and distributing them to the town's poorer residents (last year, a ninety-four-year-old recipient won $14,000, of which $10,000 was gratefully donated to the church).

In Sandro's estimation, in fact, Don Reggio cannot only do no wrong, but is "the type of traditional priest that makes the Church what it is today."

I am not quite sure what he intends by that statement, never having known him to be particularly religious. But then he goes on to recall a string of very funny movies made in the fifties about two charismatic characters: Don Camillo, a humble postwar pastor assigned to a poor, tiny village in central Calabria, and his nemesis, Beppone, the portly mayor and local Communist party chief. In one of Sandro's favorite episodes, Don Camillo is scheduled to bless the river (a traditional event in most southern Italian villages), but the bumbling Beppone abruptly cancels the festivities, saying it is too dangerous for so many people to convene along the riverbank.

On the appointed day, a defiant Don Camillo—carrying a large wooden crucifix on his back—leads a contingent of church faithful on a procession of protest. Along the way, he engages in one of his famous chats with Christ, this time complaining about the unbearable heaviness of the cross. "You're telling *me*?" Christ responds, "I had to carry that infernal thing all the way to Gethsemane."

At the river, Beppone and his cohorts have formed a human barrier, but Don Camillo simply lowers his head and forges forward. The Communists are, naturally, left with no choice but to allow him passage. "Dear God," Camillo says in the final reel of the film, "Bless these waters and also this cretin you have given us to be our mayor." As the people cheer his words, a humbled and supposedly reformed Beppone puts his arm around Don Camillo and whispers into his ear, "Well done, my dear sacerdote, well done."

"If priests took those kinds of positions today, the Church would swell with disciples," Sandro says.

"The problem is that today's positions are a little more complicated," I answer. "Traditional solutions no longer apply. Unfortunately, many priests still think we live in a world of angels and devils."

"I think in many cases, they're right. You'd be surprised how many people continue to believe there is an absolute wrong and an absolute right. As a matter of fact, you had better get used to it if you're planning to spend time in Serre San Bruno. People there live very much the same lives as their parents and grandparents before them, despite their four-wheel drives and cellular phones. Their values and belief systems have changed very little."

"But does it work?" I ask him. "Even I know there's something very attractive about believing in absolute reality. It's what makes the concept of traditions so appealing—we do it the way we've always done it and that's that. But can people truly be happy limiting themselves to a set of thoughts and beliefs that have already been prescribed? Does it really work for them?"

"Only for those who believe it works," he says. And those people are probably happier than you with all your questions and doubts."

I've never been sure how I feel about this "ignorance is bliss" type of reasoning. There is no question that, in many cases, believers have simpler and easier lives than nonbelievers. But in order to reap the benefits of a more traditional lifestyle, one must first believe, and belief is something you either have or you don't. Very circular.

One belief I can be absolutely certain about in this particular moment is that Serre San Bruno is the town for me and, further, that Sandro's Don Reggio is the perfect man to guide me in my exploration of the area's traditional festivals.

Unfortunately, the day I arrive is the day after his ninety-two-year-old brother has succumbed to cancer. "Don Reggio will only be able to spend a few moments with you," his secretary says.

I hastily scribble together a list of things I absolutely need to know now:

> Who is the area's patron saint?
> When does his or her festival take place?
> How many days does it last and do I need any tickets?
> What are the defining characteristics of the celebration?

I am not to get answers for any of my questions, at least not in the form I expect.

"Please note that I am leaving within the next five minutes and arrange your requests accordingly," Don Reggio states as soon as I am admitted to his cavernous office. His back is turned and the tone of his voice is what one might call brusque, although "rude" might serve as a more appropriate descriptor.

A small man who once might have been taller, he stands at the window, behind a desk that is larger than most king-size beds—an enormous hunk of chestnut intricately carved with dozens of haloed men and fluttery cherubs.

I blurt out my credentials. "Sandro Costa. I am a friend of Sandro Costa. His mother worked here in the rectory until her death six years ago." Unlike other places in the world where personal contacts serve as a distinct advantage—here in Italy, they are an absolute must. "Ahhh, Fortunata," he says, turning to look at me. "Yes, now I remember. Sandro called, in fact, to say you were coming." The strategy works. I may not get exactly what I came for, but his reaction guarantees I will at least get something.

"*Una santa donna, Fortunata.*" A sainted woman. Don Reggio lowers his head and makes a heartfelt sign of the cross.

"It would help ever so much if I could just have a few moments of your time later today or tomorrow," I say when he finishes his meditation. "I know your brother has just died and I am *very* very sorry."

"Yes," he says, "we all are. Nonetheless, he is now with God and I am not, so who should be sorry for whom?"

He smiles and I follow suit, not quite sure whether his sentiment is serious or a joke.

"What can I do for you?" he says, reverting to his former brusqueness.

I rattle off the list I had earlier compiled and offer to leave it for his perusal. But he cuts my sentence short in midstream.

"Traditions. According to Sandro, you have come here to witness our traditions, *vero?*"

I nod my head.

"My dear girl, God must today have cast His beatific glow in your direction. Because in the next minute, I will hurry away to to attend to a small boy who lives on the other side of Monte San Nicola. For the past two years, the boy has not been able to go to school because he cannot control his rage and just last week he hit his grandfather over the head with an iron pot. His mother lives in constant fear and the boy's own brothers and sisters have begged that he be sent away."

"Hmmm," I say for lack of a more pertinent response.

"The parents have tried everything within their power. Punishment, drugs, psychiatrists. Nothing works. The only remaining possibility is that the boy may be possessed by evil spirits. They have asked me to perform an exorcism," says Don Reggio, buckling up his briefcase. "And today I will begin that process. You may accompany me if you wish."

Nothing in my background has prepared me to deal with a statement this peculiar, so I hesitate just a minute longer than is obviously appropriate.

"Needless to say, this is not a tradition related to food, but as I understand Sandro to say, your interests lie in the overall concept of traditions. What you do not know, but what I will educate you about while driving to the boy's home, is that the patron for this town, Saint Bruno, is also the patron of the *spirdati*, which means people who have been possessed by evil spirits. Hence, you will be witnessing an event that speaks directly to the reason why this town was founded."

The trip over the mountain takes forty-five minutes, during which Don Reggio makes good on his promise to "educate me." Saint Bruno, as it turns out, came by his reputation as the patron saint of possessed people purely by fortune (or misfortune, depending on one's viewpoint). In 1522, Garetto Scopacasa di Simbario and his wife, Isabella, brought him their daughter, Maria, in hope he could rid her of the *spiriti immondi*—otherwordly spirits— which they claimed had invaded her body. After a string of communal prayers, day-long chanting, and other spiritual intercessions, Bruno apparently came upon the idea of immersing Maria in the frigid waters of *Laghetto di Mongiana*—Mongiana Lake—which lies just north of Serra San Bruno, and the girl was reportedly cured.

"For the rest of his life, people from as far north as Naples brought their possessed family members to Bruno. In fact, every one of the miracles attributed to him after his death involved people presumed to be inhabited by evil spirits."

By the time we arrive at our destination, I know more about Saint Bruno than I do about my own sister. But this is good, I tell myself. It gives me a perfect framework for the events of the next few hours, whatever they may be.

The house is a handsome, two-story split-level located on a beautifully landscaped plot along a small river. There are three cars in the driveway, one a flashy red convertible. The roof of the house contains a large satellite dish, and an electrified system of surveillance beeps softly as we make our way toward the front door.

What happens next can only be described as a "complete divergence of interpretation." I follow Don Reggio into the house, where we are effusively greeted by the boy's parents and then led into a small room where the boy—Valerio by name—is sitting on the floor, painting with magic markers. Valerio has already produced five or six pictures and they are scattered around him, wild profusions of color and form.

Prodded by his mother to acknowledge Don Reggio's presence ("Kiss Father's ring," the mother pleads more than once. "Kiss Father's ring"), the boy remains relatively silent throughout our stay and continues to ignore everything going on around him. He neither responds to the holy water subsequently sprinkled over his head nor does anything unusual during the recitation of Don Reggio's arsenal of prayers, except to mangle every other picture he finishes.

At one point, however, Valerio obviously tires of the excitement swirling around his head and begins rocking back and forth, chanting in a progressively louder, gutteral voice what sounds to me like gibberish. But at the very first utterance, his mother—hovering just outside the door—begins to cry hysterically. "It is him," she screams and is hustled away by her husband.

"The Devil," one of the aunts explains, when I turn in her direction with an obviously puzzled look. "It is the Devil fighting against the healing presence."

A few hours later, the boy has fallen asleep on the floor and Don Reggio and I are back in his car and heading toward home. "*Allora?*" he says casually as we creep along the steep mountain roads. What did you think?

"What exactly happened there?" I ask, not wanting to voice an actual opinion.

"There was no question but that we took the first step toward ridding the boy of evil spirits," he says, with admirable certainty. "Before today, I was not sure he actually had been invaded. But when I heard the presence speak, there was no further doubt."

"Why not?" I ask against my better judgment. "What made you so certain it was an evil spirit."

"You heard it yourself, did you not?"

"Yes, but to me, it was gibberish. Valerio could simply have been playing with sounds the way children often do. My friend's daughter does it all the time and she's even older."

"You are wrong," he says simply. "The voice was that of the Devil."

I am quite shaken by what has transpired and decide to call Sandro for some feedback. "Either Don Reggio has lost his mind or I have completely misinterpreted the events of the last few hours," I say in a sudden outpouring of words. "One of us is off-base and there's no question in my mind that it's not me."

"Why must either of you be off-base?" he asks.

"Because either . . . because what happened today . . . because the effects of his judgment. . ." It suddenly occurs to me that whatever I say is going to result in the same response. "It's all perception," Sandro is going to say in the same way he has said it before in response to so many other discussions about what is real and what is not.

"I know you're going to say that it's simply a difference in perception. That they believe him to be possessed while, to me, the boy just needs a firmer hand. But don't you think there's something very harmful in raising a child to think he is inhabited by the Devil?"

"Look, the reality is that exorcism is just as likely to work as psychotherapy, maybe more so. I keep telling you, belief is a powerful thing."

Don Reggio has asked me to come back the day after tomorrow. "By then, my brother will be buried and we will begin the preparations for *la festa*—The Festival of San Bruno. In the meantime, here are a few people who can help you with your quest to learn about our cuisine." He hands me a list of names, ranging from bread bakers to fishermen to pasta makers and then stretches out his arm in my direction, placing his ring at the level of my chest.

I cannot kiss it. No matter how much I'd like to since that is obviously what is done in these circumstances, I cannot. If I had never participated in the so-called exorcism, perhaps I might be able to convince myself that when in Rome . . . but I simply cannot.

"Thank you very much," I say, cupping his hand between both of mine. "I will be thinking of you steadily over the next twenty-four hours."

My first stop is the baker's, where I sample some of the local breads associated with the upcoming festival, specifically *pitta cu lu pipi di maju*—a type of focaccia baked in a wood-burning oven and filled with ricotta, pancetta, and the flowers of the Sambuca plant. The fanciful-sounding name is a blend of *pipi*, dialect for Sambuca flowers, and *maju* or May since that's the other time of year when the bread is popular (for the festival of the Madonna).

The baker, who remembers Sandro from when he was a little boy, is just about to sit down to lunch and invites me to join him in a dish of *pasta alla serrese*, a locally devised pasta dish made with capers, anchovies, olives, and chilies, followed by *luppura*, a thick frittata made from a certain type of thick, wild asparagus that grows in the woods around Serre San Bruno.

Both dishes are quite spicy, the Serrese—and Calabrians, at large—being very fond of chilies. "Calabria has always been a very poor region," Vito the baker explains, "and *peperoncini* (chilies) were all we had for flavoring, since salt has always been very expensive, not to mention a state-controlled monopoly. We used *peperoncini*, and use them still, for pasta sauces, pickled meats, and vegetables, or simply fried and eaten as is."

His point is well taken. Driving through Calabria, one can't help but notice the ubiquitous strings of chilies drying in the sun. They are everywhere, strung across balconies, draped across the hoods of cars, hanging between trees, dangling on laundry lines between undershirts and socks. Almost every Calabrian market has five or six old women dressed from head to toe in black sitting next to a pile of chilies, patiently stringing them with needle and thread.

Vito tells me about the *Sagra del Peperoncino*—Chili Pepper Festival—held in the seaside town of Diamante during the first week of September. "Every night, there is a different menu, each one spicier than the last." He starts to laugh. "The main feature, though, is the erotic artwork, which is so hot, it makes the food seem like milk custard by comparison." (I have since been to this festival and can testify that Vito's description is completely accurate. There is music, dancing, theater, satire, art, and food—all of it *molto picante!*).

To wash down our lunch, Vito serves both white Ciro (with the focaccia) and red Ciro with the pasta and frittata. "Ciro is Calabria's only D.O.C. wine," he tells me, adding quickly that "it is so good, we only need one." The white is made from the Greco grape, named after the ancient Greeks who planted the original vines. It is a very young wine—like most southern whites—but I, nonetheless, find myself drawn by the complex blend of citrus and mint.

The red is made from the robust Gaglioppo grape and is also very young—again by choice, since most Calabrians favor light, zesty wines with their spicy foods. As we sip the last few drops, Vito mentions that he saw me in the grocer's the previous evening. "How was that barolo you bought?" he says.

The reference is to a bottle of 1979 Barolo that I found on the back of the shelf in the local grocer's for 7,000 lire or approximately $4. "Don't waste your time," the owner of the store had cautioned when I pulled it out and blew off the dust. The bottle had been hidden behind a few dozen, equally inexpensive local vintages bottled in the last year or two. Having just spent the entire day with Don Reggio exorcising spirits, I wanted nothing other than a hunk of bread, a piece of cheese, and a bottle of good, robust wine. "For the same price, you can get a much newer bottle," the woman had suggested.

By that time, I was familiar with the preference for new, light wines that characterize much of Italy, but especially the South. I also knew my own tastes, which range toward wine as thick and dense as tar. "What do I have to lose?" I had said to the woman and walked out with my dinner. As it turns out, the wine was superb, as good as any I'd ever had in the Piedmont, which is barolo country. And for one-tenth the price!

Against my better judgment, I return to Don Reggio's. In the last twenty-four hours, no one has volunteered any information on the festival except to say, *"parla con don Reggio, esso sa tutta l'historia del paese."* Talk to Don Reggio. He is the only one who can tell you about the history of the town. My guess is that this is not true, that many people have the kind of information I need, but that, in matters regarding local culture, they routinely defer to Don Reggio as a traditional sign of respect.

When I am once again admitted by the secretary, Don Reggio is sitting behind his desk, shouting into the phone. *"No. Non si può permettere questo tipo di controllo! Da dove verebbero i soldi?"* We cannot permit this type of control over our affairs! Where would the money come from if we acceded?

He slams down the receiver, muttering something about "ridiculous" and then turns to greet me.

"Allora?" So?

"I can come back later today if that would be better," I say hastily.

"No, no, no. This moment is fine. I simply have to realize that some people operate on the basis of theory rather than reality." He shakes his head, eyes closed, and I know that, no matter what I say, I am going to be drawn into the story of the moment.

The gist of which is that the regional bishop objects to what Don Reggio calls a "standard and necessary" procedure employed in the course of the Saint Bruno Festival. To best illustrate his point, Don Reggio pulls out of his desk a large color photo showing the event's main float—a ten-foot-high conical tower faced with a hundred little girls in white dresses sitting so close to each other that, from far away, they form a solid palette of joy. In the photo, each girl is smiling and waving a shiny red pinwheel.

"The parents of each of those girls pays 50,000 lire, [approximately $35]" says Don Reggio, poking his index finger blindly into the sea of happy little faces. "The bishop thinks we should let them sit up there for free."

After the events of the other day, I am somewhat more practiced in the art of impassivity.

"Let *his* diocese pay for the festival then," Don Reggio shouts unexpectedly. "Let *his* diocese assume the responsibility of mounting five or six festivals every year without the involvement of the church faithful."

"Why does he object to the practice?" I ask because, at this point, I feel I have to say something.

The question has the unanticipated effect of making Don Reggio think I am on his side. "Ask His Holiness Himself," he answers as if there could be no possible reason that would justify such an absurdity.

What I learn in the next few minutes is that this is not the first time the bishop has voiced his objection. In fact, the argument is four years running and stems directly from Rome,

Pope Paul having apparently decided to clamp down on the appearance of shaky financial practices. The thrust of the bishop's objection (in a letter that Don Reggio contemptuously pulls out of his desk) was stated in a dictum that likened selling seats on festival cars to the practice of selling indulgences—the volatile sixteenth-century issue that prompted Martin Luther to post his Ninety-five Theses on the door of Wittenberg Cathedral.

"But this is not only about little girls and 50,000 lire," Don Reggio sputters to the air at large. "If we deny the faithful the opportunity to participate in their liturgy, our entire way of life will be threatened. The first tradition to vanish will be that of the festivals themselves." He turns back to me. "*You* are from Tuscany. Tell me. Do Tuscans have festivals as grand as ours? Do the people celebrate festivals with the joy and devotion you see here in Serre San Bruno?"

It is a good point. "No," I answer. "One of the things that amazes me about the South is the incredible emotional outpouring that surrounds religious festivals. In Tuscany, religious feast days are not nearly as important anymore as *palios* [contests between rival factions of a city] or costumed pageants."

"My point exactly!"

"But there must surely be a compromise point between selling favors and having to discontinue the festival."

"Compromise of any kind is a step toward death," he answers, and I know there is no sense even broaching the subject of voluntary donations.

For the rest of our time together, Don Reggio tells me much about Serre San Bruno's festivals, about the Good Friday observance—called *Schiovazzioni*—during which residents of the town carry the large wooden cross from Matrice Church to Mount Calvary, many dressed in traditional costumes; about the fireworks for the August 16 Feast of Saint Rocco; about the aforementioned Saint Bruno Festival, held on October 6, which draws almost a half million people from surrounding communities.

He also talks about traditions that are no longer alive: the grandmother-chaperones walking five steps behind young couples during nightly *passegiatte;* the baking of certain breads and cakes for various feast days (chief among these, the *nzulli,* the recipe for which no one was ever able to spirit away from either the town elders or the professional bakers); the tuna fishermen who used to kill their prey using harpoons, a method that is now largely forbidden because of protests by animal-rights groups.

This last, the harpooning of tuna, is the tradition that fascinates me most of all, mainly because of its inherent ideological grayness. According to Don Reggio, tuna fishing was once one of the area's foremost occupations, with many of Serre San Bruno's men spending entire seasons away from their families. "But the tuna industry is now in the hands of the big producers," he says. "And so the tuna die in huge nets that scoop them up from the waters as if they were nothing more than a pebble. Is that more sportsmanlike? In other cases, they're hooked on forty-mile-long fishing lines with hundreds of hooks that catch any fish that takes the bait, including thousands of tuna that don't make the weight requirement. Some 40,000 undersize tuna are discarded each year and almost all of them die in the process. Is that more humane?"

His point is a good one. But I am once again struck by the difference between his certainty about every single issue and my consistent wavering between positions. The truth is, I can see both sides equally—on the one hand, who wants to see the waters red with the blood of harpooned tuna even if the resultant product is gastronomically superior by virtue of its pure white delicacy? But the other side is equally compelling: why damn one method when the replacement solution has so many problems of its own?

"*Cara,* your problem is in lacking a spiritual rudder," says Don Reggio when I voice my duality, "a sense of tradition that would ground you in a collective world far greater than simply this moment in time. Despite what you think, most things are either right or wrong and the difference between the two is blatantly obvious."

I spend a few more days in Serre San Bruno, watching the festival floats and eating my way from one end of the town to the other. It is all wonderful to me, all of it. The girls in their communion dresses, the women in their traditional costumes, the horses draped in tapestries, the men playing cards in the betting parlor. But there is something about this and every other festival that makes me unable to feel at one with the events in motion.

"It is the part of you that has become an American," says Sandro when I call him from the road. "Your Italian side allows you to be more one of us than any Brit or German who has lived here year-round for the past three decades. But any Italian who spends a few minutes with you senses a certain pulling back, a certain inability to truly merge into the historic collective that is Italy. In a word, what you lack is a sense of tradition."

This is, for us, an old discussion. At times, its nature has been serious; at times, exuberantly light. This time, I can hear the teasing in his voice. "Is there no hope for me, then?" I say, suddenly feeling a lot better.

"I'm not sure. Come back to Tuscany and we'll see what we can do." He stops. For a moment, I think he has replaced the receiver.

"What?"

"Maybe . . ." he breaks off in hysterical laughter, ". . . maybe you should ask Don Reggio if he thinks you might be inhabited by an evil spirit."

GAMBERI IN POCETO

Shrimp in Wine and Parsley

364

❦ Venezia-Friuli Giulia ❧

AS I WANDERED FROM HOUSE TO HOUSE DURING RAVASCLETTO'S *FIESTA TAS CORTS*, *I was amazed at not only the bounty of the foods offered, but also by the diversity of the recipes. It was almost as if each house had opened the door to their most cherished secrets: the recipes handed down through generations of families and preserved in a way that was noticeably different from the same dish eaten just next door.*

At the Silvano house in Val Caldo, I ate mesta e busa *(creamy polenta with sausage, ricotta, and butter sauce),* cartufles e radic *(potatoes and radicchio dressed with sautéed lard) and the following dish of freshwater shrimp sautéed simply with white wine, parsley, and a bay leaf.*

serves 4

Time: 15 minutes

Level of Difficulty: Easy

⚖

2 tablespoons extra virgin
   olive oil

2 tablespoons unsalted butter

1 clove garlic, minced

2 tablespoons chopped fresh
   Italian parsley

1 fresh or dried bay leaf

32 large shrimp, peeled and
   deveined

Salt to taste

Freshly ground black pepper
   to taste

1/2 cup dry white wine

1/2 cup fresh Italian parsley
   leaves for garnish

1 Heat the oil and butter in a large skillet over low heat 2 to 3 minutes, or until foamy. Stir in the garlic, parsley, and bay leaf and cook for 1 minute.

2 Add the shrimp, cover, and cook for 3 to 4 minutes, or until the shrimp turn pink. Season with salt and pepper and pour in the wine. Increase the heat to high and cook until the wine has evaporated, about 3 minutes.

3 Remove the shrimp with tongs and place on a heated platter. Nap with the pan juices, garnish with parsley, and serve immediately.

How to Serve As an appetizer followed by pasta tossed with yellow pepper béchamel or as an entrée paired with bread (to soak up the white wine) and gratinéed fennel.

Wine Suggestion Dry White

CASSOLA

Fish Soup with Garlic-rubbed Bread

❦ Sardegna ❦

WHEN KING UMBERTO I VISITED SARDINIA IN 1899 (THE FIRST ITALIAN KING TO DO *so), residents of Sassari in the northwestern corner organized a grand festival to show off the island's history and traditions. Dubbed* La Cavalcata Fiabesca, *the festival lasted for three days filled with sumptuous banquets, jousting events, dancing, musical performances, and equestrian parades. In 1951, Sardinia hosted a meeting of Europe's various Rotary Club members and residents once again seized the moment to revive the idea of a lavish Cavalcata. The festival is now an institution, held every year on the third Sunday in May and attended by over 7,000 spectators. Each province in Sardinia sends a representative "division" to display its folkloric traditions; the costumes alone are worth a visit.*

serves 4

Time: 30 minutes

Level of Difficulty: Moderate

🜍

4 tablespoons extra virgin olive oil
1 small onion, minced
1 clove garlic, minced
1 fresh or dried chili, diced
1 tablespoon chopped fresh basil
1 large (28–32 ounce) can
    Italian peeled plum tomatoes,
    with liquid
Salt to taste
1 pound squid, cleaned (see page
    123) and thinly sliced
1 pound clams, scrubbed
1 pound shrimp, peeled and
    deveined
1 pound dourade (orata) or snapper
    fillets, cut into chunks
4 thick slices country-style bread,
    toasted and rubbed with garlic

1 Heat the oil in a skillet over low heat and sauté the onion, garlic, chili, and basil for 8 minutes, stirring constantly. Add the tomatoes and their liquid. Increase the heat to medium, season with salt, and cook until the mixture reaches a boil.

2 Add the squid and cook for 10 minutes, stirring constantly. Add the clams, shrimp, and dourade, cover, and cook for 5 minutes, or until the mollusks have opened. Discard any unopened shells.

3 Distribute the bread among four plates, top with the tomato mixture, and serve immediately.

How to Serve As a one-dish meal with plenty of bread to soak up the remainder of the broth.

Wine Suggestion Dry or Medium-Sweet White

MUGGINI ARROSTI NEL SALE

Mullet Roasted in Salt

❧ Sardegna ❧

AFTER I HAD WITNESSED THE GRAND PROCESSION OF HORSES AND COSTUMED *actors parading through the streets of Sassari, I strolled over to the food stalls and asked about what looked like platters of salt being removed from a makeshift oven. The old woman in charge told me that Sardinians roast fresh mullet in a casing of salt to give the flesh a flaky, almost-smoked texture. "Come," she said, and hustled me off to the kitchen where hundreds of mullets were being washed and placed on salt beds. "Taste," she ordered, handing me a forkful of already cooked mullet. I obeyed instinctively and to great satisfaction.*

serves 4

Time: 1 hour

Level of Difficulty: Moderate

8 fresh red mullets, about 1/2
    pound each, or two 2-pound
    snappers, washed, dried,
    and eviscerated (scales
    left on)
About 16 cups coarse salt
4 lemons, thinly sliced

1 Preheat the oven to 400°F.

2 Pour half the salt into an ovenproof glass or terra-cotta baking pan and smooth with a spatula. Place the mullets on the salt and cover entirely with the remaining salt.

3 Bake for 40 minutes. To release the fish, break the hardened crust with the handle of a knife or a hammer and lift out the individual mullets; the salt pulls off the scales. Serve on a bed of sliced lemons.

How to Serve With peperonata—a red-and-yellow pepper "stew" made by first sautéing an onion in olive oil, then adding roughly chopped peppers and cooking for about 30 minutes over low heat, stirring occasionally. Stir in a handful of diced parsley just before serving.

Wine Suggestion **Dry or Medium-Sweet White**

ZUPPA DI VONGOLE

Fresh Clams in Tomato-Parsley Broth

❧ Lazio ❧

EST! EST! EST! IS ONE OF THE LAZIO'S GREAT WHITE WINES AND THE ONE THAT FORMS *the central focus of Montefiascone's* Fiera del Vino *held the first two weeks of August. The story behind this wine dates back to 1111, when Enrico V was en route to Rome with his servant, Martino, whose job it was to scout out the regions' best* osterie—*small restaurants that make their own wine. When he found one, he was to write on the outside wall "est," meaning roughly "I have been here," with the understanding that the wine was good. Martino first arrived in Montepulciano, producer of one of Italy's best red wines—vino nobile—and marked it with an "Est!" His next stop was in Orvieto, where he tasted that delicately perfumed, eponymously named vintage and, with unrestrained exuberance, commented: "Est! Est!" But then he arrived in Montefiascone, a hilltop village overlooking Lake Bolsena, and tasted a moscato so superb as to render him almost speechless, except for the enthusiastic "Est! Est! Est!" scribbled onto the outside wall.*

serves 4

Time: 30 minutes

Level of Difficulty: Moderate

⚜

2 pounds Manila or other
    medium clams, scrubbed under
    running water
5 tablespoons extra virgin olive oil
2 cloves garlic, minced
1 salt-packed anchovy (see page 25)
3 tablespoons chopped fresh
    Italian parsley
1 pound ripe Italian plum tomatoes,
    peeled, seeded, and finely diced
Salt to taste
Freshly ground black pepper to taste
3 tablespoons heavy cream
8 thin slices country-style bread,
    toasted and rubbed with garlic

1 Soak the clams in 15 minutes in cold water to extract any sand. Drain and put in a large skillet, cover, and cook over medium heat for 5 minutes. Discard any unopened shells. Cool to room temperature.

2 Using a slotted spoon, remove the clams and strain the broth that will have seeped out of the shells.

3 Heat the oil in a skillet over low heat. Sauté the garlic, anchovy, and parsley for 6 minutes, stirring constantly. Add the tomatoes, clams, clam broth, salt, and pepper and mix until well blended. Cook for 10 minutes. Stir in the cream and cook until warmed through.

4 Divide the warm bread among four bowls, top with soup, and serve immediately.

How to Serve As a first course, followed by roast turkey and sautéed greens; or as a one-dish meal served with additional bread and a mixed green salad.

Wine Suggestion Dry White or Medium-bodied Red

TORTIERA DI COZZE

Baked Stuffed Mussels

❦ Puglia ❦

ONE OF ITALY'S MOST INTENSE GOOD FRIDAY OBSERVANCES TAKES PLACE IN *Foggia, a large city in northern Puglia. Over 300 actors and actresses transform the city into an Italian Jerusalem with their portrayal of the events leading up to Christ's death. There's Veronica cleaning Christ's face; Roman soldiers pushing him to move faster as he carries the cross to Calvary; the three Marys: his mother, his aunt and the prostitute who converted after her first encounter with Christ; Joseph of Arimathea, who carried the cross for Christ when his strength had given out. The scenes are reenacted in various parts of the city and occupy most of the piazzas and gardens and all of Foggia's energy and attention.*

serves 4

Time: 30 minutes

Level of Difficulty: Moderate

⚖

4 tablespoons extra virgin olive oil

2 pounds large blue mussels, scraped clean, bearded, and washed under running water

4 ounces plain breadcrumbs

2 tablespoons chopped fresh Italian parsley

3 cloves garlic, minced

Salt to taste

Freshly ground black pepper to taste

1 Heat 1 tablespoon oil in a large, heavy-gauge skillet over high heat. Add the mussels, cover, and cook for 2 to 3 minutes, or until the mussels open. Discard any unopened shells. Discard the top half of each shell (the half not containing the mussel). Strain the juice through a fine sieve or cheesecloth and set aside.

2 Preheat the oven to 350°F. Oil a large baking pan with 1 tablespoon oil.

3 Arrange the mussels in the pan in a single layer. Place the breadcrumbs, parsley, garlic, salt, pepper, and reserved mussel juices in a bowl and mix until well blended. Place a teaspoon of the mixture on top of each mussel and drizzle with the remaining oil.

4 Bake for 10 minutes. Pour some beaten egg over each mussel and bake for another 10 minutes. Garnish with parsley and serve immediately.

How to Serve As an appetizer followed by grilled snapper, saffron-flavored rice, and steamed green beans.

Wine Suggestion **Dry White**

2 large eggs, lightly beaten
8 to 12 fresh Italian parsley
  sprigs for garnish

369

ORATA AL FORNO

Oven-roasted Dourade Served on a Bed of Potato Wafers

❧ Puglia ☙

A SIMILAR PROCESSION (SEE PAGE 368) TAKES PLACE IN TARANTO, LOCATED IN THE *instep of Italy's boot.* La Processione dell'Addolorata *begins at midnight, when groups depart from the Church of San Domenico—a picturesque sanctuary built on a small island in the old part of the city and connected to the rest of Taranto by a revolving turnbridge. The procession consists of eight living dioramas representing The Via Crucis—from Christ praying in the garden of Gethsemane, to the departed Christ covered with a white blanket embroidered with golden stars. Throughout the night, bands play, church bells ring, and people stand around, eating, talking, playing cards, and praying (the disparity between one activity and another is rather startling to witness).*

I ate the following dish at a makeshift table outside the home of Elda Damore, who saw me watching from the local cafe and invited me to join her family.

serves 4

Time: 65 to 75 minutes

Level of Difficulty: Moderate

1 1/2 pounds boiling potatoes,
    peeled and thinly sliced
    into rounds
6 tablespoons extra virgin
    olive oil
2 cloves garlic
3 tablespoons chopped fresh
    Italian parsley

1 Toss the potato slices with 4 tablespoons oil and layer all but 15 to 20 slices on the bottom of a glass or terra-cotta baking pan.

2 Put the garlic and parsley on a cutting board and chop together until pastelike. Sprinkle half the paste over the potatoes and season with salt and pepper.

3 Preheat the oven to 400°F.

4 Place the fish on the bed of potatoes and overlap the remaining slices around the perimeter. Sprinkle the remaining parsley-garlic paste over the potatoes, season with salt and pepper, and drizzle with the remaining oil.

5 Bake for 45 minutes, shaking the pan occasionally to prevent sticking. Remove from the oven and serve immediately.

How to Serve Pair with a mixture of roasted vegetables including peppers, fennel and onions.

Wine Suggestion Dry or Medium-Sweet White

2 pounds dourade (orata) or snapper, scales and fins removed, eviscerated, washed, and dried with paper towels
Salt to taste
Freshly ground black pepper to taste

371

SARDE AL FORNO

Sardines Baked with Tomatoes and Parsley-Garlic Pesto

❧ Campania ☙

AFTER AN HOUR OF SELF-ADMINISTERED BEATINGS, A STATUE OF THE VIRGIN IS *carried from the church into the piazza. The statue itself has an unusual story: according to legend, it was discovered more than 400 years ago by two pigs in a field and was, initially, very heavy, but became lighter over time as more and more people turned to beating themselves as a way of doing penance. When the statue is set in place in the piazza, the* battenti *fall to their knees and accelerate their activity. Thirty minutes later, the statue is once again returned to its inner sanctum and the bloodied battenti disperse throughout the town, joining the various processions organized to honor the Assumption of Mary.*

serves 4

Time: 40 minutes

Level of Difficulty: Moderate

1¹/₂ pounds sardines

4 tablespoons extra virgin
olive oil

Salt to taste

Freshly ground black pepper
to taste

1 tablespoon freshly chopped
oregano

6 ripe Italian plum tomatoes,
peeled, seeded and
finely diced

2 cloves garlic

2 tablespoons chopped fresh
Italian parsley

1 To clean the sardines, remove the scales and cut off and discard the heads. Open flat and lift out the central bone. Discard the entrails, wash gently, and place on a cutting board or other flat surface to dry.

2 Drizzle 3 tablespoons oil in a 10-inch-round glass or porcelain baking dish. Arrange the sardines in a star pattern. Season with salt, pepper, and oregano. Distribute the tomatoes evenly over the surface.

3 Preheat the oven to 350°F.

4 Put the garlic and parsley on a cutting board and dice together to blend the flavors. Spread the mixture over the sardines and drizzle with the remaining oil.

5 Bake for 25 minutes. Remove from the oven and serve it either hot or cold.

Make Ahead The entire dish can be prepared earlier in the day, refrigerated, and served cold.

How to Serve Pair with parsleyed potatoes and a green salad.

Wine Suggestion Dry White or Medium-bodied Red

CACCIUCCO

Tuscan Fish Soup

❧ Toscana ❧

THERE ARE MANY CACCIUCCO FESTIVALS THROUGHOUT TUSCANY, BUT THIS ONE *in Montramito has always been one of my favorites because the food is prepared entirely by members of the local socialist party, who have, as of the last election, gained a little more administrative power. Years ago, the flavor of the event was one of camraderie—that particular type of camraderie engaged in by people united in an underdog struggle. Publicity was limited to a few hundred fliers attached to trees in surrounding villages. The cacciucco was prepared by groups of volunteers who stopped by after work to clean a few dozen cuttlefish and it was served in mismatched plates borrowed from local housewives. The wine was all made by locals. But now the socialists are in ascendance. And what that means for this sagra is, obviously, a far more lavish budget. Suddenly, there are professional cooks in the kitchen and quasi-famous wines for sale. There are also more than 3,000 or 4,000 people in attendance on any given night of the three-week run (generally from July 1 to around the 20). But let me not, as my mother would say, go looking for the feather in the egg. The spirit of fun is still the same as is the magnificence of this extraordinary, bouillabaisselike soup.*

serves 4

Time: About 1 hour

Level of Difficulty: Moderate

⚖

5 tablespoons extra virgin
    olive oil

1 small onion, minced

1 medium carrot, diced

1 stalk celery, diced

1 clove garlic, minced

4 tablespoons chopped fresh
    Italian parsley

1 Heat the oil in a skillet large enough to hold all the fish and shellfish over low heat. Sauté the onion, carrot, celery, garlic, parsley, and chili for 8 minutes, stirring frequently. Pour the wine over the mixture and cook until it evaporates, about 3 minutes.

2 Add the cuttlefish, octopus, and tomatoes, season with salt, and cook for 20 minutes, stirring occasionally and adding a few tablespoons of fish broth, as needed. The sauce should be thick and somewhat dry. The cuttlefish and octopus should be fork tender.

3 Add the large fish chunks and cook for 15 minutes. Then add the shrimp and cook for 3 minutes, or until pink.

4 Meanwhile, toast the bread on both sides and rub with garlic. Distribute among four bowls and top with the fish, making sure to include a few pieces of every type in each bowl. Spoon some juices over the fish, garnish with parsley, and serve immediately.

How to Serve As a one-dish meal or preceded by a cold shellfish salad.

Wine Suggestion Dry or Medium-Sweet White or even Medium-bodied Red

1 fresh chili, minced, or dried crumbled chili

1 cup dry red wine

1/2 pound cuttlefish, heads, cartilege, and ink sacks removed (see page 123 for directions) and cut into rings

1/2 pound baby octopus, eyes and ink sacks removed and peeled (ask the fishmonger to do this) and cut into 1-inch chunks

1 pound ripe Italian plum tomatoes (about 6 to 7), peeled, seeded, and diced

Salt to taste

1 cup fish broth

2 1/2 pounds assorted large fish steaks, such as sea bass, halibut, cod, and hake, cut into chunks

1/2 pound large shrimp, deveined and peeled

8 thin slices country-style bread, toasted and rubbed with garlic

SARDE A BECCAFICO

Gratinéed Sardine Rolls Stuffed with Parsley and Pignoli Pesto

❧ Sicilia ❧

TRAPANI IN WESTERN SICILY CELEBRATES GOOD FRIDAY WITH A STUNNING *procession that lasts twenty-four hours—from just after lunch on Friday to late Saturday morning. Twenty huge statues representing episodes from the Passion of Christ are carried through the streets in a slow, rhythmic pace (called* l'annacata*) by groups of folklorically costumed trade union members. Spectators number in the thousands and, afterward, everyone repairs to a local restaurant, all of which, on this day, serve fish since Catholics abstain from eating meat on Holy Saturday. This dish of gratinéed sardines left me speechless.*

serves 4

Time: 60 to 70 minutes

Level of Difficulty: Moderate

2 pounds sardines

4 tablespoons extra virgin
    olive oil

1/2 cup plain breadcrumbs

1/4 cup golden raisins, soaked for
    20 minutes in warm water
    and drained squeezed dry

6 salt-packed anchovies, filleted
    and finely chopped
    (see page 25)

2 tablespoons finely chopped
    fresh Italian parsley

1/4 cup pine nuts, finely diced

Salt to taste

Freshly ground black pepper
    to taste

3 fresh or dried bay leaves

1 To clean the sardines, remove the scales and cut off and discard the heads. Open flat and lift out the central bone. Discard the entrails, wash gently, and place on a cutting board or other flat surface to dry.

2 Heat 2 tablespoons oil in a skillet over low heat and add all but 2 tablespoons of the breadcrumbs. Cook, stirring constantly, for 5 to 7 minutes, or until toasted. Place in a bowl with the raisins, anchovies, parsley, pine nuts, salt, and pepper and mix until well blended.

3 Preheat the oven to 350°F.

4 Place about 1/2 teaspoon on each sardine. Roll into a ball, tail side up, and fasten with a tooth-pick. Arrange the sardines in a glass or terra-cotta baking pan and place a piece of bay leaf in between each roll. Sprinkle with the reserved breadcrumbs and drizzle with the remaining oil.

5 Bake for 30 minutes. Remove from the oven and cool for 5 minutes before serving.

Make Ahead The parsley-anchovy mixture can be prepared earlier in the day and refrigerated until ready to use.

How to Serve Serve as an appetizer followed by seafood risotto. To use as an entrée, pair with lukewarm parsleyed potatoes.

Wine Suggestion **Dry or Medium-Sweet White**

AGGHIOTTA DI PESCE SPADA

Swordfish Steaks Baked with Tomatoes, Raisins, and Olives

❧ Sicilia ❧

I ATE A PLATE OF THIS TASTY BAKED SWORDFISH IN A RESTAURANT, THE WALLS OF *which walls were decorated with pictures of the Risen Christ posted alongside numerous photos of young boys. "My grandchildren," answered the old woman proprietor when I asked who they were. "All boys?" I asked, surprised. "I have twenty-six grandchildren," she responded. "And twenty-four of them are boys. The only girls are twins born to my daughter, who lives in Chicago. But you know how those Americans are," she said, obviously assured that I bore no resemblance. "Too busy to even send a picture. Wait until they come to see me. 'And you?' I'll ask. 'Who the hell are you?'"*

serves 4

Time: 45 minutes

Level of Difficulty: Easy

🙢

6 tablespoons extra virgin
    olive oil

1 small onion, thinly sliced

1 clove garlic, crushed

1/4 cup pine nuts

1/4 cup sultana raisins, soaked in
    warm water for 20 minutes,
    drained, and squeezed dry

1 tablespoon brine-packed
    capers, drained

3 ounces green olives, pitted

1 Heat the oil in a skillet over low heat and sauté the onion and garlic for 8 minutes, stirring frequently. Add the pine nuts, raisins, capers, olives, and tomato fillets and stir to blend all ingredients. Cover and cook for 15 minutes.

2 Preheat the oven to 350°F. Oil a glass or terra-cotta baking pan.

3 Season the swordfish steaks with salt and pepper. Arrange the steaks in a single layer in the pan. Pour the sauce over the steaks and sprinkle with parsley.

4 Bake for 8 minutes, gently turn the steaks, and cook for another 8 minutes. Remove from the oven and serve hot.

Make Ahead The sauce can be made up to
2 days in advance and refrigerated in a sealed
container until ready to use.

How to Serve Precede with a simple fish broth and
then serve this entrée accompanied by lemony rice
and a green salad.

Wine Suggestion Medium-bodied Red

12 ounces canned Italian plum
    tomatoes, drained, and cut
    into fillets
4 swordfish steaks, about 4 ounces
    each (1 pound total)
Salt to taste
Freshly ground black pepper
    to taste
2 tablespoons chopped fresh
    Italian parsley

379

PESCE PERSICO ALLA PIEMONTESE

Panfried Royal Perch

❦ Piemonte ❧

OF ALL ITALY'S FESTIVALS, I PARTICULARY LIKE THE ONES CELEBRATING THE SEASONS, *which is why I hastened to Torre Pellice, a hillside village near Torino, when I heard they were having a Summer Festival last July 6. Seasonal festivals seem to have a no-holds-barred quality to them, held as they are at the height of an area's agricultural abundance. This one did not disappoint. In addition to the tomatoes and apricots and strawberries and new cheeses (one of the very best things I have ever tasted was brussu, new ewe's milk cheese that had been marinated for three weeks in grappa), this festival offered the following dish of royal perch battered in flour, egg, and breadcrumbs, fried in butter, and topped with a wonderful lemon-caper sauce.*

serves 4

Time: 25 minutes

Level of Difficulty: Easy

8 freshwater perch fillets

3 tablespoons unbleached
    all-purpose flour

2 large eggs, lightly beaten with
    a pinch of salt

6 tablespoons plain breadcrumbs

4 tablespoons unsalted butter

Salt to taste

1 clove garlic, minced

3 tablespoons chopped fresh
    Italian parsley

1 tablespoon capers packed in
    brine, drained

2 tablespoons lemon zest

1 Dredge the fillets in flour, dip in the eggs, and press into the breadcrumbs to coat well.

2 Heat the butter in a nonstick pan over medium heat, and when it begins to foam, fry the fish for 4 to 6 minutes per side, or until golden. Remove with tongs, salt, drain on paper towels, and keep warm.

3 Add the garlic, parsley, capers, and lemon zest to the skillet. Reduce the heat to low and cook for 3 minutes, stirring to blend the flavors. Pour over the fillets and serve immediately.

Make Ahead The fish can be floured and coated with breadcrumbs an hour before and refrigerated on a plate lined with paper towels.

How to Serve As an entrée served with mashed potatoes and marinated red peppers.

Wine Suggestion Dry White

TROTA AL ERBE

Freshwater Trout with Herbs and Lemon Fragrance

381

❧ Piemonte ❧

THE PIEDMONT IS KNOWN FOR ITS FRESHWATER TROUT BUT I HAVE NEVER ENJOYED IT *more than this exquisitely simple version prepared by Adriana Foscaro at Torre Pellice's Fiera d'Estate (see page 380). Signora Foscaro was one of the many cooks when I wandered back behind the counter and began scrutinizing each of the fish dishes being prepared. She took me under her wing, sat me down, and began feeding me. "This one is made according to my personal recipe," she said upon presenting the trout. "The secret is to use only the very freshest ingredients. Yesterday's trout is no good." That having been said, I eventually tried making it with yesterday's trout, my New York City apartment not being located on a trout-filled river. There was a difference, but the taste was still divine.*

serves 4

Time: 45 minutes

Level of Difficulty: Moderate

4 freshwater trout, about 8 ounces each, eviscerated (ask the fishmonger to do this)

4 tablespoons extra virgin olive oil

1 clove garlic, minced

1 small onion, minced

1 teaspoon chopped fresh rosemary

1 teaspoon chopped fresh sage

1 celery stalk, diced

2 tablespoons grated lemon zest

1/4 cup sultana raisins, soaked in warm water for 20 minutes, drained, and squeezed dry

Salt to taste

4 tablespoons white wine vinegar

1 cup Basic Meat Broth (page 460) or canned broth

1 lemon, thinly sliced for garnish

4 stems fresh rosemary, for garnish

1 Rinse the trout under running water and pat dry with paper towels.

2 Heat the oil in a skillet over low heat and sauté the garlic, onion, rosemary, sage, and celery for 8 minutes, stirring constantly. Add the fish, lemon zest, raisins, salt, vinegar, and broth, cover, and cook for 8 minutes. Turn the fish and cook for another 8 minutes.

3 Using a slotted spatula, transfer the fish to a heated serving platter. Bring the sauce to a boil, and reduce the sauce by half. Pour over the fish and serve on a bed of lemons and garnished with fresh rosemary.

How to Serve With parsleyed potatoes and steamed asparagus

Wine Suggestion Dry White

SARDELLE IN SAOR

Fried Sardines Marinated with Onions

382

❧ Veneto ❧

ON THE FEAST OF CHRIST THE REDEEMER, VENETIANS PREPARE THIS DELICIOUS *terrine filled with batter-fried sardines marinated in hot vinaigrette and layered with sautéed onions, pine nuts, and raisins. The day-long festival, held on the third Saturday of July, reaches its climax after the sun goes down, when exquisitely decorated gondolas carrying Venetian officials dressed in costumes dating back to 1576 form a flotilla near the Giudecca Canal. As thousands crowd the bridges and waterfronts, there is a spectacular display of fireworks that lights all of Giudecca Island.*

serves 4

Time: 45 minutes excluding the 2-day marinating period

Level of Difficulty: Moderate

⚕

1 1/2 pounds fresh sardines
Unbleached all-purpose flour
    for dredging
Olive oil for frying
4 tablespoons extra virgin olive oil
2 large yellow onions, thinly sliced
1 cup red wine vinegar, heated
    to a simmer

1 To clean the sardines, remove the scales and cut off and discard the heads. Open flat and lift out the central bone. Discard the entrails, wash gently, and dry with paper towels. Dredge in flour and fry in 1 inch of olive oil over medium heat until golden brown on all sides. Remove with tongs and drain on paper towels.

2 Heat the 4 tablespoons oil in a skillet and sauté the onions over medium heat for 5 minutes, stirring constantly. Add 3/4 cup hot vinegar and the sugar and stir until well blended. Cook for 5 minutes longer, or until the vinegar has evaporated, and remove from the heat.

Prepared this way, sardines will last without refrigeration for three to four days, but all surfaces of the fish must be completely immersed in vinaigrette; fish exposed to air will deteriorate within hours. The sardines can also be refrigerated for the two-day period.

3 Arrange a layer of sardines on the bottom of a serving bowl. Top with layers of onions, pine nuts, and raisins and drizzle with vinegar. Continue layering until all ingredients are used up. Cover tightly and marinate in a cool, dry place for 2 days* before serving.

How to Serve As an appetizer followed by pasta tossed with parsley, garlic, and Parmigiano-Reggiano, or as an entrée served with new potatoes pan-roasted until almost crisp.

Wine Suggestion Medium- or Full-bodied Red

1 tablespoon sugar

1/4 cup pine nuts

1/4 cup sultana raisins, soaked in warm water for 20 minutes, drained, and squeezed dry

383

STORIONE IN UMIDO CON LA POLENTA

Sturgeon Steaks Braised in White Wine and Tomatoes and Served with Creamy Polenta

384

❧ Trentino-Alto Adige ❧

IN 1439, THE SERENISSIMA REPUBLIC OF VENICE WAS AT WAR WITH THE VISCONTI *of Milan. In order to surprise the enemy troops with an attack from the rear, the Serenissima transported a fleet of galleys from the Adriatic Sea up the river Adige, across the mountains, and then launched them onto Lake Garda near Torbole. It was an incredible undertaking for any epoch and is remembered in history books as a near-impossible feat. Since then, every August 27, the various districts (called* quadre*) of Riva (a village on the Trentino side of Lake Garda referred to by Stendhal as "perhaps the most beautiful landscape in the world") hold three days of sailing competitions designed to choose the crew for a reenactment of this classic battle. And finally, on the evening of August 30, around 10:00 P.M., the winning quadra (dressed in period costumes) board the galley bearing Riva's coat of arms and sets off in battle against the Venetians (who, of course, must always win). The event is called* Le Notte di Fiaba—*The Night of Fairy Tales—and attracts millions of spectators.*

Afterward, both teams—along with village residents and spectators—celebrate with, among other wonderful dishes, these meaty sturgeon steaks braised in a delicious white-wine broth flavored with anchovies, tomatoes, bay leaf, parsley, and marjoram.

serves 4

Time: 75 minutes excluding the 2-hour marinating period

Level of Difficulty: Moderate

2 pounds sturgeon or swordfish, cut into 4 thick steaks

3 tablespoons chopped fresh Italian parsley

Salt to taste

1 Put the sturgeon steaks in a glass baking dish in a single layer, sprinkle with parsley, and season with salt and pepper. Pour half the oil and half the wine over the steaks and refrigerate for 2 hours, turning the steaks every 20 minutes.

2 Place the onions, garlic, and celery on a cutting board and cut into a fine dice. Heat the remaining oil in a skillet over medium heat and sauté the vegetable dice, marjoram, bay leaves, and anchovies for 8 minutes, stirring constantly.

3 Using tongs, remove the sturgeon from the marinade and add to the skillet, reserving the marinade. Cook about 10 miuntes, or until browned on both sides.

4 Stir in the tomatoes and cook for 5 minutes, or until the sauce has noticeably thickened. Add the remaining wine and the fish marinade, cover, and cook for 20 minutes.

5 Meanwhile, bring 2 quarts salted water to a rolling boil over medium heat in a heavy-gauge saucepan.* Reduce the heat to low and pour in the cornmeal steadily, whisking constantly. Cook for 30 to 40 minutes, whisking frequently until the polenta comes away from the sides of the pan and the whisk stands up by itself in the center of the polenta. Add the butter and milk, stirring until the polenta is smooth and creamy.

6 To serve, place a dollop of polenta on one half of each plate. Arrange a sturgeon steak on the other half, top with the sauce, and garnish with parsley

How to Serve Generally a one-dish meal although I like to add a mixed green salad or sautéed greens to round out the flavors.

Wine Suggestion Medium- or Full-bodied Red

Freshly ground black pepper
   to taste
3/4 cup extra virgin olive oil
2 cups dry white wine
2 medium onions
2 cloves garlic
1 celery stalk
1 teaspoon dried marjoram
2 bay leaves
4 salt-packed anchovies, filleted
   (see page 25) and diced
12 ounces canned Italian plum
   tomatoes, drained (liquid
   reserved for another use)
2 quarts salted water
2 cups coarsely ground cornmeal
4 tablespoons unsalted butter
1 cup whole milk
Parsley leaves for garnish

*See page 63 for a less time-consuming way to cook polenta.

CAPPON MAGRO

Fish and Vegetable Salad

386

❧ Liguria ❧

THE HIGHLIGHT OF CAMPO LIGURE'S SAINTS PETER AND PAUL FESTIVAL IS THE *presentation of this complex fish and vegetable salad, a classic dish of Genoa. Infinitely simpler than would appear by looking at the list of ingredients, Cappon Magro is made by alternating layers of fish with layers of vegetables and seasoning the whole with a wonderful puree made from bread, oil, anchovies, garlic, and pine nuts.*

serves 6

Time: 75 minutes excluding the 90 minutes to roast the beef

Level of Difficulty: Moderate

FISH

2 pounds dourade (orata) fillets or monkfish, skate, sole, or snapper fillets

Salt to taste

1 large lobster tail

12 large shrimp, unpeeled

2 pounds large blue mussels

1 tablespoon extra virgin olive oil

VEGETABLES

1 cup baby green beans

4 medium new red potatoes, peeled and thinly sliced

1 small head cauliflower, cored and cut into florets

1 cup salsify, peeled, cut into thin rounds (optional)

1 To make the fish, put the dourade in a skillet with just enough salted water to cover. Cook over medium heat for 8 to 10 minutes, or until the fish flakes when scraped with a fork. Drain, cool, and set aside.

2 Put the lobster in boiling salted water and cook for 10 minutes. Add the shrimp during the last minute of cooking. Drain everything and peel the shrimp. Using kitchen shears, cut the lobster tail casing lengthwise, and remove the meat in one piece. Cut the meat into thin slices widthwise and set aside with the cooked shrimp.

3 Put the mussels and 1 tablespoon oil in a skillet, cover, and cook over medium heat for 3 to 4 minutes, or until the shells open. Discard any unopened shells. Remove from the heat and extract the mussels, discarding the shells and cooking liquid, or reserve the liquid for another use. Set aside with the other fish.

4 To make the vegetables, boil the green beans in salted water for about 4 minutes, or until tender, and drain. Boil the potatoes in salted water about 7 minutes, or until tender, and drain. Boil the cauliflower florets in salted water for about 8 minutes, or until tender, and drain. Boil the salsify in salted water about 8 minutes, or until tender, and drain. Boil the artichokes in salted water about 8 minutes, or until tender, and drain. Boil the celery in salted water for about 5 minutes, or until tender, and drain. Boil the carrots in salted water about 12 minutes, or until tender, and drain. Wrap the beet in foil and oven-roast about 90 minutes, or until tender.

5 To make the sauce, peel the hard-boiled eggs, cut in half, and separate the yolks from the whites. Cut the whites and all but two of the yolks into thin slices and set aside. Place the remaining yolks in the bowl of a food processor. Add the anchovies, capers, half the olives, pine nuts, soaked bread, 2 tablespoons oil, and the vinegar and process into a semi-liquid sauce. Add water if the sauce is too thick.

6 Rub the bread with garlic and arrange in one layer on a large serving platter. Drizzle with wine and 2 tablespoons oil and season with salt and pepper. Top with a layer of dourade and a few mussels. Spread a bit of sauce over the fish and add a layer of mixed vegetables drizzled with oil and a little sauce. Then begin again with fish, sauce, vegetables, and sauce until all ingredients have been used up. Somewhere along the way, insert a layer of eggs. Top with mushrooms and the remaining olives, drizzle with lemon juice, garnish with parsley, and let sit for 15 minutes. Serve at room temperature.

Make Ahead Step 4 can be prepared up to a day in advance and refrigerated in a sealed container until ready to use.

How to Serve Makes a wonderful centerpiece for a party buffet.

Wine Suggestion Dry White

6 baby artichokes, outer leaves removed
2 celery stalks, cut into 1-inch slices
3 carrots, thickly sliced
1 medium beet

SAUCE
6 large hard-boiled eggs
8 salt-packed anchovies, filleted (see page 25)
1/4 cup capers, drained
1/2 cup green olives, pitted
1/4 cup pine nuts
4 thick slices country-style bread, soaked in milk for 20 minutes and squeezed dry
10 tablespoons extra virgin olive oil
1 teaspoon red wine vinegar
8 thin slices country-style bread
1 clove garlic, halved
2 tablespoons dry red wine
Salt to taste
Freshly ground black pepper to taste
1 cup button mushrooms, thinly sliced and marinated in 1/4 cup olive oil
Juice of 1 lemon
4 tablespoons chopped fresh Italian parsley

PESCE SPADA ALLO SPIEDINO

Breaded Swordfish Kebabs with Wedges of Red Onion

❧ Sicilia ❧

ST. PETER IS SAID TO HOLD THE KEYS TO HEAVEN AND SO TO CELEBRATE HIS *feast day on June 29, Palermo is awash in stalls selling anything and everything in the shape of keys. There are key-shaped cookies, pasta, breads, rice terrrines, and even the following swordfish kebabs threaded onto skewers with a curl on the end to resemble the keys of old. I have added the capers, which give a complimentary tang to the cheese-flavored breadcrumb batter.*

serves 4

Time: 35 minutes

Level of Difficulty: Easy

Equipment: 8 skewers

1/4 cup plain breadcrumbs

Salt to taste

Freshly ground black pepper to taste

3 tablespoons chopped fresh Italian parsley

1 tablespoon brine-packed capers, drained

3 tablespoons freshly grated caciocavallo or pecorino

2 pounds swordfish or halibut, thinly sliced

1 large red onion, cut into thin pie-shaped wedges

4 tablespoons extra virgin olive oil

1 Put the breadcrumbs in a bowl with the salt, pepper, and parsley. Remove 4 tablespoons of the mix and set aside. Add the capers, grated cheese, and oil and mix until well blended.

2 Place the swordfish between sheets of waxed paper and gently pound with a kitchen mallet until the slices are wafer thin. Cut the slices in half and spread each with the breadcrumb-caper mixture. Roll into tight cylinders and thread onto eight skewers alternating with wedges of onion.

3 Drizzle the remaining oil over the skewers and dip in the reserved breadcrumbs. Only the swordfish will become coated since the kebabs are wider than the onion wedges.

4 Prepare a charcoal grill or preheat the broiler. Coat the grill rack with vegetable oil cooking spray.

5 Grill over hot coals or broil for 5 to 10 minutes, or until golden brown and crispy on both sides. Serve immediately.

Make Ahead The coating mixture in Step 1 can be prepared up to 1 day in advance and refrigerated in a sealed container until ready to use.

How to Serve As an appetizer followed by pasta with clam sauce, or as an entrée bedded on rice and paired with panfried red and yellow peppers.

Wine Suggestion Dry or Medium-Sweet White

NASCELLO ALLA PALERMITANA

Roasted Hake with Anchovies and Rosemary

390

❦ Sicilia ❦

RESIDENTS OF PALERMO TALK ABOUT ST. PETER AS IF HE WERE A NEIGHBOR, WITH *all the same sarcasms, backbiting, and hilarity. Of all the stories told, however, my favorite is this tale of justice, recounted here exactly as it was conveyed to me by Cecco Lamarana, a very funny fisherman who lives near the Ballaró open-air market and supplies much of the fish used to celebrate* La Festa di San Pietro *(see page 388): "One day, while Peter's mother was busy cleaning leeks, an old beggar woman walked by and asked for a simple piece of bread. Well, the mother—known throughout Sicily for her incredible avarice—gave her only the tough, outer leaf of the leek. A few days later, she died unexpectedly and, of course, went right to hell. But a mother is a mother and so the bereaved Apostle begged Jesus to pardon her. And Jesus being who He is, told him to take that sheaf of leek—the only act of kindness ever performed by that miserable woman—and extend it down toward hell so she could use it as a ladder of escape. Which Peter did but when his mother began climbing up the leek, other residents of hell attached themselves to her skirts and that* malvagia—*villain—began kicking them away. 'Who do you think you are,' she bellowed. 'The Apostle is my son, not yours, and the sheaf of leek was extended to me!.' Her howling grew to such intensity that, just at the moment that she was about to clear the border of Hell, the sheaf ripped in half and she fell back down into the fires."*

serves 4

Time: 60 minutes

Level of Difficulty: Moderate

⚛

5 tablespoons extra virgin
    olive oil
4 whole hakes*,
    about 8 ounces each

1 Preheat the oven to 350°F. Oil a glass baking pan with 1 tablespoon oil.

2 Clean the hakes, removing the scales, fins, and intestines. Roll the rosemary sprigs in oil and place one inside each cavity. Season each fish with salt and pepper inside and out and place in a single layer in the baking pan.

*Snapper can be substituted for hake.

3 Heat 2 tablespoons oil in a skillet over low heat and cook the anchovies until dissolved. Pour the paste over the hakes, sprinkle with rosemary, and sprinkle with breadcrumbs.

4 Bake for 30 minutes. Remove from the oven, place on a serving platter, and surround with the lemon slices.

How to Serve Paired with semolina gnocchi (see page 146) and steamed, lemon-drizzled brussel sprouts.

Wine Suggestion Dry or Medium-bodied White

4 sprigs fresh rosemary

Salt to taste

Freshly ground black pepper to taste

5 salt-packed anchovies, filleted (see page 25) and roughly chopped

2 tablespoons chopped fresh rosemary

2 tablespoons plain breadcrumbs

1 lemon, thinly sliced for garnish

RAVIEU DE MA

Sea Bass Ravioli with Marjoram Sauce

392

❦ Liguria ❦

EACH YEAR ON THE FIRST OF MARCH, GENOVA THROWS A HUGE PARTY ON THE *piers near the acquarium to celebrate its seagoing heritage. For the most part,* Il Mare dei Tyrreni *encompasses lectures, boat tours, and demonstrations of ancient fishing implements and techniques. But mainly, it's about food. Plenty of food and all incredible fish dishes such as the following recipe for delicately stuffed homemade ravioli sauced simply with good quality olive oil and leaves of fresh marjoram.*

serves 4

Time: About 75 minutes

Level of Difficulty: Advanced

FILLING

3 tablespoons extra virgin
    olive oil

1 pound sea bass fillet

2 cloves garlic, minced

1 teaspoon chopped
    fresh rosemary

1 tablespoon chopped fresh
    Italian parsley

2 tablespoons freshly grated
    Parmigiano-Reggiano

1 large egg, lightly beaten

Salt to taste

Freshly ground black pepper
    to taste

1 Preheat the oven to 400°F. Oil a roasting pan with 1 tablespoon oil.

2 To prepare the fish, put the sea bass in the pan and top with half the minced garlic and the rosemary. Drizzle with oil and bake for 10 to 15 minutes or until the flesh is flaky.

3 Using a slotted spatula, remove the fish and put on a cutting board. Cut into fine dice and transfer to a bowl. Add the parsley, cheese, egg, salt, and pepper and mix until well blended.

4 To make the dough, heap the flour on a work surface and make a well in the center. Add the eggs and a pinch of salt and beat with a fork, incorporating an increasing amount of flour and adding water as needed to create a solid ball of dough. Knead for 5 minutes until smooth and elastic. Pass through a pasta machine according to directions on page 461.

5 Place ¹/₂ teaspoon filling at 2-inch intervals on the lower half of each sheet of dough. Fold over and press between the mounds to seal. Cut into squares with a ravioli wheel and transfer to a floured surface. Continue until all the filling has been used.*

6 To prepare the sauce, heat the oil in a skillet and add the marjoram, cooking over very low heat for 3 to 4 minutes, or just until the oil has assumed the herb flavor. Keep warm.

7 Place the ravioli in boiling salted water and cook for 3 to 4 minutes, or until they float to the surface. Drain and gently toss with the herbed oil. Serve immediately.

Make Ahead The ravioli dough can be made earlier in the day and sealed tightly in plastic until ready to use.

How to Serve As a first course followed by a medley of stuffed vegetables, such as golden peppers, ripe tomatoes, zucchini blossoms, zucchini, and artichokes.

Wine Suggestion Dry White

DOUGH

4 cups unbleached all-purpose flour

4 large eggs, lightly beaten

Salt to taste

SAUCE

4 tablespoons extra virgin olive oil

2 tablespoons chopped fresh marjoram

393

Wonton wrappers can be used instead of making your own dough. Make sure to trim the excess edges of the wrappers once they have been filled with the fish mixture.

STOCCAFISSO AL VERDE

Poached Codfish and Potatoes with Parsley Pesto

394

❧ Liguria ❧

ANOTHER OF THE TRADITIONAL DISHES SERVED AT THE *MARE DEI TYRRENI* FESTIVAL *(see page 392) is this simple and satisfying dish of cod poached with potatoes and tossed with very good quality oil and a refreshing parsley-walnut-garlic pesto. I have substituted fresh cod for* stoccafisso, *which is a type of dried, salted cod that requires seven days of soaking and three hours of cooking.*

serves 4

Time: 45 minutes

Level of Difficulty: Moderate

⊤

12 ounces boilng potatoes
2 cloves garlic
4 tablespoons chopped fresh
    Italian parsley
1/4 cup shelled walnuts
1/4 teaspoon salt
1 pound fresh cod steaks,
    at least 1 inch thick
1/2 cup dry white wine
1/2 cup water
6 tablespoons extra virgin
    olive oil

1 Boil the potatoes in salted water for 20 minutes, or until fork tender. Drain, peel, and chop into rough chunks.

2 Place the garlic, parsley, walnuts, and 1/4 teaspoon salt in a mortar and crush with a pestle until pastelike.*

3 Put the potato chunks in a skillet with the cod, wine, and 1/2 cup water. Season with salt, cover, and simmer for 10 minutes, or until the fish is tender and the liquid almost completely absorbed. Transfer to a serving platter, toss gently with the pesto and the oil, and serve.

*Pesto can also be made on a cutting board by using a chef's knife or cleaver or with a food processor.

Make Ahead The pesto, omitting the garlic, can be made up to a week in advance and refrigerated in a sealed container until ready to use. Cover the top of the pesto with a layer of oil before storing and add the garlic just before using.

How to Serve Round out this one-dish meal with a fresh green salad tossed with lemon vinaigrette.

Wine Suggestion Dry or Medium-Sweet White

COZZE RIPIENE

Mussels Stuffed with Sausage and Herbs

❦ Toscana ❦

THE MAREMMA AREA OF SOUTHERN TUSCANY IS KNOWN MAINLY FOR ITS STUNNING *panoramas, excellent red wines, and an Etruscan ancestry still visible in every village and town. One of these tiny villages, Capalbio, is located just inland from the Monte Argentario peninsula–resort and adjacent to the Maremmana Natural Park with its grazing cattle and colorful cowboys (*butteri*). The gastronomic profile resulting from this duality of maritime heritage and a pronounced love of good red meat realizes its highest potential in* La Sagra del Pesce, *held on the third weekend in July and featuring a unique menu of fish dishes, many of which also have a meat component, such as this beatific dish of mussels stuffed with prosciutto, sausage, and fresh herbs.*

serves 4

Time: About 75 minutes

Level of Difficulty: Moderate

4 tablespoons extra virgin
    olive oil

1 small onion, minced

1 pound ripe tomatoes, passed
    through a food mill

4 leaves fresh basil plus 10 to
    15 leaves for garnish

2 thick slices stale bread,
    soaked in warm water
    for 20 minutes, and
    squeezed dry

One 2-ounce slab prosciutto,
    diced

1 Heat the oil in a skillet over low heat and sauté the onion for 8 minutes, stirring constantly. Stir in the tomatoes and basil and cook for 15 minutes, or until the liquid has thickened.

2 Meanwhile, put the bread, prosciutto, sausage, parsley, thyme, basil, garlic, egg, salt, and pepper in a large bowl and mix until well blended.

3 Put the mussels in a large skillet and cook, covered, over medium heat for 4 to 5 minutes, or until the mussels open, shaking the pan once or twice. Remove from the heat and discard any mussels that do not open. Stuff the mussel shells with the meat-and-herb mixture and tie each partially closed with a piece of string to hold in the stuffing.

4 Preheat the oven to 350°F.

5 Pour the tomato sauce into a glass or terra-cotta baking pan. Arrange the mussels over the sauce and bake for 30 minutes, basting the mussels with sauce two or three times. Remove the string, arrange in a star pattern on a serving platter, drizzle with sauce, and intersperse the basil leaves.

Make Ahead The stuffing in Step 2 can be made up to a day in advance and refrigerated in a sealed container. Omit the garlic, however, and add instead just before using.

How to Serve As an appetizer followed by dourade or any other white baked on a layer of thyme and olive-oil-scented potatoes; or as an entrée with rice and a mixed green salad.

Wine Suggestion Medium-bodied Red

4 ounces fennel sausage, removed from casing and crumbled
3 tablespoons chopped fresh Italian parsley
1 teaspoon chopped fresh thyme
1 teaspoon chopped fresh basil
2 cloves garlic, minced
1 large egg, lightly beaten
Salt to taste
Freshly ground black pepper to taste
2 pounds large blue mussels, scraped, bearded, and washed under running water

ACCIUGHINI COL PROSCIUTTO

Fried Sage Sandwiches with Anchovies and Prosciutto

❦ Toscana ❦

SAGE GROWS WILD THROUGHOUT TUSCANY AND, IN SOME CASES, THE LEAVES ARE *large enough to serve as the "bread" slices in tasty sandwiches. So perfect are these dusty green bread stand-ins in fact, that Tuscans have devised dozens of different sage-sandwich varieties. I had never before tasted this particular version, stuffed with anchovies and prosciutto, dipped in a wine and meringue batter and fried until crisp, but I knew as soon as it was placed on my plate at Capalbio's Fish sagra (see page 400) that I would love it. And love it I did, indeed.*

serves 4

Time: About 45 minutes

Level of Difficulty: Moderate

ЛѢ

2 ounces thinly sliced prosciutto,
   fat removed

6 salt-packed anchovies, filleted
   and cut in half (see page 25)

24 large sage leaves, uniform
   in size

1/2 cup dry white wine

2 tablespoons extra virgin olive oil

1/3 cup unbleached
   all-purpose flour

1 large egg white

Olive oil for frying

1 lemon, thinly sliced for garnish

*To test the temperature of the oil, you can put a cube of bread into the skillet. When it sizzles around the edges and turns golden almost immediately, the oil is the right temperature.

1 Cut the prosciutto into 12 pieces the same size as the sage leaves. Place one piece of anchovy and one piece of prosciutto on each of 12 sage leaves. Cover the filling with the leaves that remain, making a sandwich.

2 Blend the wine with the oil and whisk in the flour until smooth. Beat the egg white into stiff peaks and fold into the oil batter, which should be smooth and semiliquid.

3 Heat 1 inch of oil in a heavy skillet to 375°F.* Dip the sage sandwiches into the batter, making sure that both sides are coated. Using tongs, carefully place them in the hot oil and fry 2 to 3 minutes per side, or until golden brown. Using a slotted spoon or tongs, remove from the oil, drain on paper towels, and serve on a bed of lemon slices.

How to Serve Makes wonderful finger food for parties.

Wine Suggestion Dry or Medium-Sweet White

ZUPPA DI CERNIA

Spicy Sea Bass Soup

❖ Molise ❖

I WAS SURPRISED TO FIND THIS SOUP AT TERMOLI'S *SAGRA DEL PESCE* (SEE PAGE 396). *Molise is not one of the southern Italian regions known for particularly spicy cooking. But when I asked one of the cooks whether this was an authentic regional dish, he became instantly defensive. "What do you think, that only the Calabrians know how to use chili peppers? The difference is that we know how and when to use them instead of throwing them into everything we make."*

serves 4

Time: 1 hour

Level of Difficulty: Moderate

4 tablespoons extra virgin olive oil

1 clove garlic, minced

3 tablespoons finely chopped
    Italian parsley

1¹/₂ pounds sea bass fillets,
    cut into large chunks

1 dried chili, crumbled

Salt to taste

¹/₂ cup fish broth

8 thin slices country-style
    bread, toasted

1 Heat the oil in a skillet over low heat and sauté the garlic for 5 minutes, stirring constantly. Add the parsley and fish and cook for about 8 minutes, or until the fish is lightly browned on all sides.

2 Stir in the chili, salt, and broth, cover, and cook for 30 minutes.

3 Divide the bread among four bowls. Top with pieces of fish, pour over the broth, and let rest for 4 minutes before serving.

How to Serve As a first course followed by broiled halibut steaks and pan-fried broccoli florets.

Wine Suggestion **Dry White**

INSALATA DI FRUTTI DI MARE

Shellfish Salad with Lemon-Mustard Vinaigrette

❧ Molise ❧

TO LIST THE COMPONENTS FEATURED IN TERMOLI'S *SAGRA DEL PESCE* WOULD MAKE *it seem like any of the hundreds of other fish festivals throughout Italy. Yes, there are lots of spectators; yes, there is a band and, yes, the food is spectacular (particularly this wonderful cold salad dressed with an ingredient rare in Italian cooking: mustard). What makes it different is Termoli itself, a small, charming town located on the Adriatic coast and containing not only a magnificent lighthouse, but also a small contingent of ferries en route to the undiscovered Tremiti Islands, just twenty miles offshore. The festival is very much a local event, held right on the water on the last Sunday in August—on a picturesque stretch of beach overtaken at dawn and dusk by cantankerous seagulls.*

serves 4

Time: 55 minutes excluding the 2-hour refrigeration time

Level of Difficulty: Moderate

2 pounds blue mussels, scraped, bearded, and washed under cold running water

2 pounds Manila or other medium clams, scrubbed and washed under running water

6 tablespoons extra virgin olive oil

1/2 cup water

1 Put the mussels and clams in a large skillet with 2 tablespoons oil and 1/2 cup water and cook, covered, over medium heat for 4 to 5 minutes, or until the mussels open, shaking the skillet once or twice. Remove from the heat and discard any mollusks that do not open. Remove the meat from the shells and put in a bowl, discarding all but 8 or 9 of the shells for garnish. Strain the the broth and return to the skillet.

2 Reduce the heat. Add the squid, cover, and cook over low heat for 15 minutes. Add the shrimp during the last 2 minutes of cooking and cook until pink. Drain and discard the liquid. Put the shrimp, squid, and shellfish into a bowl.

3 Parboil the fennel in salted water for 5 minutes, or until slightly soft. Drain and add to the bowl with the fish. Add the pepper and carrot.

4 Place the oil, mustard, lemon juice, parsley, salt, and pepper in a small bowl and whisk until emulsified. Pour over the fish and vegetables and toss until well blended. Transfer to a serving platter and refrigerate for 2 hours. To serve, garnish with parsley and the reserved shells.

How to Serve As an appetizer followed by pasta tossed with cauliflower béchamel or as a light summer entrée served with crusty bread and a platter of steamed baby vegetables.

Wine Suggestion Dry White

1 pound squid, cleaned (see page 123) and cut into thin slices

2 pounds large shrimp, peeled and deveined

1 medium fennel, fronds removed, halved, cored, and thinly sliced

1 red pepper, stemmed, cored, seeded, and thinly sliced

1 medium carrot, scraped and julienned

1 teaspoon prepared mustard

Juice of 1 lemon

2 tablespoons finely minced Italian parsley

Salt to taste

Freshly ground black pepper to taste

5 to 6 sprigs fresh Italian parsley for garnish

401

BACCALÀ MANTECATO

Codfish Salad with Fried Polenta Wedges

❦ Friuli-Venezia Giulia ❧

THE *SAGRE DI PLACE* IS CELEBRATED ON THE FIRST SUNDAY OF SEPTEMBER IN *Paluzza, a tiny village north of Udine, near the border with Austria. Referred to not very long ago as a* festa paesana—*a small, local event—it has since become a huge draw for Austrian tourists whose presence has resulted in a blending of Italian and Austrian festival traditions. The first festival of its kind was held in 1293 to celebrate the village's having been granted a permit to operate a food market for three days in honor of the feast of San Daniele, Paluzza's patron saint. Paluzza is not a coastal village, and the mantecata I tasted was made with dried codfish* (baccalà). *I have refashioned the recipe using fresh codfish in consideration of the amount of work required to soak and cook the dried version. Since the taste was then much fresher, I substituted fried polenta wedges for the heap of polenta with which the mantecata was originally served.*

serves 4

Time: 1 hour

Level of Difficulty: Moderate

⚖

2 quarts salted water
2 cups coarsely ground cornmeal*
2 pounds codfish steaks
1/2 cup extra virgin olive oil
1 clove garlic, finely minced
3 tablespoons finely chopped
    Italian parsley
Salt to taste
Freshly ground black pepper
    to taste
Olive oil for frying

1 Bring 2 quarts salted water to a rolling boil over medium heat in a heavy-gauge saucepan.** Reduce the heat to low and pour in the cornmeal steadily, whisking constantly. Cook for 30 to 40 minutes, whisking frequently, until the polenta comes away from the sides of the pan and the whisk stands up by itself in the center of the polenta. Pour onto a flat surface, smooth to 1/4 inch thick, and cool to room temperature.

2 Meanwhile, preheat the broiler. Coat the grill rack with vegetable oil cooking spray. Broil the codfish for 3 to 4 minutes per side. Transfer to a plate and cool completely. Using a fork, flake the cooled flesh and drizzle with the oil, a little at a time,

*Already cooked polenta can be substituted.

**See page 63 for a less time-consuming method for cooking polenta.

mashing with a fork until the oil is completely absorbed. Add the garlic, parsley, salt, and pepper and mix until the consistency becomes a thick paste.

403

3 Cut the cooled polenta into triangles. Heat 1 inch of oil in a skillet over medium heat and fry the triangles for 4 to 6 minutes per side, or until golden and crispy. Remove with a slotted spatula and drain on paper towels.

4 To serve, place a mound of *mantecata* (fish paste) on the center of a plate and surround with 4 or 5 polenta triangles.

Make Ahead The polenta can be made a day in advance, wrapped in plastic wrap, and refrigerated until ready to use.

How to Serve As a one-dish meal rounded out with lemon-and-parsley drizzled steamed carrots.

Wine Suggestion **Dry White**

CALAMARETTI PICANTE

Spiced Baby Shrimp

❦ Basilicata ❧

ON CHRISTMAS EVE, THE YOUNG MEN OF CASSANO ALLO JONIO PARADE THROUGH *the town playing various types of pan flutes. The flute music is alternated with percussive rounds created by seashells used as castanets. The "band" is backed up by amazing choruses of older men singing* cupi cupi, *which is a low, gutteral sound whose intensity grows and grows until it creates an almost deafening wall of sound. The women, meanwhile, open their kitchens to whoever chooses to partake of a vast variety of meatless treats. This little delight comes from the festive kitchen of Mariarosa Brogna.*

serves 4

Time: 10 minutes

Level of Difficulty: Easy

½ cup olive oil

2 cloves garlic, crushed

2 pounds tiny shrimp, peeled
    and deveined

½ cup dry white wine

Salt to taste

1/4 teaspoon dried chili powder

Juice of ½ lemon

2 tablespoons chopped fresh
    Italian parsley

16 wedges country-style
    bread, toasted

1 Heat the oil in a skillet over low heat and sauté the garlic for 3 minutes, stirring constantly. Just before the garlic is about to brown, remove and discard it.

2 Increase the heat to high, add the shrimp, and cook for 2 to 3 minutes, shaking the pan constantly. Pour in the wine and cook for about 2 minutes, or until it evaporates. Transfer to a bowl and toss with the salt, chili powder, lemon juice, and parsley. Divide among four plates, surround with toast, and serve immediately.

How to Serve Makes a wonderful appetizer followed by a dense fish soup; to serve as an entrée, pair with a platter of steamed baby vegetables.

Wine Suggestion **Dry White**

TONNO FRESCO ALLA MARINARA

Tuna Steaks Baked with Olives, Capers, and Fresh Tomatoes

❧ Sicilia ❧

IN SICILY'S COASTAL VILLAGES, THE KILLING OF A TUNA (CALLED A *MATANZA*) WAS *always cause for great celebration. The tuna were killed in the traditional way, using harpoons, which left the waters around the island red with the blood of the dying fish. Highly prized for its white (blood-free) color and clean, delicate taste (impossible with tuna caught in driftnets or on fishing lines), the tuna was chopped into large pieces and boiled for an hour in salted water. Then it was left to dry for a day in the sun or on a* cannaria, *a kind of stretcher made of wood and reeds. But the growing attention to environmental questions and the problems associated with training new generations in traditional harpooning methods have combined to bring about a sharp decrease in the amount of white tuna available. What quantities remain can only be found in Favignana, off the coast of Trapani, and the Egadi Islands.*

serves 4

Time: 40 minutes

Level of Difficulty: Easy

---

¹/₂ cup extra virgin olive oil

Four 1-inch-thick tuna steaks (about 2 pounds), washed and dried

2 tablespoons freshly chopped basil

¹/₂ **cup gaeta or other black olives, pitted and chopped**

3 tablespoons capers, drained

1¹/₂ **pounds ripe Italian plum tomatoes, peeled, seeded, and diced**

Salt to taste

Freshly ground black pepper to taste

2 tablespoons plain breadcrumbs

1 Preheat the oven to 325°F.

2 Pour half the oil in the bottom of a glass or terra-cotta baking pan. Add the tuna steaks in a single layer. Top with the basil, olives, capers, and tomatoes, distributing the ingredients evenly over the surface of the steaks. Season with salt and pepper, sprinkle with breadcrumbs, and drizzle with the remaining oil.

3 Bake for 20 to 30 minutes, or until the fish is cooked throughout and the sauce thickened. Remove from the oven and serve immediately.

How to Serve With parsleyed potatoes and a mixed green salad.

Wine Suggestion Dry White

Desserts

CROSTATA DI RICOTTA
Creamy Ricotta Tart

SFORMATO TRASTEVERINO
Kiwi Custard Tart

ZALETI
Cornmeal Scones

PERSEGHINI
Butter Ring Cookies

CASTAGNACCIO
*Chestnut Cake
with Pignolis
and Raisins*

SBRISULONA
Almond-Rum Cake

MIRTILLI ALLA GRAPPA
*Grappa-marinated
Blueberries*

CASSATA
*Chocolate Ricotta
Refrigerator Cake*

TORRONE AL CIOCCOLATO
Hazelnut Honey Nougat

FRITELLE AL GRANTURCO
Sweet Polenta Fritters

ROCCIATA DI ASSISI
*Marsala-flavored Fruit
and Nut Rolls*

ZELTEN
Alpine Fruit Bread

TORTA DI MELE
*Open-faced Christmas
Apple Pie*

GELATO AL COCOMERO
*Watermelon and
Pistachio Sorbet*

FICHI AL CIOCCOLATO
*Chocolate-covered
Walnut-stuffed Figs*

CANNOLI ALLA SICILIANA
*Pastry Cylinders Filled
with Sweet Ricotta
and Chocolate*

OFFELLE DI PASTA SFOGLIA
*Puff Pastry Rounds
Stuffed with Apricots*

GIANDUJA
*Hazelnut Chocolate
Pudding Cake*

LIMONI CANDITI
Whole Candied Lemons

PASTICCIOTTI DI FICU VIRDI
Fig and Nut Wafers

MASCARPONE ALLO ZABAIONE
*Mascarpone Cheese Cake
with Marsala*

FICHI ALLO SCIROPPO
*Fresh Figs Preserved
in Rum Syrup*

CROCCANTE DI MANDORLE
Crunchy Almond Brittle

FRITTELLE DI MELE ALLA GRAPPA
*Apple Doughnuts
Scented with Grappa*

AMARETTUS
*Sardinian Amaretti
(Almond Cookies)*

TORTA DEGLI ADDOBBI
Sweet Rice and Almond Cake

SICILY
Of Boundaries and Separation

"SICILY—A NATION APART!" SCREAMED THE NEWSPAPER HEADLINE. "Sgarbi vows never to return to what he characterizes as 'a separate enclave ruled by brigands and governed by despots!'"

"Sgarbi" is Vittorio Sgarbi, Italian parliamentarian and host of a rather unusual television piece aired for ten minutes every afternoon. Highly articulate, strongly opinionated, and quite good-looking, this eloquent government minister stands in front of an antique wood table littered with dozens of disheveled newspapers, faces the camera squarely—a clouded blue sky as his fantastical backdrop—and simply speaks his mind on whatever political issue interests him at that moment. The script never varies: two minutes of initial presentation conveyed in a calm, precise manner; a few emphatic readings excerpted from that day's newspapers; and a final segment that, more often than not, finds Sgarbi cholerically pounding the table behind him, his voice raised to the rafters in absolute outrage, his left hand furiously thrusting back his long, chestnut hair.

On the particular day in question, Sgarbi stood before the cameras, recounting the story of having flown to Sicily on government business and at the personal invitation of that island's governor on whose private plane he had made the trip. As the cameras zoomed in for a closeup, Sgarbi faced the lens squarely and informed us that upon landing, his plane had been boarded by armed guards representing the Sicilian state. "The sergeant-in-charge asked for my papers," Sgarbi stated to us with as much innocence as he could muster. "And, imagining some type of error, I told him who I was and that I was here at the personal invitation of the mayor.

"'*Pazienza*,' the man replied. (Patience) 'I must still check your documents. It is all part of our anti-Mafia program; no one can enter or leave the island via private plane without passing first through police customs.'"

The television cameras zoomed in even closer.

"Customs!" Sgarbi screamed at his viewing audience. "Customs are what you go through when you journey to foreign countries. Customs are what you endure when your identity is in question. Since when are customs necessary when one is an agent of the state traveling on state business from one Italian region to another?"

He carefully repositioned his hair. "Do the Roman police demand to see Armani's private plane when he flies down from Milan for a fashion show? Does anyone ask for Agnelli's papers when he flies up to Turin for a board meeting? Are we not all part of the same country?"

Five minutes and numerous outbursts later, Sgarbi concluded with these dispirited comments: "I am sorry that Sicily wastes its anti-Mafia energy on invited guests of the national government instead of on the scoundrels who so obviously have infiltrated every enterprise from fishing to politics to bridge building. I am sorry that Sicilians continue to be held hostage by bandits who isolate the considerable energies and talents of an extraordinary people. But I am most sorry that, as Italians, we must unfortunately give up the dream of one nation and accept the existence of a separate country on our southern shores. For Sicily is, indeed, a separate country."

"Let's put it this way," says Rosario DeVito, head of the Sicilian tourist office. "Sgarbi is not wrong. In theory, the guards should never request documents from people traveling from one Italian region to another—state business or not. But the fact is that Sicily has finally decided to do something about organized crime, and, frankly, most Mafiosi use private planes."

DeVito continues, "The sergeant's misfortune was in coming up against Vittorio Sgarbi, who is one of the biggest loudmouths and foremost prima donnas ever to grace the halls of parliament." He pokes my shoulder with his index finger. "Let's give this thing the right title. Sgarbi doesn't give a fig about whether or not Sicily is a separate country. His gripe has solely to do with the fact that he, the great parliamentarian, was not immediately recognized and had to produce documents testifying to his identity."

Again the poke. "I'll bet my teenage son that that *presumptuoso* [presumptuous one] treated the sergeant in charge like a dog. You can just hear him, '*Ma lei non sa chi sono io.* You obviously have no idea who I am.'"

Leaving aside Sgarbi's pronouncements about its being a separate country, Sicily is today more poised to join its mainland cousins than at any previous time in its long, turbulent history. To some people, however, the more sensible proposition might be the mainland joining *it*. "Without seeing Sicily," Goethe declared, "one cannot get a clear idea of what Italy is."

Luigi Barzini created an even more compelling case for Sicily serving as the model for the rest of Italy when he observed that Sicilians embody every single Italian quality and defect, only magnified and more brightly colored.

Barzini continues: "The islanders are so expert that they neutralize each other. The simplest project, something which could be carried out anywhere else by means of a letter and a couple of conversations, becomes among Sicilians an enterprise of heroic proportions, each participant inventing diabolical schemes of his own to get the better of his opponent and, at the same time, forsee all possible schemes which his opponent will try to employ against him. The result is almost always the immobility of two wrestlers of equal strength, the melancholic immutability. . . .the feeling of death."

Certainly it is true that Sicily makes Italy look tame, that Sicilians dazzle all who witness their capacity for grasping situations with lightning speed, that they are masters at inventing a way out of intricate triangles by creating even more intricate octagons, that they instinctually gauge the relative power of contending parties and then side with the stronger of the two, that they weave wonderfully complex intrigues purely for the sake of amusement, that they coldly control even their smallest acts, emotions, and words only to, when safe, abandon themselves with reckless enthusiasm.

Given all this, how much a part of Italy can Sicily be?

"Obviously, the two can never be *physically* united," says Nicola Puzzi, head of the Sicilian tourist office. "Even if—and it is a big if—the proposed tunnel under the Straits of Messina ever becomes a reality, Sicily's essence is too much tied to southern Mediterranean cultures."

"Actually, union with the rest of Italy is not at all part of the goal," adds her assistant. "After all, with tourist dollars now propping up every facet of the economy, distinctiveness is our main asset."

Puzzi nods his head. "There's a difference, however, between exotic distinction and fear-provoking distinction. What we have to do is exchange the latter for the former."

As they talk, I can't help but wonder at the extraordinary number of words expended on the only real subject, which is basically that, for as long as I can remember, every conversation about Sicily's connection (or lack of connection) to the mainland has always segued into one about the Mafia.

And yet, on this particular trip, I notice many changes. True, it has been a long time since I last ventured to this, the crossroads of Mediterranean civilization. Six years ago, Judges Giovanni Falcone and Paolo Borsellino were still alive and galvanizing public opinion against the age-old code of silence, *omerta*. When the two were brutally murdered in 1992, just as their investigation was zeroing in on dozens of underworld figures, this island nation entered a period of profound self-examination that ultimately led to stricter laws, greater police power, and a determination among local citizens that the Mafia had outlived its usefulness.

"In truth," says Puzzi, "the Mafia never had a chance against the nineties. For one thing, its power requires a certain level of social ignorance that no longer exists, even in the most rural societies. In the old days, people relied on the Mafia to deal with issues that are, today, handled by campaign consultants and investment analysts."

But, he continues, the Mafia's greatest present-day drawback "lies in its growing lack of relevance. Today's adolescents want Armani jeans, access to the Internet, and a white-collar future. No longer are they willing to live in poverty, isolation, and a social construction based on loyalty to local *mafiosi*."

As testimony to its decreasing importance, he tells me, the word *mafia* is now used less in its upper case form (as in "The Mafia was responsible") and more as simply a lower case adjective to describe a certain state of mind—an exhibition of manly pride, a flamboyant display of force, the unmistakable attitude of invincibility. "What a *mafioso* car," a young Sicilian might exclaim, upon seeing a bright red Ferrari racing against the light down one of Parlermo's boulevards.

That the Mafia is in serious decline is no longer questioned by anyone. Well, that's not exactly true. Despite what is obviously the dawn of another golden age for this spectacular island paradise, guidebooks to Sicily continue to warn against everything from an "exorbitant rate of pickpocketing" to "ever present dangers lurking in the shadows of dimly lit streets." "Never walk through the streets of Messina alone in either daytime or at night," one guidebook cautions. "When night falls over the dusty streets of Palermo, restrict yourself to brightly lit boulevards and never carry a camera," advises another.

In previous trips to Sicily, I had always straddled the fine line between heeding the advice of these experts and doing as I please. While not about to stay locked in my hotel room after sunset, I was also not about to go wandering through dark, unpopulated streets. Either I have always been wrong or Sicily has changed much more than I was led to believe.

"There is a new openness here," my friend Tommaso had said by way of luring me back to Sicily. According to him, it was visible everywhere, a statement I found very hard to believe.

The fact is, it is not easy for Sicilians to embrace outsiders. Their history has taught them much about the price one pays for hoping and trusting. Unlike other parts of Italy, Sicily was conquered and subjugated by a long roster of foreign occupiers. Originally a Greek city-state, the island fell under the rule of the Byzantines in the sixth century; the Arabs in the ninth; the Normans in the eleventh; Germans in the twelfth; the Aragons in the thirteenth; and the Bourbons in the nineteenth. Each culture left its imprint on everything from architecture to mores.

For better or worse, Sicily's architecture has evolved into a kaleidoscope of majestic Greek columns existing placidly alongside stunning Byzantine towers. The mesmerizing faces of its people constitute a human map of genetic heterogeneity; their personalities, a melting pot of music and language and dance and painting.

Its greatest area of diversity, however, lies in its food, in a refreshing blend of ingredients and techniques rarely encountered on the mainland. The Arabs exerted the most significant influence in terms of introducing new crops; in the tenth and eleventh centuries, they arrived in Sicily armed with wheat, barley, grapes, lemons, and oranges. Using highly refined farming and irrigation techniques, they were able to adapt crops previously grown in humid climates to the dry heat of the Mediterranean. The Greeks brought olive trees used for producing oil, and cereals, especially barley ("Triticum" and "Marzuolo"), which was used to supply Greek and African cities.

"Sicily is just like New York," Tomasso had declared before his first visit to the States, when I told him he could eat his way through most of the cuisines of Europe within a five-block radius of my apartment. "Ten nations are present in every one of our dishes."

"Yes, but I'm talking about different dishes entirely, not different elements of the same dish."

"Is it not better to have all the influences blended in one harmonious dish than to be pulled in ten different directions?" It is the perfect rationale in support of fusion food and out of the mouth of a Sicilian, nonetheless.

Tomasso is a psychiatrist—normally, we two meet in Tuscany, where the good doctor comes every year for a series of psychiatric seminars. But he is also a dedicated gourmand in both senses of the word: While never one to push away a plate regardless of its contents, he also possesses a verifiable appreciation for life's finer tastes. "An epicure," he once identified himself after learning the word's definition.

"If you come to Sicily, I'll take you on the gastronomic tour of your life," he had boasted, before knowing I was, indeed, planning a return trip. "There are ingredients here you haven't even dreamed of." Oh, that Sicilian bravado!

I saw him as soon as I got off the ferry in Messina, leaning against a white convertible Lancia, smoking a long, thin cigar. He was, of course, wearing Armani sunglasses and his hair was cut so perfectly as to seem sculpted by Giotto himself. I do not see Tomasso often, but every time I do, I am amazed at his physical perfection. It is not so much a natural perfection but a created one, a perfection resulting from one-third desire, one-third work (in terms of both research and implementation), and one-third money. Not unusual for a Sicilian male who, much more than a Roman, more than a Neapolitan, and even more than a Tuscan, loves to preen. And nobody preens better than Tomasso.

True to his word, we wind our way to Palermo via a varied and fascinating tour of Sicilian ingredients. Our first stop is a *latticino*—cheesemaker—on the road to Taormina, where he has arranged for us to sample two of Sicily's premier cheeses: pecorino, which, the owner tells us, was given the *denominazione d'origine controllata* (D.O.C.) in 1955 and Ragusa caciocavallo, honored in 1962 with the almost-as-prestigious *denominazione tipica*.

"Tell me how this caciocavallo is different from the one in Puglia or Calabria," I ask the owner.

I should have foreseen his answer. "No comparison," he says in true Sicilian fashion. "This one is so much better as to make the use of the same name a crime." He cuts a large wedge from the pear-shaped cheese and, upon tasting it, it *does* seem better. But then again, I am so enamored of food in general that I sometimes doubt my ability to exert any degree of critical judgment.

"If you like something, who cares whether it's better or worse than what you ate somewhere else," Tomasso scolds me with an obvious "Oh, those Americans" look. "Food is to enjoy, not to analyze."

From there, we journey to Avola on the southwest side of Mt. Etna, famous for the quality of its shelled almonds. "Almonds are one of the most important foods of Sicily," Tomasso explains. "Without them, we would not be as famous as we are for our desserts."

Sicily is, in fact, very famous for its desserts, especially for its *torrone mandorlato* (almond nougat candy), *cassata al gelato* (almond ice cream cake), and, most prized of all, *pasta reale* (marzipan). "You probably didn't know this, but marzipan was invented by the nuns of Palermo's Martorana Church, hence its name," Tomasso informs me in that smarmy, know-it-all manner that either makes me chuckle with delight or drives me completely insane.

I was tempted to say that of course I knew about the famous Martorano nuns—"Who doesn't know that they were responsible for inventing marzipan?"—but I accept his provocation with grace. At least, for the time being.

He goes on to tell me that the last few years have seen an enormous decline in the production of almonds. "Vineyards," he says, shaking his head in dismay. "Most people are uprooting centuries-old almond trees to plant grapes because they can make more money selling wine." He points to a grove of dry, dusty trees. "In there, however, you'll find three of the finest almond varieties in the world. Pizzuta, d'Avola, and Fascionello. All three produce succulent, long, slender nuts."

We filch a few samples and enjoy them with the flask of excellent Donnafrugata wine Tomasso brought along for moments just like these.

A few miles further along the same road, the landscape changes abruptly, and suddenly the horizon becomes a profusion of citrus trees. "Lemons and oranges are probably the most cherished fruits of all to Sicilians," says Tomasso, parking the car in front of what looks like a tree bearing large tangerines.

"They're called Mapos," he says upon noticing my confusion at what looks and smells like a bloated clementine. "A cross between the tangerine and the grapefruit. In the next few months, they'll get a lot bigger, and in October, when they are fully ripe, every Sicilian table will bear a large bowl filled to overflowing."

He picks one from the tree and, even in its unripe state, the crisp, clean zesty flavor is unmistakable. "Besides lemons, which, as you know, are like a religion here in Sicily, only tarocco oranges are more popular."

"I'm sure you already know that Americans call taroccos 'blood oranges?'" I tease him.

"Of course they do," he rebounds without hesitation. "The Americans are, above all, practical people. What other name makes more sense for an orange with bright red pulp?" A very good comeback, I decide.

Our last stop is a pistachio orchard located on Mt. Etna, 900 feet above sea level. It's hard for me to imagine anything growing amidst those lava formations, but Tomasso maintains that pistachios prefer to locate in areas with extreme climatic conditions. "Pistachios love the contrast between sharp cold winters and high summer temperatures," he states in what seems like nonsense. Not that I doubt his culinary knowledge; it would be insane to doubt any Sicilian's knowledge of food. It just seems as if I had always known pistachios to be warm-weather plants.

"California grows pistachios, too," I tell him. "But the climate there is much more temperate."

"Yes, but are they the same varieties?" he counters. "Here we grow Napoletana, Femminella, and Agostana. Larger than most of their counterparts, all three. Certainly larger than your California nuts."

I wonder how Tomasso would fare in Texas. Seems to me, his braggadocio would fit right in.

On the way to Palermo, he tells me we will be making one final stop. "I have arranged for us to visit the grandson of one of the last *monzùs*, who died in 1978," he says with the great pride of one who knows he has done well. "It's time you Northern Italians saw the more aristocratic side of Sicily."

The original monzùs, he had told me years earlier, were French chefs who came to Sicily during the nineteenth-century Bourbon occupation. Few in number when they first arrived, they are, today, reduced to one or two representatives and it is hard to believe Tomasso has actually found a real-life descendant. But what I know about my friend is that, like Sicilians at large, his generosity knows no bounds. For the rest of your life, you may be required to offer profuse and grandiloquent thanks, but there are no limits to what he will do to please you.

Also like a typical Sicilian, Tomasso is very proud of his homeland and always eager to show its best face. "Not to say that the monzù tradition is intrinsically better than our more rustic one," he says defensively. "But monzùs are, in fact, part of a Sicily known to very few— of an elegant Sicily, an aristocratic Sicily, a Sicily that lives in lavish villas and speaks in precise, refined diction."

A corruption of the French *monsieur*, the word *monzù* was used to address the small group of French chefs employed by Sicilian aristocrats during the reign of Napoleon's brother-in-law, King Joachim Murat, in the early 1800s. Armed with their beloved béchamel and other Gallic exoticisms, the monzùs added yet another set of ingredients and techniques to a cuisine already rich with Greek, Arabic, and Spanish influences.

But with Napoleon's death and the subsequent collapse of the Napoleonic empire, King Murat was murdered and Sicily fell under the rule of the repressively tyrannical Bourbons. The monzùs, however, continued to ply their trade for the next few decades, until eventually it became politically dangerous to hire French chefs. When they finally departed, they left their beloved toques to the Sicilians who had long labored as their second in commands. The period was glamorously portrayed in *The Leopard*, Giovanni de Lampedusa's epic tale of nineteenth-century Sicilian aristocracy, which was later made into a very successful film starring Burt Lancaster.

"While the first monzù was undoubtedly chef to King Murat himself," says Tomasso, "the last remaining practicioner is thought to be Mario Lo Menzo, who currently lives and works at Regaleali, a lavish wine estate near Palermo, which belongs to Count Giuseppe Tasca d'Almerita."

Signore Lo Menzo—or Mario, as Tomasso tells me he prefers to be called—is Sicilian born, in his early sixties, and internationally known for blending Sicilian ingredients, such as anchovies and baby octopus, with such distinctly non-Sicilianisms as white wine marinades, truffled poultry, and great quantities of creamy béchamel.

"But everyone knows Mario," Tomasso says with the rationalization of one who undoubt-edly tried and failed to get us an appointment there. "So instead, we're going to have lunch with Roberto Fiucci, the grandson of Monzù Vito Fiucci, a contemporary of Mario Lo Menzo who worked for the Lanza family about fifty years ago."

Not familiar with the Lanzas—a fact Tomasso takes as a cultural slight ("not knowing the Lanzas is like saying you don't know the Medicis")—I am treated to what seems like their entire curriculum vitae including that they were one of Sicily's first families, having arrived over one thousand years ago. "Lanzas fought at the side of Frederick II of Hohenstaufen, king of Sicily and emperor in the thirteenth century. Members of the family also served as advisors to kings and emperors, viceroys, generals, and admirals. The family owns thousands of acres of land, entire towns, rivers, castles, palaces, and villas."

"Thank you," I say, as we career off the autostrada headed for Palermo. "Now that I know the Lanzas, who are these people the Medicis?"

Roberto Fiucci turns out to be a very likable fellow, but hardly what I expect from a descendant of the notoriously haughty monzùs. The head chef of an obviously successful restaurant, Porta Bella, located just outside Palermo, he is modest in the extreme and it is hard even to get him to admit that he prepared the dishes we ordered. "There are four of us in the kitchen," he says when I compliment his fried artichokes. "We all work together."

When lunch is finished, he sits briefly down to talk with us about his illustrious grandfather. "*Il Nonno* died without leaving any written record of his recipes," Roberto tells us with obvious displeasure. "The monzùs, all of them, were apparently very secretive. One reason was that there existed a very high level of competition among them. I suppose there had to be. The aristocracy places a great deal of importance on exclusivity, on having something no one else has."

Roberto also explains that his grandfather rarely fraternized with other chefs, even the ones who were second in command in his own kitchen. "The monzùs went to great pains to arrange their work staffs so that no one knew all the steps inherent in creating the most famous dishes. If those who worked with my grandfather learned any of his culinary tricks, they did so by being sneaky and observing when *Nonno* wasn't looking."

"So why aren't you also considered a monzù?" I ask him, confused by the dicotomy between his feeling for his grandfather and the obvious fact of his not considering himself to be at that same level.

"To be a monzù, you have to espouse a particular blend of Gallic and Sicilian ingredients," he answers. "And, although I revere my grandfather and even revere the complexity and technical perfection of that kind of food, my own cooking style is more simple and quintessentially local."

"And better," Tomasso chimes in. "Much better."

"How would *you* know?" I ask him, when Roberto is temporarily out of hearing. "How many times have you ever eaten a meal prepared by a monzù?"

"I don't have to fall in the river to know the water is cold," he replies with an irresistibly impish grin.

At the end of our meal, Roberto thanks us for our interest in his grandfather. "I cannot say I knew him very well. That was a difficult thing to do. But I would have liked to and it makes me very angry that he died without letting any of us—neither my father, who is also a chef, nor I—get close to his great wisdom."

Today is the Festival of Saint Rosalia, which is the reason I journeyed to Sicily in the first place. But after four days of gastronomic touring with Tomasso—every one of the ten meals we ate together took place in a different restaurant whose owners he knew and in none of them did we order from the menu—I want nothing more than to simply lie by the pool and rest.

"Absolutely the wrong attitude," Tomasso says, when he arrives first thing in the morning to serve as my festival escort.

We start the day by wandering through the maze of back streets surrounding the cathedral in search of candles to hold at tonight's procession. I wave at old men leaning from their second-story windows and wish them *buon giorno.* True to what Tomasso described, there is a marked difference in their response from just a few years ago. Still more cautious than a Tuscan addressed in the same way, today's Sicilians are, nonetheless, as likely to grace me with a slight nodding of their heads as they are to ignore me.

Palermo is an explosive joy of a city. Lying in the shadow of Mt. Pellegrino, which Goethe deemed "the most beautiful promontory in the world," its charms are not always immediately apparent and day visitors are sometimes put off by the continuing presence of World War II rubble strewn through the city's streets. But anyone enamored of probing beneath tourbook superficialities can't help but fall in love with such hidden facets as the unhurried charm of *granita* vendors so tickled by your patronage that they offer a second bowl of the delicious lemony slush for free; by the colors and textures and smells of the four markets that wind their way through the streets like snakes (the market vendors calling out their wares in a haunting singsong that reverberates through the pencil-thin alleys); by the fountains and cupolas and parks and huge open piazzas; by the wide, busy boulevards pulsing with what seems like millions of cars, all in a hurry; by the Quattro Canti, the heart of the old center and a virutal open-air museum of baroque cornices, ornate balustrades, and sooty allegorical statues.

"Isn't Palermo just the most perfect city?" Tomasso exults as we stop for yet another "must taste" gelato. "Climate, beauty and the virtue of being largely undiscovered."

Over the course of the next few hours, it will become ever harder to believe the "undiscovered" part. Before the point of total exhaustion—which will come at about 4:00 tomorrow morning—we will join more than a million people who have flooded into this city to witness arches alive with over 500,000 lights, festival cars dating back to 1624 (the first year Palermo celebrated St. Rosalia's feast day), and a main float that is thirty feet high, twenty-seven feet wide, and burdened with the weight of—among other riders—a sixty-person symphony orchestra.

We will participate in a lottery with prizes that range from valuable paintings to $6,000 in cash. We will wander through the streets of Palermo eating fried chick pea cakes, pasta with spicy tomatoes, and marinated sea bass prepared in stalls decorated with hand-painted murals. We will shuffle along beneath building facades draped with colorful rugs and woven tapestries. There will be strolling musicians, stationary accordian players, and men with live monkeys dressed in eighteenth-century brocaded coats. At Piazza Vigliena—the heart of the city's historic district—the police will try their best to maintain the free flow of vehicular traffic only to give up within an hour and repair to the local cafe. By midafternoon, the city will be at an absolute, free-for-all standstill, and I will be infused with so much energy that, come midnight, I will be begging Tomasso to stay out "just another half hour."

But for now, confronted with his outstretched hand offering me the Palermitan version of an ice cream sandwich—a large puffy brioche stuffed with creamy vanilla gelato—the city seems like a small, quaint village the inhabitants of which have nothing better to do than to sit at a sunny streetside table and count the clouds wafting across the magnficent Sicilian sky.

Who cares whether they want to check my passport upon entry?

CROSTATA DI RICOTTA

Creamy Ricotta Tart

❧ Lazio ❧

ON JULY 16, ALL OF ITALY CELEBRATES THE FEAST DAY OF *LA MADONNA DEL CARMINE.* *"Carmine" comes from the Hebrew "karmel," which is the name of the mountain where the prophet Elias first saw a vision of the Madonna. The apparition so moved Elias that he immediately established a monastic order dedicated to the not-yet-born Virgin, although papal approval of the order did not come until 1226, after the Virgin had already appeared a few times and was credited with a number of miracles. In Rome, the festival is called* Madonna de noantri—*Our Own Madonna—because, according to a legend dating back to the sixteenth century, three Roman men fishing in the Tiber pulled up a wooden case containing a statue of the Madonna. That very statue today resides in the Church of St. Agatha and, on the Saturday before July 16, is paraded through the streets to St. Crisogono, where it spends the next eight days before journeying back home.*

This buttery ricotta tart is one of the many desserts associated with this very popular feast. In the Lazio and throughout the south, ricotta is made from whey left over from the milk of sheep, goats, water buffalos, and cows.

yields 10 slices

Time: 60 minutes, excluding refrigeration time

Level of Difficulty: Moderate

꠸

PASTA FROLLA*
**2 cups unbleached
 all-purpose flour**
1/2 cup sugar
Pinch of salt

1 To make the pasta frolla, put the flour, sugar, and pinch of salt in the container of a food processor and pulse once or twice to blend. Add the butter, egg yolks, and lemon zest and pulse just until a ball forms. Remove from the food processor and knead by hand for 1 minute. Wrap in plastic wrap and refrigerate for 30 minutes.

2 To make the filling, put the ricotta in a large bowl and beat with a fork until soft. Stir in the sugar, butter, eggs, candied fruit, and cinnamon until all ingredients are well blended.

*Pasta frolla is a shortbreadlike dense pastry used in making many Italian desserts.

3 Preheat the oven to 350°F. Butter an 8-inch-round springform pan.

4 Unwrap the pasta frolla and break off three-quarters of it. On a lightly floured surface, roll the larger piece into a 10-inch circle that is $1/8$ inch thick. Line the pan with the dough, patting the excess against the sides and working the top edge into a rolled crust. Avoid overhandling or the dough will toughen.

5 Fill the pan with the ricotta mixture, tapping the pan against the counter to level the surface. Roll the remaining dough into a 10 x 12-inch rectangle that is $1/8$ inch thick. Cut the dough into $1/2$-inch-wide strips and arrange as latticework on the filling.

6 Bake for 30 minutes, remove from the oven, and cool to room temperature. Refrigerate for 1 to 2 hours and serve cold.

Make Ahead Pasta frolla can be made up to 2 days in advance, wrapped in plastic wrap, and refrigerated until needed. It can also be frozen for up to 3 weeks. Thaw in the refrigerator when ready to use.

8 tablespoons (1 stick) unsalted butter at room temperature

3 large egg yolks, lightly beaten

1 tablespoon grated lemon zest

FILLING

1 pound fresh sheep's milk, cow's milk, or goat's milk ricotta

$1/2$ cup sugar

6 tablespoons unsalted butter, at room temperature

2 large eggs, lightly beaten

$1/2$ cup candied fruit, diced

$1/8$ teaspoon ground cinnamon

Butter for greasing

SFORMATO TRASTEVERINO

Kiwi Custard Tart

❦ Lazio ❧

THE FEAST OF THE MADONNA DEL CARMINE (SEE PAGE 420) IS WIDELY AND *vigorously celebrated throughout Rome, but especially in the Trastevere district. Food stalls line the streets and the piazzas are fully scheduled with street theater and musical performances. Hordes of tourists participate, having no idea of the day's religious significance, but enjoying, nonetheless, the sense of having stumbled onto something authentically local. This nonsectarian aspect dates back only to the 1920s, when Fascists first attempted to instill nationalist pride by supporting popular traditions rather than more religious ones.*

Traditionally, this tart was made with other types of fruit (mainly strawberries), but Italy has since become one of the world's greatest exporters of kiwis and so, now, it is most often found adorned with these perfect little rounds of green.

yields 10 slices

Time: 45 minutes, excluding 1-hour refrigeration time

Level of Difficulty: Moderate

8 tablespoons (1 stick) unsalted butter, melted

1 1/4 cups crumbled ladyfingers or light, crumbly biscuits

Juice of 2 lemons

3 teaspoons plus 1/2 cup sugar

1 Combine half the butter and and the crumbled ladyfingers in a bowl and beat to form a smooth dough. Press the dough into a 10-inch-round fluted tart pan with a removable bottom. Press the dough against the ridged sides. Refrigerate for 1 hour.

2 Put the lemon juice and the 3 teaspoons sugar in a small saucepan and cook over low heat, stirring constantly, for 5 minutes, or until the mixture thickens. Cool to room temperature.

3 Preheat the oven to 425°F.

4 Combine the remaining butter with the ricotta, the remaining sugar, egg, and lemon syrup in a bowl. Mix until well blended and smooth. Pour into the chilled tart shell.

5 Bake for 20 minutes. Remove from the oven and cool to room temperature. Remove from the pan, decorate the top by arranging the kiwi slices in a circular pattern with the edges overlapping slightly, slice, and serve.

Make Ahead The entire tart (excluding the kiwi topping) can be made earlier in the day and refrigerated until baked.

2^1/2 cups sheep's milk, cow's milk, or goat's milk ricotta

^{1}/2 cup sugar plus 3 teaspoons sugar

1 large egg, lightly beaten

2 kiwis, peeled and thinly sliced

421

ZALETI

Cornmeal Scones

❧ Friuli Venezia Giulia ❧

IN CELTIC TIMES, THE BEGINNING OF NOVEMBER MARKED THE NEW YEAR.
For those who wonder why an annual cycle would begin in the middle of autumn, Giacomo Breso, a Friuli farmer, explains, "Because autumn signals the end of one growing season and the beginning of the new. The corn and wheat have been planted by then; the seeds have sunk into the earth and begun their long ascent toward the sun. The forces of life ferment below the ground." But, Breso says, the Church was not happy with having its followers celebrate this pagan concept. "So, in 998, Odilone of Cluny issued a doctrine replacing the New Year with the Feast of All Saints on November 1 and the Feast of All Souls on November 2. And since then, believe it or not, the dead have been buried in beautiful clothes so that they can far bella figura [make a good showing] when they rise up and parade through the town on the night between the two. Now I ask you, is this not the height of ridiculouness?" Self-declared anticlerics, Breso and his wife celebrate a very local Capodanno (Celtic New Year's Festival) in the tiny village of Sauris near the Austrian border. "Everyone in our small group makes something using various grains, and then we meet in the cemetery where we eat together and commune with our ancestors."

These wonderful corn flour scones are Giacomo Breso's contribution.

makes 12 to 15 scones

Time: 60 to 70 minutes

Level of Difficulty: Moderate

⚕

2 large eggs, lightly beaten
³/₄ cup sugar
1 cup finely ground corn flour,
    sifted
1 cup unbleached all-purpose
    flour, sifted

1 Using an electric mixer, beat the eggs and the sugar until smooth, creamy, and doubled in volume.

2 Put the corn flour and the all-purpose flour in a large bowl, add the lemon zest, salt, and melted butter and stir until well blended. Add the raisins and incorporate the egg mixture, a few tablespoons at a time. If the dough is too dry, add 1 to 2 tablespoons milk. The finished dough should be smooth and soft.

3 Preheat the oven to 375°F. Butter a 12 x 16-inch baking sheet.

4 Divide the dough into two sections and roll each into a long tube 2^1/$_2$- to 3-inches wide. Cut diagonally into 3-inch-long segments. Arrange the segments on the baking sheet.

5 Bake for 40 minutes. Remove from the oven and cool the scones to room temperature, sprinkle with confectioner's sugar, and serve.

Make Ahead The dough can be prepared through Step 2 earlier in the day or even a day or two in advance. Wrap in plastic wrap and refrigerate, but return to room temperature before using.

2 tablespoons grated lemon zest

Pinch of salt

8 tablespoons (1 stick) unsalted butter, melted

^{1}/$_3$ cup sultana raisins, soaked in warm water for 20 minutes, drained, and squeezed dry

About ^{1}/$_2$ cup whole milk

Butter for greasing

2 tablespoons confectioner's sugar for sprinkling

423

PERSEGHINI

Butter Ring Cookies

424

❧ Friuli Venezia Giulia ❧

CIVIDALE NEL FRIULI IS ABOUT SIXTY MILES AWAY FROM SAURIS (SEE PAGE 422), *but the Breso's friends, Marta and Pietro Casone, brought a little of their hometown with them when they arrived for last year's Celtic New Year celebration. These simply delicious butter cookies are a Cividale specialty, served either with prosecco or with chilled Tocai wine.*

makes about 30 cookies

Time: 45 minutes

Level of Difficulty: Moderate

4 cups unbleached
    all-purpose flour
16 tablespoons (2 sticks)
    unsalted butter, at room
    temperature and cut into
    thin pats
Pinch of salt
1/4 cup sugar
1/2 teaspoon active dry yeast

1 Heap the flour on a work surface, or put in a bowl, and make a well in the center. Add all but 1 tablespoon of the butter, salt, sugar, and yeast. Using a pastry blender or fork, blend the ingredients to form a soft, smooth dough. Avoid overhandling or the dough will toughen.

2 Preheat the oven to 350°F. Butter a 12 x 16-inch baking sheet with the remaining butter.

3 Pinch off a walnut-size piece of dough and roll into a 7 x 1/2-inch string. Form the string into a circle and pinch the dough to seal. Repeat until all the dough has been used. Arrange the cookies on the baking sheet, about 1 inch apart.

4 Bake for 20 minutes, or until a toothpick inserted in the center comes out clean. Remove from the oven, cool to room temperature, and serve with dessert wine.

Make Ahead The dough can be made up to 2 days in advance, wrapped in plastic wrap, and refrigerated until used. It can also be frozen for up to 3 weeks. Return to room temperature before using.

CASTAGNACCIO

Chestnut Cake with Pignolis and Raisins

❦ Toscana ❦

FOR TWO WEEKS IN MID-SEPTEMBER, LUCCA CELEBRATES THE FEAST OF THE VOLTO *Santo, an ancient wooden crucifix created, according to legend, by Nicodemus, who sculpted everything except Christ's face, which was supposedly completed by an angel. Nearing death, Nicodemus entrusted the crucifix to a Christian who hid it in his house, where it lay for 700 years. In 742, the legend continues, Bishop Gualfredo of Rome journeyed to Palestine, then occupied by Moslems, where an angel told him not only of the crucifix's existence, but also of its location. Gualfredo finally succeeded in smuggling the crucifix to Naples, but there he was greeted by Bishop Giovanni of Lucca who had been directed by an angelic apparition to transport the crucifix to Lucca, where it now resides in the Cathedral of San Michele. The festival's climax comes on the second Monday of September, when the Volto Santo is carried through Lucca's narrow cobblestone streets and almost every window of every house is lit with candles. The effect is mesmerizing.*

yields 8 slices

Time: 75 minutes

Level of Difficulty: Moderate

4 cups chestnut flour*
4 tablespoons sugar
Pinch of salt
4 tablespoons extra virgin olive oil
3 tablespoons water
Butter for greasing
Breadcrumbs for sprinkling
1/4 cup pine nuts
1/4 cup sultana raisins, soaked in warm water for 20 minutes, drained, and squeezed dry
1 tablespoon chopped fresh rosemary
1 cup fresh ricotta, preferably sheep's milk or goat's milk

1 Put the flour, sugar, and pinch of salt in a bowl and blend. Add 3 tablespoons oil and 3 tablespoons warm water, 1 tablespoon at a time, as needed to form a smooth, semiliquid batter. Stir constantly.

2 Preheat the oven to 350°F. Butter an 8-inch-round cake pan and sprinkle with breadcrumbs.

3 Pour in the batter, tapping the pan on a flat counter to level the surface. Top with pine nuts, raisins, and rosemary and drizzle with the remaining oil.

4 Bake for 1 hour. Remove from the oven and serve immediately with a dollop of ricotta.

*Chestnut flour can be found in specialty food stores.

SBRISULONA

Almond-Rum Cake

❦ Lombardia ❦

DURING ROMAN TIMES, THE LOMBARDIAN VILLAGE OF BERNAREGGIO SERVED AS *winter quarters for the Royal Regiment of the Milan duchy. Today, it is a charming low-key village, but one that pulls out all the stops for its week-long annual festival,* La Sagra del Paese, *held during the second week of September. Everyone participates to create a riot of events encompassing musical performances, sporting competitions, folkloric demonstrations, arts-and-crafts displays, and a wonderful exposition of ancient wind instruments called firlinfeu.*

A number of desserts are typically associated with this festival, among them, this crumbly, rum-and-lemon infused cake.

yields 10 slices

Time: 75 minutes

Level of Difficulty: Moderate

Butter for greasing

2 tablespoons plain breadcrumbs

2 cups finely ground cornmeal

2 cups unbleached all-purpose flour

1 cup sugar

Grated zest of 1/2 lemon

2 cups finely chopped almonds

Pinch of salt

1 tablespoon pure vanilla extract

16 tablespoons (2 sticks) unsalted butter, at room temperature and cut into thin pats

2 large egg yolks, lightly beaten

1 cup white rum

1 Preheat the oven to 350°F. Grease a 10-inch-round springform pan and sprinkle with breadcrumbs, shaking out the excess.

2 Put the cornmeal, flour, sugar, lemon zest, almonds, and salt in a bowl and mix well. Heap the mixture onto a work surface and make a well in the center. Add the vanilla, butter, eggs, and rum and mix with a fork, incorporating the flour a little at a time, until the mixture is well blended and crumbly. Pour the batter into the pan.

3 Bake for 1 hour. Remove the cake from the pan, cool to room temperature, and serve.

MIRTILLI ALLA GRAPPA

Grappa-marinated Blueberries

❦ Lombardia ❧

THE HIGH POINT OF BERNAREGGIO'S ANNUAL FESTIVAL COMES ON SUNDAY, AFTER *the procession in honor of the town's patron, St. Maria Nascente. Tables heaped with desserts, wine, and other drinks are set up in Piazza Repubblica and local priests distribute the bounty to any and all interested parties. Later in the afternoon, there is a six-mile race and an assortment of musical performances.*

This simple dessert was one of my favorites.

serves 4

Time: 10 minutes, excluding the 3-hour refrigeration time

Level of Difficulty: Easy

2 pounds fresh blueberries
(or other types of berries)
1/2 cup sugar
Juice of 1 lemon
1 1/2 cups grappa
1 tablespoon lemon zest
for garnish
8 to 12 sprigs fresh mint
for garnish

1 Put the blueberries in a large bowl. In a separate bowl, mix the sugar with the lemon juice and grappa until the sugar is completely dissolved. Pour over the blueberries, cover with plastic wrap, and refrigerate for 3 hours, stirring 4 or 5 times.

2 Distribute among four dessert glasses and serve with a sprinkling of lemon zest and a sprig of fresh mint.

CASSATA

Chocolate Ricotta Refrigerator Cake

❧ Sicilia ❧

FIFTEEN MILES FROM PALERMO LIES MARINEO WITH ITS ANNUAL FESTIVAL *celebrating St. Ciro, an Egyptian medic, who was murdered by Diocletian. Ciro's sanctuary subsequently became one of the ancient world's most popular, because of his reputation as a magical healer. When the Arabs invaded Egypt, Ciro's bones were entrusted to Neapolitan Jesuits and in 1665, his head was donated to the village of Marineo, which promptly made the martyr its patron. The feast day, held on the next-to-last Sunday of August, opens with a fascinating procession of horses and donkeys draped in regal garments and pulling ancient carts filled with grain offered to the Lord in thanksgiving for an abundant harvest.*

yields 10 generous slices

Time: 1 hour, excluding the 2-hour refrigeration time

Level of Difficulty: Moderate

2 cups sugar
1 vanilla bean
1 3/4 pounds fresh cow's milk ricotta
1/8 teaspoon ground cinnamon
8 ounces bittersweet chocolate, grated
1/2 cup candied fruit, diced
2 tablespoons pistachios, diced
1/2 cup maraschino cherry juice

1 Put the sugar and vanilla bean in a saucepan and cook over low heat, stirring constantly with a wooden spoon, until the sugar has dissolved. Remove from the heat and discard the vanilla bean.

2 Pour the ricotta into a large bowl and beat with a wooden spoon until creamy. Stir in the dissolved sugar and cinnamon until completely incoporated, then add half the chocolate, the candied fruit, pistachios, and maraschino juice. Mix well.

3 Line a 10-inch-round springform pan with waxed paper. Slice the sponge cake into three layers, each 1/2 inch thick, and arrange one layer in the bottom of the cake pan. Cut the remaining layers into 2-inch-long strips and line the sides of the pan, fitting the cake snugly enough to form a solid ring.

4 Pour in the ricotta mixture, smooth the surface with a spatula, and top with a layer of sponge cake. Wrap in plastic wrap and refrigerate for 2 hours.

5 After refrigeration, put the apricot preserves and confectioner's sugar in a saucepan and heat for 7 minutes, or until dissolved. Unwrap the cake and remove the sides. Spread the apricot sauce evenly over the entire surface.

6 Place the remaining chocolate in a saucepan, add the orange juice, and melt over low heat, stirring constantly with a wooden spoon. Pour over the center of the cake and, using a spatula, spread over the entire surface.

7 When the chocolate has firmed, decorate the surface with the orange slices and serve.

Make Ahead The ricotta mixture can be made a day ahead and the sponge cake can be placed in the pan earlier in the day.

One 10-inch-round sponge cake, 1^1/$_2$ inches thick (or with different dimensions, cut to size)

3 tablespoons apricot preserves

2 tablespoons confectioner's sugar

2 tablespoons orange juice

10 to 15 candied orange slices

429

TORRONE AL CIOCCOLATO

Hazelnut Honey Nougat

430

❦ Abruzzo ❦

THE FESTIVAL OF THE *PERDONANZA ALL'AQUILA* DATES BACK TO JULY 5, 1294, WHEN *the Vatican's Sacred College unexpectedly elevated to the papacy a hermit who lived on a mountaintop near Aquila. After five months, the hermit—by then known as Celestino V—found himself helpless in the face of the Vatican's notorious political machine and renounced the papacy. But the people of Aquila never forgot him and, in fact, stole his body from a nearby town where he had been buried and brought it back to L'Aquila's Basilica of Santa Maria di Collemaggio, where it resides today. Every year, on August 28 and 29, L'Aquila remembers their hometown pope who, during his reign, had obtained from King Carlos II of Naples not only complete pardon for any offense ever committed by any Aquilano resident, but a guarantee of greater autonomy for the town and its own defense force. Moreover, Celestino's legacy grants spiritual pardon to "anyone who enters Santa Maria Basilica on August 29 and confesses himself to be sorry for his sins." Needless to say, this is a very well-attended festival.*

You can purchase this wonderful hazelnut nougat candy from any of the dozens of food stalls lining the square.

makes about 12 to 16 squares

Time: 45 minutes, excluding the 2-hour refrigeration time

Level of Difficulty: Moderate

⚖

3 cups hazelnuts
1 1/2 cups sugar
4 tablespoons water
1/4 cup honey, preferably chestnut
1/4 cup bittersweet chocolate, grated

1 Preheat the oven to 350°F. Line a 6-inch-square pan with waxed paper.

2 Toast the hazelnuts on a baking sheet for 15 minutes, or until the skins are slightly burned. Rub the nuts against each other to remove the outer skin and discard.

3 Meanwhile, place 1/4 cup sugar and 2 tablespoons water in a small saucepan and cook over low heat until the sugar dissolves, stirring constantly with a wooden spoon. Keep warm.

4 Heat the honey in another saucepan over low heat for 3 minutes, or until the honey liquefies.

5 Put the remaining sugar in a saucepan with 2 tablespoons water and cook over low heat about 10 minutes, or until caramelized to a light amber color. Add to the honey with the chocolate and the nuts.

6 Using an electric mixer, beat the egg whites and the salt about 2 minutes, or until foamy. Add the cream of tartar and continue to beat until stiff peaks form. Gently fold into the chocolate mixture.

7 Pour the chocolate-nut mixture into the pan and cool to room temperature. Cut into 3-inch squares and refrigerate for 2 hours before removing from the pan.

Make Ahead The entire nougat recipe can be prepared as long as 2 weeks in advance and kept in a sealed container or wrapped in plastic wrap.

2 egg whites
$1/4$ teaspoon salt
$1/4$ teaspoon cream of tartar

431

FRITELLE AL GRANTURCO

Sweet Polenta Fritters

❦ Umbria ❦

MAY 1 HAS BEEN AN INTERNATIONAL HOLIDAY SINCE 1889 WHEN THE WORLD'S *socialists proclaimed it "Worker's Day" in honor of those who had died in Chicago's Haymarket Square massacre. In Assisi, the* Calendomaggio *festival used to consist simply of street performances featuring musicians chosen from among Assisi's many church choruses. But since 1954, it has been enlarged to encompass a series of musical contests between the town's two factions, Upper and Lower. Musicians are dressed in traditional costumes and perform with ancient musical instruments. There are also equestrian competitions and a beautiful display of flagmanship that takes place at Rocca Maggiore, a huge rock platform which towers above the town.*

These frugal polenta fritters are very much in keeping with Assisi's patron, St. Francis, who preached asceticism, poverty, chastity, and "an abundance of the divine."

makes 10 to 12 fritters

Time: 30 to 45 minutes

Level of Difficulty: Moderate

2 cups finely ground cornmeal
1/2 cup sugar
Pinch of salt
1/2 teaspoon active dry yeast
1 large egg, lightly beaten
1/3 cup sultana raisins, soaked in warm water for 20 minutes, drained, and squeezed dry

1 Put the cornmeal, sugar, pinch of salt, and yeast in a bowl and mix with a fork, adding as many tablespoons of warm water as needed to form a thick, creamy batter. Stir in the egg and raisins and mix well.

2 Heat 2 inches of oil in a heavy skillet to 375°F. Carefully add 4 or 5 level tablespoons of batter spaced about 2 inches apart. When they puff up and turn golden, remove with a slotted spoon and drain on paper towels. Dust with confectioner's sugar and serve.

Make Ahead The fritter batter can be prepared a few hours in advance and kept covered until ready to use. If it becomes too dense, stir in a tablespoon or two of warm water.

Olive oil for frying
Confectioner's sugar for dusting

433

ROCCIATA DI ASSISI

Marsala-flavored Fruit and Nut Rolls

❦ Umbria ❦

BEFORE ASSISI'S MAY DAY celebration evolved into its present-day format *including multiple music and sporting events, the simple choral festival was transmitted by radio to San Francisco, where many Umbrians had emigrated years earlier. The first such transmission took place on April 30, 1930, and afterward became an annual event and, to this day, hundreds of grateful letters written by Umbrian immigrants grace the walls of Assisi's city hall.*

Rocciata is an almost literal translation of "rugelach," the small Jewish pastries encasing a variety of fruits and nuts. In this delicious version, however, the slices are larger and the pastry made from thinner, more elastic dough.

yields about 24 rolls

Time: 75 minutes, excluding resting and cooling

Level of Difficulty: Moderate

PASTRY

2 cups unbleached all-purpose flour, sifted with a pinch of salt

1 large egg, lightly beaten

1 tablespoon extra virgin olive oil

1 tablespoon water

1 Heap the flour on a work surface and make a well in the center. Add the egg, oil, and 1 tablespoon water and mix with a fork, incorporating flour a little at a time and adding warm water as needed to form a soft, smooth dough; some flour may remain. Knead for 10 minutes, cover with a clean cloth, and let rest for 1 hour.

2 Put the fruits and nuts in a bowl with the lemon zest, cinnamon, sugar, and Marsala and mix until the ingredients are well blended.

3 Preheat the oven to 350°F. Butter a 16 x 20-inch baking pan.

4 Roll the dough into a 1/8-inch-thick rectangle. Distribute the fruit and nut mixture evenly over the surface leaving a 1 1/2-inch border on all sides. Roll up from the short side and press the edges sealed. Arrange the roll in the pan, seam side down.

5 Bake for 30 minutes. Remove from the oven and cool for 15 minutes. Cut into 1-inch-thick slices. Arrange on a platter and garnish with dried fruits and nuts.

Make Ahead The dough can be prepared 2 days in advance, wrapped in plastic wrap, and kept refrigerated until ready to use. It can also be frozen for up to 3 weeks. Return to room temperature before using.

435

FILLING

2 medium Granny Smith apples, peeled, cored, and thinly sliced

10 dried prunes, pitted and chopped

2 dried figs, stems removed and chopped

1/4 cup pine nuts, chopped

6 hazelnuts, shelled, peeled, and chopped

6 walnuts, shelled and chopped

1 teaspoon grated lemon zest

1/8 teaspoon ground cinnamon

1/2 cup sugar

5 tablespoons Marsala

Butter for greasing

Assorted dried fruits and nuts for garnish

ZELTEN

Alpine Fruit Bread

❦ Trentino-Alto Adige ❦

BOLZANO, MERANO, AND BRESSANONE ARE THE THREE TOWNS IN ALTO ADIGE *that host* Christkindlmärkte—*open-air markets held during the Christmas season and featuring a great variety of arts and crafts. All three include living Nativity dioramas and charmingly decorated stands selling vin brulé, grilled fruit kebabs, and this traditional Christmas fruit bread made with almonds, raisins, dates, and grappa. The markets are open every day during the Advent season, in December.*

yields about 24 slices

Time: 1 hour, 45 minutes

Level of Difficulty: Moderate

⚕

1/2 cup sultana raisins

1 cup candied citron, diced

1/2 cup grappa

1/4 cup water

8 tablespoons (1 stick)
    unsalted butter

3 large eggs

2 cups confectioner's sugar

4 cups unbleached all-purpose
    flour, sifted with
    2 tablespoons active
    dry yeast

1/2 cup pine nuts

1 Soak the raisins and citron in the grappa for 1 hour.

2 Meanwhile, heat 1/4 cup water until boiling and add the butter. Stir until the butter melts. Keep warm.

3 Beat the eggs with the confectioner's sugar in a bowl until smooth and creamy. Stir in the flour-yeast mixture, a little at a time. Pour in the melted butter and stir until well blended. Drain the raisins and citron and add to the dough with the pine nuts, almonds, dates, walnuts, cinnamon, cloves, and milk. Mix well.

4 Preheat the oven to 350°F. Butter and flour a 12 x 16-inch baking sheet, shaking off the excess flour.

5 Shape the dough into 4 oval loaves about
1 inch high. Place in the prepared pan about
3 inches apart and bake for 30 minutes, or until a
toothpick inserted in the center comes out clean.
Remove from the oven, cool to room temperature,
cut into thin slices, and serve.

Make Ahead The loaves can be made earlier in the
day, wrapped in plastic wrap, and refrigerated until
ready to bake. The finished loaves can be frozen for
up to 3 weeks, cut or uncut, and heated through just
before serving.

$1/2$ cup almonds, crushed
$1/2$ cup pitted dates, diced
$1/2$ cup walnuts, crushed
$1/8$ teaspoon ground cinnamon
$1/8$ teaspoon ground cloves
3 tablespoons whole milk
Flour for sprinkling

437

TORTA DI MELE

Open-faced Christmas Apple Pie

❧ Trentino-Alto Adige ❧

THERE ARE MANY HIGH POINTS TO THE CHRISTMAS SEASON IN THIS ALPINE REGION *(see page 436), but the one most favored by children takes place on the night of December 6, The Feast of St. Nicholas, Protector of Small Children. According to legend, Nicholas roams the villages of Alto Adige distributing gifts to good boys and girls. But in the typical push-pull between good and evil that characterizes most religious holidays, Nicholas is accompanied by Krampus, a horrendously ugly, hirsute figure representing the devil. Krampus starts his prowl on the night of December 5, when he can be seen combing the streets (and scaring small children to death) in search of those who have been bad so he can spirit them away to his mountain lair and eat them.*

yields 10 slices

Time: 75 minutes

Level of Difficulty: Moderate

1 large egg
3/4 cup sugar
Pinch of salt
Grated zest of 1 lemon
12 tablespoons (1 1/2 sticks)
 unsalted butter, melted
2 cups unbleached all-purpose
 flour, sifted with
 1 tablespoon active
 dry yeast

1 Place the egg, sugar, pinch of salt, and lemon zest in the bowl of a food processor and process. With the motor running, pour the melted butter through the feed tube and immediately pour in the flour-yeast mixture, vanilla, and milk. Process until the ingredients form a soft dough.

2 Preheat the oven to 375°F. Butter a 10-inch-round cake pan with sides about 2 inches high. Sprinkle with flour, shaking off the excess.

3 Arrange the dough on the bottom of the pan and level with a spatula.

4 Make a series of superficial incisions on the surface of each apple half, cutting first lengthwise, then widthwise. This forms a grid pattern, but the cuts should not go through to the bottom. Press one apple half into the center of the tart without piercing the bottom of the crust. Press the remaining apples in a circular pattern around the center.

5 Bake for 10 minutes, then reduce the temperature to 350°F and bake for 40 to 45 minutes more, or until a toothpick inserted into the dough comes out clean.

6 Meanwhile, place the apricot preserves and water in a saucepan and cook over low heat, stirring constantly, for 4 to 5 minutes, or until the preserves are melted.

7 Remove the pie from the oven and baste the entire surface with the preserves. Return to the oven and bake for 2 to 3 minutes. Remove from the oven, cool to room temperature, and serve.

1 teaspoon pure vanilla extract
6 tablespoons warm whole milk
Butter for greasing
Flour for dusting
4 small Granny Smith apples,
    peeled, cored, and halved
2 tablespoons apricot preserves
2 tablespoons water

439

GELATO AL COCOMERO

Watermelon and Pistacchio Sorbet

❧ Sicilia ❧

IN MESSINA, THE FEAST OF THE ASSUMPTION IS PRECEDED BY ANOTHER, MORE *secular festival called* I Giganti—*The Giants. Every August 13 and 14, two enormous statues made of wood and papier-mâché are paraded through the town*—U Gialanti e'u Gilantissa *(or as they are more affectionately nicknamed, Mata and Grifone)—the mythological god and goddess who founded the town and to whom many Messanesi still pay tribute. According to legend, Grifone was a black African warrior who routinely ravaged and terrorized the villages around Messina. But one day, while engaged in one of his rampages, he spotted a beautiful young woman running away in fear and asked her to be his wife. "On one condition," she said. "That you stop this reign of terror." And so the legendary couple made their home on the southern coast, thus founding the city of Messina.*

This watermelon sorbet is widely served throughout Messina on this quirky festival day.

serves 6

Time: 60 minutes, excluding the 2-to-3 hour refrigeration time

Level of Difficulty: Easy

1 pound watermelon flesh
2 cups sugar
1 cup grated bittersweet chocolate
1/2 cup shelled and crushed pistachios
1/4 teaspoon ground cinnamon

1 Pass the watermelon through a food mill and discard the seeds. Stir the sugar into the resultant mash, transfer to an ice cream freezer, and freeze according to the manufacturer's directions.

2 Remove the sorbet from the freezer, add the chocolate, pistachios, and half the cinnamon and mix until blended. Place in a ring mold and freeze for 2 to 3 hours. When ready to serve, dip the bottom of the mold in hot water, unmold onto a serving platter, dust with the remaining cinnamon, and cut into wedges.

Make Ahead The entire gelato can be made up to a week in advance and kept frozen until ready to use.

FICHI AL CIOCCOLATO

Chocolate-covered Walnut-stuffed Figs

❧ Campania ❧

THE SECOND SUNDAY OF JULY, MINTURNO CELEBRATES THE *SAGRA DELLE REGNE*—*being Campanese dialect for "sheafs of grain." Minturno is a wheat-growing area located near the border between Lazio and Campania; in ancient times, the festival was a strictly pagan one, celebrating the abundance of nature. But since 1378, when the Church dedicated the day to the Madonna delle Grazie in an effort at Christianizing pagan ceremonies, farmers have placed statues of the Madonna in their fields hoping for a good harvest. On the actual day of the sagra, farmers don traditional clothes and travel in horse-drawn wooden carts to Minturno's main piazza, where they arrange their statues on a huge stage erected in the center. Then they separate the grain from the chaff, using ancient methods, and offer it to the assembled Madonnas in a moving ritual, the solemnity of which brought tears to the eyes of many spectators (myself included). Afterward, there is much eating, drinking, and traditional dancing.*

makes 16 to 24 chocolate-coated figs

Time: 30 minutes

Level of Difficulty: Easy

16 to 24 ripe figs

1 cup shelled walnuts, finely chopped

4 to 5 ounces bittersweet chocolate

2 tablespoons water

6 to 8 fresh mint leaves for garnish

1 Preheat the oven to 200°F.

2 Clean the figs gently with a damp cloth and dry in the oven for 2 to 3 minutes. The figs' skins must be extremely dry. Cut the figs in half lengthwise, but avoid cutting all the way through. The figs should open and close like a book. Stuff the figs with the chopped walnuts and bring the two sides together so that the figs appear whole.

3 Put the chocolate in a saucepan, add 2 tablespoons water, and melt over very low heat. Dip the figs in the chocolate and rotate until all sides are coated. Place on waxed paper until dry and serve garnished with fresh mint.

Make Ahead The figs can be stuffed earlier in the day.

CANNOLI ALLA SICILIANA

Pastry Cylinders Stuffed with Sweet Ricotta and Chocolate

❦ Sicilia ❦

THE DAY AFTER THE GIGANTI FESTIVAL (SEE PAGE 440), THE FEAST OF THE *Assumption takes over, with its amazing forty-five-foot high float carrying a diorama displaying the death and assumption of the Virgin Mary. The float, crowned by fourteen small children dressed in white, is pulled by a thousand barefoot residents and is probably the largest and most intricate festival float in all of Italy. Its magnitude reflects the particular devotion experienced by the people of Messina toward the Virgin Mary—a devotion that, according to legend, began when Mary herself wrote a letter of thanks to a group of Messinanesi who visited Jerusalem in A.D. 43. Preserved for over twelve centuries in the city's cathedral, the letter was destroyed in the great fire of 1253; its memory is kept alive, however, by a separaie festival in honor of* La Madonna della Lettera, *held on June 3.*

These cannoli are associated with many of Sicily's festivals, but never in such great numbers as the thousands I saw ready for distribution in Messina's Piazza del Duomo.

makes 12 to 15 cannolis

Time: About 2 hours

Level of Difficulty: Advanced

Equipment: 12 to 15 cannoli rings*; Large pastry bag fitted with a standard tip

⨳

CANNOLI SHELLS
1¹/2 cups unbleached
    all-purpose flour
1¹/2 tablespoons unsalted
    butter, melted
Pinch of salt

1 To make the shells, heap the flour on a work surface and make a well in the center. Add the butter, pinch of salt, sugar, vinegar, cocoa, and coffee. Mix with a fork, incorporating the flour a little at a time and adding Marsala as needed to form a dense dough; some flour may remain. Knead about 15 minutes, or until the dough becomes smooth and elastic. Wrap in plastic wrap and refrigerate for 30 minutes.

2 Roll the dough into an ¹/8-inch-thick rectangle. Using a 4-inch-round cookie cutter, cut the dough into circles. When all the dough is cut, gather any remaining dough into a ball, and repeat the procedure. Continue until all the dough has been used.

Cannoli forms can be found in specialty kitchen stores.

3 Gently pull each circle into an oval. Grease the cannoli rings with butter and wrap each circle around a ring, basting the ends with egg white and pressing to seal.

4 Heat 2 inches of oil to 375°F in a large skillet over medium heat and fry the dough-wrapped rings, a few at a time, turning frequently until all surfaces are golden brown. Remove with a slotted spoon, drain on paper towels, cool to room temperature, and gently slide off the metal tubes.

5 To make the filling, pass the ricotta through the finest disk of a food mill, add the remaining ingredients, and mix well. Refrigerate for 30 minutes.

6 Spoon the filling into a pastry bag and pipe into each of the cannolis. Arrange on a platter, dust with confectioner's sugar, and serve.

Make Ahead The cannoli dough can be made up to 2 days in advance, wrapped tightly in plastic wrap, and refrigerated until ready to use. It can also be frozen for up to 3 weeks, but, in either case, it should be returned to room temperature before using. The fried cannoli shells can be stored in an airtight container for up to a week. Although the filled cannolis can be made earlier in the day and refrigerated until ready to serve, they should be filled as close to serving time as possible to preserve the crispness of the shell.

1 tablespoon sugar

1 teaspoon white wine vinegar

1 teaspoon unsweetened cocoa powder

1 teaspoon ground espresso

About $1/2$ cup Marsala or white wine

Butter for greasing

1 large egg white, lightly beaten

Olive oil for frying

FILLING

$1^1/2$ cups fresh ricotta

1 tablespoon pure vanilla extract

$1/2$ cup sugar

$1/3$ cup diced candied fruit

$1/4$ cup grated bittersweet chocolate

$1/8$ teaspoon ground cinnamon

4 tablespoons confectioner's sugar

443

OFFELLE DI PASTA SFOGLIA

Puff Pastry Rounds Stuffed with Apricots

❦ Lombardia ❦

ON JANUARY 6, MILAN CELEBRATES THE *CORTEO DEI RE MAGI*—THE FESTIVAL OF *the Three Kings. Revived in 1963 by Don Spreafico of Saint Eustorgio Church after almost thirty years of abandonment, the festival dates back to the fourth century, when St. Eustorgio, Milan's favorite son, presented himself before Emperor Constantine, who was to crown him Bishop of Milan. As a sign of friendship, Constantinople's emperor gave Eustorgio a gold box containing the relics of the Three Kings—the same box that is today preserved in the knave of Saint Eustorgio Church. The festival begins at 10 A.M. with a sprightly procession led by the Three Kings and including everything from drum majorettes to caged lions to Milan's Civic Band. The route weaves between the churches of St. Ambrogio and St. Eustorgio, where gifts are laid before the Living Nativity. Food stalls line the piazza and spectators number in the tens of thousands.*

These puff pastry rounds are as associated with this festival as they are with traditional end-of-year celebrations.

makes about 20 rounds

Time: 50 minutes

Level of Difficulty: Easy

❦

Butter for greasing
Flour for dredging
1 pound frozen puff pastry
1 cup apricot preserves

1 Preheat the oven to 400°F. Butter and flour a baking pan, shaking off the excess.

2 Spread out the pastry sheets and roll with a rolling pin until flat. Cut into rounds, using either a 2-inch cookie cutter or the rim of a 6-ounce water glass.

3 Arrange the pastry rounds 1 inch apart in the pan and bake for 10 minutes. Reduce the temperature to 325°F and bake for another 10 minutes. Reduce the temperature to 300°F and bake for 5 to 10 minutes more, or until the puff pastry turns golden brown. If the pastries seem to be turning too brown, cover with aluminum foil, and continue baking. Remove from the oven and cool to room temperature.

4 Spread half the rounds with the apricot preserves and cover with the remaining rounds. Transfer to a decorative platter and serve.

445

GIANDUJA

Hazelnut Chocolate Pudding Cake

❦ Piemonte ❦

THE *FESTIVAL DELLE SAGRE ASTIGIANE*—FESTIVAL OF ALL FOODS—TAKES PLACE
*on the second weekend of September in fifty different piazzas throughout the province of Asti. This is
truly the festival of festivals, with no focus other than food, food, and more food. Described by Asti's
Pro Loco (Pro Locos are organizations devoted to organizing and maintaining traditional festivals)
as a "gastronomic orgy," the festivals present foods and wines typical of the Asti region, such as this
sinfully rich chocolate pudding cake.*

serves 6

Time: 50 minutes, excluding
2 hours refrigeration time

Level of Difficulty: Moderate

1/4 cup hazelnuts
1 large egg
1 large egg yolk
1/2 cup sugar
2 cups grated bittersweet
    chocolate
8 tablespoons (1 stick)
    unsalted butter
16 ladyfingers, crumbled

1 Preheat the oven to 350°F. Butter a 9-inch
springform pan.

2 Put the hazelnuts in a baking pan and toast
10 or 12 minutes, or until the skins are brown.
Remove and rub them on a hard mesh sieve to
remove the skins. Discard the skins, transfer the nut
meats to the bowl of a food processor, and pulse until
the nuts are roughly chopped.

3 Put the egg, egg yolk, and sugar in a bowl and
beat with an electric mixer about 5 minutes, or until
the mixture is light yellow and fluffy.

4 Melt the chocolate and butter in the top of a
double boiler over simmering water. Remove from
the heat, cool for a few minutes, and add to the egg
mixture, whisking constantly until light and fluffy.
Add the nuts and crumbled ladyfingers and mix well.

5 Pour in the chocolate mixture. Wrap in plastic
wrap and refrigerate for 2 hours. Unmold and serve.

LIMONI CANDITI

Whole Candied Lemons

❦ Sicilia ❧

'U FISTINU (SMALL FEAST) IS THE LOCAL NAME GIVEN TO THE FESTIVAL OF SAINT *Rosalia, which consumes Palermo for one entire week until it climaxes on July 8. But Palermo is not alone in its love affair with Rosalia. When Goethe first climbed Mt. Pellegrino and laid eyes on the immense statue of the saint that was donated to the city by Carlo III of Bourbon and now resides in the Sanctuario over the cave where Rosalia performed her ablutions, he rhapsodized thusly in his epic memoir,* Italian Journey, *"That image seemed to possess an extraordinary power over me; I never tired of contemplating it." The following confection makes wonderful use of the exceptional lemons that grow in Conca d'Oro, the dense fertile plain that surrounds Palermo and is planted almost exclusively with lemon and orange groves.*

makes 1 pint

Time: 2 hours actual working time, 24 hours marinating time, and 3 to 5 days seasoning

Level of Difficulty: Easy

3 organic lemons
(about 3/4 pound total),
preferably of uniform
size and shape
1/4 cup water
1/2 cup sugar

1 Wash and dry the lemons, trim both ends, and make 5 or 6 incisions in the skin. Using a citrus squeezer, squeeze out all the juice (reserve for another use) and eliminate any remaining seeds. Do not tear the skin beyond the incisions already made.

2 Place the lemons in a glass jar, fill with cold water to cover, cap the jar, and let the lemons rest for 24 hours, changing the water 2 or 3 times.

3 Drain the lemons and place in a stainless steel saucepan. Cover with water and cook, covered, over low heat for 1 1/2 hours. Drain and air dry for 2 hours.

4 Place the lemons in a stainless steel saucepan, add the 1/4 cup water, sugar, and cook over low heat until the mixture thickens but does not caramelize. Pour into a 1-pint glass jar and seal. Store in a cool, dark, dry place for 3 to 5 days. Cut into strips and serve with cookies or ice cream.

Make Ahead Lemons prepared in this way keep for 3 weeks.

PASTICCIOTTI DI FICU VIRDI

Fig and Nut Wafers

❧ Sicilia ❧

ST. ROSALIA (SEE PAGE 447) WAS A YOUNG NORMAN PRINCESS WHO SOUGHT ASCETIC *seclusion on Mt. Pellegrino, an isolated mass of limestone rising from the sea. Her bones were discovered on July 15, 1624, by a paralyzed woman who had been carried to the mountaintop after a dream in which Rosalia had appeared to her. The following year, as Palermo lay in the throes of a raging plague, Rosalia appeared again, this time to a dying man, to whom she promised to heal the city if her bones were carried through the town in solemn procession. The plague was vanquished and Palermo has since honored the saint with a massive procession held on July 15, her feast day. The procession's main float is shaped like an actual-size ship and covered with statues of saints above which stands the towering Rosalia sculpted of pure white marble. Inside the float, Palermo's band plays a rather odd sort of liturgical music that often seems to segue into popular lounge songs.*

makes about 24 wafers

Time: 2 hours

Level of Difficulty: Moderate

DOUGH

2 1/2 cups unbleached
    all-purpose flour, sifted
    with 1 teaspoon active
    dry yeast

2/3 cup sugar

2 large eggs

6 tablespoons unsalted butter,
    at room temperature and
    thinly sliced

1 Put the flour and sugar in a food processor and pulse once or twice to blend. Add the eggs and and butter and pulse just until a ball forms. Knead by hand for 2 minutes, or until smooth. Wrap in plastic wrap and refrigerate for 30 minutes.

2 Meanwhile, place the figs in a saucepan, add the sugar and lemon zest, and cook over very low heat for 20 to 30 minutes, or until the consistency is thick and smooth. Cool to room temperature and stir in the citron and nuts.

3 Preheat the oven to 350°F. Butter a 16 x 20-inch baking sheet.

4 On a lightly floured surface, roll the dough into a $^1/_8$-inch-thick rectangle. Using a 4-inch cookie mold, cut out a series of circles. Place a teaspoon of filling in the center of half the circles. Baste the edges with water, top with the remaining wafers, and press the edges to seal.

5 Bake for 20 minutes, or until the tops are light golden brown. Sprinkle with confectioner's sugar and cool completely before serving.

Make Ahead The dough can be made up to 2 days in advance, wrapped tightly in plastic wrap, and refrigerated until ready to use. It can also be frozen for up to 3 weeks. Thaw in the refrigerator before using. The filling can also be prepared up to 2 days in advance and kept refrigerated in a sealed container.

FILLING

$^3/_4$ pound green figs, (not quite ripe), peeled and diced

$^1/_3$ cup sugar

1 tablespoon grated lemon zest

2 ounces candied citron, finely diced

$^1/_4$ cup blanched almonds, finely diced

$^1/_4$ cup shelled walnuts, finely diced

Butter for greasing

Confectioner's sugar for dusting

MASCARPONE ALLO ZABAIONE

Sweet Mascarpone Cheese Cake Flavored with Marsala

450

❧ Lombardia ❧

MILAN'S CARNIVAL IS THE WORLD'S LONGEST IN DURATION, ENDING ON THE FIRST *Saturday of Lent rather than on* Martedi Grasso—*Mardi Gras. The custom originates with Saint Ambrogio, the city's patron who made a number of changes to the Church liturgy, the most popular being the shortening of Lent by four days. On that final Saturday, there is a huge parade led by Meneghin and Cecca, festival characters representing Milan. The parade ends in Piazza del Duomo, which is lined with food stalls offering sweets, such as this very rich and very scrumptious cheese cake.*

makes 10 slices

Time: 35 to 45 minutes, excluding the 12-hour refrigeration time

Level of Difficulty: Moderate

1 cup mascarpone* at room
    temperature
4 large egg yolks
4 tablespoons sugar
12 tablespoons Marsala
One 10-inch-round sponge cake,
    cut horizontally into
    2 layers

1 Put the mascarpone in a large bowl and beat with a fork until creamy.

2 Beat the eggs and the sugar until light and fluffy. Add 8 tablespoons of the Marsala, pouring in a steady stream and whisking until smooth. Place this egg mixture in the top of a double boiler over simmering water and cook for 10 minutes, stirring constantly until the temperature reaches 160°F. Remove from the heat, transfer to a bowl, and cool to room temperature. Fold into the mascarpone, mixing until well blended.

3 Arrange a layer of sponge cake in a 10-inch-round springform pan. Drizzle the remaining Marsala over the surface. Pour the mascarpone mixture into the pan and smooth the surface with a spatula. Cover with the remaining sponge layer. Refrigerate for 12 hours, remove the sides of the pan, and serve.

Mascarpone is a very rich, triple-cream cheese with a texture and color that is like that of heavy whipped cream. In the "decadent" '80s, mascarpone came to define the Lombardian kitchen, where it was used in everything from desserts to pasta sauces to risottos.

FICHI ALLO SCIROPPO

Fresh Figs Preserved in Rum Syrup

❦ Calabria ❦

WHAT MAKES BOVALINO MARINA'S TWO-WEEK FESTIVAL IN HONOR OF ITS PATRON *saint unusual is the magnificent procession that takes place on August 15, the final day. The Ionian Sea is carpeted with boats, both large and small, all come to pay tribute to Saint Francesco of Paola, whose statue is prominently displayed on the prow of the colorful lead boat. Afterward, the shore is lined with long tables and participants purchase food from the various stalls, eating together under makeshift umbrellas.*

makes 1 quart

Time: 2 hours 40 minutes, excluding the 2- to 6-month seasoning period

Level of Difficulty: Easy

1 pound fresh figs, not too ripe
1¹/2 cups sugar
1 cup water
3 tablespoons white rum

1 Gently wash and dry the figs, making sure not to break the skin.

2 Put the sugar in a large stainless steel saucepan with 1 cup water and cook over low heat for 10 to 15 minutes, stirring frequently. Add the rum and figs and cook for 2 hours, gently turning the figs every 15 minutes. Be careful to avoid tearing the skin.

3 Transfer the figs and syrup to a glass jar, seal, and store in a cool, dark, dry place for 2 to 6 months before serving. Works well on its own or when paired with rum raisin ice cream.

CROCCANTE DI MANDORLE

Crunchy Almond Brittle

❦ Liguria ❦

BANCARELLE ARE FOOD STALLS SET UP ON FESTIVAL DAYS TO SELL ANYTHING FROM *sliced pork-roast sandwiches to grilled skewers threaded with small song birds. The nature of the food generally depends on the festival*—cenci, *for example, are most closely associated with carnival in the Tuscan seaside village of Viareggio. But there is one food, nut brittles, that seems to be inherent to festivals everywhere, whether in the Piedmont or Calabria. Wherever you go, you see* bancarelle *hawking seven or eight varieties, generally arranged alongside four or five types of nougat candy. The only difference seems to be the type of nuts. What makes this almond brittle Ligurian is that, according to legend, it was first made by a Genovese housewife whose seafaring husband had brought the nuts back from Asia.*

makes 20 to 30 pieces brittle

Time: 40 minutes

Level of Difficulty: Easy

1 tablespoon extra virgin
  olive oil
1 cup shelled almonds, peeled*
  and roughly chopped
1 cup sugar

1 Preheat the oven to 350°F. Oil an 8-inch-square baking pan.

2 Put the almonds in a baking pan and toast for 5 to 6 minutes. Melt the sugar in a skillet over medium heat about 5 minutes, or until caramelized to a light amber color. Add the almonds to the melted sugar and toss to coat.

3 Pour the almond-sugar mixture into the pan and, working very quickly, smooth the surface with a spatula. Cut into diamonds, but leave the sheet intact until the mixture hardens before separating.

To peel almonds, immerse in boiling water for 5 minutes. Drain and rub away the skin.

FRITTELLE DI MELE ALLA GRAPPA

Apple Doughnuts Scented with Grappa

❦ Val d'Aosta ❧

THERE ARE INFINITELY MORE APPLE TREES IN AND AROUND GRESSAN THAN THERE *are people and, on the second Sunday of every October, their small, round fruits take center stage. La Festa delle mele (Apple Festival) consists of fruit growers offering their best varieties for a judging that takes place in one of the central market warehouses. Afterward there is plenty of apple cider and an infinite variety of apple-based desserts, among which the following was my favorite.*

makes 20 to 25 doughnuts

Time: 20 to 30 minutes, excluding the 1-hour rest period

Level of Difficulty: Moderate

2 large eggs

1/2 cup sugar

11/2 cups unbleached all-purpose flour

1/8 teaspoon ground cinnamon

1/2 cup grappa or brandy

1/2 cup whole milk

4 large Granny Smith apples, peeled, cored, and cut horizontally into 1/2-inch-thick slices

Olive oil for frying

Confectioner's sugar for dusting

1 Whisk the eggs and the sugar in a bowl until light and fluffy. Add the flour, cinnamon, grappa, and milk and continue whisking until the batter is smooth and foamy. Cover with a clean towel and let rest for 1 hour.

2 Heat 2 inches of oil in a heavy skillet to 375°F.* Dip the apple slices in the batter to coat and fry until golden. Remove with a slotted spoon, drain on paper towels, sprinkle with confectioner's sugar, and serve hot.

To test the temperature of the oil, you can put a cube of bread into the skillet. When it sizzles around the edges and turns golden almost immediately, the oil is the right temperature.

AMARETTUS

454

Sardinian Amaretti (Almond Cookies)

❧ Sardegna ☙

BY NOW IT MUST BE OBVIOUS TO ANYONE PERUSING THIS BOOK THAT I LOVE *festivals. Even I, however, have my favorites and generally, they tend to be* Sagre Gastronomiche *(Gastronomic Festivals), where I can stroll among tables laden with all manner of regional homemade or home-crafted specialties. In Santadi, I happened upon just such an event, held every August 1 in Piazza Marconi. There were local wines, cured pork products, steaming pasta casseroles made by black-clad widows eager to tell me their secret preparations, grilled meats, roasted vegetables, and one entire table filled with desserts—all as wonderful as these lighter-than-air amaretti.*

makes about 20 amaretti

Time: 1 hour

Level of Difficulty: Moderate

1 pound shelled almonds, peeled
   (see page 452)
3 egg whites
1/2 teaspoon salt
1/2 teaspoon cream of tartar
1/2 cup unbleached
   all-purpose flour
4 cups sugar

1 Preheat the oven to 300°F.

2 Place the almonds on a baking sheet and toast for 15 minutes. Transfer to a bowl of a food processor and process on high speed until the almonds have been pulverized.

3 Using an electric mixer, beat the egg whites with the salt about 3 minutes, or until foamy. Add the cream of tartar and beat into stiff peaks. Gently fold the almonds, flour, and sugar into the egg whites until the mixture is well blended and smooth.

4 Raise the oven temperature to 350°F. Line a 16 x 20-inch baking sheet with parchment paper.

5 Drop the almond batter by teaspoonfuls spaced 2¹/₂ inches apart. Partially flatten the tops with a wet spatula.

6 Bake for 20 minutes, or until golden brown. Remove from the oven, cool to room temperature, and serve.

Make Ahead The almonds can be crushed into flour a few hours before using. To keep fresh, they should be stored in a sealed glass container.

455

TORTA DEGLI ADDOBBI

Sweet Rice and Almond Cake

❦ Emilia-Romagna ❦

AT THE ENTRANCE TO THE *SAGRA DELL'UOVO*—EGG FESTIVAL—EVERYONE IS *handed a colored hard-boiled egg to use in the* battitura—*a couple's game with the ultimate object of breaking the partner's egg before he or she breaks yours. The festival takes place on both Easter Sunday morning and Monday night in Tredozio. On Sunday, the events center on the egg-breaking contest and a match to see who can eat the most hard-boiled eggs. Monday evening is the* Palio dell'Uovo, *a tournament among the town's four rival quarters: Borgo, Casone, Nuovo, and Piazza. Each quarter arrives in the main piazza regally dressed in their traditional medieval costumes and proceeds through a series of competitions all involving eggs: rolling eggs up an incline, finding an egg in a mound of hay, and flipping an egg in a frying pan. Sounds bizarre, but is great fun and the food— all egg-based—ranges from fresh egg pasta with wild boar sauce to egg-stuffed pheasant to this wonderful dessert named* addobbi, *which comes from the days when aristocrats dressed in fine jewels and ornaments* (addobbati) *would watch the tournament from their balconies.*

yields 10 slices

Time: 90 minutes

Level of Difficulty: Moderate

1 cup Arborio rice
2¹/2 cups whole milk
2 large eggs, lightly beaten
1 teaspoon pure vanilla extract
³/4 cup sugar
²/3 cup shelled almonds, peeled
    (see page 452 for directions)

1 Put the rice and milk in a medium saucepan and cook over low heat for 15 to 18 minutes, or until the rice softens. Transfer to a bowl and cool to room temperature.

2 Preheat the oven to 325°F. Butter and flour a 9-inch springform pan.

3 Add the beaten eggs to the cooled mixture, 1 tablespoon at a time, stirring constantly. Add the vanilla, sugar, and almonds and mix until well blended. Pour the rice mixture into the pan.

4 Bake for 30 minutes. Remove from the oven and pour the Marsala over the top. Cool to room temperature, remove from the pan, and garnish with fresh mint.

Butter for greasing
Flour for dusting
1 cup Marsala or fruit brandy
8-10 sprigs mint for garnish

457

appendix A

Basic Recipes

NINETY PERCENT OF ITALIAN COOKING REVOLVES AROUND A FEW BASIC RECIPES. Making a meat broth. Churning up a batch of dough. Concocting a polenta. No matter how innovative the dish or distinct its ingredients, the basics—and a cook's understanding of them—are the most important factors in whether a dish will turn out well. Not only that, but a freezer filled with broths and doughs enables you to take a few simple ingredients and turn them into a masterpiece in thirty minutes or less.

BRODO DI VERDURA

Basic Vegetable Broth

THIS BROTH CAN BE MADE WITH ALMOST ANY VEGETABLES, BUT MUST INCLUDE AN *onion, carrot, and celery, which form the base of the flavor. For a fresh summer flavor, try substituting basil and tomatoes for the leeks, turnips, and parsley. If using organic ingredients (and it is always best to do so), add the onion and carrot peels as well.*

makes about 1¹/2 quarts

3 tablespoons extra virgin olive oil
1 medium onion
1 carrot
1 stalk celery
2 leeks, cleaned and halved
    lengthwise
1 turnip, chopped
1 cup chopped fresh parsley leaves
    (stems discarded)
1 bay leaf
8 whole peppercorns
1 teaspoon salt
2 quarts water

1 Put the oil in a large, heavy soup pot. Sauté the onion, carrot, and celery for 8 minutes over low heat, stirring frequently. Add the remainder of the ingredients, increase the heat to medium, and bring to a boil.

2 Reduce the heat to low, cover, and cook for 30 minutes. Adjust the seasonings, adding more salt if needed.

3 Remove from the heat and strain through a fine mesh sieve. Cool to room temperature and store in the refrigerator or freeze. Before using, scrape any fat from the surface and discard.

Variations For a lighter taste, eliminate the initial sauté. Place all ingredients into the pot cold and proceed from Step 2.

Storage This broth will keep for up to 4 days if stored in the refrigerator in a sealed container. It can also be frozen for up to 3 months.

BRODO DI CARNE

Basic Meat Broth

THERE ARE VERY FEW HOMES THROUGHOUT ITALY THAT MAKE IT THROUGH ANY *given week without cooking up a big pot of basic meat broth. Used as the basis for soups, as a soup in itself, and as the most important ingredient in making risotto, basic meat broth is to Italians what butter and cream are to the French—indispensable. You can omit the beef bones, if you like, and simply turn this same recipe into basic chicken broth.*

makes about 1¹/2 quarts

1 chicken (preferably free-range), cleaned and with internal organs removed

2 pounds beef bones (any type), roasted for 30 minutes in a 400°F oven

1 onion, halved

3 carrots

2 stalks celery

2 fresh (or canned) tomatoes

5-6 sprigs fresh flat leaf parsley

2 quarts water (or enough to cover the chicken)

1 teaspoon salt

4 whole peppercorns

1 Place all ingredients in a heavy-gauge soup pot, cover, and cook over medium heat for 2 hours. From time to time, skim off any scum from the surface.

2 Strain through a colander, discarding the solids, and cool to room temperature. Before using, scrape off and discard the layer of fat on the surface.

Variations For a broth that is lighter (more yellow) in color, eliminate the tomatoes.

Storage This broth will keep for up to 4 days if stored in the refrigerator in a sealed container. It can also be frozen for up to 3 months.

PASTA ALL'UOVA

Basic Egg Pasta

461

makes about one pound pasta

1 cup semolina˙

2 cups unbleached all-purpose
   flour

4 large eggs

1 teaspoon extra virgin olive oil

¹/₂ teaspoon salt

1 tablespoon water

1 Blend the two flours in a bowl, then heap them on a work surface. Using your fingers, make a well in the center. Beat the eggs, oil, salt, and water in a bowl and pour them into the well. Beat with a fork, incorporating the flour a little at a time until the dough becomes too dense to continue. Be careful not to break through the wall. Once you have formed a dense dough ball, begin kneading with your hands, incorporating as much of the remaining flour as necessary, a little at a time, until the dough is smooth and elastic. Some flour may remain.

2 Continue to knead for about 2 to 3 minutes. Divide the ball into four pieces and wrap three in plastic wrap to keep from drying out.

3 Set your pasta machine˙˙ on the widest opening. Flatten the unwrapped dough with your hands; this makes it easier to fit into the machine. Dust very lightly with flour on both sides.

4 Pass the dough through the rollers, feeding with one hand and cranking with the other, unless the machine is motorized. The first pass will produce a very rough dough that is somewhat pocked and uneven in color.

5 Fold the dough into thirds the long way, dust both sides lightly with flour, and pass again through the rollers. Fold again into thirds and repeat two more times.

˙*If you cannot find semolina, increase the amount of all-purpose flour to 3 cups.*

˙˙*If not using a pasta machine, roll each ball on a lightly floured surface into a large ¹/₈-inch thick (or thinner) rectangle. To create noodles, roll the rectangle from the long side into a tight cylinder and cut into noodles.*

462

6 Set the rollers to the next thinner size and roll the dough through, dusting both sides lightly with flour before placing through the rollers. Make sure to support the pasta with one hand as you feed it through the machine with the other. At this point, the pasta will be smoother and more velvety, with a homogenized color and texture.

7 Keep setting the rollers to the next thinner size and passing the dough through. With one hand cranking and one gently pulling, extrude the dough until it becomes too long to handle. Cut into lengths approximately 12 inches long and keep rolling each piece until you are down to the next thinnest setting.

8 Repeat with the remaining balls of dough until all ingredients are used up. Cut into noodles or leave as is, depending on recipe.

Variations Color can be added in Step 1. Using pureed spinach for green, concentrated tomato paste for red, squid ink for black, or beet juice for purple, add 1 tablespoon color to the bowl with the egg mixture and proceed to make the pasta.

Storage Egg pasta is best when cooked within 1 hour of making. To store for longer periods, toss with flour, place loosely in a plastic refrigerator bag, and freeze for up to 3 weeks. To dry egg pasta, toss with flour and air dry for at least 2 hours. Seal tightly in a plastic bag and store in a cool, dry pantry for up to 2 weeks. Dried pasta can also be frozen for up to a month.

PASTA DI PANE

Basic Pizza Dough

THE ITALIAN TRANSLATION FOR THIS PIZZA DOUGH IS, LITERALLY, "DOUGH FOR *making bread.*" *That's because it can be used for either purpose, although Italians generally make their breads with at least some semolina to give the finished product a greater shelf life. With a drizzle of oil or a few chopped olives thrown in, this dough can also be used for making a wonderful focaccia.*

makes about two 10-inch-round pizzas

1 teaspoon active dry yeast

1/2 cup plus 3/4 cup warm water

4 cups unbleached all-purpose flour

1/2 teaspoon salt

2 tablespoons extra virgin olive oil

1 Dissolve yeast in 1/2 cup warm water. Stir in 1 tablespoon flour, place the cup in a larger bowl of very hot water so that the water comes two-thirds of the way up the sides of the cup, and let sit for 10 to 15 minutes, or until the yeast is foamy.

2 Pour the flour and salt into a large bowl and add the yeast, oil, and 3/4 cup warm water. Stir with a fork for a thick dough that does not stick to the sides of the bowl.

3 Turn the dough out onto a floured surface and, with floured hands, knead energetically for 7 to 8 minutes. If too sticky, add more flour to the work surface. When done, the dough should be smooth, dry, and elastic. Oil a bowl with olive oil and place the dough in the bowl, rolling it around to coat all sides. Cover with a damp cloth and let rise until doubled, about 1 hour.

Variations Place the flour and salt in Step 2 in a food processor with a strong motor. With motor running, pour the yeast, oil, and water through the feed tube one at a time and process until dough forms a ball. Proceed with Step 3.

Storage Can be made earlier in the day, wrapped tightly in plastic wrap, and refrigerated. Can also be frozen for up to 1 month. In either case, return to room temperature before using.

appendix
B

Italian Wines

ITALIANS ARE INCREDIBLY EGALITARIAN WHEN IT COMES TO WINE ON THE TABLE. Wine is an everyday beverage (no meal is served without wine) and—except for special occasions—there is no great stress laid on the prestige of estate-bottled wines or great vintages. Much more relaxed than their French or German neighbors when it comes to scrutinizing labels, Italians take their wine where and when they find it.

All this notwithstanding, most wine sellers agree that the most exciting developments in wine today are happening on the Italian peninsula. Italian wines are now talked about and pursued with the same fervor once applied to those from France. The world's largest producer of wine, Italy is not only the geographical origin of wine production, with over 3,000 years of experience, but the current source of over 2,500 different labels from 18 regions and 98 provinces. Many are classified as D.O.C., which means that the wine has been made according to stringent laws governing where and how the wine can be made. More recently, the Italian government has taken yet another step toward upgrading vinification standards and has moved beyond D.O.C. regulations to the even more prestigious D.O.C.G.; the "G" stands for *garantita*, meaning that tasting control boards guarantee the wine's stylistic authenticity.

Each recipe, except the dessert recipes, in this book concludes with a Wine Suggestion. In adding this piece of information, I have tried to adhere to the Italian style of having wine be an integral part of the meal without making any great fuss over producers and vintages. Each recipe simply states Dry White, Medium-Sweet White, Medium-bodied Red or Full-bodied Red. In my mind, those specifications speak for themselves. But then I realized that, since each recipe originates from a certain geographic region, some of you might want to lend your dishes a further degree of authenticity by pairing them with an appropriately regional wine. And so I present the following list of wines catalogued by both type and region. Keep in mind that wines assume different personalities based on both growing conditions and the style of the producer. So that, for example, while I have listed "Montepulciano d'Abruzzo" under "Medium-bodied Red," the same type of wine could also be astoundingly full-bodied given a different method of vinification.

Dry White

Prosecco
(Friuli-Venezia Giulia)

Frascati (Lazio)

Trebbiano (Many regions)

Verdicchio (Le Marches)

Soave
(Friuli-Venezia Giulia)

Lacrima Christi (Lazio)

Grechetto (Umbria)

Vernaccia (Tuscany)

Gavi (Piedmont)

Locorotondo (Puglia)

Alcamo (Sicily)

Franciacorta White
(Lombardy)

Cinqueterre (Liguria)

Montecarlo White
(Tuscany)

Medium-Sweet

Tocai (Friuli-Venezia
Giulia)

Est! Est! Est! (Lazio)

Colomba Platino (Sicily)

Vermentino (Many regions)

Orvieto (Umbria)

Arneis (Piedmont)

Galestro (Tuscany)

Pomino White (Tuscany)

Fiano di Avellino
(Campania)

Greco di Tufo
(Campania)

Cirò White
(Calabria)

Medium-bodied Red

Dolcetto (Piedmont)

Bardolino (Friuli-Venezia
Giulia)

Montepulciano d'Abruzzo
(Abruzzo)

Santa Maddalena
(Trentino-Alto Adige)

Lago di Caldaro
(Trentino-Alto Adige)

Nebbiolo (Piedmont)

Carema (Piedmont)

Valpolicella
(Friuli-Venezia Giulia)

Lambrusco (Emilia-
Romagna)

Rosso Conero (Le Marches)

Torgiano (Umbria)

Rosso di Montefalco
(Umbria)

Falerno (Campania)

Cirò Red (Calabria)

Pomino Red (Tuscany)

Full-Bodied Red

Barolo (Piedmont)

Barbaresco (Piedmont)

Chianti Classico (Tuscany)

Brunello di Montalcino
(Tuscany)

Carmignano (Tuscany)

Vino Nobile di
Montepulciano (Tuscany)

Amarone (Lombardy)

Aglianico (Basilicata)

Cannonau (Sardinia)

Gattinara (Piedmont)

Torgiano Riserva (Umbria)

Taurasi (Campania)

Salice Salentino (Puglia)

Recioto (Lombardy)

Barbarossa VdT
(Emilia-Romagna)

Sassicaia (Tuscany)

Ornellaia (Tuscany)

appendix C

Calendar of Festivals

January

1/6—Abruzzo, many small villages. *Pasquelle* (Twelfth Night). Religious processions.

1/6—Faenza (Emilia-Romagna). *La Nott de Biso.* Twelfth Night celebration featuring music, fireworks, and drinking of hot mulled wine.

1/6—Milan (Lombardy). Feast of The Three Kings. Huge procession including everything from drum majorettes to caged lions to Milan's Civic Band to the Three Kings themselves.

1/17—Novoli (Puglia). Feast of St. Anthony. Huge bonfire in main piazza.

1/17—Cansana (Abruzzo). Feast of St. Anthony. Benediction of animals held in the main piazza.

Sunday after 1/17—Tuscania (Lazio). *Sagra della Fritella di Tuscania.* Processions including cowboys, marching bands, cattle exhibits, and the preparation of cauliflower fritters.

February

Last Friday before Lent—Verona (Lombardy). *Baccanal del Gnoco.* Gnocchi Festival encompassing music, dancing and the election of the *Papá del Gnoco,* the Festival Father.

Fat Tuesday—Mamoiada (Sardinia). Carnival. Musicians, medieval costumes, historic reenactments.

Fat Tuesday—Tossignano and Borgo di Tossignano (Emilia-Romagna). Dual celebrations taking place two miles from each other, both involving music and dancing: Polenta Sagra in the former and Maccheroni Sagra in the latter.

Fat Tuesday—Zignago (Liguria). *Ballo Mascherato*—masked ball. Costumed ball held in main piazza.

Halfway through Lent—San Lorenzo in Campo (Le Marche). *Mezzaquaresima.* Celebration of having arrived halfway through a period of fasting. Puppet-burning, music, games.

March

3/1—Genoa (Liguria). *Il Mare dei Tyrreni.* Harborside festival featuring nautical lectures, boat tours, demonstrations of ancient fishing implements.

Holy Thursday/Good Friday—San Fratello (Sicily). Costumed reenaction of Christ's passion takes place throughout the city.

Good Friday—Gubbio (Umbria). Choral Procession. Two nationally renowned choruses square off side by side. Heavily attended.

Good Friday—Foggia (Puglia). Historic reenactment of the events leading up to Christ's death.

Good Friday—Taranto (Puglia). Procession involving eight living dioramas representing Christ's journey on route to his crucifixion.

Holy Saturday—Modica (Sicily). *Vasa vasa.* Staged dramatizations throughout the city depicting Christ's suffering and death.

Easter Sunday/Monday—Tredozio (Emilia-Romagna). Egg Festival. Games, sporting competitions, costumes, processions, and the famous "Egg Contest," wherein participants attempt—in groups of two—to wrestle eggs from each other without breaking them.

Monday after Easter—Ottaviano (Campania). Feast of the Madonna dell'Arco. Elaborate prayer services, dramatizations, and musical performances.

April

First weekend—Canossa (Emilia-Romagna). *Il Perdono di Canossa.* Staged reenactment of a thirteenth-century event in the history of Canossa.

Second weekend—Chivasso (Piedmont). Egg Festival. A local event featuring egg throws, egg swaps, and egg marathons.

4/23—Susa, Bagnasco a Fenestrelle, and Rocca Grimalda, all in western Piedmont.
San Giorgio Festival/Dance of the Sabers. Costumes, dancing, swordplay.

4/30—Bolzano (Trentino-Alto Adige). Flower Festival. Flower exhibits, judgings, music, dance.

Ongoing, eight weekends through April and May—Terlano (Trentino-Alto Adige).
Asparagus Festival featuring *vino degli asparagi*—asparagus wine—bottled specifically for this event.

May

5/1—Assisi (Umbria). *Calendomaggio.* May Day celebration, featuring music contests involving ancient instruments, equestrian competitions, and flagmanship. Heavily attended.

5/1—Gualdo Tadino (Emilia-Romagna). Celebration of May revolving around the installation of a huge tree in the main piazza.

5/4—Bagnone (Tuscany). Onion and Wild Asparagus Festival. Music, dancing.

5/4—Cagliari (Sardninia). *Sagra di Sant Efisio.* Procession in traditional dress.

First Thursday—Cocullo (Abruzzo). Snake Festival. Music, dancing, people exhibiting snakes. Heavily attended.

First Sunday—Santa Sofia d'Epiro (Calabria). Festival of St. Athanasius. Albanian festival held in traditional dress.

Second Sunday—Camogli (Liguria). World's Largest Fish Fry. Tons of fish cooked in huge frying pan on beach. Heavily attended.

5/14—Marta (Lazio). *Le Passate.* Trade union festival featuring costumes, plays, tool exhibits, and demonstrations.

5/15—Gubbio (Umbria). Feast of St. Ubaldo. Procession with candles and dioramas.

5/17—Milan (Lombardy). Feast of St. Ambrogio/ *O bei, o bei.* Costumed procession marks the opening day of La Scala Opera season. Very heavily attended.

One Sunday in mid-May—Throughout Piedmont and Tuscany. *Cantine Aperte.* Open wine and food tastings at many of the two regions' fine wineries.

5/20—Sagliano Micca (Piedmont). Cherry Sagra. Music, dancing.

Around the third Sunday—Santena (Piedmont). *Sagra Primaverile*. Spring Festival.

5/29—Milan (Lombardy). Liberation Festival. Procession of regally costumed horses. Heavily attended.

Third Sunday—Recco (Liguria). Focaccia Festival. Centerpiece of this event is a twelve-foot-round focaccia baked in the central piazza.

Third Sunday—Sassari (Sardinia). *Cavalcatta*. Celebration of folkloric traditions with costumes, jousts, dancing, musical performances, and equestrian parades.

Third Sunday—Acquapendente (Lazio). Festival of the Mid-May Madonna. Music, dancing.

Third weekend—Lavezzola (Emilia-Romagna). *Sagra dei Tortellini*. Festival featuring all types of stuffed pasta.

Last Sunday—Ferrara (Lombardy). St. George's Palio. Horse and donkey racing, historical costumes. Heavily attended.

End of May—Taormina (Sicily). Festival of Costumes and Sicilian Carts. Procession of historic carts with medieval costumes and horses adorned in traditional banners. Heavily attended.

Every weekend—Scarparia (Tuscany). *Sagra della ricotta*. Ricotta festival featuring music and dancing.

Last weekend May, first weekend June—Valli di Ostellato (Emilia-Romagna). *Le Valli in Tavola*. Competition involving professional chefs, prix-fixe meals judged by general public.

June

First Sunday—Pontedassio (Liguria). Basil Sagra. Music, dancing.

6/13—Throughout Sicily. Feast of St. Anthony of Padova. Generally involves city-wide processions.

Second weekend—Combai (Lombardy). Festival of Verdiso Wine. Tastings, lectures, music.

Three days in mid-June—Arbus (Sardinia). Feast of St. Anthony of Santadi. Twenty-three-mile-long procession of ox-drawn carts, costumed horsemen, and musicians.

Mid-June—Milano Marritima (Emilia-Romagna). *Piadina d'autore.* Piadina bakeoff (piadina is a simple, flat focaccia native to this region.)

Mid-June—Brinidisi (Puglia). *Corpus Domini.* Costumed equestrians, carpets of flowers, procession.

Mid-June—Campobasso (Molise). *Corpus Domini.* Procession of the mysteries. Religious procession over a carpet of flowers.

Mid-June—Spello (Umbria). *Corpus Domini.* Extravagant procession on fresh flower carpets. Heavily attended.

6/15—Garbigna (Piedmont). Cherry Sagra. Music, dancing, cherry-tart bakeoff.

Third weekend—Bëileun (Val d'Aosta). *Sagra della Fiocca.* Whipped cream festival, 6.2 mile race through the mountains, trip to natural grottoes for cream whipping demonstration and tasting.

Third weekend—Mottalciata (Piedmont). Grape, Bean and Rice Festival. Music, dancing.

6/22—Nola (Campania). Lily Festival. Procession involving eight 75-foot bell towers, plays, dancing, final benediction by bishop. Heavily attended.

6/24—Mondello (Sicily). Feast of St. John the Baptist. Singing, dancing.

6/24—Florence (Tuscany). Feast of St. John the Baptist. Local soccer tournament. Heavily attended.

6/29—Aragona (Sicily). Feast of St. Paul. Snake exhibitions, ox-drawn carts, procession of musicians playing ancient musical instruments.

6/29—Palermo (Sicily). Feast of St. Peter. Music, dancing, stalls selling foods and knicknacks in the shape of keys (St. Peter was said to hold the keys to heaven).

July

7/6—Torre Pellice (Piedmont). Summer Festival. Featuring music, dancing and seasonal produce.

7/8—Palermo (Sicily). Festival of St. Rosalia. City-wide celebration involving processional floats, music and staged presentations. Very heavily attended.

7/16—Throughout Italy. Madonna del Carmine. Processions, most involving statues of the Madonna and floats.

First two weekends—Massarosa (Tuscany). Crab Festival. Music, dancing.

Second Sunday—Minturno (Campania). Wheat Festival. Demonstrations of ancient wheat-harvesting techniques.

Second weekend—Frosolone (Molise). Mountain Festival and Caciocavallo Cheese Fair. Cultural presentations, sporting events, cheesemaking demonstrations.

Mid-July to mid-August—Villa Basilica (Tuscany). *Sagra del Pane.* Bread Festival featuring music and dancing.

Third Saturday—Venice (Friuli-Venezia-Giulia). Feast of Christ the Redeemer. Flotilla of gondolas carrying costumed participants. Very heavily attended.

7/24—Caltagirone (Sicily). *Festa di San Giacomo.* Procession involving St. James's relics culminating in a mass candlelighting ritual in Santa Maria del Monte Church.

Next-to-last Sunday—Perloz (Val d'Aosta). *Festa du pan ner.* Black Bread Festival involving a 600-year-old outdoor oven used to bake the bread.

Last weekend—Lucca (Tuscany). Folkloric Festival. Musical performances, costumes, crafts demonstrations.

August

8/1—Santadi (Sardinia). Gastronomic Festival. Local produce and traditional foods.

First two weeks—Montefiascone (Lazio). Wine Festival celebrating Est! Est! Est!, one of the Lazio's great white wines.

8/10—Cervia (Emilia-Romagna). Feast of Saint Lorenzo. Procession through a pine forest followed by a communal swim.

First weekend—Villanovafranca (Sardinia). *La Festa dell'emigrato*—Immigrant Festival celebrating those who left, many of whom return for this event. Folkloric costumes, music, and dancing.

Second weekend—Sestri Levante (Liguria). Minestrone Sagra. Music, dancing.

8/13–14—Messina (Sicily). *I Giganti.* Giant's Day. Procession of two giant papier-mâché statues representing the legendary god and goddess who founded the town. Followed the next day (8/15) by the Feast of the Assumption, which encompasses a 45-foot-high float pulled by 1,000 residents. Heavily attended.

8/14—Sassari (Sardinia). Feast of the Assumption of the Virgin/*I Candalieri di Sassari.* Fireworks, procession, flagmanship.

8/15—Throughout Italy. The Feast of the Assumption. National holiday signifying the start of summer vacations.

8/15—Bovalino Marina (Calabria). Feast of St. Francis of Paola. Procession of boats.

8/16—Palmi (Calabria). Feast of Saint Rocco of Montpellier. Procession of *spinati*—people encased in spiny twig cases for purposes of self-mutilation.

8/16—Camogli (Liguria). Feast of Saint Rocco, patron of animals. Procession of animals and communal benediction in church.

Third week—Sanframondi (Campania). *I Battenti di Guardia Sanframondi.* Procession and liturgical reenactment. Most noted for 3,000 men and women who beat themselves penitently in the main piazza.

Third Sunday—Livenza (Friuli-Venezia-Giulia). *Sagra degli Osei.* Festival of Small Birds. Open-air concerts, art shows, outdoor cabaret.

Third Sunday—Marina di Gioiosa (Calabria). Festival of the Madonna del Carmine. Procession of boats.

Third Sunday—Ravascletto (Friuli-Venezia Giulia). *Fiesta Tas Corts.* Open-door festival. Local housewives cook traditional foods for visitors whom they invite into their homes.

Third weekend—Mazaro del Vallo (Sicily). St. Vito's Day. Procession led by fishermen starts at 4 A.M. on beach followed by living float processions throughout the town (actors and actresses reenacting scenes from the life of Christ).

Third weekend—San Vito (Sardinia). *Sagra delle Launeddas.* Music festival featuring ancient wind instruments.

Next-to-last Sunday—Marineo (Sicily). Feast of St. Ciro. Procession of adorned horses and donkeys pulling ancient carts.

Last Sunday—Termoli (Molise). Fish festival held on waterfront.

Last two weekends—Caprarola (Lazio). Walnut Sagra. Music and dancing.

8/27—Riva (Trentino-Alto Adige). Night of Fairy Tales. Sailing competition and reenactment of 1439 battle against Venetians. Very heavily attended.

8/28–29—L'Aquila (Abruzzo). *Perdonanza all'Aquila.* Staged dramatizations of historical events.

September

First Sunday—Venice (Friuli-Venezia Giulia). *Regata Storica.* Procession of magnificently decorated boats and gondolas, and two-oared gondola race. Very heavily attended.

First Sunday—Paluzza (Friuli-Venezia Giulia). *Sagre di Place.* Italian-Austrian festival.

First Sunday—Fagagna (Friuli-Venezia Giulia). *Palio degli asini.* Historic donkey palio (race).

9/3—Viterbo (Lazio). Feast of Saint Rosa. Candlelit procession involving thirty-five-foot-high stone statue.

9/7—Tindari (Sicily). Feast of the Black Madonna. Procession to mountain sanctuary followed by festival in the main piazza.

9/7—Avellino (Campania). Feast of the Madonna of Monte Virgine. Pilgrimage up 3,600-foot mountain at 3 A.M.

First two weeks—Budoia (Friuli-Venezia Giulia). *Festa dei funghi.* Mushroom festival involving exhibits and a judging.

Second Monday—Lucca (Tuscany). Feast of the Volto Santo. City-wide candlelight procession with costumes and flags. Heavily attended.

Second week—Bernareggio (Lombardy). *La Sagra del Paese.* Local city-wide festival featuring musical performances, sporting competitions, folkloric demonstrations, and exhibits of ancient wind instruments.

Second weekend—Asti (Piedmont). Festival of All Foods. Fifty towns throughout the province of Asti celebrate foods and wine of the region.

9/19—Naples (Campania). Feast of San Gennaro. Huge procession after viewing of Gennaro's blood liquefaction. Very heavily attended.

Mid-September—Gessate (Lombardy). *Palio del pane.* Bread bakeoff.

Mid-September—San Georgio Morgeto (Calabria). Immigrants Festival honors returning those who left in earlier part of century.

Third Saturday—Viterbo (Lazio). *Festa del Salvatore.* Local procession, tables outside houses.

Third Sunday—Setterquerce (Trentino-Alto Adige). *Sagra dell uva.* Wine festival, floats, historic games.

9/29—Campo Catino (Abruzzo). Feast of St. Michael the Archangel. Local harvest festival.

October

First Sunday—Marino (Lazio). Wine and Harvest Festival. Parade through town, theatrical reenactments, music, horse-drawn cortege.

First Sunday—Alba (Piedmont). Truffle Festival/Donkey Palio. Donkey race and truffle exhibits. Very heavily attended.

10/7—Throughout Veneto. Feast of Sacred Rosary. Processions and local food offerings.

Second Sunday—Gressari (Val d'Aosta). Apple Festival. Varietal judging.

10/16—Caposele (Campannia). Feast of Saint Gerard. Pilgrimage to Materdomini Sanctuary.

Third Sunday—Croix Noire (Val d'Aosta). *La bataille des reines.* Cattle show, music, dancing.

Mid-October—Sillano (Tuscany). Cypress Tree Festival. Local harvest celebration.

Last Sunday—Rufina (Tuscany). Feast of Saint Michael. Benediction of wine, open admission to wine museum, and antique shows.

Late October—Road between Asti and Alba (Piedmont). Harvest Festival, dance contests, bocce competition.

Late October—Roncegno (Trentino-Alto Adige). Chestnut Festival. Music, dancing.

10/31—Throughout Italy. All Soul's Day. Family gatherings at local cemeteries.

November

11/1—Throughout Italy. All Saint's Day. National holiday. Family gatherings for festive meals to honor ancestors.

Beginning of month—Sauris (Friuli-Venezia Giulia.) *Capodanno.* Local Celtic New Year festival celebrating the start of the growing season.

11/18—Frediano (Tuscany). Feast of Saint Frediano. Winter festival involving musical performances, poetry recitals, and communal lunch.

Middle of month—Mone Corona (Umbria). Truffle Sagra. Music, dancing.

Sunday nearest the 25th—Gorgonzola (Lombardy). Feast of St. Catherine. Music, dancing.

Last Sunday—Spello (Umbria). Olive Festival and Bruschetta Sagra. Music and dancing.

December

All December—Bolzan/Merano/Bressanone (Trentino-Alto Adige). *Christkindlmärkte.* Open-air Christmas market.

All December—Throughout Tuscany. Open-air Christmas nativity displays.

12/6—Throughout Puglia. Feast of Saint Nicholas. Pugliese Christmas.

12/8—Rome (Lazio). Feast of the Immaculate Conception. National holiday; in Rome, people lay sampling of traditional foods and flowers at the base of the Spanish Steps. Fireworks in Trastevere.

12/9—Ascoli Piceno (Le Marche). Feast of the Madonna of Loreto. Open-door parties wherein visitors wander in and out of local houses.

12/24—Cassano allo Jonio (Basilicata). On Christmas Eve, young men parade through town after dark playing various types of pan flutes while old men sing traditional songs.

12/24—Nereto (Le Marche). *'Ndocciata.* Torchlight procession for Christmas eve.

12/31—Gambarie (Calabria). *La Pupa.* Procession with trumpets led by *la pupa* (an old witchlike Santa Claus) handing out cookies to children.

appendix
D

Mail-Order Sources

IF YOU CANNOT FIND SPICY SICILIAN OLIVES and smoked chestnut flour in the specialty shops and gourmet stores in your area, you might try one of the following:

Balducci's
424 Avenue of the Americas
New York, NY 10011
800/822-1444 or 800/247-2450

Buon Italia
75 Ninth Avenue
New York, NY 10011
212/633-9090
Fax 212/633-9717

Dean & DeLuca
560 Broadway
New York, NY 10012
800/221-7714

Manganaro Foods
488 Ninth Avenue
New York, NY 10018
212/563-5331

Todaro Brothers
555 Second Avenue
New York, NY 10016
212/679-7766

B & L Specialty Foods
500 Denver Avenue South
Seattle, WA 98108
800/328-7278

Vivande
2125 Fillmore Street
San Francisco, CA 94115
415/346-4430

Zingerman's
422 Detroit Street
Ann Arbor, MI 48104
313/769-1625

And for Italian cookware, from pasta machines to pizzelle irons:

Cucina Mia Cookware
P.O. Box 603468
Cleveland, OH 44103
800/766-0300

appendix E

Index

Almond:
    Brittle, Crunchy, 452
    Cookies (Amaretti),
        Sardinian, 454–55
    and Rice Cake, Sweet,
        456–57
    Rum Cake, 426
Anchovy(ies):
    Cheese, and Caper-stuffed
        Calzones, 46–47
    Fried Sage Sandwiches with
        Prosciutto and, 398
    and Olive Savory Pie,
        266–67
    Roasted Hake with
        Rosemary and, 390–91
    Rolls, Deep-fried, 224–25
    Sauce, Panfried Spring
        Lamb with Herbs and,
        324–25
Appetizers, xxii
    Baby Shrimp with Garlic
        Sauce, 42–43
    Blood Orange and Red
        Onion Salad, 32–33
    Bruschetta with Truffles,
        24–25
    Cheese, Anchovy, and
        Caper-stuffed
        Calzones, 46–47
    Farro Salad, 48
    Fontina Cheese and White
        Truffle Fondue, 8–9
    Frittata Kebabs Stuffed with
        Creamed Chick Peas,
        12–13
    Green Olives Stuffed with
        Meat, Battered, and

Fried, 38–39
    Mixed Green Salad Topped
        with Ricotta Rolled in
        a Pistachio Crust,
        40–41
    Olive and Blood Orange
        Salad, 50–51
    Pancetta-wrapped Mussels
        Grilled on Skewers, 49
    Pecorino Empanadas, 22–23
    Polenta Rounds with
        Walnut Sauce, 30–31
    Porcini Canapés Served
        with Wild Boar
        Prosciutto, 26–27
    Porcini Mushroom Sauté,
        16–17
    Rosemary Crepes, 44–45
    Rounds of Robbiola Cheese
        Marinated in Tomato
        Sauce and Balsamic
        Vinegar, 10–11
    Sardinian Semolina Terrine,
        20–21
    Sicilian Rice and Pecorino
        Cheese Croquettes,
        14–15
    Stuffed Zucchini Blossoms,
        36–37
    Tuna Carpaccio with
        Lemon-Parsley Sauce,
        34–35
    Walnut, Mozzarella, and
        Prosciutto Sandwiches,
        28–29
    Zucchini Carpaccio with
        Green Peppercorn
        Dressing, 18–19

Apple:
    Doughnuts Scented with
        Grappa, 453
    Pie, Open-faced Christmas,
        438–39
Apricots, Puff Pastry Rounds
    Stuffed with, 444–45
Artichoke(s):
    Cauliflower, Leeks, and
        Broccoli Rabe Braised
        in Balsamic Vinegar
        and Dusted with
        Anise, 164–65
    Fish and Vegetable Salad,
        386–87
    Frittata, 262–63
    and Potato Tart, 190–91
    Spring, Baby Peas Sautéed
        with, 174–75
    Veal Sausages with Fresh
        Fava Beans and, 306–7
Asiago, Baked Gnocchi Made
    with Asparagus, Taleggio
    and, 148–49
Asparagus:
    Baked Gnocchi Made with
        Taleggio, Asiago and,
        148–49
    with Fried Eggs, 259
    Wild, Risotto with, 84–85

Balsamic vinegar, xvii–xviii
    Cauliflower, Artichokes,
        Leeks, and Broccoli
        Rabe Braised in, and
        Dusted with Anise,
        164–65

478

Rounds of Robbiola Cheese Marinated in Tomato Sauce and, 10–11
Sauce, Smoked Provolone Panfried with Oregano and, 292–93
Barley, Chestnut, and White Bean Minestrone, 208–9
Basic recipes, 458–63
Egg Pasta, 461–62
Meat Broth, 460
Pizza Dough, 463
Vegetable Broth, 459
Basil:
Summer Vegetable and Pasta Soup Perfumed with Pesto Cream, 202–3
Trenette with Pesto Sauce, 138–39
Bass, Sea:
Ravioli with Marjoram Sauce, 392–93
Soup, Spicy, 399
Bean(s):
Cannelini, Braised with Prosciutto and Herbs, 172–73
Cold Soup of Dried Favas and Wild Fennel, 213
Fava, and Sausage Soup, 218–19
Fava, Sausage, and Potato Winter Stew, 188–89
Fresh Fava, Veal Sausages with Artichokes and, 306–7
and Rice, Piedmont-style, 82–83
The Virtues (Many Vegetable Soup), 220–21
White, Barley and Chestnut Minestrone, 208–9
White, Winter Pasta with Chick Peas, Lentils and, 134–35
see also Chick Peas
Beef:
Broth with Tiny Meatballs, 212

Goulash with Polenta, 73
Mozzarella-stuffed Meatballs Braised in Fresh Tomatoes, 320–21
Polenta Layered with Meat Sauce, 70–71
Polenta with Skewered Meats, 68–69
Sirloin Braised in Barolo, 304–5
Stew, Creamy Polenta with, 76–77
Blueberries, Grappa-marinated, 427
Boar, Wild:
Braised with Pine Nuts, Raisins, Chocolate, and Prunes, 346–47
Prosciutto, Porcini Canapés Served with, 26–27
Borage Fritters, 170
Bread (prepared):
Frittata, Light Golden, 264
Garlic-rubbed, Fish Soup with, 365
and Mozzarella Soup, Sardinian, 216–17
Squares Stuffed with Mozzarella and Olive Paste, Fried, 284
Breads, 192
Alpine Fruit, 436–37
Braided Pepper Biscuits, 226–27
Butternut Squash, 246–47
Deep-fried Anchovy Rolls, 224–25
Onion and Mozzarella Ring, 232–33
Toasted Flat, 234–35
see also Focaccias
Broccoli Rabe:
Cauliflower, Artichokes, and Leeks Braised in Balsamic Vinegar and Dusted with Anise, 164–65
Gnocchetti with Chick Peas and, 116–17
Broths, basic:

Meat, 460
Vegetable, 459
Bruschetta with Truffles, 24–25
Buckwheat:
Pasta with Potatoes and Cabbage, 126–27
Polenta, Baked, 74
Butternut Squash:
Bread, 246–47
Cream of, Soup, 214–15
Gnocchi, 144–45
Marinated, Chioggia-style, 169

Cabbage:
Buckwheat Pasta with Potatoes and, 126–27
Twelfth Night Stuffed Savoy, 184–85
Winter, Polenta with Braised Duck and, 67
Caciocavallo:
Country-style Cheese and Prosciutto Pie, 272–73
Lightly Smoked, 290
Scamorza, and Potato Terrine, 291
and Scamorze Cheeses, Baked Kebabs Made with, 288–89
Cakes:
Almond-Rum, 426
Chestnut, with Pignolis and Raisins, 425
Chocolate Ricotta Refrigerator, 428–29
Hazelnut Chocolate Pudding, 446
Sweet Mascarpone Cheese, Flavored with Marsala, 450
Sweet Rice and Almond, 456–57
Calabria, 353–63
Calendar of Festivals, 466–75
Calzones:
Cheese, Anchovy, and Caper-stuffed, 46–47
Eggplant, Red Pepper, and Black Olive, 280–81
Campania, 249–57

Caper(s):
  Braised Escarole with Black Olives and, 178–79
  Cheese, and Anchovy-stuffed Calzones, 46–47
  Escarole, Curly Endive, and Black Olive Tart, 268–69
  Parsley Sauce, Veal Scaloppine with, 322–23
  Red Peppers Roasted with Olives, Fresh Oregano and, 186–87
  Tuna Steaks Baked with Olives, Fresh Tomatoes and, 405
Cardoons, Gratinéed, 162–63
Cauliflower:
  Artichokes, Leeks, and Broccoli Rabe Braised in Balsamic Vinegar and Dusted with Anise, 164–65
  Fish and Vegetable Salad, 386–87
  Fritters, 171
  Hollow Spaghetti with, 136–37
Chard:
  Green Gnocchi with Butter and Sage Sauce, 142–43
  and Mint Ravioli with Sardinian Pecorino, 106–7
  and Ricotta Tart, 278–79
  Stuffed Pizza Made with Sundried Tomatoes and, 270–71
  The Virtues (Many Vegetable Soup), 220–21
Cheese(s), xviii–xix, 248
  Anchovy, and Caper-stuffed Calzones, 46–47
  Baked Gnocchi Made with Asparagus, Taleggio, and Asiago, 148–49

Cake Flavored with Marsala, Sweet Mascarpone, 450
Chard and Mint Ravioli with Sardinian Pecorino, 106–7
Chard and Ricotta Tart, 278–79
Chocolate Ricotta Refrigerator Cake, 428–29
Creamy Ricotta Tart, 418–19
Egg Dumplings with Smoked Ricotta and Dark Chocolate, 110–11
Fontina, and Polenta Kebabs, Fried, 66
Fontina, and White Truffle Fondue, 8–9
Fried Bread Squares Stuffed with Mozzarella and Olive Paste, 284
Fried Mozzarella Rounds, 285
Lightly Smoked Caciocavallo, 290
Mixed Green Salad Topped with Ricotta Rolled in a Pistachio Crust, 40–41
Mozzarella-stuffed Meatballs Braised in Fresh Tomatoes, 320–21
Onion and Mozzarella Ring Bread, 232–33
Oven-poached Eggs with Prosciutto and, 258
Pasta Dumplings with Mascarpone, 114–15
Pastry Cylinders Stuffed with Sweet Ricotta and Chocolate, 442–43
Pecorino, and Rice Croquettes, Sicilian, 14–15
Pecorino, Spaghetti with Black Pepper and, 113
Pecorino Empanadas, 22–23

Potato Gnocchi with Gorgonzola Sauce, 150–51
and Prosciutto Pie, Country-style, 272–73
Rounds of Robbiola, Marinated in Tomato Sauce and Balsamic Vinegar, 10–11
Sardinian Bread and Mozzarella Soup, 216–17
Scamorza, Caciocavallo, and Potato Terrine, 291
Scamorze and Caciocavallo, Baked Kebabs Made with, 288–89
Shepherd's Pasta with Fresh Ricotta, 112
Smoked Provolone Pan-fried with Oregano and Balsamic Vinegar Sauce, 292–93
Soup, Thick and Creamy Alpine, 204
Stracchino, Fried Polenta with, 72
-stuffed Focaccia, 242–43
Sweet Ricotta Fritters, 282–83
Timballo, St. John's Day, 276–77
Walnut, Mozzarella, and Prosciutto Sandwiches, 28–29
Wedges, Fried, 286–87
Cherries, Black, Risotto with, 90–91
Chestnut(s):
  Barley, and White Bean Minestrone, 208–9
  Cake with Pignolis and Raisins, 425
  Wine-braised, 168
Chicken:
  Breast Stuffed with Vegetables and Braised in White Wine and Heavy Cream, Rolled, 340–41

Broth with Grated Pasta,
206–7
Green Olives Stuffed with
Meat, Battered, and
Fried, 38–39
Lamb, and Pork Kebabs
Grilled with Sage and
Pancetta, 348
Sautéed, with Poached
Shrimp and Fried
Eggs, 334–35
Stuffed with Walnuts,
336–37
Veal, Pork, and Guinea Hen
Cooked with Tomatoes
and Herbs, 310–11
Chick Peas:
Couscous with, 108–9
Creamed, Frittata Kebabs
Stuffed with, 12–13
Gnocchetti with Broccoli
Rabe and, 116–17
The Virtues (Many
Vegetable Soup),
220–21
Winter Pasta with Lentils,
White Beans and,
134–35
Chocolate:
-covered Walnut-stuffed
Figs, 441
Dark, Egg Dumplings with
Smoked Ricotta and,
110–11
Duck Cooked in White
Wine and, 312–13
Hazelnut Pudding Cake,
446
Pastry Cylinders Stuffed
with Sweet Ricotta
and, 442–43
Ricotta Refrigerator Cake,
428–29
Wild Boar Braised with
Pine Nuts, Raisins,
Prunes and, 346–47
Clams:
Fresh, in Tomato-Parsley
Broth, 367

Shellfish Salad with
Lemon-Mustard
Vinaigrette, 400–401
Codfish:
and Potatoes, Poached, with
Parsley Pesto, 394–95
Salad with Fried Polenta
Wedges, 402–3
Cookies:
Almond (Amaretti),
Sardinian, 454–55
Butter Ring, 424
Cornmeal, xxi
Scones, 422–23
Couscous with Chick Peas,
108–9
Crepes, Rosemary, 44–45
Croquettes:
Fried Risotto, 88–89
Sicilian Rice and Pecorino
Cheese, 14–15
Custard Tart, Kiwi, 420–21

Desserts, 406
Almond-Rum Cake, 426
Alpine Fruit Bread, 436–37
Apple Doughnuts Scented
with Grappa, 453
Butter Ring Cookies, 424
Chestnut Cake with
Pignolis and Raisins,
425
Chocolate-covered Walnut-
stuffed Figs, 441
Chocolate Ricotta
Refrigerator Cake,
428–29
Cornmeal Scones, 422–23
Creamy Ricotta Tart,
418–19
Crunchy Almond Brittle, 452
Fig and Nut Wafers,
448–49
Fresh Figs Preserved in
Rum Syrup, 451
Grappa-marinated
Blueberries, 427
Hazelnut Chocolate
Pudding Cake, 446

Hazelnut Honey Nougat,
430–31
Kiwi Custard Tart, 420–21
Marsala-flavored Fruit and
Nut Rolls, 434–35
Open-faced Christmas
Apple Pie, 438–39
Pastry Cylinders Stuffed
with Sweet Ricotta and
Chocolate, 442–43
Puff Pastry Rounds Stuffed
with Apricots, 444–45
Sardinian Amaretti
(Almond Cookies),
454–55
Sweet Mascarpone Cheese
Cake Flavored with
Marsala, 450
Sweet Polenta Fritters,
432–33
Sweet Rice and Almond
Cake, 456–57
Watermelon and Pistachio
Sorbet, 440
Whole Candied Lemons,
447
Doughnuts, Apple, Scented
with Grappa, 453
Dourade, Oven-Roasted,
Served on a Bed of Potato
Wafers, 370–71
Duck:
Braised, Polenta with
Winter Cabbage and,
67
Cooked in White Wine and
Chocolate, 312–13
Sauce, Spaghetti Tubes
with, 120–21
Dumplings:
Egg, with Smoked Ricotta
and Dark Chocolate,
110–11
Pasta, with Mascarpone,
114–15
Egg Dumplings with Smoked
Ricotta and Dark
Chocolate, 110–11
Egg Pasta, Basic, 461–62

Eggplant:
  Four Variations of Pizza
    Tartlets, 240–41
  Red Pepper, and Black
    Olive Calzone, 280–81
  Red Pepper, and Prosciutto
    Terrine, 166–67
  Red Pepper, Potato, and
    Black Olive Stew,
    180–81
  Timballo, 132–33
Eggs, 248
  Artichoke Frittata, 262–63
  Fried, Asparagus with, 259
  Fried, Sautéed Chicken
    with Poached Shrimp
    and, 334–35
  Frittata Kebabs Stuffed with
    Creamed Chick Peas,
    12–13
  Light, Golden Bread
    Frittata, 264
  Oven-poached, with
    Prosciutto and Fontina,
    258
  Sliced Frittata Rounds
    Made with Rice and
    Thyme-scented Oven-
    dried Tomatoes,
    260–61
  White Truffle Frittata, 265
Emilia–Romagna, 95–103
Empanadas, Pecorino, 22–23
Endive, curly:
  Escarole, Capers, and
    Black Olive Tart,
    268–69
  The Virtues (Many
    Vegetable Soup),
    220–21
Escarole:
  Braised, with Capers and
    Black Olives, 178–79
  Curly Endive, Capers, and
    Black Olive Tart,
    268–69
Farro:
  Salad, 48
  Soup, 205

Fava bean(s):
  Dried, Cold Soup of Wild
    Fennel and, 213
  Fresh, Veal Sausages with
    Artichokes and, 306–7
  Sausage, and Potato Winter
    Stew, 188–89
  and Sausage Soup, 218–19
  The Virtues (Many
    Vegetable Soup),
    220–21
  Winter Pasta with Chick
    Peas, Lentils, and
    White Beans, 134–35
Fennel, Wild, Cold Soup of
  Dried Favas and, 213
Festivals, Calendar of, 466–75
Fig(s):
  Chocolate-covered Walnut-
    stuffed, 441
  Fresh, Preserved in Rum
    Syrup, 451
  and Nut Wafers, 448–49
Fish, 352
  Breaded Swordfish Kebabs
    with Wedges of Red
    Onion, 388–89
  Codfish Salad with Fried
    Polenta Wedges, 402–3
  Freshwater Trout with
    Herbs and Lemon
    Fragrance, 381
  Fried Sardines Marinated
    with Onions, 382–83
  Gratinéed Sardine Rolls
    Stuffed with Parsley
    and Pignoli Pesto,
    376–77
  Mullet Roasted in Salt, 366
  Oven-Roasted Dourade
    Served on a Bed of
    Potato Wafers, 370–71
  Panfried Royal Perch, 380
  Poached Codfish and
    Potatoes with Parsley
    Pesto, 394–95
  Roasted Hake with
    Anchovies and
    Rosemary, 390–91

Saint Vito's Day Pizza,
  238–39
Sardines Baked with
  Tomatoes and Parsley-
  Garlic Pesto, 372–73
Sea Bass Ravioli with
  Marjoram Sauce,
  392–93
Soup, Tuscan, 374–75
Soup with Garlic-rubbed
  Bread, 365
Spaghetti with Tuna and
  Porcini Mushrooms,
  118–19
Spicy Sea Bass Soup, 399
Sturgeon Steaks Braised in
  White Wine and
  Tomatoes and Served
  with Creamy Polenta,
  384–85
Swordfish Steaks Baked
  with Tomatoes,
  Raisins, and Olives,
  378–79
Tuna Carpaccio with
  Lemon-Parsley Sauce,
  34–35
Tuna Steaks Baked
  with Olives, Capers,
  and Fresh Tomatoes,
  405
and Vegetable Salad,
  386–87
see also Anchovy
Focaccias, 192
  Cheese-stuffed, 242–43
  with Green Olives, 244–45
  Rosemary, 230–31
Fondue, Fontina Cheese and
  White Truffle, 8–9
Fontina Cheese:
  Oven-poached Eggs with
    Prosciutto and, 258
  and Polenta Kebabs, Fried,
    66
  and White Truffle Fondue,
    8–9
Frittata(s):
  Artichoke, 262–63

482

Kebabs Stuffed with
Creamed Chick Peas,
12–13
Light, Golden Bread, 264
Rounds Made with Rice
and Thyme-scented
Oven-dried Tomatoes,
Sliced, 260–61
White Truffle, 265
Fritters:
Borage, 170
Cauliflower, 171
Sweet Polenta, 432–33
Sweet Ricotta, 282–83
Fruit:
Bread, Alpine, 436–37
and Nut Rolls, Marsala-
flavored, 434–35
see also specific fruits

Game, 294
Chicken, Veal, Pork, and
Guinea Hen Cooked
with Tomatoes and
Herbs, 310–11
Duck Cooked in White
Wine and Chocolate,
312–13
Gratinéed Rabbit, 342–43
Guinea Hen Cooked in
Terra-cotta, 350–51
Hare with Red Wine Sauce,
330–31
Oven-roasted Rabbit
Stuffed with
Prosciutto, 316–17
Panfried Quail with
Buttered Rice, 338–39
Ragù of Venison with Herbs
and Juniper Berries,
318–19
Roast Pigeon with Black
Olives, 314–15
Truffled Pheasant, 332–33
Wild Boar Braised with
Pine Nuts, Raisins,
Chocolate, and Prunes,
346–47
Garlic:
Parsley Pesto, Sardines

Baked with Tomatoes
and, 372–73
-rubbed Bread, Fish Soup
with, 365
Sauce, Baby Shrimp with,
42–43
Gnocchetti with Chick Peas
and Broccoli Rabe, 116–17
Gnocchi, 94
Baked, Made with
Asparagus, Taleggio,
and Asiago, 148–49
Baked Semolina, 146–47
Butternut Squash, 144–45
Green, with Butter and
Sage Sauce, 142–43
Potato, with Gorgonzola
Sauce, 150–51
Gorgonzola Sauce, Potato
Gnocchi with, 150–51
Goulash with Polenta, 73
Grappa:
Apple Doughnuts Scented
with, 453
-marinated Blueberries, 427
Guinea Hen:
Chicken, Veal, and Pork
Cooked with Tomatoes
and Herbs, 310–11
Cooked in Terra-cotta,
350–51

Hake, Roasted, with
Anchovies and Rosemary,
390–91
Hare with Red Wine Sauce,
330–31
Hazelnut:
Chocolate Pudding Cake,
446
Honey Nougat, 430–31
Herbs, xix
Honey Hazelnut Nougat,
430–31

Ingredients, xvii–xxi

Juniper Berries, Ragù of
Venison with Herbs and,
318–19

Kiwi Custard Tart, 420–21
Lamb:
Chicken, and Pork Kebabs
Grilled with Sage and
Pancetta, 348
Panfried Spring, with Herbs
and Anchovy Sauce,
324–25
Ragù, 308–9
Lasagne, Stuffed, 140–41
Leeks, Cauliflower, Artichokes,
and Broccoli Rabe Braised
in Balsamic Vinegar and
Dusted with Anise,
164–65
Lemon(s):
Fragrance, Freshwater Trout
with Herbs and, 381
Mustard Vinaigrette,
Shellfish Salad with,
400–401
Parsley Sauce, Tuna
Carpaccio with, 34–35
Whole Candied, 447
Zest, Veal Shanks with
Dried Porcini and,
328–29
Lentils:
The Virtues (Many
Vegetable Soup),
220–21
Winter Pasta with Chick
Peas, White Beans and,
134–35

Mail-Order Sources, 476
Marjoram Sauce, Sea Bass
Ravioli with, 392–93
Mascarpone:
Pasta Dumplings with,
114–15
Sweet, Cheese Cake
Flavored with Marsala,
450
Meat(s), 294
Beef Broth with Tiny
Meatballs, 212
Beef Sirloin Braised in
Barolo, 304–5

Broth, Basic, 460

Chicken, Lamb, and Pork Kebabs Grilled with Sage and Pancetta, 348

Chicken, Veal, Pork, and Guinea Hen Cooked with Tomatoes and Herbs, 310–11

Creamy Polenta with Beef Stew, 76–77

Goulash with Polenta, 73

Gratinéed Rabbit, 342–43

Green Olives Stuffed with, Battered, and Fried, 38–39

Grilled Bundles of Herb-stuffed Pork, 349

Hare with Red Wine Sauce, 330–31

Lamb Ragù, 308–9

Mozzarella-stuffed Meatballs Braised in Fresh Tomatoes, 320–21

Oven-roasted Rabbit Stuffed with Prosciutto, 316–17

Panfried Spring Lamb with Herbs and Anchovy Sauce, 324–25

Ragù of Venison with Herbs and Juniper Berries, 318–19

Risotto with Spareribs, 92–93

Sauce, Baked Polenta with, 64–65

Sauce, Polenta Layered with, 70–71

Skewered, Polenta with, 68–69

Veal in Red Wine Ragù, 326–27

Veal Scaloppine with Parsley-Caper Sauce, 322–23

Veal Shanks with Lemon Zest and Dried Porcini, 328–29

Wild Boar Braised with Pine Nuts, Raisins, Chocolate, and Prunes, 346–47

see also Pancetta; Prosciutto

Meatballs:

Mozzarella-stuffed, Braised in Fresh Tomatoes, 320–21

Tiny, Beef Broth with, 212

Mint and Chard Ravioli with Sardinian Pecorino, 106–7

Mozzarella cheese:

and Bread Soup, Sardinian, 216–17

Country-style Cheese and Prosciutto Pie, 272–73

Fried Bread Squares Stuffed with Olive Paste and, 284

and Onion Ring Bread, 232–33

Rounds, Fried, 285

St. John's Day Cheese Timballo, 276–77

-stuffed Meatballs Braised in Fresh Tomatoes, 320–21

Walnut, and Prosciutto Sandwiches, 28–29

Mullet Roasted in Salt, 366

Mushrooms, *see* Porcini mushroom

Mussels:

Baked Stuffed, 368–69

Pancetta-wrapped, Grilled on Skewers, 49

Shellfish Salad with Lemon-Mustard Vinaigrette, 400–401

Soup Made with Fresh Tomatoes and, 222–23

Stuffed with Sausage and Herbs, 396–97

Mustard-Lemon Vinaigrette, Shellfish Salad with, 400–401

Nougat, Hazelnut Honey, 430–31

Nut:

and Fig Wafers, 448–49

and Fruit Rolls, Marsala-flavored, 434–35

see also specific nuts

Olive(s):

and Anchovy Savory Pie, 266–67

Black, Braised Escarole with Capers and, 178–79

Black, Eggplant, Red Pepper and Potato Stew, 180–81

Black, Eggplant and Red Pepper Calzone, 280–81

Black, Escarole, Curly Endive, and Capers Tart, 268–69

Black, Roast Pigeon with, 314–15

and Blood Orange Salad, 50–51

Green, Focaccia with, 244–45

Green, Stuffed with Meat, Battered, and Fried, 38–39

Paste, Fried Bread Squares Stuffed with Mozzarella and, 284

Red Peppers Roasted with Capers, Fresh Oregano and, 186–87

Swordfish Steaks Baked with Tomatoes, Raisins and, 378–79

Tuna Steaks Baked with Capers, Fresh Tomatoes and, 405

Olive oil, xviii

Onion(s):

Fried Sardines Marinated with, 382–83

and Mozzarella Ring Bread, 232–33

Red, and Blood Orange Salad, 32–33

483

Red, Breaded Swordfish Kebabs with Wedges of, 388–89

Sweet, Cooked with Marsala Wine, 183

Orange, Blood:
and Olive Salad, 50–51
and Red Onion Salad, 32–33

Orecchiette, Homemade, with Sundried Tomato Sauce, 104–5

Oregano, fresh:
Red Peppers Roasted with Olives, Capers and, 186–87
Smoked Provolone Pan-fried with Balsamic Vinegar Sauce and, 292–93

Pancetta:
Chicken, Lamb, and Pork Kebabs Grilled with Sage and, 348
Green Olives Stuffed with Meat, Battered, and Fried, 38–39
Polenta with Skewered Meats, 68–69
-wrapped Mussels Grilled on Skewers, 49

Parmigiano-Reggiano cheese, xviii

Parsley:
Caper Sauce, Veal Scaloppine with, 322–23
Garlic Pesto, Sardines Baked with Tomatoes and, 372–73
Lemon Sauce, Tuna Carpaccio with, 34–35
Pesto, Poached Codfish and Potatoes with, 394–95
and Pignoli Pesto, Gratinéed Sardine Rolls Stuffed with, 376–77
Shrimp in Wine and, 364

Tomato Broth, Fresh Clams in, 367

Pasta, 94
Basic Egg, 461–62
Buckwheat, with Potatoes and Cabbage, 126–27
Chard and Mint Ravioli with Sardinian Pecorino, 106–7
Couscous with Chick Peas, 108–9
Dumplings with Mascarpone, 114–15
Egg Dumplings with Smoked Ricotta and Dark Chocolate, 110–11
Eggplant Timballo, 132–33
Grated, Chicken Broth with, 206–7
Hollow Spaghetti with Cauliflower, 136–37
Homemade Orecchiette with Sundried Tomato Sauce, 104–5
Oven-baked, Pie Filled with Porcini Mushrooms and Truffles, 124–25
Oven-baked Sweet Ravioli Filled with Quince, 130–31
Sea Bass Ravioli with Marjoram Sauce, 392–93
Shepherd's, with Fresh Ricotta, 112
Spaghetti Tubes with Duck Sauce, 120–21
Spaghetti with Black Pepper and Pecorino Cheese, 113
Spaghetti with Squid and Squid Ink, 122–23
Spaghetti with Tuna and Porcini Mushrooms, 118–19
Stuffed Lasagne, 140–41
and Summer Vegetable Soup Perfumed with Pesto Cream, 202–3

Trenette with Pesto Sauce, 138–39
The Virtues (Many Vegetable Soup), 220–21
Wide Ribbon Noodles with Prosciutto, 128–29
Winter, with Chick Peas, Lentils, and White Beans, 134–35

Pastry:
Cylinders Stuffed with Sweet Ricotta and Chocolate, 442–43
Puff, Rounds Stuffed with Apricots, 444–45

Peas, Baby, Sautéed with Spring Artichokes, 174–75

Pecorino cheese, xviii
Anchovy, and Caper-stuffed Calzones, 46–47
Country-style Cheese and Prosciutto Pie, 272–73
Empanadas, 22–23
and Rice Croquettes, Sicilian, 14–15
Sardinian, Chard and Mint Ravioli with, 106–7
Spaghetti with Black Pepper and, 113

Pepper(s), bell:
Four Variations of Pizza Tartlets, 240–41
Red, Eggplant and Black Olive Calzone, 280–81
Red, Eggplant and Prosciutto Terrine, 166–67
Red, Eggplant, Potato, and Black Olive Stew, 180–81
Red, Roasted with Olives, Capers, and Fresh Oregano, 186–87

Pepper, peppercorn(s), xx–xxi
Biscuits, Braided, 226–27
Black, and Prosciutto Pizza, 228–29
Black, Spaghetti with Pecorino Cheese and, 113

Green, Dressing, Zucchini Carpaccio with, 18–19
Perch, Panfried Royal, 380
Pesto:
    Cream, Summer Vegetable and Pasta Soup Perfumed with, 202–3
    Parsley, Poached Codfish and Potatoes with, 394–95
    Parsley and Pignoli, Gratinéed Sardine Rolls Stuffed with, 376–77
    Parsley-Garlic, Sardines Baked with Tomatoes and, 372–73
    Sauce, Trenette with, 138–39
Pheasant, Truffled, 332–33
Pie, Open-faced Christmas Apple, 438–39
Piedmont, 1–7
Pies, savory:
    Country-style Cheese and Prosciutto, 272–73
    Olive and Anchovy, 266–67
    Spinach, 274–75
Pigeon, Roast, with Black Olives, 314–15
Pignoli(s) (Pine Nuts):
    Chestnut Cake with Raisins and, 425
    and Parsley Pesto, Gratinéed Sardine Rolls Stuffed with, 376–77
    Wild Boar Braised with Raisins, Chocolate, Prunes and, 346–47
Pistachio:
    Crust, Mixed Green Salad Topped with Ricotta Rolled in, 40–41
    and Watermelon Sorbet, 440
Pizza(s), 192
    Dough, Basic, 463
    Prosciutto and Black Pepper, 228–29
    Saint Vito's Day, 238–39

Stuffed, Made with Chard and Sundried Tomatoes, 270–71
    Tartlets, Four Variations of, 240–41
Pizzette, Fried Potato, 236–37
Polenta, 52
    Baked, with Meat Sauce, 64–65
    Baked, with Sausage and Raisins, 75
    Baked Buckwheat, 74
    with Braised Duck and Winter Cabbage, 67
    Creamy, Sturgeon Steaks Braised in White Wine and Tomatoes and Served with, 384–85
    Creamy, with Beef Stew, 76–77
    Fried, and Fontina Cheese Kebabs, 66
    Fried, with Stracchino Cheese, 72
    Fritters, Sweet, 432–33
    Goulash with, 73
    Layered with Meat Sauce, 70–71
    Rounds with Walnut Sauce, 30–31
    Served on a Wooden Board, 62–63
    with Skewered Meats, 68–69
    Wedges, Fried, Codfish Salad with, 402–3
Pomegranates, Roast Turkey with, 344–45
Porcini mushroom(s), xxi
    Canapés Served with Wild Boar Prosciutto, 26–27
    Cutlets, Pan-fried, 182
    Dried, Veal Shanks with Lemon Zest and, 328–29
    Oven-baked Pasta Pie Filled with Truffles and, 124–25
    Risotto, Twice-cooked, 86–87

Sauté, 16–17
    Spaghetti with Tuna and, 118–19
Pork:
    Baked Polenta with Meat Sauce, 64–65
    Chicken, and Lamb Kebabs Grilled with Sage and Pancetta, 348
    Chicken, Veal, and Guinea Hen Cooked with Tomatoes and Herbs, 310–11
    Green Olives Stuffed with Meat, Battered, and Fried, 38–39
    Herb-stuffed, Grilled Bundles of, 349
    Polenta with Skewered Meats, 68–69
    Risotto with Spareribs, 92–93
Potato(es):
    and Artichoke Tart, 190–91
    Baked Rice Casserole with Zucchini and, 80–81
    Buckwheat Pasta with Cabbage and, 126–27
    Eggplant, Red Pepper, and Black Olive Stew, 180–81
    Fava Bean, and Sausage Winter Stew, 188–89
    Fish and Vegetable Salad, 386–87
    Gnocchi with Gorgonzola Sauce, 150–51
    Pizzette, Fried, 236–37
    Poached Codfish and, with Parsley Pesto, 394–95
    Scamorza, and Caciocavallo Terrine, 291
    Wafers, Oven-Roasted Dourade Served on a Bed of, 370–71
Poultry, 294
    Chicken, Veal, Pork, and Guinea Hen Cooked with Tomatoes and Herbs, 310–11

Duck Cooked in White
Wine and Chocolate,
312–13
Guinea Hen Cooked in
Terra-cotta, 350–51
Panfried Quail with
Buttered Rice, 338–39
Polenta with Braised Duck
and Winter Cabbage,
67
Roast Pigeon with Black
Olives, 314–15
Roast Turkey with
Pomegranates, 344–45
Spaghetti Tubes with Duck
Sauce, 120–21
Truffled Pheasant, 332–33
see also Chicken
Prosciutto:
and Black Pepper Pizza,
228–29
Cannelini Beans Braised
with Herbs and,
172–73
and Cheese Pie, Country-
style, 272–73
Eggplant, and Red Pepper
Terrine, 166–67
Fried Sage Sandwiches with
Anchovies and, 398
Green Olives Stuffed with
Meat, Battered, and
Fried, 38–39
Oven-poached Eggs with
Fontina and, 258
Oven-roasted Rabbit
Stuffed with, 316–17
Walnut, and Mozzarella
Sandwiches, 28–29
Wide Ribbon Noodles with,
128–29
Wild Boar, Porcini Canapés
Served with, 26–27
Provolone:
Country-style Cheese and
Prosciutto Pie, 272–73

Smoked, Pan-fried
with Oregano and
Balsamic Vinegar
Sauce, 292–93
Prunes, Wild Boar Braised with
Pine Nuts, Raisins,
Chocolate and, 346–47
Puglia, 295–303

Quail, Panfried, with Buttered
Rice, 338–39
Quince, Oven-baked Sweet
Ravioli Filled with,
130–31

Rabbit:
Gratinéed, 342–43
Oven-roasted, Stuffed with
Prosciutto, 316–17
Ragù:
Lamb, 308–9
Red Wine, Veal in, 326–27
of Venison with Herbs and
Juniper Berries, 318–19
Raisins:
Baked Polenta with Sausage
and, 75
Chestnut Cake with
Pignolis and, 425
Swordfish Steaks Baked
with Tomatoes, Olives
and, 378–79
Wild Boar Braised with
Pine Nuts, Chocolate,
Prunes and, 346–47
Ravioli:
Chard and Mint, with
Sardinian Pecorino,
106–7
Oven-baked Sweet, Filled
with Quince, 130–31
Sea Bass, with Marjoram
Sauce, 392–93
Rice:
and Almond Cake, Sweet,
456–57

and Beans, Piedmont-style,
82–83
Buttered, Panfried Quail
with, 338–39
Casserole with Zucchini
and Potatoes, Baked,
80–81
and Pecorino Cheese
Croquettes, Sicilian,
14–15
Sliced Frittata Rounds
Made with Thyme-
scented Oven-dried
Tomatoes and, 260–61
Tomatoes Stuffed with, and
Baked with Fresh
Herbs, 176–77
see also Risotto
Ricotta cheese, xviii–xix
and Chard Tart, 278–79
Chocolate Refrigerator
Cake, 428–29
Country-style Cheese and
Prosciutto Pie, 272–73
Fresh, Shepherd's Pasta
with, 112
Fritters, Sweet, 282–83
Mixed Green Salad Topped
with, Rolled in a
Pistachio Crust, 40–41
Smoked, Egg Dumplings
with Dark Chocolate
and, 110–11
Sweet, Pastry Cylinders
Stuffed with Chocolate
and, 442–43
Tart, Creamy, 418–19
Risotto, 52
with Black Cherries, 90–91
Croquettes, Fried, 88–89
with Spareribs, 92–93
with Truffles, 78–79
Twice-cooked Porcini
Mushroom, 86–87
with Wild Asparagus,
84–85

Robbiola Cheese Marinated in Tomato Sauce and Balsamic Vinegar, Rounds of, 10–11

Rosemary:
Crepes, 44–45
Focaccia, 230–31
Roasted Hake with Anchovies and, 390–91

Rum:
Almond Cake, 426
Syrup, Fresh Figs Preserved in, 451

Sage:
and Butter Sauce, Green Gnocchi with, 142–43
Chicken, Lamb, and Pork Kebabs Grilled with Pancetta and, 348
Sandwiches with Anchovies and Prosciutto, Fried, 398

Salads, xxii
Blood Orange and Red Onion, 32–33
Codfish, with Fried Polenta Wedges, 402–3
Farro, 48
Fish and Vegetable, 386–87
Mixed Green, Topped with Ricotta Rolled in a Pistachio Crust, 40–41
Olive and Blood Orange, 50–51
Shellfish, with Lemon-Mustard Vinaigrette, 400–401

Salt, xix–xx

Sandwiches:
Fried Sage, with Anchovies and Prosciutto, 398
Walnut, Mozzarella, and Prosciutto, 28–29

Sardine(s):
Baked with Tomatoes and

Parsley-Garlic Pesto, 372–73
Fried, Marinated with Onions, 382–83
Rolls Stuffed with Parsley and Pignoli Pesto, Gratinéed, 376–77
Saint Vito's Day Pizza, 238–39

Sardinia, 193–201

Sausage(s):
Baked Polenta with Meat Sauce, 64–65
Baked Polenta with Raisins and, 75
Fava Bean, and Potato Winter Stew, 188–89
and Fava Bean Soup, 218–19
Mussels Stuffed with Herbs and, 396–97
Polenta Served on a Wooden Board, 62–63
Polenta with Skewered Meats, 68–69
Veal, with Artichokes and Fresh Fava Beans, 306–7

Scamorza(e):
Caciocavallo, and Potato Terrine, 291
and Caciocavallo Cheeses, Baked Kebabs Made with, 288–89
St. John's Day Cheese Timballo, 276–77

Scones, Cornmeal, 422–23

Sea Bass:
Ravioli with Marjoram Sauce, 392–93
Soup, Spicy, 399

Seafood, 352
Baby Shrimp with Garlic Sauce, 42–43
Baked Stuffed Mussels, 368–69

Fresh Clams in Tomato-Parsley Broth, 367
Mussels Stuffed with Sausage and Herbs, 396–97
Pancetta-wrapped Mussels Grilled on Skewers, 49
Sautéed Chicken with Poached Shrimp and Fried Eggs, 334–35
Shellfish Salad with Lemon-Mustard Vinaigrette, 400–401
Shrimp in Wine and Parsley, 364
Soup Made with Mussels and Fresh Tomatoes, 222–23
Spaghetti with Squid and Squid Ink, 122–23
Spiced Baby Shrimp, 404
see also Fish

Semolina, xxi
Gnocchi, Baked, 146–47
Terrine, Sardinian, 20–21

Shrimp:
Baby, with Garlic Sauce, 42–43
Poached, Sautéed Chicken with Fried Eggs and, 334–35
Shellfish Salad with Lemon-Mustard Vinaigrette, 400–401
Spiced Baby, 404
in Wine and Parsley, 364

Sicily, 407–17

Sorbet, Watermelon and Pistachio, 440

Soups, 192
Barley, Chestnut, and White Bean Minestrone, 208–9
Beef Broth with Tiny Meatballs, 212

488

Chicken Broth with Grated
Pasta, 206–7
Cold, of Dried Favas and
Wild Fennel, 213
Cream of Butternut Squash,
214–15
Farro, 205
Fish, with Garlic-rubbed
Bread, 365
Made with Mussels and
Fresh Tomatoes,
222–23
Many Vegetable (The
Virtues), 220–21
Sardinian Bread and
Mozzarella, 216–17
Sausage and Fava Bean,
218–19
Spicy Sea Bass, 399
Summer Vegetable and
Pasta, Perfumed with
Pesto Cream, 202–3
Thick and Creamy Alpine
Cheese, 204
Tuscan Fish, 374–75
Zucchini Leaf and Fresh
Tomato, 210–11
Spaghetti:
with Black Pepper and
Pecorino Cheese, 113
Hollow, with Cauliflower,
136–37
with Squid and Squid Ink,
122–23
Tubes with Duck Sauce,
120–21
with Tuna and Porcini
Mushrooms, 118–19
Spareribs, Risotto with, 92–93
Spinach Pie, Savory, 274–75
Squash, see Butternut Squash;
Zucchini
Squid:
Shellfish Salad with
Lemon-Mustard
Vinaigrette, 400–401
and Squid Ink, Spaghetti
with, 122–23

Stracchino Cheese, Fried
Polenta with, 72
Sturgeon Steaks Braised in
White Wine and
Tomatoes and Served with
Creamy Polenta, 384–85
Swordfish:
Breaded Kebabs with
Wedges of Red Onion,
388–89
Steaks Baked with
Tomatoes, Raisins,
and Olives, 378–79

Taleggio:
Baked Gnocchi Made with
Asparagus, Asiago
and, 148–49
Cheese-stuffed Focaccia,
242–43
Tarts, dessert:
Creamy Ricotta, 418–19
Kiwi Custard, 420–21
Tarts, savory, 248
Chard and Ricotta, 278–79
Escarole, Curly Endive,
Capers, and Black
Olive, 268–69
Four Variations of Pizza
Tartlets, 240–41
Potato and Artichoke,
190–91
Stuffed Pizza Made with
Chard and Sundried
Tomatoes, 270–71
Terrines:
Eggplant, Red Pepper,
and Prosciutto, 166–67
Sardinian Semolina, 20–21
Scamorza, Caciocavallo, and
Potato, 291
Thyme-scented Oven-dried
Tomatoes, Sliced Frittata
Rounds Made with Rice
and, 260–61
Timballos:
Eggplant, 132–33
St. John's Day Cheese, 276–77

Tomato(es):
canned, xix
Chicken, Veal, Pork, and
Guinea Hen Cooked
with Herbs and,
310–11
Four Variations of Pizza
Tartlets, 240–41
Fresh, and Zucchini Leaf
Soup, 210–11
Fresh, Mozzarella-stuffed
Meatballs Braised in,
320–21
Fresh, Soup Made with
Mussels and, 222–23
Fresh, Tuna Steaks Baked
with Olives, Capers
and, 405
Parsley Broth, Fresh Clams
in, 367
Saint Vito's Day Pizza,
238–39
Sardines Baked with
Parsley-Garlic Pesto
and, 372–73
Sauce, Rounds of Robbiola
Cheese Marinated in
Balsamic Vinegar and,
10–11
Stuffed with Rice and
Baked with Fresh
Herbs, 176–77
Sturgeon Steaks Braised in
White Wine and,
Served with Creamy
Polenta, 384–85
Sundried, Sauce,
Homemade
Orecchiette with,
104–5
Sundried, Stuffed Pizza
Made with Chard and,
270–71
Swordfish Steaks Baked
with Raisins, Olives
and, 378–79
Thyme-scented Oven-dried,
Sliced Frittata Rounds

Made with Rice and,
260–61
The Virtues (Many
Vegetable Soup),
220–21
Trenette with Pesto Sauce,
138–39
Trentino–Alto Adige, 53–61
Trout, Freshwater, with Herbs
and Lemon Fragrance,
381
Truffle(s), truffled:
Bruschetta with, 24–25
Oven-baked Pasta Pie
Filled with Porcini
Mushrooms and,
124–25
Pheasant, 332–33
Risotto with, 78–79
White, and Fontina Cheese
Fondue, 8–9
White, Frittata, 265
Tuna:
Carpaccio with
Lemon-Parsley Sauce,
34–35
Spaghetti with Porcini
Mushrooms and,
118–19
Steaks Baked with Olives,
Capers, and Fresh
Tomatoes, 405
Turkey, Roast, with
Pomegranates, 344–45
Tuscany, 153–61

Veal:
Chicken, Pork, and Guinea
Hen Cooked with
Tomatoes and Herbs,
310–11
Green Olives Stuffed with
Meat, Battered, and
Fried, 38–39
Polenta with Skewered
Meats, 68–69
in Red Wine Ragù,
326–27

Sausages with Artichokes
and Fresh Fava Beans,
306–7
Scaloppine with
Parsley-Caper Sauce,
322–23
Shanks with Lemon Zest
and Dried Porcini,
328–29
Vegetable(s), 152
Baby Peas Sautéed with
Spring Artichokes,
174–75
Borage Fritters, 170
Braised Escarole with
Capers and Black
Olives, 178–79
Broth, Basic, 459
Cannelini Beans Braised
with Prosciutto and
Herbs, 172–73
Cauliflower, Artichokes,
Leeks, and Broccoli
Rabe Braised in
Balsamic Vinegar and
Dusted with Anise,
164–65
Cauliflower Fritters, 171
Eggplant, Red Pepper, and
Prosciutto Terrine,
166–67
Eggplant, Red Pepper,
Potato, and Black
Olive Stew, 180–81
Fava Bean, Sausage, and
Potato Winter Stew,
188–89
and Fish Salad, 386–87
Gratinéed Cardoons,
162–63
Many, Soup (The Virtues),
220–21
Marinated Butternut
Squash, Chioggia-style,
169
Pan-fried Porcini
Mushroom Cutlets,
182

Potato and Artichoke Tart,
190–91
Red Peppers Roasted with
Olives, Capers, and
Fresh Oregano, 186–87
Rolled Chicken Breast
Stuffed with, and
Braised in White Wine
and Heavy Cream,
340–41
Summer, and Pasta Soup
Perfumed with Pesto
Cream, 202–3
Sweet Onions Cooked with
Marsala Wine, 183
Tomatoes Stuffed with Rice
and Baked with Fresh
Herbs, 176–77
Twelfth Night Stuffed
Savoy Cabbage,
184–85
Wine-braised Chestnuts,
168
Venison, Ragù of, with Herbs
and Juniper Berries,
318–19

Walnut(s):
Chicken Stuffed with,
336–37
Mozzarella, and Prosciutto
Sandwiches, 28–29
Sauce, Polenta Rounds with,
30–31
-stuffed Figs, Chocolate-
covered, 441
Watermelon and Pistachio
Sorbet, 440
Wild Boar:
Braised with Pine Nuts,
Raisins, Chocolate, and
Prunes, 346–47
Prosciutto, Porcini Canapés
Served with, 26–27
Wine, 464–65
Beef Sirloin Braised in
Barolo, 304–5
-braised Chestnuts, 168

Marsala, Sweet Onions
    Cooked with, 183
Marsala-flavored Fruit and
    Nut Rolls, 434–35
Red, Ragù, Veal in,
    326–27
Red, Sauce, Hare with,
    330–31
Shrimp in Parsley and,
    364
Sweet Mascarpone
    Cheese Cake Flavored
    with Marsala, 450

White, Duck Cooked
    in Chocolate and,
    312–13
White, Rolled Chicken
    Breast Stuffed with
    Vegetables and Braised
    in Heavy Cream and,
    340–41
White, Sturgeon Steaks
    Braised in Tomatoes
    and, Served with
    Creamy Polenta,
    384–85

Zucchini:
    Baked Rice Casserole
        with Potatoes and,
        80–81
    Blossoms, Stuffed, 36–37
    Carpaccio with Green
        Peppercorn Dressing,
        18–19
    Four Variations of
        Pizza Tartlets,
        240–41
    Leaf and Fresh Tomato
        Soup, 210–11